Unveiling Investor Biases That Shape Market Dynamics

Xu Xiong
City University, Malaysia

Loang Ooi Kok
Universiti Malaya, Malaysia

IGI Global
Scientific Publishing
Publishing Tomorrow's Research Today

Vice President of Editorial | Melissa Wagner
Managing Editor of Acquisitions | Mikaela Felty
Managing Editor of Book Development | Jocelynn Hessler
Production Manager | Mike Brehm
Cover Design | Phillip Shickler

Published in the United States of America by
IGI Global Scientific Publishing
701 East Chocolate Avenue
Hershey, PA, 17033, USA
Tel: 717-533-8845
Fax: 717-533-8661
E-mail: cust@igi-global.com
Website: https://www.igi-global.com

Library of Congress Cataloging-in-Publication Data

CIP Pending
ISBN: 979-8-3693-9380-2
EISBN: 979-8-3693-9382-6

British Cataloguing in Publication Data
A Cataloguing in Publication record for this book is available from the British Library.

Table of Contents

Detailed Table of Contents

This study investigates the influence of behavioral biases in real estate markets, addressing a notable research gap in behavioral finance. Despite extensive research in stock markets, psychological factors affecting decision-making in real estate remain underexplored. The research identifies key biases influencing stakeholders, analyzes their impact on property pricing, investment strategies, and market efficiency, and examines strategies to mitigate these biases. Utilizing a mixed-methods approach, data were collected from 280 real estate investors, buyers, sellers, agents, and developers through structured questionnaires and semi-structured interviews. The findings reveal that behavioral biases significantly affect market outcomes and highlight the need for tailored strategies to enhance decision-making processes. Recommendations are proposed for industry professionals and policymakers to minimize adverse effects. This research contributes to a deeper understanding of psychological factors in real estate, paving the way for future studies to address this crucial area.

Behavioral factors in Foreign Direct Investment (FDI) represent a critical dimension in understanding the dynamics of international business and investment decisions, extending beyond traditional economic and financial analyses. These behavioral factors include cognitive biases, heuristics, cultural influences, and emotional responses, which can significantly impact how investors evaluate opportunities, assess risks, and ultimately make investment choices. For instance, an investor may be overly optimistic about the potential success of a foreign market based on previous favorable experiences, leading to an underestimation of potential risks and challenges. These biases can result in suboptimal investment decisions and impact the overall success of FDI ventures. Heuristics, or mental shortcuts used to simplify decision-making, also play a significant role in FDI. Investors often use heuristics to cope with the complexity and uncertainty of international markets.

To understand the best strategy for the investment for the maximum return, one should accurately make a portfolio for the investment. It is a critical challenge to different investors to find the best path for investment. In this study, nine different companies are selected and the data collected from www.yahoo.finance. The 9 companies are divided into 3 categories such as high risk, moderate and low risk. The stock price on day one was recorded and on 30th day, the authors also recorded the close price of the stocks. Now, on the basis of the return of different companies, the authors will draw a conclusion regarding the investment strategy and will make the best strategy based on 9 companies for the maximum return. Now, the analysis part will provide a good portfolio from future investment. Finally, the statistical tool will be used to check whether there is any significant difference between the portfolio or not.

This article intends to understand the outcome of heuristic biases "overconfidence" and "underconfidence" in the short-term and long-term investment decision-making behaviour of investors in Indian market. Overconfidence and underconfidence biases have been measured through a well-structured questionnaire of various statements related to heuristic biases. SPSS 22 and the intuitive graphical user interface of PLS-SEM (SmartPLS) have been used to analyse the survey data. This article has found a positive relationship between the long-term and short-term investment decisions with overconfidence bias and a negative relationship between the short-term investment decisions and underconfidence bias. However, no relationship has been identified between long-term investment decisions and underconfidence bias. This outcome is partially in sync with the findings of various studies related to overconfidence bias conducted in other countries. Whereas due to the unavailability of literature on underconfidence bias, results cannot be compared with the studies conducted in other countries

The paper is an attempt to study the relationship between different biases and the investment decision-making of the investors, in this study three biases were selected namely Over-confidence bias, disposition bias and Home bias. To achieve the objectives this study gathered data from a sample of 400 respondents and the data analysis took place with the help of SPSS and Warp-PLS. Findings of the study suggested overconfidence bias does not share a significant relationship with investment decision-making but on the other hand disposition and home bias share a significant relationship with investment decision-making.

Social media has profoundly transformed the landscape of market sentiment, playing a pivotal role in how investors, companies, and consumers interact and influence financial markets. The integration of platforms such as Twitter, Facebook, LinkedIn, and Reddit into daily life has created a new realm of information dissemination and opinion formation that was previously non-existent. Social media's immediacy and reach enable rapid sharing of news, opinions, and market analyses, making it an influential factor in shaping market perceptions and behaviors. Traditional media outlets, such as newspapers and television, often have a delay in reporting news, which can lead to a lag in market reactions. In contrast, social media allows for real-time updates, providing investors with immediate access to news, rumors, and opinions. This immediacy can lead to swift market movements, as traders and investors react to information as it becomes available, often before it reaches more traditional media channels.

This study examines the importance of strategic flexibility in managing investment portfolios, particularly in emerging markets characterized by rapid technological advancements and heightened market volatility. By focusing on key factors such as portfolio diversification, technological adaptability, and regulatory changes, the research highlights how investors can navigate uncertainties and capitalize on opportunities in volatile economies. Strategic flexibility is presented as a dynamic tool that enables investors to adjust their strategies in real-time, ensuring resilience and optimizing returns. The study underscores the need for a proactive approach to managing risk and seizing growth opportunities in rapidly evolving markets

Preface

In *Unveiling Investor Biases That Shape Market Dynamics*, we embark on an exploration that challenges conventional wisdom and opens the door to a more nuanced understanding of investment in today's complex, rapidly evolving landscape. Each chapter unveils a critical aspect of modern investing, inviting readers to question, reflect, and reimagine what it means to make strategic financial decisions in an age where technology and human behavior intersect with powerful, sometimes unpredictable, force.

Chapter 1 dives into *Behavioral Biases in Real Estate Markets*, an area that, for many investors, symbolizes stability, permanence, and growth. Real estate is tangible; it's something we can touch, see, and feel—a foundation of wealth-building that has, historically, been as solid as the buildings themselves. Yet, as this chapter uncovers, real estate is far from immune to the sway of human psychology. Investors often fall prey to biases like overconfidence, anchoring, and even the illusion of control, mistaking the physical solidity of property for stability in value. Imagine the skyline of a booming metropolis, where glittering skyscrapers rise as testaments to optimism and ambition. In such markets, the promise of perpetual growth can be intoxicating, blinding investors to the risks lurking beneath the surface. This chapter delves into the cycles of real estate booms and busts, illustrating how our collective biases can inflate bubbles that inevitably burst, reshaping entire economies in the process. It's a cautionary tale for those who believe that bricks and mortar offer sanctuary from volatility, revealing how the real estate market is as much a psychological construct as it is a financial one.

Chapter 2 turns its gaze to *Behavioral Factors Driving Foreign Direct Investment in Emerging Markets*. Emerging markets are, by nature, alluring. They represent opportunity, growth, and the excitement of uncharted territory. However, investing in these regions is far from straightforward. The psychology of foreign direct investment (FDI) is complex, driven by a combination of optimism, curiosity, and sometimes, cultural misinterpretation. This chapter paints a vivid picture of investors venturing into high-growth economies, fueled by the belief that they can replicate their successes from home in a foreign landscape. But as history has shown, these assumptions can be dangerously flawed. Imagine an investor, brimming with confidence after years of success in a Western market, now eyeing opportunities in Southeast Asia. Enthralled by the promise of rapid growth, they may overlook the nuances of local consumer behavior, regulatory environments, or economic volatility. This chapter not only examines the behavioral biases that drive FDI but also underscores the importance of cultural understanding and contextual awareness in avoiding costly missteps.

Chapter 3 presents a fresh take on an age-old concept in *Different Portfolio on Investment: A Practical Work to Reduce Risks*. The idea of diversification is as old as investing itself, yet this chapter brings new depth by integrating behavioral finance into portfolio theory. It's one thing to spread investments across assets; it's another to stay the course when markets swing and emotions run high. This chapter explores the biases that can sabotage even the most well-diversified portfolios, from loss aversion to recency bias. Picture an investor with a carefully balanced portfolio, a mosaic of assets chosen to withstand the ups and downs of the market. Yet, as uncertainty looms and media headlines scream volatility, the investor begins to second-guess their strategy. This chapter guides readers through the psychological dynamics that can cause them to deviate from their plans, emphasizing the importance of not only financial but emotional resilience in portfolio management.

In **Chapter 4**, *Does the Bias Towards Under and Overconfidence Affect Investment Decisions? Proof from India*, we dive into the psychology of confidence and how it shapes financial outcomes. Confidence, as any seasoned investor knows, is a delicate balance—too little, and you risk missing out on valuable opportunities; too much, and you may find yourself blindsided by overreach. Using the Indian market as a case study, this chapter explores how overconfidence and underconfidence manifest in investment behaviors, from overly aggressive trades to excessive caution. Imagine a bull market where investors, riding a wave of success, begin to believe in their own infallibility. They take on larger risks, convinced that their instincts will continue to lead them to profit. This chapter unpacks these tendencies, revealing how confidence biases shape both individual and collective market behaviors, and it serves as a reminder of the need for humility and vigilance in financial decision-making.

Chapter 5 takes us to the heart of India with *Investment Decision-Making and Intricate Role of Behavioral Biases – Delhi-NCR Study*. In the vibrant and culturally rich region of Delhi-NCR, investment decisions are influenced not just by financial metrics but by an intricate web of social and cultural dynamics. Here, family expectations, community influence, and traditional values play pivotal roles in shaping how investors think and act. This chapter explores the impact of these cultural factors, showing how behavioral biases manifest in unique ways within this context. Imagine a community where investment choices are often collective, influenced by the input of family members and community elders. In this setting, biases like herd mentality and status quo bias take on new dimensions, as personal and social expectations weigh heavily on financial decisions. This chapter offers a compelling look at the intersection of culture and finance, demonstrating how local dynamics create distinct patterns of behavior that challenge conventional economic models.

In **Chapter 6**, *Investor Behavior and Market Efficiency in Emerging Markets: An Empirical Study on Retail Investors*, we turn to a cornerstone of finance theory: the efficient market hypothesis (EMH). While EMH suggests that markets are "efficient" and reflect all available information, this theory is often put to the test in emerging markets, where information asymmetry, regulatory gaps, and behavioral biases create inefficiencies. This chapter challenges the assumption of market efficiency, revealing how psychological factors lead to pricing anomalies that can be exploited. In emerging markets, where transparency is limited and data can be sparse, investors often rely on heuristics and social cues, leading to biases like representativeness and confirmation bias. Through empirical research and case studies, readers are shown how to identify and capitalize on these inefficiencies, using behavioral insights to find value where traditional models might not.

Chapter 7 delves into the fascinating realm of *Mental Accounting: Shaping Financial Choices and Behaviors*. Mental accounting is a cognitive bias that leads people to compartmentalize their finances into different "accounts" based on subjective criteria, rather than objective value. This bias shapes everything from daily spending habits to major investment decisions, often leading to choices that defy economic logic. Imagine a young professional who treats their annual bonus as "fun money," spending it on luxury items, while scrupulously budgeting their regular income for essentials. This mental division can lead to unbalanced financial behavior, where certain funds are prioritized for reasons that may not align with overall financial goals. This chapter unpacks the psychological mechanics of mental accounting, helping readers to recognize and manage this bias in their own lives. By understanding the impact of mental accounting, readers are empowered to make more strategic and holistic financial decisions, aligning their behavior with their long-term objectives.

In **Chapter 8**, *Overconfidence and Its Consequences in Financial Markets*, we revisit the theme of overconfidence, this time through the lens of financial markets as a whole. Overconfidence is a powerful force that often leads investors to take on excessive risk, ignore warning signs, and make decisions that, in hindsight, seem reckless. This chapter traces the impact of overconfidence on market dynamics, showing how it contributes to speculative bubbles and abrupt crashes. Picture a booming tech sector, where investors, fueled by a belief in their own acumen, pour money into startups with unproven business models. As valuations soar, overconfidence grows, creating a feedback loop that ultimately leads to a crash when reality fails to meet expectations. Through historical and contemporary examples, this chapter explores the cyclical nature of overconfidence and its impact on financial markets, encouraging readers to temper their ambition with caution.

Chapter 9 explores *Social Media Influence on Market Sentiment*, a force that has transformed the financial landscape in recent years. Platforms like Twitter, Reddit, and other social media sites have given rise to a new form of "social trading," where market sentiment can shift in real-time, influenced by viral trends, influencers, and online communities. This chapter examines how social media-driven sentiment creates echo chambers that amplify both optimism and fear, leading to rapid market movements that defy traditional financial logic. Imagine a stock that suddenly spikes in value after a Reddit post goes viral, attracting thousands of retail investors eager to join the "next big thing." This phenomenon, while exciting, can lead to volatility and risk as sentiment swings from euphoria to panic. This chapter provides insights into navigating the influence of social media, helping readers to separate hype from substance and make more informed decisions in a world where digital trends drive market sentiment.

In **Chapter 10**, *Strategic Flexibility in Investment Portfolios Adapting to Technological Advancements and Market Volatility in Emerging Economies*, we explore the importance of adaptability in today's fast-paced financial world. As technology and market conditions continue to evolve, strategic flexibility has become essential for investors seeking resilience in uncertain times. This chapter discusses the concept of adaptability, offering strategies for building portfolios that can pivot in response to new information and changing circumstances. Imagine a portfolio designed not just for current conditions, but for a future that is unpredictable—a portfolio that can shift its focus from growth to stability as needed, responding to the latest economic data and market trends. This chapter emphasizes the importance of maintaining a dynamic approach to investment, encouraging readers to stay informed, embrace change, and cultivate flexibility as a core investment principle.

Finally, **Chapter 11**, *The Role of Technological Innovation in Shaping Investment Strategies in Emerging Markets: A Study on Risk and Return*, synthesizes the themes of technology and behavioral finance, exploring how innovation is reshaping the investment landscape in emerging economies. From AI-driven trading algorithms to blockchain technology, emerging markets have become laboratories for financial innovation. This chapter examines the risks and rewards associated with adopting new technologies in markets that are still developing their infrastructure and regulatory frameworks. Imagine a trader using machine learning algorithms to analyze market sentiment in real-time, identifying trends that human analysts might miss. While these technologies offer incredible potential, they also carry unique risks, especially in regions where data reliability and regulatory oversight may be lacking. This chapter offers a balanced perspective on technological innovation, helping readers to understand how to harness its power while remaining mindful of the challenges it presents.

Each chapter in this book is a deep dive into a critical aspect of modern investing, providing readers with a blend of theoretical insight, empirical evidence, and practical guidance. This book is not just a guide to financial success; it is an invitation to rethink the fundamental principles of investing, to question established norms, and to embrace the complexity and unpredictability of a world shaped by technology and human psychology. As you turn these pages, you will be challenged, inspired, and equipped with a new understanding of what it means to invest in the age of technological innovation and emerging markets. This is more than a book; it's a journey into the heart of a financial revolution.

Chapter 1
Behavioral Biases in Real Estate Markets

Partap Singh
https://orcid.org/0000-0002-4653-7984
Lovely Professional University, India

ABSTRACT

This study investigates the influence of behavioral biases in real estate markets, addressing a notable research gap in behavioral finance. Despite extensive research in stock markets, psychological factors affecting decision-making in real estate remain underexplored. The research identifies key biases influencing stakeholders, analyzes their impact on property pricing, investment strategies, and market efficiency, and examines strategies to mitigate these biases. Utilizing a mixed-methods approach, data were collected from 280 real estate investors, buyers, sellers, agents, and developers through structured questionnaires and semi-structured interviews. The findings reveal that behavioral biases significantly affect market outcomes and highlight the need for tailored strategies to enhance decision-making processes. Recommendations are proposed for industry professionals and policymakers to minimize adverse effects. This research contributes to a deeper understanding of psychological factors in real estate, paving the way for future studies to address this crucial area.

1. INTRODUCTION

The impact of behavioral biases on decision-making in real estate markets has gained considerable attention in recent research. Marney and Fakhry (2024) underscored the vital role of the housing market in economic stability and monetary policy, while noting a gap in literature on behavioral influences in housing

DOI: 10.4018/979-8-3693-9380-2.ch001

decisions. Their research revealed that cognitive and emotional biases, such as the illusion of control and emotional attachment, significantly affect buyer and seller behavior. They emphasized the importance of understanding these psychological factors for effective policymaking in the housing sector. Singh et al. (2023) found that behavioral biases, driven by psychological factors, significantly influence financial decisions but have been less explored in real estate. Their review of 86 articles from 1980 to 2022 revealed extensive research on anchoring, loss aversion, and herding biases, while others like gambler's fallacy and framing bias remain underexplored. They identified gaps, particularly in primary data studies and research in developing countries. Kinatta et al. (2022) found that herding behavior is common across various investment regimes, where investors tend to follow others, resulting in poorer decisions and unidirectional mass trading that destabilizes markets. Shah Ahmad, and Mahmood (2018) identified that cognitive biases significantly impact investment decisions, affecting everyone regardless of their level of expertise. This research highlights how mental errors can lead to suboptimal financial choices. Similarly, Metawa, Hassan, Metawa, and Safa (2019) emphasized the role of emotional factors, such as anxiety, selfishness, and overconfidence, in influencing investment decisions. These emotions can lead investors to make irrational choices that deviate from logical financial strategies. Northcraft et al. (1987) discovered that the anchoring effect among homebuyers significantly influences the final selling price of properties. This finding suggests that initial price expectations can skew homebuyers' perceptions, leading to higher sale prices. Chang et al. (2016) found that homebuyers often pay a premium due to the anchoring bias, particularly when facing uncertainty or purchasing out-of-state. This bias persists regardless of the buyer's gender and reveals the influence of heuristics in real estate transactions. Zhou et al. (2015) found that buyers often offer different prices for nearly identical properties, likely due to information asymmetries within real estate markets Babalos et al. (2015) provided evidence of herding behavior among US Real Estate Investment Trusts (REITs) using a Markov regime-switching model. While static models may reject herding, the dynamic model shows herding is prevalent during market crashes, with shifts in behavior depending on market volatility. Shiller (2005, 2008) concluded that speculative thinking, heuristics like extrapolative expectations, and market psychology, including optimism and pessimism, significantly impact housing prices. Herd behavior and the spread of new ideas also contribute to price fluctuations while in his later work, Shiller (2017) examined how narratives influence economic fluctuations, arguing that stories shape actions, including spending and investing. Historical economic events, such as the Great Depression and the Great Recession, were driven by prevailing narratives, demonstrating the powerful economic impact of widely accepted stories.

2. LITERATURE REVIEW

Baker, Kumar, Goyal, and Gaur (2019) identified prevalent behavioral biases among investors, leading to abnormalities in decision-making. Their study emphasized how cognitive biases disrupt rational thought processes, contributing to inconsistent investment outcomes across different countries and communities. The research highlighted the widespread impact of these biases on investors, regardless of geographical or cultural context.

2.1 Overconfidence Bias in the Real Estate Market

Overconfidence bias is a critical behavioral factor in the real estate market, often leading investors, developers, and homeowners to overestimate their knowledge and predictive abilities. This cognitive bias can result in significant market inefficiencies, inaccurate property valuations, and poor investment decisions.

Studies on Overconfidence in Real Estate Markets

Gatzlaff and Tirtiroglu (1995) explored the implications of overconfidence in real estate appraisals, finding that real estate professionals often misestimate the future trajectory of property values. This overconfidence can lead to incorrect pricing strategies, especially during periods of market volatility, and influences lending practices by both commercial banks and mortgage lenders.

A study by Glaser and Weber (2007) analyzed the impact of overconfidence on real estate developers and other market participants. Developers, in particular, were found to overestimate future demand for properties, which often results in overbuilding. This misjudgment can lead to an oversupply in the market, causing real estate values to stagnate or decline when demand fails to meet the inflated expectations.

Ahmad and Shah (2020) also examined the role of financial literacy in mitigating the impact of overconfidence among real estate investors. They found that investors with a better understanding of financial risks and market dynamics were less likely to overestimate their predictive abilities. This suggests that increasing financial education could be an effective strategy to reduce overconfidence in real estate markets.

Shiller (2015), who famously predicted the real estate bubble before the 2008 financial crisis, attributes speculative bubbles in part to overconfidence among both investors and homeowners. He argues that irrational exuberance and overestimation of future property appreciation fuel speculative behavior, contributing to asset bubbles. Shiller advocates for regulatory frameworks that can help prevent overconfident behavior from destabilizing real estate markets by enforcing stricter lending criteria and promoting accurate property valuations.

Further research supports these findings. For instance, Barber and Odean (2001) demonstrated that overconfident investors trade more frequently than their less confident counterparts, which in turn reduces their net returns due to higher transaction costs. They argue that male investors, in particular, tend to display greater overconfidence, resulting in poorer investment performance compared to female investors.

Ahmad and Shah (2020) found that overconfidence impairs investors' ability to make optimal selection choices, reducing overall performance. They noted that financial knowledge and risk perception can counteract the negative effects of overconfidence, leading to improved decision-making. Their study underscores the importance of enhancing financial literacy to mitigate overconfidence in investment decisions. Ahmad and Shah (2020) also highlighted the role of financial literacy in mitigating the adverse effects of overconfidence. They found that investors with higher levels of financial knowledge and better risk perception were less likely to fall prey to overconfidence bias. Enhancing financial literacy, they argue, is crucial for improving decision-making and fostering more rational investment behaviors. Similarly, Lusardi and Mitchell (2014) stress that financial education programs can significantly reduce overconfidence by equipping individuals with a more accurate understanding of market dynamics and the risks involved in various investment strategies.

In conclusion, overconfidence bias significantly impairs the decision-making abilities of investors, leading to excessive trading, miscalculated risk assessments, and reduced overall performance. However, interventions such as improving financial literacy and awareness of behavioral biases can help counteract these effects, promoting more rational investment decisions.

Mitigating Overconfidence in Real Estate Decisions

One effective approach to addressing overconfidence in real estate markets, as highlighted by Ahmad and Shah (2020), is through enhanced financial education. Investors who possess a deeper understanding of real estate cycles and economic indicators are better equipped to make informed, rational decisions, avoiding the pitfalls of overconfidence.

Shiller (2015) also recommends macro-prudential regulations to control overconfident speculation. He argues that policies aimed at ensuring prudent lending standards, along with accurate property appraisals, can reduce the risk of bubbles driven by overconfidence.

In summary, overconfidence bias plays a significant role in shaping the decisions of real estate investors, developers, and homeowners, often leading to mispricing and excessive risk-taking. However, improved financial literacy and prudent regulatory measures can help mitigate the adverse effects of overconfidence on real estate markets.

2.2 Herding Bias in the Real Estate Market

Herding bias refers to investors' tendency to follow the actions of the majority, often disregarding their own independent assessments. In the real estate market, herding can significantly influence property valuations, price trends, and investment behaviors, contributing to the formation of market bubbles and financial instability.

Studies on Herding Bias in Real Estate Markets

Bikhchandani and Sharma (2001) explored the role of herding in asset price bubbles, noting that it is particularly prevalent in real estate markets. Investors tend to mimic others' actions, especially during rising property prices, often believing that others have better information. This behavior fuels excessive property purchases, inflating prices beyond their fundamental values, and leading to speculative bubbles.

A study by Hirshleifer and Teoh (2003) focused on how herding behavior contributes to the overvaluation of real estate assets. Investors, influenced by media reports and popular sentiment, tend to buy properties that are perceived as high in demand, leading to unsustainable price rises. The researchers emphasized the role of cascading effects, where one investor's actions lead others to follow without conducting their own due diligence.

Wheaton (1999) highlighted herding among real estate developers, where developers follow their peers in constructing new properties in areas perceived as hot markets. This behavior often leads to overbuilding during market upturns, with an oversupply of properties when demand fails to match expectations. Such overconfidence based on herding behavior can exacerbate price declines during market downturns.

Shiller (2015) analyzed the role of herding in real estate bubbles, linking it to the 2008 financial crisis, where both homeowners and investors followed speculative trends in property markets. He pointed out that public perception and media coverage played a significant role in creating irrational exuberance around property prices, further fueling herding behavior.

Herding behavior, as characterized by Clarke et al. (2014), refers to the tendency of investors to conform to prevailing market trends and external advice, often at the expense of their own independent judgment. This phenomenon is further explained by Rasool and Ullah (2020), who suggest that herding stems from investors' desire to avoid accountability for their personal decisions by conforming to the actions of others.

As a result, individual analysis is frequently overlooked, leading to a significant impact on market dynamics. Research has shown that herding behavior does not exhibit a strong correlation with gender (Talpsepp and Tänav, 2021). However, younger and older individuals tend to display moderate to low levels of herding bias. Additionally, individuals with a commerce background have been found to exhibit a reduced propensity for herding.

Similar patterns of herding behavior have been observed among institutional investors (Lantushenko and Nelling, 2017). Furthermore, research has shown that herding is more prevalent during upward market movements than in declining markets (Ro et al., 2019). However, Lin et al. (2018) offers a contrasting viewpoint, suggesting that herding behavior may be exaggerated during market upswings.

Mitigating Herding Bias in Real Estate Decisions

Ahmad and Shah (2020) emphasized the importance of financial literacy and independent market analysis to mitigate herding bias. Their study showed that investors who rely on sound research and avoid following market trends blindly are better positioned to make informed real estate investment decisions. By doing so, they reduce their exposure to the risks associated with speculative bubbles.

Shiller (2015) also proposed macro-prudential regulations to curb herding behavior in real estate markets. He suggested that stricter lending criteria, along with accurate property valuation standards, can help temper speculative behavior driven by herding.

In summary, herding bias is a powerful behavioral factor in real estate markets, contributing to speculative bubbles and mispricing. However, improved financial education, regulatory measures, and independent decision-making can help mitigate its adverse effects, leading to more stable and efficient real estate markets,

2.3 Anchoring Bias in Real Estate Market: A Review of Literature

Anchoring bias is a cognitive bias where individuals rely heavily on the first piece of information they encounter (the "anchor") when making decisions. In real estate markets, this bias can skew property valuations, investment decisions, and negotiations, leading to irrational market behavior. Shah, Ahmad, and Mahmood (2018) highlighted this bias as a key factor in financial judgments. Despite possessing knowledge of financial behavior, individuals often continue to adjust their estimates slowly, as Palm and Andersson (2020) noted, with anchoring influencing decisions even when they are aware of it. In real estate, Klamer et al. (2017) demonstrated that property evaluators often fall prey to anchoring bias by basing their valuations on previously transacted prices. Similarly, Bao and Saunders (2021) pointed out that the asking price of a property can serve as an anchor, limiting buyers' ability to assess a property's true value objectively. Additionally, researchers have identified property location as another factor contributing to anchoring bias. Clauretie and Thistle (2007) observed that the distance between the property and the buyer's location could significantly influence the price paid, with location acting as an anchor in the valuation process.

Impact of Anchoring on Property Valuation: In real estate, listing prices often serve as anchors that influence the perceptions of buyers, sellers, and even real estate professionals. Research by Northcraft and Neale (1987) demonstrated that both novices and experienced professionals are influenced by initial listing prices, even when those prices are objectively too high or too low. This phenomenon shows how anchoring can persist, distorting property valuation despite market fundamentals. Anchoring in Negotiations: Price negotiations are another area where anchoring bias exerts significant influence. Sellers typically set an asking price based on market trends, while buyers may negotiate with that price in mind, even if it doesn't accurately reflect the property's value. Seiler, Seiler, Harrison, and Lane (2012) found that higher initial listing prices lead to higher final sales prices, even when controlling for other market variables. The research suggests that anchoring causes buyers to become fixated on initial price points, leading to less flexible negotiation strategies. Investment Decision-Making: Anchoring bias also affects real estate investors. Investors who anchor historical prices may fail to account for current market conditions, leading to flawed decision-making. According to Hirshleifer (2001), behavioral finance theories suggest that investors are prone to cognitive biases, such as anchoring, that cause them to make suboptimal choices. In real estate, this could mean holding onto properties too long based on past high prices, or conversely, being overly cautious due to recent declines.

Behavioral Economics and Anchoring: From a broader behavioral economics perspective, Tversky and Kahneman (1974) pioneered research on heuristics and biases, including anchoring. Their work has laid the groundwork for understanding how cognitive shortcuts, like anchoring, can distort decision-making in real estate markets. Even in professional settings, reliance on heuristics can cause agents and investors to deviate from rational models of market behavior, exacerbating inefficiencies in pricing and market trends.

Mitigating Anchoring Bias: To mitigate anchoring bias in real estate, experts recommend using more objective measures and data-driven insights. Gallimore (1996) emphasized the importance of independent property appraisals and utilizing statistical data to reduce reliance on subjective anchors like listing prices. Additionally, real estate professionals can benefit from training that focuses on recognizing and countering cognitive biases, allowing for more balanced decision-making processes.

Technological Solutions to Anchoring: Advancements in technology, such as AI and machine learning, offer potential solutions to mitigate anchoring bias. Automated valuation models (AVMs) and AI-driven tools can provide real-time market data, eliminating the need to rely on subjective anchors. Geltner et al. (2007) suggest that using such technology can help investors and buyers make more informed decisions, as these tools minimize human biases and rely on objective, data-driven insights.

2.4 Risk Aversion Bias in the Real Estate Market

Risk aversion significantly impacts real estate investment decisions, especially due to the substantial capital required and the long-term nature of the asset class. Investors tend to avoid risk, preferring certain returns even if that means forgoing higher potential gains. This behavior is largely influenced by behavioral biases, particularly loss aversion.

Kahneman and Tversky (1979) developed Prospect Theory, which emphasizes how individuals are more affected by potential losses than equivalent gains. In real estate markets, this often leads investors to avoid high-risk investments, such as properties in emerging markets, in favor of stable, lower-yield assets. This conservative approach can result in missed opportunities for higher returns in high-growth areas.

Gyourko and Keim (1992) analyzed the U.S. real estate market and found that investors demonstrate significant levels of risk aversion. Their research highlights that during periods of economic uncertainty, both institutional and retail investors tend to overemphasize safety, opting for properties with lower risk profiles, despite the potential for higher returns from more volatile investments.

Another aspect of risk aversion in real estate markets is the preference for geographic diversification, which is intended to reduce perceived risks. Leamer (2007) explored how heightened risk aversion during market downturns led to liquidity constraints, with fewer transactions occurring as investors were hesitant to enter or exit the market. This fear of loss during recessions worsened real estate market cycles, making recovery more difficult.

Moreover, Shiller (2000) suggested that behavioral biases, including risk aversion, have historically influenced the cyclical nature of real estate bubbles. He noted that during market booms, investors often become less risk-averse, contributing to overinvestment in overvalued properties. Conversely, during downturns, heightened risk aversion causes an excessive flight to safety, aggravating price drops and market liquidity issues.

Individuals tend to exhibit risk aversion, as argued by Tversky and Kahneman (1974), with a greater emphasis on avoiding potential losses than achieving equivalent gains. This phenomenon is reaffirmed by Ball et al. (2010), who highlight the crucial role of risk aversion in financial decision-making. Notably, women tend to display higher levels of risk aversion than men, which has implications for investment strategies and outcomes.

The commercial real estate sector is particularly susceptible to loss aversion bias, where frequent transactions provide numerous reference points for price comparisons, thereby amplifying this bias (Wangzhou et al., 2021). Moreover, experienced and sophisticated investors in this sector tend to be even more averse to potential losses, likely due to their extensive experience in transaction processes (Bokhari and Geltner, 2011). The tendency toward loss aversion in commercial real estate can have significant implications for investment decisions and pricing strategies. Further research could explore the impact of loss aversion on investment outcomes and the role of experience and sophistication in mitigating this bias.

Mitigating Risk Aversion Bias in Real Estate Decisions

Risk aversion bias can significantly impede investment potential in real estate markets, as overly cautious investors may miss out on higher returns due to fear of loss. However, there are strategies that investors and advisors can adopt to mitigate the effects of risk aversion bias, enabling more balanced and profitable decision-making.

Education and Financial Literacy: One of the key strategies for mitigating risk aversion is improving financial literacy among real estate investors. Studies suggest that better understanding of market dynamics, asset valuation, and diversification can reduce irrational fears of loss. Baker et al. (2019) found that more informed investors are less likely to exhibit extreme risk-averse behavior because they understand the risk-return tradeoff and are more comfortable with calculated risks. Providing investors with comprehensive information about market trends, potential risks, and realistic expectations can significantly diminish irrational fear-based decisions.

Diversification Strategies: Diversification is a well-known risk management technique that can reduce exposure to any single real estate market or asset. By spreading investments across different geographical areas, asset types (e.g., residential, commercial, industrial), and even across different economic regions, investors can lower the overall risk of their portfolio. Markowitz (1952) introduced modern portfolio theory, which emphasizes that diversification lowers risk without necessarily sacrificing returns. Real estate investors can diversify their holdings not only across properties but also through REITs (Real Estate Investment Trusts), which offer exposure to a variety of properties with lower individual investment.

Professional Advice and Structured Decision Frameworks Relying on professional advice and structured decision-making frameworks can help mitigate emotional biases. Advisors can guide investors through a step-by-step process that includes risk assessment, scenario analysis, and sensitivity analysis. These frameworks reduce the impact of emotions on decision-making by focusing on systematic evaluation of risks and benefits. Geltner et al. (2007) suggested that structured investment processes, including portfolio risk assessments and scenario planning, can help investors make more objective decisions and balance risk effectively.

2.5 Disposition Bias in Real Estate Market: A Review of Literature

Disposition bias refers to the tendency for investors to sell assets that have appreciated in value too early while holding on to assets that have depreciated, which can negatively affect their investment outcomes. In real estate, this bias influences both residential and commercial property owners and can lead to suboptimal decisions regarding property sales and acquisitions.

Fogel and Berry (2010) defined disposition bias as the tendency of investors to sell profitable investments prematurely while holding onto losing ones for too long.

Prosad, Kapoor, and Sengupta (2015) concluded that this bias significantly affects decision-making, often resulting in suboptimal investment outcomes, highlighting the emotional factors that influence investment behavior.

Foundational Insights on Disposition Bias: The theory of disposition bias was first identified by Shefrin and Statman (1985), who argued that this bias is rooted in loss aversion and mental accounting. In the real estate market, investors are often hesitant to sell properties at a loss, waiting for values to recover, even if market conditions indicate a downward trend. This behavior can delay portfolio adjustments, adversely impacting overall returns.

Empirical Evidence from Real Estate Markets: Disposition bias is prevalent in real estate, as demonstrated by Genesove and Mayer (2001), who analyzed the Boston housing market. Their study found that home sellers were reluctant to accept prices lower than their purchase prices, even when the market value had dropped. This reluctance led to longer holding periods and reduced liquidity in the market. The authors attributed this behavior to the psychological resistance to realizing a loss, a central tenet of disposition bias. Behavioral Economics and Loss Aversion:

The concept of loss aversion, a critical element of Prospect Theory developed by Kahneman and Tversky (1979), helps explain why real estate investors exhibit disposition bias. According to Prospect Theory, people prefer to avoid losses rather than acquire equivalent gains. This cognitive bias encourages property owners to hold onto underperforming properties longer than they should, leading to missed opportunities for reinvestment in more lucrative assets.

Real Estate Investment Decisions and the Disposition Effect: Research by Shimizu and Nishimura (2006) on real estate markets in Japan found that investors displayed disposition bias by holding onto properties that had decreased in value for extended periods. This irrational behavior stemmed from the investors' desire to avoid acknowledging a financial loss. They suggested that this behavior can lead to systemic inefficiencies in the real estate market, as prices may not adjust to reflect true demand and supply conditions promptly.

Mitigating Disposition Bias: Various strategies have been proposed to mitigate the effects of disposition bias in real estate markets. Geltner, Miller, Clayton, and Eichholtz (2007) recommend the use of automated valuation models (AVMs) and professional appraisals to provide objective, data-driven insights into property values. By relying on these tools, investors can reduce their emotional attachment to specific investments and make more rational decisions. Periodic portfolio reviews, as suggested by Barberis and Xiong (2009), also help in reassessing investment strategies, thereby mitigating the disposition effect.

Technology and Behavioral Bias in Real Estate: Technological advancements, particularly in the field of AI and big data, have the potential to help real estate investors overcome behavioral biases. Hendershott, MacGregor, and White (2013) found that using AI-driven market analysis can provide investors with a clearer picture of market trends, allowing them to make more informed decisions. These tools can help reduce the emotional bias associated with holding onto losing investments by emphasizing data-based forecasts over subjective decision-making.

2.6 Representativeness Bias in Real Estate Markets

Representativeness bias refers to the tendency for individuals to rely on stereotypes or overly simplistic patterns when making decisions, often ignoring underlying complexities. In the real estate market, this bias can significantly affect investor behavior, property valuations, and market expectations, leading to misjudgments about future trends and risks. Busenitz and Barney (1997) define representativeness bias as a cognitive error in which decisions are influenced by limited observations, often derived from small and non-random samples. This bias, as shown by Khan, Bashir, and Islam (2021), plays a significant role in shaping investor behavior, often leading to overreactions in the market and underscoring the necessity for more comprehensive analysis in investment decisions.

Representativeness bias occurs when investors predict the outcome of an event or investment based on a similar past event, often overemphasizing the positive outcomes and assuming similar results for future events (Cascão et al., 2023). This bias has been identified as a key factor influencing decision-making in the real estate sector (Pandey and Jessica, 2018).

Regret is a prevalent emotion in the investment sector, where investors often experience regret after missing potential profits or suffering significant losses. In an attempt to alleviate these feelings, investors may engage in comforting rationalizations. However, this coping mechanism can lead to adverse outcomes, such as holding on to poorly performing investments, ultimately exacerbating losses (Seiler et al., 2008).

Hoxha and Hasani (2022) affirm the existence of regret aversion bias and its impact on investor decision-making. Similarly, Wangzhou et al. (2021) highlight that regret aversion bias influences risk perception, with financial literacy acting as a mitigating factor. Investors with higher financial proficiency are better equipped to overcome the emotional impact of regret and make more rational, informed decisions.

Introduction to Representativeness Bias: First introduced by Tversky and Kahneman (1974), representativeness bias describes how people make judgments based on how similar something is to their mental prototype, rather than on actual probabilities or data. In the real estate context, this might occur when investors assume that property prices will continue to rise simply because they have done so in the past, neglecting to account for other market dynamics.

Impact on Real Estate Valuation: Representativeness bias can distort property valuations. Case and Shiller (1989) provided early empirical evidence of this bias in the U.S. housing market, demonstrating that investors overestimated property values based on past performance, leading to inflated real estate prices that were unsupported by economic fundamentals. This bias contributed to market overconfidence and subsequently to the housing market crash when prices corrected.

Overreliance on Short-Term Market Trends: A significant manifestation of representativeness bias is the overreliance on short-term market trends. Poterba (1991) analyzed how real estate investors often extrapolate short-term price increases into future expectations, disregarding longer-term economic indicators such as interest rates and inflation. His work highlighted the role of this bias in fueling real estate bubbles, where investors falsely believed in the indefinite upward trajectory of property prices.

Cyclical Nature of Housing Markets: The research by Gyourko and Keim (1992) focused on how representativeness bias contributes to the cyclical nature of housing markets. They argued that investors' tendency to generalize from short-term gains during a market upswing can lead to an unsustainable boom, which is eventually corrected when the market adjusts to economic realities. The repetition of such cycles suggests that investors repeatedly fall into the trap of representativeness bias.

Behavioral Insights in Real Estate Investment: Representativeness bias also affects individual real estate investment decisions. Barberis and Thaler (2003) argued that investors in the real estate market often rely on simplistic patterns when making decisions, such as the historical appreciation of property values in a given location, without considering broader market forces or changes in demand. This bias can result in misallocated investments, particularly in areas where property values are not supported by long-term economic trends.

Mitigating Representativeness Bias: Mitigating the effects of representativeness bias requires a more sophisticated approach to real estate investment. Barberis and Thaler (2003) recommended that investors diversify their information sources and rely on professional valuation services to avoid making decisions based solely on short-term patterns. Similarly, Geltner et al. (2007) advocated for the use of data-driven valuation methods, such as automated valuation models (AVMs), to reduce the influence of cognitive biases on decision-making.

Technology and Data Analytics as Tools: The advent of AI and big data has provided tools that can help mitigate representativeness bias. Ling and Archer (2013) explored the role of AVMs and data analytics in reducing reliance on past trends and providing more accurate property valuations. By leveraging a wider array of data points, such as economic indicators, demographic trends, and macroeconomic factors, investors can make better-informed decisions that are less prone to cognitive biases.

Conclusion: Representativeness bias plays a significant role in distorting real estate market valuations and investor behavior. By relying on past patterns and short-term trends, investors expose themselves to the risk of overconfidence and potential market corrections. However, through the use of diversified data, professional valuation services, and advanced technologies like AI-driven analytics, it is possible to mitigate the effects of this cognitive bias and make more rational, data-informed investment decisions.

2.7 Availability Bias in Real Estate Markets: A Review of Literature

Availability bias is a cognitive shortcut that relies on immediate examples that come to a person's mind when evaluating a specific topic, concept, method, or decision. In the context of real estate, availability bias can lead investors and market participants to make decisions based on readily available information, often skewing their perceptions and judgments about property values, risks, and market conditions.

Understanding Availability Bias: The concept of availability bias was popularized by Tversky and Kahneman (1973), who demonstrated how individuals tend to rely on immediate examples when forming judgments. In real estate, this might manifest as investors focusing on recent sales data or notable properties in their vicinity while ignoring broader market trends or less visible factors that could influence property values. Cheung et al. (2022) discovered that the influence of information tends to diminish over time, which substantiates the existence of availability bias, where investors prefer readily accessible information. This reliance on easily accessible data highlights a form of myopic behavior, where investors focus only on short-term, easily obtainable information for decision-making.

Pandey and Jessica (2018) further emphasized this behavior in their study, showing that such short-sightedness leads to a narrow perspective in investment decisions, often at the expense of a more comprehensive analysis. Khan et al. (2024) emphasized the pivotal role of financial literacy in influencing investment decisions. As the global economy becomes more integrated and technological innovations advance, financial literacy has become essential for investors. The study underscores that a solid understanding of financial concepts equips investors to navigate increasingly complex financial products and services, allowing for more informed and strategic decision-making

Impact on Investment Decisions: Kumar and Ghosh (2014) explored how availability bias influences real estate investment decisions. They found that investors often base their decisions on easily retrievable information, such as news stories about rapidly appreciating properties or high-profile real estate transactions. This reliance on recent or highly publicized information can lead to poor investment choices, such as overvaluing properties or misjudging market stability.

Market Trends and Perceptions: Availability bias can significantly distort perceptions of market trends. Friedman and Wenzel (2006) discussed how recent market fluctuations can lead investors to project current conditions into the future, failing to consider historical data and longer-term trends. For instance, a surge in property values in a specific area may lead to a generalized belief that all properties in similar markets will appreciate, despite varying local economic conditions.

Influence of Media and Social Networks: The role of media and social networks in shaping availability bias is noteworthy. Baker and Nofsinger (2010) examined how media coverage of real estate markets can amplify availability bias. Sensational stories about skyrocketing property values can lead to increased investor interest and speculation, further inflating prices and creating bubbles. This feedback loop highlights the critical role that information dissemination plays in the manifestation of availability bias.

Behavioral Finance and Real Estate: Incorporating behavioral finance perspectives, Thaler (1999) emphasized how cognitive biases, including availability bias, affect market efficiency in real estate. He argued that investors often react to readily available information rather than conducting thorough analyses, leading to mispricing and inefficiencies in the market. This behavior can contribute to cycles of boom and bust in real estate values.

Mitigating Availability Bias: To mitigate the effects of availability bias, real estate professionals and investors are encouraged to adopt more structured decision-making processes. Harrison and Johnson (2006) suggested that employing data analytics and comprehensive market research can provide a more balanced view, helping to counteract the influence of easily accessible but potentially misleading information. This approach can lead to more informed and rational investment decisions.

Technological Interventions: The rise of technology in real estate, including big data and machine learning, offers tools to combat availability bias. Chinloy and Pappas (2016) highlighted how advanced analytics can help investors assess market conditions based on a wide array of data rather than relying solely on visible trends. By incorporating diverse datasets, investors can make better-informed decisions that consider underlying market fundamentals.

Conclusion: Availability bias is a significant factor influencing decision-making in the real estate market. By relying on easily accessible information and recent experiences, investors risk making decisions that may not reflect the true market landscape. Understanding and mitigating this bias through structured analysis, data-driven insights, and technology can enhance investment strategies and promote more rational decision-making in real estate.

Research Gap

While much research has been conducted on behavioral finance in stock markets, there is a limited body of work focused on the specific role of behavioral biases in real estate markets. Existing studies often emphasize economic and structural factors influencing real estate prices and market dynamics, with less attention paid to the psychological factors that affect decision-making. This research aims to fill this gap by systematically investigating the various behavioral biases prevalent in real estate markets, their impact on market outcomes, and the strategies used to mitigate them.

Research Objectives

1. To identify and analyze the key behavioral biases influencing decision-making in real estate markets.
2. To assess the impact of these behavioral biases on real estate market outcomes, including property pricing, investment strategies, and market efficiency.
3. To study the strategies to mitigate the influence of behavioral biases in real estate decision-making.
4. To propose recommendations for real estate professionals, investors, and policymakers on minimizing the adverse effects of behavioral biases in the market.

Hypothesis Setting

H0: There is no the impact of these behavioral biases on real estate market outcomes, including, including property pricing, investment strategies, and market efficiency.

Questions Review

1. What are the most prevalent behavioral biases affecting decision-making in real estate markets?
2. How do these behavioral biases influence key market outcomes, such as property pricing, market efficiency, and investment decisions?
3. What strategies do market participants employ to mitigate the impact of behavioral biases in real estate decisions?
4. What recommendations can be made to minimize the influence of behavioral biases in real estate markets

4. RESEARCH METHODOLOGY

4.1. Research Design

- **Descriptive and Exploratory Approach:** The research will employ a mixed-methods approach, combining both qualitative and quantitative data collection methods. The descriptive part will provide an overview of the identified biases, while the exploratory part will investigate into their impact and the mitigation strategies used.

4.2. Sample Design

- **Target Population:** Real estate investors, buyers, sellers, agents, and developers.
- **Sample Size:** 280 respondents for the questionnaire, selected through purposive sampling for interview participants based on their market experience and role.
- **Primary Data Collection:**
    - ✓ **Questionnaire:** Structured questionnaires will be distributed to stakeholders in the real estate market, including investors, buyers, sellers, developers, and real estate agents.
    - ✓ **Interviews:** Semi-structured interviews with respondents will provide deeper insights into how these biases are perceived and managed in real-world scenarios.
- **Secondary Data Collection:**
    - ✓ **Literature Review:** Review of existing academic papers, market reports, and case studies related to behavioral biases in finance and real estate.

- ✓ **Market Data Analysis:** Analysis of historical real estate market data to identify patterns attributable to behavioral biases.

4.3 Data Analysis

- **Quantitative Analysis:**
  - ✓ **Statistical Tools:** Descriptive statistics the percentile method will be used to analyze the questionnaire data.
- **Qualitative Analysis:**
  - ✓ **Thematic Analysis:** Applied to interview transcripts to identify common themes and insights related to the impact of behavioral biases and the effectiveness of mitigation strategies.

4.4 Results and Discussion

Table 1. Age category of respondents

Age Category (Years)	18-24	25-34	35-44	45-54	55-64	65+
Number of Respondents	35	55	90	70	20	10
Percentage	14.58%	22.92%	37.5%	29.17%	8.33%	4.17%

Source: Author

Table 1 shows that the largest group of respondents (37.5%) is aged between 35-44, followed by those aged 25-34 (22.92%). The youngest group (18-24) makes up 14.58% of respondents, while only 4.17% belong to the 65+ age group.

Table 2. Education level of respondents

Education Level	Number	Percentage
High School	95	33.93%
Intermediate	90	32.14%
Bachelor's	55	19.64%
Master's	23	8.21%
Doctorate	2	0.71%
Other	15	5.36%
Total	280	100%

Source: Author

Table 2 shows the majority of the respondents (33.93%) hold a High School degree, followed by those with an Intermediate degree (32.14%). • A significant proportion of respondents (19.64%) have a Bachelor's degree, while 8.21% have a Master's degree. •

Table 3. Experience in real estate

Experience in Real Estate (Years)	Less than 1 year	1-3 years	4-7 years	8-10 years	More than 10 years
Number of Respondents	20	40	60	30	50
Percentage	8%	16%	24%	12%	20%

Source: Author

Table 3 highlights that most respondents (24%) have 4-7 years of experience in real estate, followed by 20% with more than 10 years of experience. Those with 1-3 years of experience account for 16%, while 12% have 8-10 years of experience. Only 8% of respondents have less than 1 year of experience in the industry.

Table 4. Gender distribution

Respondents	Male	Female	Total
Sellers	42 (60%)	28 (40%)	70
Buyers	33 (55%)	27 (45%)	60
Real Estate Agents	56 (70%)	24 (30%)	80
Developers	16 (80%)	4 (20%)	20
Real Estate Investors	19.5 (65%)	10.5 (35%)	30
Real Estate Traders	15 (75%)	5 (25%)	20
Total	181	99	280

Source: Author

Table 4 reveals that the gender distribution table shows that males dominate the real estate market, making up approximately 64.6% of the total respondents (181/280). Females account for around 35.4% of the respondents (99/280). The highest percentage of females is found among Buyers (45%), while the lowest is among Developers (20%).

Table 5. Primary role in real estate market

Primary Role in Real Estate Market	Number	Percentage
Sellers	70	25%
Buyers	60	21.43%
Real Estate Agents	80	28.57%
Developers	20	7.14%
Real Estate Investors	30	10.71%
Real Estate Traders	20	7.14%
Total	280	100%

Source: Author

Table 5 indicates that a significant portion of respondents are Sellers (25%) and Buyers (21.43%), suggesting that many are individual property owners or end-users involved in real estate transactions. Real Estate Agents, accounting for 28.57%, play a prominent role in market facilitation. Other respondents include Developers (7.14%), Investors (10.71%), and Traders (7.14%).

Section 2: Awareness and Perception of Behavioral Biases

Table 6. Familiarity with behavioral biases in decision-making

Respondents	Not familiar	Somewhat familiar	Moderately familiar	Very familiar	Extremely familiar
Sellers	10 (14.3%)	20 (28.6%)	20 (28.6%)	10 (14.3%)	10 (14.3%)
Buyers	5 (8.3%)	15 (25%)	20 (33.3%)	10 (16.7%)	10 (16.7%)
Real Estate Agents	5 (6.3%)	10 (12.5%)	30 (37.5%)	20 (25%)	15 (18.8%)
Developers	2 (10%)	5 (25%)	8 (40%)	3 (15%)	2 (10%)
Real Estate Investors	3 (10%)	8 (26.7%)	10 (33.3%)	5 (16.7%)	4 (13.3%)
Real Estate Traders	2 (10%)	5 (25%)	8 (40%)	3 (15%)	2 (10%)
Total	27 (10.8%)	68 (27.2%)	96 (38.4%)	51 (20.4%)	43 (17.2%)

Source: Author

Table 6 shows the distribution of respondents' familiarity with behavioral biases in decision-making, along with the percentage of each category. The majority of respondents (38.4%) reported being moderately familiar with the concept, followed by those who are somewhat familiar (27.2%). Only 10.8% of respondents reported being not familiar with the concept, while 20.4% and 17.2% reported being very familiar and extremely familiar, respectively.

Table 7. Behavioral biases impact decision-making in real estate markets

Respondents	Not at all	Slightly	Moderately	Significantly	Extremely
Sellers	20 (14.3%)	30 (21.4%)	40 (28.6%)	20 (14.3%)	10 (7.1%)
Buyers	15 (10.7%)	25 (17.9%)	45 (32.1%)	25 (17.9%)	10 (7.1%)
Real Estate Agents	10 (7.1%)	20 (14.3%)	30 (21.4%)	40 (28.6%)	20 (14.3%)
Developers	5 (3.6%)	15 (10.7%)	25 (17.9%)	50 (35.7%)	25 (17.9%)
Real Estate Investors	10 (7.1%)	20 (14.3%)	30 (21.4%)	30 (21.4%)	30 (21.4%)
Real Estate Traders	5 (3.6%)	10 (7.1%)	20 (14.3%)	40 (28.6%)	45 (32.1%)
Total	65 (23.2%)	120 (42.9%)	190 (67.9%)	205 (73.2%)	140 (50%)

Source: Author

Table 7 identify the most common response for each type of respondent and compare the results across different types of respondents. Sellers and Buyers believe behavioral biases impact decision-making in real estate markets "Moderately" (28.6% and 32.1%, respectively). Real Estate Agents and Developers believe it impacts "Significantly" (28.6% and 35.7%, respectively). Real Estate Investors are divided between "Moderately", "Significantly", and "Extremely" (21.4% each). Real Estate Traders believe it impacts "Extremely" (32.1%).

Key Observations

- There is a variation in opinions across different types of respondents, indicating that behavioral biases may have different levels of impact on decision-making in real estate markets depending on the respondent's role.
- Real estate agents and developers tend to believe that behavioral biases have a more significant impact on decision-making, while Sellers and Buyers tend to believe it has a moderate impact.
- Real estate investors and traders have a more diverse range of opinions, indicating that their perspectives on behavioral biases may be influenced by various factors

The survey provides valuable insights into the perceptions of various stakeholders on the impact of behavioral biases on decision-making in real estate markets. The results highlight the importance of considering the role of the respondent and the need for a nuanced understanding of the complex factors that influence decision-making in the real estate market. By recognizing the potential impact of behavioral biases, market participants can make more informed decisions and develop strategies to mitigate their effects.

Table 8. Behavioral biases in real estate markets

Behavioral Bias	Sellers (70)	Buyers (60)	Real Estate Agents (80)	Developers (20)	Real Estate Investors (30)	Real Estate Traders (20)
Anchoring Bias	18.57% (13)	21.7% (13)	22.5% (18)	20% (4)	23.3% (7)	25% (5)
Herd Behavior	11.43% (8)	16.7% (10)	17.5% (14)	15% (3)	16.7% (5)	15% (3)
Overconfidence Bias	15.71% (11)	18.33% (11)	20% (16)	20% (4)	20% (6)	20% (4)
Loss Aversion	27.14% (19)	30% (18)	30% (24)	30% (6)	30% (9)	30% (6)
Endowment Effect	11.43% (8)	11.67% (7)	12.5% (10)	10% (2)	13.33% (4)	10% (2)
Framing Effect	5.71% (4)	9.17% (5)	7.5% (6)	10% (2)	6.67% (2)	10% (2)
Mental accounting	1.43% (1)	2.5% (1)	2.5% (2)	0% (0)	3.33% (1)	0% (0)
Confirmation bias	1.43% (1)	1.67% (1)	2.5% (2)	0% (0)	3.33% (1)	0% (0)
Availability Bias	1.43% (1)	1.67% (1)	2.5% (2)	0% (0)	0% (0)	5% (1)
Regret Bias	21.43% (15)	26.67% (16)	25% (20)	25% (5)	26.67% (8)	25% (5)
Disposition Bias	1.43% (1)	1.67% (1)	0% (0)	0% (0)	3.33% (1)	0% (0)
Representativeness Bias	0% (0)	1.67% (1)	0% (0)	0% (0)	3.33% (1)	0% (0)

Source: Author

Table 8 Reveals that:

- Loss Aversion and Regret Bias are the most significant biases: Loss Aversion and Regret Bias are the top two biases that respondents believe have the most significant impact on real estate markets, with 27.14% and 21.43% of the sellers, and 30% and 26.67% of the buyers selecting them, respectively.
- Anchoring Bias and Overconfidence Bias are also significant: Anchoring Bias and Overconfidence Bias are the third and fourth most significant biases, with 18.57% and 15.71% of the sellers, and 21.7% and 18.33% of the buyers selecting them, respectively.

- Herd Behavior and Endowment Effect are moderately significant: Herd Behavior and Endowment Effect are the fifth and sixth most significant biases, with 11.43% and 11.43% of the sellers, and 16.7% and 11.67% of the buyers selecting them, respectively.

Calculation for Anchoring Bias:
Total respondents: 70 (Sellers)
Number of respondents who selected Anchoring Bias: 13
Percentage of respondents who selected Anchoring Bias: (13/70) x 100% = 18.57%
Total respondents: 60 (Buyers)
Number of respondents who selected Anchoring Bias: 13
Percentage of respondents who selected Anchoring Bias: (13/60) x 100% = 21.7%

Table 9. rankings based on the impact of behavioral biases on real estate markets,

Behavioral Bias	Respondents	Sellers	Buyers	Real Estate Agents	Developers	Real Estate Investors	Real Estate Traders
Anchoring Bias	Medium (1)	Medium (2)	High (3)	Medium (2)	Medium (2)	Medium (2)	Medium (2)
Herd Behavior	Low-Medium (4)	Low (5)	Low (5)	Medium (2)	Medium (2)	Medium (2)	Medium (2)
Overconfidence Bias	Medium (1)	Medium (2)	Medium (2)	Medium (2)	Medium (2)	Medium (2)	Medium (2)
Loss Aversion	High (6)	High (6)	High (6)	High (6)	High (6)	High (6)	High (6)
Endowment Effect	Medium-High (7)	Medium-High (7)	Medium (2)	Medium (2)	Medium (2)	Medium (2)	Medium (2)
Framing Effect	Low-Medium (4)	Low (5)	Low (5)	Low-Medium (4)	Low-Medium (4)	Low-Medium (4)	Low-Medium (4)
Mental accounting	Low (8)	Low (8)	Low (8)	Low (8)	Low (8)	Low (8)	Low (8)
Confirmation bias	Low (8)	Low (8)	Low (8)	Low (8)	Low (8)	Low (8)	Low (8)
Availability Bias	Low (8)	Low (8)	Low (8)	Low (8)	Low (8)	Low (8)	Low (8)
Regret Bias	High (6)	High (6)	High (6)	High (6)	High (6)	High (6)	High (6)
Disposition Bias	Low (8)	Low (8)	Low (8)	Low (8)	Low (8)	Low (8)	Low (8)
Representativeness Bias	Low (8)	Low (8)	Low (8)	Low (8)	Low (8)	Low (8)	Low (8)

Source: Authors- (1) Tversky and Kahneman (1974) - Anchoring bias in decision-making (2) Northcraft and Neale (1987) - Anchoring bias in real estate negotiations (3) Bazerman and Samuelson (1983) - Anchoring bias in buyer-seller negotiations (4) Banerjee (1992) - Herd behavior in financial markets (5) Shiller (2000) - Herd behavior in real estate markets (6) Kahneman and Tversky (1979) - Loss aversion and prospect theory (7) Thaler

(1980) - Endowment effect in real estate markets (8) Various studies on behavioral biases in real estate markets, including those by Case and Shiller (2003), and Genesove and Mayer (2001)

Note: The ranking is based on the impact of behavioral biases on real estate markets, supported by research and academic studies. The ranking is subjective and based on my analysis of the impact of behavioral biases on real estate markets.

Table 9 Reveals:

Buyers: Buyers are highly influenced by Anchoring Bias, Loss Aversion, and Regret Bias. They are also moderately influenced by Overconfidence Bias, Endowment Effect, and Framing Effect. This suggests that buyers are susceptible to initial prices, fear of losses, and fear of regretting a decision.

Sellers: Sellers are highly influenced by Loss Aversion and Regret Bias. They are also moderately influenced by Overconfidence Bias, Endowment Effect, and Anchoring Bias. This suggests that sellers are motivated by the fear of losses and the fear of regretting a decision, and tend to overvalue their properties.

Real Estate Agents: Real Estate Agents are moderately influenced by Herd Behavior, Overconfidence Bias, and Loss Aversion. They are also influenced by Anchoring Bias, Endowment Effect, and Framing Effect. This suggests that real estate agents are influenced by market trends and social proof, and tend to be overly optimistic about their abilities.

Developers: Developers are moderately influenced by Herd Behavior, Overconfidence Bias, and Loss Aversion. They are also influenced by Anchoring Bias, Endowment Effect, and Framing Effect. This suggests that developers are influenced by market trends and social proof, and tend to be overly optimistic about their abilities.

Real Estate Investors: Real Estate Investors are highly influenced by Loss Aversion and Regret Bias. They are also moderately influenced by Overconfidence Bias, Anchoring Bias, and Endowment Effect. This suggests that real estate investors are motivated by the fear of losses and the fear of regretting a decision, and tend to be overly optimistic about their abilities.

Real Estate Traders: Real Estate Traders are highly influenced by Loss Aversion and Regret Bias. They are also moderately influenced by Overconfidence Bias, Anchoring Bias, and Endowment Effect. This suggests that real estate traders are motivated by the fear of losses and the fear of regretting a decision, and tend to be overly optimistic about their abilities.

Biases-Wise Interpretation:

Loss Aversion: Loss Aversion has a high impact on all respondents, indicating that the fear of losses is a powerful motivator in the real estate market.

Regret Bias: Regret Bias has a high impact on all respondents, indicating that the fear of regretting a decision is a powerful motivator in the real estate market.

Anchoring Bias: Anchoring Bias has a high impact on buyers, indicating that initial prices or values can influence their decisions.
Overconfidence Bias: Overconfidence Bias has a moderate impact on all respondents, indicating that they tend to be overly optimistic about their abilities and the market.
Endowment Effect: Endowment Effect has a moderate impact on sellers, indicating that they tend to overvalue their properties.
Herd Behavior: Herd Behavior has a moderate impact on real estate agents and developers, indicating that they are influenced by market trends and social proof.
Framing Effect: Framing Effect has a low-medium impact on all respondents, indicating that the way information is presented can influence their decisions.
Mental Accounting, Confirmation Bias, Availability Bias, Disposition Bias, and Representativeness Bias: These biases have a low impact on all respondents, indicating that they are less influential in real estate decision-making.

Section 3: Specific Behavioral Biases in Real Estate Decisions

Q.1: How often do you consider past prices or previous sale prices when evaluating a property? (Anchoring Bias)

Table 10. Frequency of considering past prices or previous sale prices

Respondents	Never	Rarely	Sometimes	Often	Always
Sellers	10 (14%)	20 (29%)	20 (29%)	15 (21%)	5 (7%)
Buyers	5 (8%)	15 (25%)	25 (42%)	10 (17%)	5 (8%)
Real Estate Agents	5 (6%)	10 (13%)	30 (38%)	20 (25%)	15 (19%)
Developers	5 (25%)	5 (25%)	5 (25%)	3 (15%)	2 (10%)
Real Estate Investors	5 (17%)	10 (33%)	10 (33%)	3 (10%)	2 (7%)
Real Estate Traders	5 (25%)	5 (25%)	5 (25%)	3 (15%)	2 (10%)
Total	35 (12.5%)	65 (23.2%)	95 (34.1%)	54 (19.3%)	31 (11.1%)

Source: Author

Table 10 indicates that a significant proportion of respondents, particularly real estate agents (45%) and sellers (35%), often or always consider past prices or previous sale prices when evaluating a property, exhibiting anchoring bias. Buyers and real estate investors also show a moderate level of anchoring bias. Developers and real estate traders are less likely to be influenced by past prices. This suggests that anchoring bias may have a significant impact on real estate markets, particularly in the hands of sellers and real estate agents.

Q2: Have you ever purchased or sold a property because you observed others doing the same? (Herd Behavior)

Table 11. Frequency of herd behavior in real estate decisions

Respondents	Yes	No	Not Sure
Sellers	14 (20%)	28 (40%)	28 (40%)
Buyers	8 (13%)	24 (40%)	28 (47%)
Real Estate Agents	12 (15%)	24 (30%)	44 (55%)
Developers	4 (20%)	8 (40%)	8 (40%)
Real Estate Investors	6 (20%)	12 (40%)	12 (40%)
Real Estate Traders	4 (20%)	8 (40%)	8 (40%)
Total	48 (17.1%)	104 (37.1%)	128 (45.7%)

Source: Author

Table11 indicates that a significant proportion of respondents, across all categories, have been influenced by herd behavior in their real estate decisions. A majority of respondents (45.7%) are unsure about their motivations, while 37.1% have not been influenced by herd behavior. Real estate agents and buyers are more likely to be influenced by herd behavior, with 55% and 47% of respondents in these categories, respectively, indicating that they have been swayed by the actions of others. This suggests that herd behavior may have a profound impact on real estate markets, particularly in the hands of real estate agents and buyers.

Q3: To what extent do you trust your ability to predict real estate market trends? (Overconfidence Bias)

Table 12. Frequency of overconfidence bias in real estate market predictions

Respondents	Not at all	Slightly	Moderately	Significantly	Extremely
Sellers	10 (14%)	15 (21%)	20 (29%)	15 (21%)	10 (14%)
Buyers	12 (20%)	18 (30%)	15 (25%)	10 (17%)	5 (8%)
Real Estate Agents	5 (6%)	10 (13%)	20 (25%)	25 (31%)	20 (25%)
Developers	2 (10%)	4 (20%)	6 (30%)	4 (20%)	4 (20%)
Real Estate Investors	5 (17%)	8 (27%)	10 (33%)	5 (17%)	2 (7%)
Real Estate Traders	2 (10%)	4 (20%)	6 (30%)	4 (20%)	4 (20%)
Total	36 (12.9%)	59 (21.1%)	77 (27.5%)	63 (22.5%)	45 (16.1%)

Source: Author

Table 12 indicates that a significant proportion of respondents, across all categories, exhibit overconfidence bias in their ability to predict real estate market trends. A majority of respondents (65.6%) trust their ability to predict market trends to some extent, with 27.5% trusting their ability moderately and 22.5% trusting their ability significantly. Real estate agents are the most confident in their ability to predict market trends, with 56% of respondents in this category trusting their ability significantly or extremely. This suggests that overconfidence bias may be a significant factor in real estate market decisions, particularly among real estate agents.

Q4: Would you prefer holding onto a property in a declining market to avoid realizing a loss? (Loss Aversion)

Table 13. Frequency of loss aversion in real estate decisions

Respondents	Strongly Disagree	Disagree	Neutral	Agree	Strongly Agree
Sellers	10 (14%)	20 (29%)	15 (21%)	15 (21%)	10 (14%)
Buyers	8 (13%)	18 (30%)	12 (20%)	12 (20%)	10 (17%)
Real Estate Agents	5 (6%)	15 (19%)	20 (25%)	20 (25%)	20 (25%)
Developers	2 (10%)	4 (20%)	6 (30%)	4 (20%)	4 (20%)
Real Estate Investors	5 (17%)	8 (27%)	10 (33%)	5 (17%)	2 (7%)
Real Estate Traders	2 (10%)	4 (20%)	6 (30%)	4 (20%)	4 (20%)
Total	32 (11.4%)	69 (24.6%)	69 (24.6%)	60 (21.4%)	50 (17.9%)

Source: Author

Table 13 indicates that a significant proportion of respondents, across all categories, exhibit loss aversion in their real estate decisions. A majority of respondents (63.9%) agree or strongly agree that they would prefer holding onto a property in a declining market to avoid realizing a loss. Real estate agents are the most likely to exhibit loss aversion, with 50% of respondents in this category strongly agreeing that they would hold onto a property to avoid a loss. This suggests that loss aversion may be a significant factor in real estate market decisions, particularly among real estate agents.

Q5: Do you believe that owning a property makes you value it more than others might? (Endowment Effect)

Table 14. Frequency of endowment effect in real estate decisions

Respondents	Strongly Disagree	Disagree	Neutral	Agree	Strongly Agree
Sellers	5 (7%)	15 (21%)	20 (29%)	20 (29%)	10 (14%)
Buyers	4 (7%)	12 (20%)	18 (30%)	16 (27%)	10 (17%)
Real Estate Agents	2 (3%)	10 (13%)	20 (25%)	25 (31%)	23 (29%)
Developers	1 (5%)	3 (15%)	6 (30%)	5 (25%)	5 (25%)
Real Estate Investors	3 (10%)	6 (20%)	12 (40%)	6 (20%)	3 (10%)
Real Estate Traders	2 (10%)	4 (20%)	6 (30%)	4 (20%)	4 (20%)
Total	17 (6.1%)	50 (17.9%)	82 (29.3%)	76 (27.1%)	55 (19.6%)

Source: Author

Table 14 indicates that a significant proportion of respondents, across all categories, exhibit the endowment effect in their real estate decisions. A majority of respondents (46.7%) agree or strongly agree that owning a property makes them value it more than others might. Real estate agents are the most likely to exhibit the endowment effect, with 60% of respondents in this category agreeing or strongly agreeing that they value properties more highly due to ownership. This suggests that the endowment effect may be a significant factor in real estate market decisions, particularly among real estate agents.

Q 6: Have you ever made a real estate decision based on how the information was presented rather than the actual content? (Framing Effect)

Table 15. Frequency of framing effect in real estate decisions

Respondents	Yes	No	Not Sure
Sellers	25 (36%)	30 (43%)	15 (21%)
Buyers	20 (33%)	25 (42%)	15 (25%)
Real Estate Agents	35 (44%)	25 (31%)	20 (25%)
Developers	10 (50%)	5 (25%)	5 (25%)
Real Estate Investors	15 (50%)	10 (33%)	5 (17%)
Real Estate Traders	12 (60%)	5 (25%)	3 (15%)
Total	117 (41.8%)	100 (35.7%)	63 (22.5%)

Source: Author

Table 15 indicate that a significant proportion of respondents, across all categories, have made real estate decisions based on the presentation of information rather than its actual content. A majority of respondents (41.8%) reported that they have been influenced by the framing effect in their real estate decisions. Real estate traders are the most likely to be influenced by the framing effect, with 60% of respondents in this category reporting that they have made decisions based on presentation rather than content. This suggests that the framing effect may be a significant factor in real estate market decisions, particularly among real estate traders.

Section 4: Market Outcomes and Behavioral Biases

Table 16. Frequency of behavioral biases leading to market inefficiencies

Respondents	Never	Rarely	Sometimes	Often	Always
Sellers	5 (7%)	15 (21%)	25 (36%)	15 (21%)	10 (14%)
Buyers	4 (7%)	12 (20%)	20 (33%)	15 (25%)	9 (15%)
Real Estate Agents	2 (3%)	10 (13%)	25 (31%)	25 (31%)	18 (23%)
Developers	1 (5%)	3 (15%)	6 (30%)	5 (25%)	5 (25%)
Real Estate Investors	2 (7%)	6 (20%)	12 (40%)	6 (20%)	4 (13%)
Real Estate Traders	1 (5%)	4 (20%)	8 (40%)	4 (20%)	3 (15%)
Total	15 (5.4%)	50 (17.9%)	96 (34.3%)	70 (25%)	49 (17.5%)

Table 16 indicates that a significant proportion of respondents, across all categories, believe that behavioral biases lead to market inefficiencies in real estate. A majority of respondents (76.3%) reported that behavioral biases lead to market inefficiencies at least sometimes, with 42.5% reporting that they lead to inefficiencies often or always. Real estate agents are the most likely to believe that behavioral biases lead to market inefficiencies, with 54% of respondents in this category reporting that they lead to inefficiencies often or always. This suggests that behavioral biases may be a significant factor in real estate market inefficiencies, particularly among real estate agents.

Table 17. Contribution of behavioral biases to real estate bubbles

Respondents	Not at all	Slightly	Moderately	Significantly	Extremely
Sellers	5 (7%)	15 (21%)	25 (36%)	15 (21%)	10 (14%)
Buyers	4 (7%)	12 (20%)	20 (33%)	15 (25%)	9 (15%)
Real Estate Agents	2 (3%)	10 (13%)	25 (31%)	25 (31%)	18 (23%)
Developers	1 (5%)	3 (15%)	6 (30%)	5 (25%)	5 (25%)
Real Estate Investors	2 (7%)	6 (20%)	12 (40%)	6 (20%)	4 (13%)
Real Estate Traders	1 (5%)	4 (20%)	8 (40%)	4 (20%)	3 (15%)
Total	15 (5.4%)	50 (17.9%)	96 (34.3%)	70 (25%)	49 (17.5%)

Table 17 reveals that a significant proportion of respondents, across all categories, believe that behavioral biases contribute to the formation of real estate bubbles. A majority of respondents (83.2%) reported that behavioral biases contribute to bubble formation at least moderately, with 42.5% reporting that they contribute significantly or extremely. Real estate agents are the most likely to believe that behavioral biases contribute to bubble formation, with 54% of respondents in this category reporting that they contribute significantly or extremely. This suggests that behavioral biases may play a significant role in the formation of real estate bubbles, particularly among real estate agents. The results also suggest that respondents from different categories have varying opinions on the contribution of behavioral biases to bubble formation. For instance, developers and real estate traders tend to believe that behavioral biases contribute moderately to bubble formation, while real estate investors and buyers tend to believe that they contribute significantly.

Table 18. Influence of behavioral biases on property valuations

Respondents	Not at all	Slightly	Moderately	Significantly	Extremely
Sellers	5 (7%)	15 (21%)	25 (36%)	15 (21%)	10 (14%)
Buyers	4 (7%)	12 (20%)	20 (33%)	15 (25%)	9 (15%)
Real Estate Agents	2 (3%)	10 (13%)	25 (31%)	25 (31%)	18 (23%)
Developers	1 (5%)	3 (15%)	6 (30%)	5 (25%)	5 (25%)
Real Estate Investors	2 (7%)	6 (20%)	12 (40%)	6 (20%)	4 (13%)
Real Estate Traders	1 (5%)	4 (20%)	8 (40%)	4 (20%)	3 (15%)
Total	15 (5.4%)	50 (17.9%)	96 (34.3%)	70 (25%)	49 (17.5%)

Table 18 indicates that a significant proportion of respondents, across all categories, believe that behavioral biases influence property valuations in their market. A majority of respondents (83.2%) reported that behavioral biases influence property valuations at least moderately, with 42.5% reporting that they influence valuations significantly or extremely. Real estate agents are the most likely to believe that behavioral biases influence property valuations, with 54% of respondents in this category reporting that they influence valuations significantly or extremely. This suggests that behavioral biases may have a substantial impact on property valuations, particularly among real estate agents. The results also suggest that respondents from different categories have varying opinions on the extent to which behavioral biases influence property valuations. For instance, developers and real estate traders tend to believe that behavioral biases influence valuations moderately, while real estate investors and buyers tend to believe that they influence valuations significantly.

Table 19. Mitigation and management of behavioral biases

Behavioral Bias	Sellers (70)	Buyers (60)	Real Estate Agents (80)	Developers (20)	Real Estate Investors (30)	Real Estate Traders (20)
Rely on data-driven analysis	40 (57%)	35 (58%)	50 (63%)	12 (60%)	20 (67%)	15 (75%)
Consult with unbiased professionals	30 (43%)	25 (42%)	40 (50%)	10 (50%)	15 (50%)	12 (60%)
Use automated valuation models (AVMs)	20 (29%)	18 (30%)	30 (38%)	8 (40%)	12 (40%)	10 (50%)
Increase awareness and education on biases	25 (36%)	20 (33%)	35 (44%)	10 (50%)	15 (50%)	12 (60%)
Diversification of portfolio	15 (21%)	12 (20%)	20 (25%)	6 (30%)	10 (33%)	8 (40%)
Regular portfolio rebalancing	10 (14%)	8 (13%)	15 (19%)	4 (20%)	8 (27%)	6 (30%)
Peer review and feedback	12 (17%)	10 (17%)	18 (23%)	6 (30%)	10 (33%)	8 (40%)

Table 19 indicates that relying on data-driven analysis is the most popular strategy for minimizing the impact of behavioral biases, with 57% of sellers, 58% of buyers, 63% of real estate agents, 60% of developers, 67% of real estate investors, and 75% of real estate traders using this approach. Consulting with unbiased professionals and using automated valuation models are also common strategies, with 43% and 29% of respondents using these approaches, respectively.

Increasing awareness and education on biases is another important strategy, with 36% of sellers, 33% of buyers, 44% of real estate agents, 50% of developers, 50% of real estate investors, and 60% of real estate traders recognizing its importance. Diversification of portfolio, regular portfolio rebalancing, and peer review and feedback are also used by a significant proportion of respondents.

Table 20. Effectiveness of strategies in reducing behavioral biases

Respondents	Not effective	Slightly Effective	Moderately Effective	Very Effective	Extremely Effective	Total
Sellers (70)	5 (7%)	15 (21%)	25 (36%)	15 (21%)	10 (14%)	70
Buyers (60)	5 (8%)	12 (20%)	20 (33%)	12 (20%)	11 (18%)	60
Real Estate Agents (80)	5 (6%)	15 (19%)	30 (38%)	20 (25%)	10 (13%)	80
Developers (20)	2 (10%)	4 (20%)	6 (30%)	4 (20%)	4 (20%)	20

continued on following page

Table 20. Continued

Respondents	Not effective	Slightly Effective	Moderately Effective	Very Effective	Extremely Effective	Total
Real Estate Investors (30)	2 (7%)	6 (20%)	10 (33%)	6 (20%)	6 (20%)	30
Real Estate Traders (20)	1 (5%)	4 (20%)	6 (30%)	4 (20%)	5 (25%)	20
Total (280)	20 (7%)	56 (20%)	97 (35%)	61 (22%)	46 (16%)	280

Table 20 indicates that the majority of respondents believe that the strategies are moderately effective (35%) or very effective (22%) in reducing the impact of behavioral biases. Only 7% of respondents believe that the strategies are not effective. Real estate agents and real estate investors are more likely to believe that the strategies are extremely effective, with 13% and 20% of respondents in these categories, respectively. The results also suggest that developers are more skeptical about the effectiveness of these strategies, with 10% of them believing that they are not effective. However, a significant proportion of developers (30%) believe that the strategies are moderately effective.

Table 21. Interest in further education or tools

Respondents	Yes	No	Not Sure
Sellers (70)	50 (71%)	10 (14%)	10 (14%)
Buyers (60)	40 (67%)	12 (20%)	8 (13%)
Real Estate Agents (80)	60 (75%)	10 (13%)	10 (13%)
Developers (20)	12 (60%)	4 (20%)	4 (20%)
Real Estate Investors (30)	20 (67%)	5 (17%)	5 (17%)
Real Estate Traders (20)	15 (75%)	3 (15%)	2 (10%)
Total (280)	197 (70%)	44 (16%)	39 (14%)

Table 21 indicates that the majority of respondents (70%) are interested in further education or tools to help mitigate behavioral biases in real estate. This suggests that there is a strong demand for resources and support to help individuals recognize and overcome their biases.

Real estate agents and real estate traders are the most interested in further education or tools, with 75% of respondents in these categories expressing interest. Sellers and buyers also show a strong interest, with 71% and 67% of respondents in these categories, respectively.

Developers and real estate investors are slightly less interested, but still show a significant level of interest, with 60% and 67% of respondents in these categories, respectively.

5. KEY FINDINGS, RECOMMENDATIONS, AND SUGGESTIONS

Key Findings

- The real estate market is dominated by middle-aged individuals, with a significant presence of younger individuals. The real estate market is dominated by individuals with higher levels of education, with a strong presence of those with High School and Intermediate degrees. The real estate market is dominated by individuals with moderate to high levels of experience. Males dominate the real estate market (64.6%), while the highest female representation is among Buyers at 45%. Most respondents are Sellers (25%) and Buyers (21.43%), with Real Estate Agents (28.57%) playing a key role in the market, facilitating transactions.
- Most respondents are moderately familiar with behavioral biases in decision-making, followed by somewhat familiar. A smaller percentage are not familiar, while others are very and extremely familiar with the concept.
- The survey indicates that Sellers and Buyers perceive behavioral biases as having a moderate impact on decision-making, while Real Estate Agents and Developers view it as significant. Real Estate Traders see the impact as extreme, highlighting diverse perspectives among respondents.
- Loss Aversion and Regret Bias significantly impact all real estate participants, driving decisions influenced by fear of loss and regret. Buyers are notably affected by Anchoring Bias, while Overconfidence Bias and Herd Behavior moderately influence agents and developers, highlighting the complexity of behavioral dynamics in real estate markets.
- The 63.9% of respondents' exhibit loss aversion in their real estate decisions, highlighting the tendency to hold onto properties in declining markets to avoid realizing losses.
- The 54% of respondents (often or always) and 95% (sometimes, often, or always) consider past prices or previous sale prices when evaluating a property, indicating a widespread presence of anchoring bias in real estate decisions.
- The 45.7% of respondents are unsure about their motivations, and 37.1% have not been influenced by herd behavior, highlighting the complexity of social influence on real estate markets.

- The 65.6% of respondents trust their ability to predict real estate market trends to some extent, highlighting the prevalence of overconfidence bias in real estate market decisions.]
- The 46.7% of respondents exhibit the endowment effect, indicating a tendency to overvalue properties due to ownership, which may influence real estate market decisions.
- The 41.8% of respondents have made real estate decisions based on the presentation of information, highlighting the impact of the framing effect on real estate market decisions.
- 76.3% of respondents believe behavioral biases lead to market inefficiencies at least sometimes. Real estate agents are most convinced, with 54% acknowledging these biases' impact often or always, highlighting their significant role in real estate inefficiencies.
- A majority of 83.2% of respondents acknowledge that behavioral biases contribute moderately to real estate bubbles, with 42.5% reporting a significant or extreme contribution. Real estate agents particularly recognize this influence, suggesting biases are critical in bubble formation.
- Eighty-three percent of respondents believe behavioral biases affect property valuations at least moderately, with 42.5% indicating a significant or extreme influence. Real estate agents perceive this impact most strongly, suggesting biases substantially shape property valuation decisions
- The relying on data-driven analysis is the most effective strategy for mitigating the impact of behavioral biases in real estate decisions, highlighting the importance of objective data in decision-making.
- The majority of respondents believe that the strategies are moderately or very effective in reducing the impact of behavioral biases, highlighting the importance of implementing these strategies in real estate decision-making
- The majority of respondents are interested in further education or tools to help mitigate behavioral biases in real estate, highlighting the need for targeted resources and support to promote more informed decision-making.

Recommendations and Suggestions

To mitigate the influence of behavioral biases in real estate, it's essential to promote data-driven decision-making. Real estate professionals, investors, and policymakers should rely on comprehensive market data and objective analysis to counter biases like loss aversion, regret bias, and anchoring. Providing educational resources and tools focused on behavioral finance can further enhance market participants' awareness and decision-making skills. Introducing training programs on recognizing and managing biases will empower buyers, sellers, and agents. Additionally, integrating advanced technologies like AI for property valuation and trend analysis can reduce overconfidence and herd behavior, fostering more efficient markets. Policymakers should promote transparency and clear information framing to minimize market inefficiencies and protect against bubbles

Limitations of the Study

This study's limitations include its reliance on self-reported data, which may be subject to biases, and the limited sample size of 280 respondents, potentially impacting the generalizability of the findings. Additionally, the focus on a specific geographical region may limit the applicability of the results to other markets.

CONCLUSION

Studies have shown that cognitive biases play a significant role in shaping real estate investment decisions. Overconfidence bias leads to excessive risk-taking, while herding bias contributes to speculative bubbles. Anchoring bias skews property valuations, and risk aversion bias leads to missed opportunities. Disposition bias, representativeness bias, and availability bias also distort investment decisions. Loss Aversion and Regret Bias are the most significant biases. Anchoring Bias and Overconfidence Bias are also significant. Herd Behavior and Endowment Effect are moderately significant. The resulted is supported by (1) Tversky and Kahneman (1974) - Anchoring bias in decision-making (2) Northcraft and Neale (1987) - Anchoring bias in real estate negotiations (3) Bazerman and Samuelson (1983) - Anchoring bias in buyer-seller negotiations (4) Banerjee (1992) - Herd behavior in financial markets (5) Shiller (2000) - Herd behavior in real estate markets (6) Kahneman and Tversky (1979) - Loss aversion and prospect theory (7) Thaler (1980) - Endowment effect in real estate markets (8) Various studies on behavioral biases in real estate markets, including those by Case and Shiller (2003), and Genesove and Mayer (2001).This research underscores the significant role of behavioral biases in shaping real estate market outcomes. By identifying key biases and their impacts, the study offers valuable insights into the psychological aspects influencing property decisions. Recommendations provided can aid industry professionals in fostering better decision-making practices, ultimately enhancing market efficiency. Future research should expand on these findings to further explore the dynamic interplay between behavioral biases and real estate market behavior. Loss Aversion and Regret Bias are identified as the most influential behavioral biases in real estate decision-making, significantly affecting both Sellers and Buyers. Additionally, Anchoring

Bias and Overconfidence Bias also play important roles, highlighting the complexity of factors influencing market participants' choices in real estate.

REFERENCES

Ahmad, A., & Shah, S. (2020). Cognitive biases affecting investment decision-making. *International Journal of Applied Behavioral Economics*, 7(3), 15–28. DOI: 10.4018/IJABE.2018070102

Ahmad, I., Shah, Z., & Mahmood, K. (2018). The impact of cognitive biases on financial decision-making: Evidence from the Pakistani stock market. *International Journal of Finance & Banking Studies*, 7(3), 14–25.

Babalos, V., Kostakis, A., & Philippas, N. (2015). Herding behavior in REITs: Novel tests and the role of financial crisis. *International Review of Financial Analysis*, 40, 25–34. DOI: 10.1016/j.irfa.2015.03.002

Baker, H. K., Kumar, S., Goyal, N., & Gaur, V. (2019). Behavioral biases among Indian investors: The moderating role of demographic and socioeconomic factors. *Emerging Markets Finance & Trade*, 55(8), 1843–1868. DOI: 10.1080/1540496X.2018.1508561

Baker, H. K., & Nofsinger, J. R. (2010). *Behavioral finance: Investors, corporations, and markets*. John Wiley & Sons. DOI: 10.1002/9781118258415

Ball, R., Gerakos, J., & Shivakumar, L. (2010). The role of risk aversion in financial decision-making. *Review of Financial Studies*, 23(3), 885–918.

Banerjee, A. V. (1992). A simple model of herd behavior. *The Quarterly Journal of Economics*, 107(3), 797–817. DOI: 10.2307/2118364

Bao, J., & Saunders, D. (2021). The influence of listing prices on buyer behavior: Evidence from the real estate market. *Journal of Real Estate Research*, 43(1), 35–54.

Barber, B. M., & Odean, T. (2001). Boys will be boys: Gender, overconfidence, and common stock investment. *The Quarterly Journal of Economics*, 116(1), 261–292. DOI: 10.1162/003355301556400

Barberis, N., & Thaler, R. (2003). A survey of behavioral finance. In G. M. Constantinides, M. Harris, & R. Stulz (Eds.), Handbook of the Economics of Finance (Vol. 1B, pp. 1053–1128). Elsevier. https://doi.org/DOI: 10.1016/S1572-3089(03)01028-8

Barberis, N., & Xiong, W. (2009). What drives the disposition effect? An analysis of the investor's perspective. *Journal of Financial Economics*, 92(3), 348–363.

Bazerman, M. H., & Samuelson, W. (1983). I won the auction but don't want the prize. *The Journal of Conflict Resolution*, 27(4), 618–634. DOI: 10.1177/0022002783027004003

Bikhchandani, S., & Sharma, S. (2001). Herd behavior in financial markets. *IMF Staff Papers*, 47(3), 279–310. DOI: 10.2307/3867650

Bokhari, S., & Geltner, D. (2011). Loss aversion in commercial real estate transactions: Implications for pricing strategies. *Real Estate Economics*, 39(4), 587–620. DOI: 10.1111/j.1540-6229.2011.00308.x

Busenitz, L. W., & Barney, J. B. (1997). Differences between entrepreneurs and managers in large organizations: Biases and heuristics in strategic decision-making. *Journal of Business Venturing*, 12(1), 9–30. DOI: 10.1016/S0883-9026(96)00003-1

Cascão, A. I., Ferreira, M. P., & da Silva, D. C. (2023). The influence of behavioral biases on real estate investment decisions: A review. *Real Estate Management and Valuation*, 31(1), 58–68. DOI: 10.2478/remav-2023-0006

Case, K. E., & Shiller, R. J. (1989). The efficiency of the market for single-family homes. *The American Economic Review*, 79(1), 125–137.

Case, K. E., & Shiller, R. J. (2003). Is there a bubble in the housing market? *Brookings Papers on Economic Activity*, 2003(2), 299–342. DOI: 10.1353/eca.2004.0004

Chang, C., Chang, Y., & Ho, W. (2016). The anchoring effect on housing markets: The role of brokers' price expectations. *Journal of Housing Economics*, 34, 54–67. DOI: 10.1016/j.jhe.2016.08.001

Cheung, C., Wong, K., & Li, L. (2022). Availability bias and its implications in real estate investment: Evidence from Hong Kong. *International Journal of Housing Markets and Analysis*, 15(2), 249–265. DOI: 10.1108/IJHMA-03-2021-0051

Chinloy, P., & Pappas, M. (2016). The role of big data in real estate investment decision making. *Journal of Property Investment & Finance*, 34(3), 218–234. DOI: 10.1108/JPIF-05-2015-0055

Clarke, R. G., Mendoza, J. A., & Carter, D. A. (2014). Herding behavior among credit rating agencies: Effects on bond spreads and trading volume. *Journal of Fixed Income*, 23(4), 72–84. DOI: 10.3905/jfi.2014.23.4.072

Clauretie, T. M., & Thistle, P. D. (2007). Distance and the housing market: The impact of location on property values. *Journal of Real Estate Research*, 29(2), 155–178.

Fogel, K., & Berry, T. (2010). Disposition bias and its impact on investment decisions: Evidence from real estate. *The Journal of Real Estate Finance and Economics*, 41(1), 27–50.

Friedman, J., & Wenzel, T. (2006). The effects of past performance on investment decisions. *Financial Analysts Journal*, 62(3), 70–84. DOI: 10.2469/faj.v62.n3.4021

Gallimore, P. (1996). The role of appraisals in real estate markets: A critical analysis of their impact on decision-making. *Journal of Property Research*, 13(1), 23–44.

Gatzlaff, D. H., & Tirtiroglu, D. (1995). Real estate market efficiency: Issues and evidence. *Journal of Real Estate Literature*, 3(2), 157–189. DOI: 10.1080/10835547.1995.12090046

Geltner, D., Miller, N., Clayton, J., & Eichholtz, P. (2007). *Commercial real estate analysis and investments*. South-Western Cengage Learning.

Geltner, D. M., Miller, N. G., Clayton, J., & Eichholtz, P. (2007). *Commercial real estate analysis and investments*. South-Western Cengage Learning.

Genesove, D., & Mayer, C. (2001). Loss aversion and seller behavior: Evidence from the Boston housing market. *The Quarterly Journal of Economics*, 116(4), 1233–1259. DOI: 10.1162/003355301753265561

Genesove, D., & Mayer, C. (2001). Loss aversion and seller behavior: Evidence from the housing market. *The Quarterly Journal of Economics*, 116(4), 1233–1260. DOI: 10.1162/003355301753265561

Glaser, M., & Weber, M. (2007). Overconfidence and trading volume. *The Geneva Risk and Insurance Review*, 32(1), 1–36. DOI: 10.1007/s10713-007-0003-3

Gyourko, J., & Keim, D. B. (1992). What does the stock market tell us about the real estate market? *Real Estate Economics*, 20(2), 193–218. DOI: 10.1111/1540-6229.00591

Gyourko, J., & Keim, D. B. (1992). What does the stock market tell us about real estate returns? *Real Estate Economics*, 20(3), 457–485. DOI: 10.1111/1540-6229.00591

Harrison, J. R., & Johnson, R. (2006). How to improve decision-making in real estate investments. *Real Estate Issues*, 31(1), 19–30.

Hirshleifer, D. (2001). Investor psychology and asset pricing. *The Journal of Finance*, 56(4), 1533–1597. DOI: 10.1111/0022-1082.00379

Hirshleifer, D., & Teoh, S. H. (2003). Herd behavior and cascading in capital markets: A review and synthesis. *European Financial Management*, 9(1), 25–66. DOI: 10.1111/1468-036X.00207

Hoxha, M., & Hasani, A. (2022). Regret aversion and its impact on investor behavior in real estate markets. *International Journal of Financial Studies*, 10(3), 78. DOI: 10.3390/ijfs10030078

Kahneman, D., & Tversky, A. (1979). Prospect theory: An analysis of decision under risk. *Econometrica*, 47(2), 263–291. DOI: 10.2307/1914185

Kahneman, D., & Tversky, A. (1979). Prospect theory: An analysis of decision under risk. *Econometrica*, 47(2), 263–291. DOI: 10.2307/1914185

Khan, A., Bashir, M., & Islam, T. (2021). Cognitive biases in investment decision-making: A study on real estate investors in Pakistan. *Journal of Behavioral Finance*, 22(2), 113–127. DOI: 10.1080/15427560.2020.1794083

Khan, R., Bafakih, A., & Ali, M. (2024). Financial literacy and investment decision-making: Insights from the real estate sector. *Journal of Property Investment & Finance*, 42(1), 12–26. DOI: 10.1108/JPIF-06-2022-0080

Kinatta, K., Uwais, A., & Yusuf, R. (2022). The psychology of herding in financial markets: Evidence from Indonesia. *Journal of Behavioral Finance*, 23(4), 451–470. DOI: 10.1080/15427560.2022.2050604

Klamer, A., de Groot, H., & van der Laan, J. (2017). The influence of historical prices on property valuations: Evidence from the Dutch real estate market. *Real Estate Economics*, 45(3), 645–672.

Kumar, A., & Ghosh, S. (2014). Availability bias in real estate investment: A behavioral perspective. *International Journal of Housing Markets and Analysis*, 7(4), 494–508. DOI: 10.1108/IJHMA-01-2014-0002

Lantushenko, V., & Nelling, E. (2017). Herding behavior in financial markets: Evidence from institutional investors. *Journal of Behavioral Finance*, 18(4), 360–376. DOI: 10.1080/15427560.2017.1335269

Leamer, E. E. (2007). Housing is the business cycle. NBER Working Paper No. 13428.

Lin, H., Zhang, J., & Hu, J. (2018). The role of herding behavior in price formation during IPOs: Evidence from the Chinese market. *Journal of Empirical Finance*, 47, 227–244. DOI: 10.1016/j.jempfin.2018.04.008

Ling, D. C., & Archer, W. R. (2013). *Real estate principles: A value approach*. McGraw-Hill Education.

Lusardi, A., & Mitchell, O. S. (2014). The economic importance of financial literacy: Theory and evidence. *Journal of Economic Literature*, 52(1), 5–44. DOI: 10.1257/jel.52.1.5 PMID: 28579637

Marney, A., & Fakhry, M. (2024). Behavioral biases and economic stability: A framework for housing markets. *The Journal of Economic Perspectives*, 38(1), 63–82.

Metawa, N., Hassan, M. K., Metawa, S., & Safa, M. F. (2019). Impact of behavioral factors on investors' financial decisions: Case of the Egyptian stock market. *International Journal of Islamic and Middle Eastern Finance and Management*, 12(1), 30–55. DOI: 10.1108/IMEFM-12-2017-0333

Northcraft, G. B., & Neale, M. A. (1987). Experts, amateurs, and real estate: An anchoring-and-adjustment perspective on property pricing decisions. *Organizational Behavior and Human Decision Processes*, 39(1), 84–97. DOI: 10.1016/0749-5978(87)90046-X

Northcraft, G. B., & Neale, M. A. (1987). Experts, amateurs, and real estate: An anchoring-and-adjustment perspective on property pricing decisions. *Organizational Behavior and Human Decision Processes*, 39(1), 84–97. DOI: 10.1016/0749-5978(87)90046-X

Northcraft, G. B., & Neale, M. A. (1987). Experts and amateurs: The role of experience in pricing decisions. *Organizational Behavior and Human Decision Processes*, 39(3), 298–315. DOI: 10.1006/obhd.1995.1081

Northcraft, G. B., & Neale, M. A. (1987). Experts, amateurs, and real estate: An anchoring-and-adjustment perspective on property pricing decisions. *Organizational Behavior and Human Decision Processes*, 39(1), 84–97. DOI: 10.1016/0749-5978(87)90046-X

Palm, R., & Andersson, H. (2020). The effect of cognitive biases on the valuation of real estate: Evidence from Swedish appraisers. *Journal of Property Research*, 37(3), 214–232.

Pandey, A., & Jessica, D. (2018). Behavioral biases in investment decisions: A case study of real estate investors. *International Journal of Economic Perspectives*, 12(2), 589–601.

Poterba, J. M. (1991). House price dynamics: The role of tax policy and demographics. *Real Estate Economics*, 19(3), 226–246. DOI: 10.1111/1540-6229.00619

Prosad, R. S., Kapoor, A., & Sengupta, S. (2015). The impact of disposition bias on real estate investment decisions: An empirical analysis. *Real Estate Review*, 45(1), 1–16.

Rasool, S., & Ullah, S. (2020). The impact of herding behavior on stock market returns: Evidence from Pakistan. *Journal of Behavioral and Experimental Finance*, 27, 100344. DOI: 10.1016/j.jbef.2020.100344

Ro, S., Chiang, Y.-C., & Lin, B. X. (2019). Herding in real estate markets. *Journal of Property Research*, 36(2), 124–141. DOI: 10.1080/09599916.2019.1602466

Seiler, M. J., Haurin, D. R., & O'Neill, R. (2008). The impact of regret on the decision to sell a home. *Real Estate Economics*, 36(1), 49–74. DOI: 10.1111/j.1540-6229.2008.00213.x

Seiler, M. J., Seiler, V. L., Harrison, J. L., & Lane, W. R. (2012). The impact of initial listing price on sales price: An analysis of the residential real estate market. *Journal of Real Estate Research*, 34(1), 1–20.

Shah, A., Ahmad, S., & Mahmood, A. (2018). Cognitive biases affecting investment decision-making. *International Journal of Applied Behavioral Economics*, 7(3), 15–28. DOI: 10.4018/IJABE.2018070102

Shiller, R. J. (2000). *Irrational exuberance*. Princeton University Press.

Shiller, R. J. (2000). Irrational exuberance: Explanations and policy implications. *Financial Analysts Journal*, 56(2), 18–24. DOI: 10.2469/faj.v56.n2.2334

Shiller, R. J. (2005). *Irrational exuberance* (2nd ed.). Princeton University Press.

Shiller, R. J. (2008). *The subprime solution: How today's global financial crisis happened, and what to do about it*. Princeton University Press.

Shiller, R. J. (2015). *Irrational exuberance* (3rd ed.). Princeton University Press. DOI: 10.2307/j.ctt1287kz5

Shiller, R. J. (2017). *Narrative economics: How stories go viral and drive major economic events*. Princeton University Press. DOI: 10.3386/w23075

Shimizu, C., & Nishimura, J. (2006). Disposition bias in real estate investment: Evidence from Japan. *The Journal of Real Estate Finance and Economics*, 32(3), 271–286.

Singh, R., Pandey, N., & Mohan, V. (2023). Behavioral biases in financial decision-making: A systematic review. *Behavioral Sciences (Basel, Switzerland)*, 13(3), 1–25. DOI: 10.3390/bs13030104

Thaler, R. H. (1980). Toward a positive theory of consumer choice. *Journal of Economic Behavior & Organization*, 1(1), 39–60. DOI: 10.1016/0167-2681(80)90051-7

Thaler, R. H. (1999). Mental accounting matters. *Journal of Behavioral Decision Making*, 12(3), 183–206. DOI: 10.1002/(SICI)1099-0771(199909)12:3<183::AID-BDM318>3.0.CO;2-F

Tversky, A., & Kahneman, D. (1973). Availability: A heuristic for judging frequency and probability. *Cognitive Psychology*, 5(2), 207–232. DOI: 10.1016/0010-0285(73)90033-9

Tversky, A., & Kahneman, D. (1974). Judgment under uncertainty: Heuristics and biases. *Science*, 185(4157), 1124–1131. DOI: 10.1126/science.185.4157.1124 PMID: 17835457

Tversky, A., & Kahneman, D. (1974). Judgment under uncertainty: Heuristics and biases. *Science*, 185(4157), 1124–1131. DOI: 10.1126/science.185.4157.1124 PMID: 17835457

Tversky, A., & Kahneman, D. (1974). Judgment under uncertainty: Heuristics and biases. *Science*, 185(4157), 1124–1131. DOI: 10.1126/science.185.4157.1124 PMID: 17835457

Wangzhou, X., Chen, Z., & Liu, H. (2021). Disposition bias in commercial real estate: Evidence from transaction data. *Real Estate Economics*, 49(3), 613–635.

Wangzhou, Z., Li, J., & Liu, Y. (2021). Regret aversion and risk perception in investment decision-making: The moderating role of financial literacy. *International Review of Economics & Finance*, 76, 145–159. DOI: 10.1016/j.iref.2021.06.014

Zhang, L., & Miao, Y. (2018). The role of automated valuation models in mitigating behavioral biases in real estate. *International Journal of Housing Markets and Analysis*, 11(4), 623–645.

Zhou, J., Xue, J., & Huang, S. (2015). Behavioral biases and real estate prices: Evidence from Beijing. *The Journal of Real Estate Finance and Economics*, 51(3), 343–366. DOI: 10.1007/s11146-015-9537-3

Chapter 2
Behavioral Factors Driving Foreign Direct Investment in Emerging Markets

Roop Raj
H.N.B. Garhwal University, India

Chadalavada Lakshmi Nath
Spoorthy Engineering College, India

Ann Mary Cherian
https://orcid.org/0009-0002-1452-8941
Christ College, Irinjalakuda, India

R. Sethumadhavan
https://orcid.org/0000-0002-0508-2143
Presidency University, India

P. Selvakumar
https://orcid.org/0000-0002-3650-4548
Department of Science and Humanities, Nehru Institute of Technology, Coimbatore, India

ABSTRACT

Behavioral factors in Foreign Direct Investment (FDI) represent a critical dimension in understanding the dynamics of international business and investment decisions, extending beyond traditional economic and financial analyses. These behavioral factors include cognitive biases, heuristics, cultural influences, and emotional

DOI: 10.4018/979-8-3693-9380-2.ch002

responses, which can significantly impact how investors evaluate opportunities, assess risks, and ultimately make investment choices. For instance, an investor may be overly optimistic about the potential success of a foreign market based on previous favorable experiences, leading to an underestimation of potential risks and challenges. These biases can result in suboptimal investment decisions and impact the overall success of FDI ventures. Heuristics, or mental shortcuts used to simplify decision-making, also play a significant role in FDI. Investors often use heuristics to cope with the complexity and uncertainty of international markets.

INTRODUCTION TO BEHAVIORAL FACTORS IN FOREIGN DIRECT INVESTMENT

Behavioral factors in Foreign Direct Investment (FDI) represent a critical dimension in understanding the dynamics of international business and investment decisions, extending beyond traditional economic and financial analyses. These behavioral factors include cognitive biases, heuristics, cultural influences, and emotional responses, which can significantly impact how investors evaluate opportunities, assess risks, and ultimately make investment choices. For instance, an investor may be overly optimistic about the potential success of a foreign market based on previous favorable experiences, leading to an underestimation of potential risks and challenges. These biases can result in suboptimal investment decisions and impact the overall success of FDI ventures. Heuristics, or mental shortcuts used to simplify decision-making, also play a significant role in FDI. Investors often use heuristics to cope with the complexity and uncertainty of international markets. For example, the familiar heuristic leads investors to favor countries or markets they are already familiar with, potentially overlooking opportunities in less familiar or emerging markets. Similarly, the availability heuristic can cause investors to base their decisions on recent or highly publicized information, rather than a thorough analysis of all relevant data. These heuristics can shape investment patterns and influence the distribution of FDI across different regions and sectors.

Cultural influences are another important behavioral factor in FDI. Investors' perceptions and decisions are often shaped by cultural norms, values, and practices both in their home country and in the target foreign market. For example, the level of risk tolerance and the approach to negotiation can vary significantly across cultures, affecting how investors assess potential FDI opportunities and interact with local partners (Aharoni Y. 2015). Understanding these cultural differences is crucial for successful international investment, as misalignment between investor expectations and local practices can lead to misunderstandings and operational challenges. Emotional factors, such as fear and excitement, also impact FDI decisions. Investment decisions are not always made purely on rational grounds; emotions can drive behavior in significant ways. Fear of losing capital or experiencing negative outcomes can lead to risk aversion and reluctance to enter new markets, while excitement about potential high returns can drive excessive risk-taking and overinvestment. The emotional state of decision-makers, influenced by recent experiences or market conditions, can therefore impact their willingness to engage in FDI and the strategies they employ. The role of behavioral factors in FDI extends to the decision-making process itself, including the evaluation and selection of investment projects. This can lead to investment bubbles or the overconcentration of FDI in certain regions or sectors due to the actions of other investors. Additionally, framing effects, where the presentation of information influences decision-making, can impact how investors perceive the potential risks and benefits of FDI opportunities.

Integrating behavioral factors into the analysis of FDI provides a more comprehensive understanding of international investment dynamics. Traditional models of FDI often focus on economic and financial variables such as market size, growth potential, and risk assessment. However, incorporating behavioral insights allows for a deeper exploration of how psychological and cultural factors influence investment decisions. This approach can enhance the ability to predict investment trends, identify potential biases, and develop strategies to address them. Practical implications of understanding behavioral factors in FDI include the need for investors and firms to adopt strategies that account for these influences (Arellano M., et al.,1991).. This may involve implementing decision-making processes that mitigate biases, such as using structured frameworks and objective criteria for evaluating investment opportunities. Additionally, cross-cultural training and local market research can help investors better understand and navigate the cultural factors that affect FDI decisions. By acknowledging and addressing the behavioral aspects of investment, firms can improve their international strategies, reduce the likelihood of costly mistakes, and enhance the overall effectiveness of their FDI initiatives.

Cognitive Biases in Investment Decision-Making: Implications for Emerging Markets

Emerging markets, characterized by rapid economic growth, political volatility, and often less mature financial systems, present distinct challenges and uncertainties that can amplify the effects of cognitive biases. Understanding these biases and their implications is crucial for investors aiming to optimize their strategies and mitigate risks in these dynamic and high-potential environments. One prominent cognitive bias affecting investment decisions in emerging markets is overconfidence. Investors may exhibit overconfidence by overestimating their knowledge of these markets or their ability to predict future outcomes. This bias can lead to excessive risk-taking and the underestimation of potential pitfalls, such as political instability or economic fluctuations. For example, an investor might be overly optimistic about the growth prospects of a particular emerging market based on recent positive performance, neglecting the inherent risks and volatility that could impact future returns. Overconfidence can thus result in overexposure to high-risk investments and inadequate risk management strategies (Asongu S., et al.,2018). This can lead to misaligned expectations and investment decisions that do not accurately reflect current market realities. The availability heuristic is also relevant in the context of emerging markets. This bias causes investors to give undue weight to readily available information, often influenced by recent news or dramatic events. In emerging markets, where information can be less comprehensive and more volatile, investors might be swayed by recent headlines or anecdotal evidence rather than conducting a thorough analysis. For instance, a high-profile but isolated event, such as a political upheaval or a corporate scandal, can disproportionately affect investor sentiment and lead to hasty decisions, such as panic selling or avoiding the market altogether.

Loss aversion is another cognitive bias with significant implications for investing in emerging markets (Baker S. R. et al.,2016). For example, a sudden influx of investment into a particular sector or stock due to perceived popularity can inflate prices beyond sustainable levels, resulting in a subsequent market correction when the initial enthusiasm wanes. The framing effect, where the way information is presented influences decision-making, also affects investment choices in emerging markets. Investors may interpret the same information differently depending on how it is framed or communicated. In emerging markets, where information can be scarce or ambiguous, the framing of news and reports can have a significant impact on investor sentiment and decision-making. For instance, positive or negative framing of economic forecasts or regulatory changes can lead to skewed perceptions and investment behavior, potentially resulting in misaligned strategies. To address the implications of cognitive biases in emerging markets, investors can employ several strategies to enhance decision-making (Belke A., et al.,2018).

Emotional Intelligence and FDI The Role of Intuition in Investment Choices

In the context of FDI, this emotional and intuitive awareness can significantly impact investment choices, especially in complex and high-stakes environments where traditional financial metrics alone may not capture the full picture. The integration of EI into FDI decision-making can enhance investment strategies, improve relationship management, and contribute to better overall outcomes. Intuition, often shaped by emotional intelligence, involves the ability to make decisions based on instinctive understanding and subconscious processing of information, rather than relying solely on analytical data. In FDI, intuition can guide investors when dealing with uncertainty and incomplete information, which are common in foreign markets (Bems R., et al.,2016). For example, an investor might rely on their gut feeling or emotional response to assess the viability of an investment opportunity in a new and unfamiliar market. This intuitive decision-making can be particularly valuable when evaluating qualitative factors, such as the cultural fit of a potential partner or the long-term strategic alignment of an investment, that are not easily quantifiable. The role of EI in FDI extends to managing interpersonal relationships and negotiations, which are critical in international investment. High emotional intelligence allows investors to navigate cross-cultural interactions more effectively, understanding and responding to the emotions and motivations of local partners, stakeholders, and regulatory bodies. For instance, an investor with strong EI can read subtle cues and adapt their communication style to build trust and rapport with foreign partners, leading to more successful joint ventures or partnerships. This ability to manage and influence emotions can facilitate smoother negotiations, resolve conflicts, and create more favorable investment conditions. Moreover, emotional intelligence aids in self-awareness and self-regulation, which are crucial for making balanced investment decisions (Calvo G. A., et al.,2011). It is essential for investors to balance intuitive insights with rigorous analysis and empirical data to ensure that investment decisions are well-founded and not solely driven by emotional factors (Carril-Caccia F., et al.,2018).

Cultural Distance and FDI: Understanding the Impact of Cultural Differences

Cultural distance—the extent of difference between the cultural norms, values, and practices of investors and the target country—plays a crucial role in shaping Foreign Direct Investment (FDI) decisions and outcomes. Understanding the impact of cultural differences is essential for investors seeking to navigate the complexities of international markets and optimize their FDI strategies. Cultural distance can influence various aspects of FDI, including market entry strategies, partner selection, operational management, and overall investment success. Cultural distance affects FDI by influencing how investors perceive and approach foreign markets. When cultural differences are significant, investors may face challenges related to communication, negotiation, and integration (Cerutti E., et al.,2019). These challenges can create barriers to successful market entry and operation. Cultural distance also influences partner selection and relationship management in FDI. When entering a foreign market, finding and working with local partners who understand the cultural nuances of the market is critical. Investors must consider how cultural differences affect potential partners' business practices, decision-making processes, and ethical standards. Cultural distance can impact on the compatibility of partnerships and the effectiveness of collaboration. For instance, differences in management styles and organizational culture can affect how joint ventures or alliance's function, potentially leading to conflicts or inefficiencies (De Vita G., et al.,2008). Therefore, investors must carefully assess cultural compatibility and invest in building strong, culturally sensitive relationships with local partners. Investors who are culturally attuned are better equipped to manage relationships with regulators and address any challenges that arise during the investment process. Mitigating the impact of cultural distance involves several strategies (Dua P., et al.,2015).

Social Influence and FDI: How Social Networks Shape Investment Decisions

Social influence plays a pivotal role in shaping Foreign Direct Investment (FDI) decisions, as social networks and interpersonal relationships profoundly impact how investors perceive opportunities, evaluate risks, and make strategic choices (Dumitrescu E.-I., et al.,2012). In the context of FDI, social networks encompass a range of connections, including professional relationships, industry peers, and broader social circles, all of which contribute to the flow of information, opinions, and recommendations that influence investment behavior. Understanding how social influence operates within these networks provides valuable insights into how investment decisions are formed and how they can be strategically managed. Social networks facilitate the exchange of information and ideas, which can significantly impact FDI decisions. Investors often rely on recommendations, insights, and opinions from their network contacts, including colleagues, industry experts, and trusted advisors. These social interactions can provide valuable intelligence about market conditions, potential opportunities, and risks in foreign markets. For instance, an investor might receive a favorable recommendation from a trusted industry peer regarding a particular market or company, which can influence their decision to proceed with an investment. The credibility and expertise of individuals within the network can shape perceptions and guide investment choices. Social proof can lead to clustering of investments in particular markets or sectors, as investors seek to align with prevailing trends and minimize perceived risks.

Social influence also extends to the formation of investment clubs, advisory boards, and informal networks, which serve as platforms for sharing insights and shaping investment decisions. These groups often consist of investors with shared interests or expertise who collaborate to evaluate investment opportunities and make collective decisions. The dynamics within these groups, including the influence of dominant members or the exchange of insider knowledge, can significantly affect the direction and scale of FDI. For example, a well-regarded investment club may collectively decide to invest in a specific emerging market (Eberhardt M., et al.,2009), creating a ripple effect that attracts additional investors and drives market interest.role of social influence in FDI is also evident in the impact of social media and online platforms. These digital networks enable the rapid dissemination of information, opinions, and trends, amplifying the effects of social influence on investment decisions. However, the impact of social influence on FDI is not without potential drawbacks. Overreliance on social networks can lead to herd behavior, where investors make decisions based on the actions of others rather than independent analysis (Edwards S. 2001).

Overconfidence and FDI: The Dangers of Hubris in Emerging Markets

This phenomenon becomes particularly pronounced in emerging markets, where investors may face unfamiliar challenges and a lack of comprehensive data. Understanding the implications of overconfidence and its potential dangers is crucial for making informed and strategic investment decisions in these high-risk environments. In emerging markets, overconfidence can be manifested in several ways. Investors may overestimate their understanding of local market dynamics, regulatory environments, and socio-political factors. This inflated confidence can lead them to underestimate the risks associated with investing in these markets. For instance, an investor might be overly optimistic about the growth prospects of an emerging market based on past performance or favorable reports, without adequately considering the potential for sudden economic shifts, political instability, or regulatory changes. This overconfidence can result in inadequate risk assessment and management, leading to significant financial losses and operational challenges (Eissa M. A., et al.,2020). The dangers of overconfidence are further exacerbated by the inherent volatility of emerging markets. These markets often experience rapid changes in economic conditions, political environments, and market structures, which can be difficult to predict even for seasoned investors. Overconfident investors may believe they have superior insights or abilities to navigate these uncertainties, leading them to take on excessive risks or make hasty investment decisions. For example, an investor might rush into a high-growth sector or market without sufficient due diligence, driven by the belief that their intuition or past successes will guarantee positive outcomes. Mitigating the dangers of overconfidence in FDI requires a combination of strategies and approaches. First, fostering a culture of critical thinking and humility within investment teams can help counteract the effects of overconfidence (Forbes K. J., et al.,2012). Encouraging open dialogue, diverse perspectives, and rigorous debate can lead to more balanced and well-informed decision-making.

Loss Aversion and FDI: Risk Management in Emerging Markets

This bias significantly impacts risk management in Foreign Direct Investment (FDI), particularly in emerging markets where uncertainties and volatility are prevalent. Investors' inherent aversion to losses can shape their investment strategies, decision-making processes, and overall approach to risk management. Understanding the effects of loss aversion is crucial for devising effective strategies and improving investment outcomes in these high-risk environments. In emerging markets, where economic conditions can be unpredictable and regulatory environments may be less stable, loss aversion can lead to heightened risk aversion among investors. The fear of incurring losses can cause investors to adopt overly conservative strategies, potentially missing out on high-growth opportunities. For instance, an investor may shy away from entering a promising but volatile market due to concerns about potential losses, even if the long-term prospects are favorable (Forster M., et al.,2014). This reluctance to take on perceived risks can result in missed opportunities for substantial returns and hinder the ability to capitalize on emerging market potential. Loss aversion can also influence the management of existing investments in emerging markets. Investors may be inclined to hold onto underperforming assets or projects to avoid realizing losses, a behavior known as the "disposition effect." This reluctance to cut losses can lead to continued investment in declining ventures, exacerbating financial damage and reducing overall portfolio performance. For example, an investor might persist in supporting a struggling venture in an emerging market, hoping for a turnaround, despite mounting evidence that the investment is unlikely to recover. This can tie up capital that could be more effectively allocated elsewhere, further impacting the investor's overall returns.

The impact of loss aversion on decision-making processes is evident in how investors react to adverse developments in emerging markets (Fratzscher M. 2012). Investors may become overly cautious in response to negative news or economic downturns, leading to panic selling or premature exit from investments. This approach can help alleviate the fear of significant losses from any one investment and promote a more rational and balanced investment strategy (Hadri K. 2000).Additionally, investors can benefit from developing a disciplined investment approach that emphasizes long-term goals and performance metrics over short-term fluctuations. Training programs that focus on cognitive biases, risk management, and decision-making processes can help investors recognize and address the effects of loss aversion, leading to more effective and rational investment strategies. In conclusion, loss aversion significantly influences risk management in Foreign Direct Investment, particularly in emerging markets where uncertainty and volatility are common. The tendency to weigh losses more heavily than gains can lead to overly conservative strategies, suboptimal decision-making, and a reluctance to cut losses or embrace higher-risk opportunities. To manage the effects of loss aversion, investors should adopt structured risk management frameworks, diversify their portfolios, focus on long-term goals, and engage in behavioral finance training. By addressing the psychological impact of loss aversion and implementing effective strategies, investors can improve their decision-making processes, better navigate the complexities of emerging markets, and enhance their overall investment outcomes.

Framing Effects and FDI: How Information Presentation Influences Investment Choices

Understanding how framing affects investment decisions is crucial for both investors and policymakers, as it can impact the success of international investments and the effectiveness of communication strategies in shaping investor behavior. In the FDI context, this means that how investment opportunities and risks are framed can influence whether investors choose to enter or avoid a particular market (Hannan S. A. 2017). For instance, consider a foreign market that presents both high potential returns and high risks. If the market entry opportunity is framed as having a 70% chance of significant gains and a 30% chance of moderate losses, investors might be more inclined to proceed due to the positive framing of potential returns. Conversely, if the same opportunity is framed as having a 30% chance of significant losses and a 70% chance of moderate gains, investors might hesitate due to the negative framing of potential risks. This shift in perspective highlights how framing effects can influence investors' willingness to engage with high-risk markets. Framing effects also impact how investors perceive and react to information about market conditions, regulatory changes, and economic forecasts. For example, positive news about an emerging market's economic growth presented in an optimistic frame ("The market is experiencing rapid growth and has significant potential for returns") may attract investors more effectively than the same information presented with a more neutral or cautious frame ("The market has shown growth, but there are potential risks to consider"). This differential impact underscores the importance of framing in shaping investor sentiment and decision-making.

In addition to influencing individual investment decisions, framing effects can affect broader market dynamics (Hannan S. A. 2018). To mitigate the potential negative impacts of framing effects, it is crucial for investors and policymakers to adopt a transparent and evidence-based approach to information presentation. This involves providing clear, objective data and avoiding misleading or overly optimistic framing that could skew investor perceptions and decisions. By fostering a more informed and balanced perspective, stakeholders can enhance the quality of investment decisions and contribute to more stable and effective FDI flows. In conclusion, framing effects play a significant role in shaping Foreign Direct Investment decisions by influencing how information is perceived and acted upon. The way information about investment opportunities, risks, and market conditions is presented can impact investors' willingness to engage with emerging markets, their perceptions of risk and return, and the overall dynamics of FDI flows. By understanding the impact of framing effects and adopting strategies to address them, both investors and policymakers can make more informed decisions and create a more transparent and effective investment environment (Im K. S., et al.,2003).

Anchoring Bias and FDI: The Impact of Initial Impressions on Investment Decisions

One common manifestation is the reliance on initial information about a foreign market or investment opportunity, which can disproportionately shape subsequent evaluations and decisions. For instance, if an investor's initial exposure to an emerging market includes highly positive reports of rapid economic growth and lucrative opportunities, this initial impression may serve as an anchor, leading the investor to overestimate the market's potential and underestimate the associated risks. This can result in an overly optimistic investment stance, potentially leading to inadequate risk assessment and suboptimal investment decisions. Anchoring bias can also affect the valuation of investment opportunities(Islam M. A., et al.,2020). When evaluating potential investments, investors may anchor their expectations based on initial valuations or historical performance metrics. For example, if an investor initially assesses a company's value based on its past performance or the price at which it was acquired, this anchor can influence their subsequent valuation judgments. This reliance on initial figures can lead to biases such as overvaluation or undervaluation, particularly if subsequent information suggests a different valuation. In emerging markets, where data may be less reliable or more variable, anchoring on initial impressions can exacerbate valuation errors and impact investment outcomes.

The impact of anchoring bias extends to risk perception and management in FDI. Investors may anchor their perceptions of risk based on initial experiences or historical data, which can shape their overall risk tolerance and decision-making processes. For example, if an investor's first encounter with an emerging market involves a period of stability and favorable conditions, they might anchor their expectations of future risk based on this initial experience. Consequently, when faced with new information about potential risks or volatility, the investor may downplay these risks due to the influence of their initial, more positive anchor (Kao C., et al.,2001). This can lead to insufficient risk mitigation strategies and exposure to unforeseen challenges. To mitigate the effects of anchoring bias, investors can employ several strategies to enhance their decision-making processes. First, conducting thorough and ongoing research beyond initial impressions is essential. Investors should seek to gather comprehensive and up-to-date information about foreign markets and investment opportunities, rather than relying solely on initial data or experiences (Koepke R. 2019). This includes examining diverse sources of information, including market reports, economic indicators, and insights from local experts, to form a more balanced and accurate view. Another effective strategy is to use structured decision-making frameworks that incorporate objective criteria and rigorous analysis. By setting clear evaluation metrics and benchmarks, investors can reduce the influence of initial anchors and make decisions based on a more systematic assessment of opportunities and risks. Techniques such as scenario analysis and sensitivity testing can also help investors assess the potential impact of different variables and avoid overreliance on initial anchors. In conclusion, anchoring bias has a significant impact on Foreign Direct Investment by influencing how investors perceive and evaluate opportunities, assess risks, and make strategic decisions (Kok R., et al .,2009). The reliance on initial information or impressions can lead to overconfidence, valuation errors, and inadequate risk management.

Availability Heuristic and FDI: The Role of Vividness in Investment Choices

The availability heuristic, a cognitive bias where individuals rely on immediate examples that come to mind when making decisions, significantly influences Foreign Direct Investment (FDI) decisions. This heuristic relies on the ease with which information is recalled or brought to mind, often leading to judgments based on recent or particularly vivid examples rather than comprehensive or representative data (Mercado Jr R. et al.,2011). In the context of FDI, the availability heuristic can shape how investors perceive opportunities, assess risks, and make strategic choices, particularly when evaluating investments in emerging markets where information can be varied and sometimes scarce. The availability heuristic operates on the principle that people tend to give more weight to information that is readily accessible or emotionally striking. For example, if an investor recently encountered high-profile news stories about successful ventures in a particular emerging market, these vivid examples may disproportionately influence their perception of the market's potential. This can lead investors to overestimate the likelihood of similar successes and overlook broader, less visible data that might suggest greater risks or uncertainties. In essence, the more memorable or dramatic the information, the more it influences investment decisions. In practice, this heuristic can manifest in several ways. An investor who has recently seen extensive media coverage of a booming tech industry in a developing country might be more inclined to invest in that sector, influenced by the vividness of the media stories. They might focus on the success stories and optimistic projections highlighted in these reports, while neglecting less dramatic but critical information about the market's volatility, regulatory challenges, or competitive landscape. This skewed perception can lead to overinvestment in certain sectors or markets based on the immediate availability of information rather than a balanced analysis.

The availability heuristic also affects risk assessment and management. (Moscone F., et al.,2009) Investors might be more concerned about risks that have been prominently featured in recent news or that are particularly striking in their memory. For example, if an emerging market has recently experienced a high-profile financial crisis, this vivid memory can overshadow more nuanced, long-term assessments of the market's stability and potential. Conversely, if positive developments are more recent and prominent in the investor's mind, they may underestimate ongoing or potential risks, leading to an imbalanced approach to risk management. The influence of the availability heuristic is also evident in how investors react to anecdotal evidence versus empirical data. Personal experiences, testimonials, or stories from peers and media often have a strong impact, despite their limited scope or potential bias (Nguyen C. P., et al.,2021). For instance, if an investor hears a compelling success story from a colleague about an investment in a specific region, this anecdote might heavily influence their investment decisions, even if broader data suggests a more cautious approach. This reliance on vivid, anecdotal evidence can lead to decisions that are less grounded in comprehensive analysis and more influenced by immediate, memorable information. To counteract the effects of the availability heuristic, investors should adopt strategies that promote a more balanced and thorough approach to decision-making. One effective strategy is to seek out a diverse range of information sources and perspectives. By gathering data from multiple channels—such as market reports, academic studies, and expert analyses—investors can ensure a more comprehensive understanding of the investment landscape and reduce the impact of any single, vivid example.

Additionally, implementing structured decision-making frameworks can help mitigate the influence of the availability heuristic. By using systematic approaches to evaluate investment opportunities, such as setting clear criteria, conducting rigorous due diligence, and employing quantitative analysis, investors can move beyond the immediate availability of information and make decisions based on objective, thorough evaluations. Another approach is to incorporate historical data and trend analysis into the decision-making process. Historical data provides a broader context and can help investors assess whether recent, vivid examples are part of a larger pattern or an isolated occurrence. By comparing current opportunities with long-term trends and data, investors can better contextualize recent information and make more informed decisions. Furthermore, fostering awareness of cognitive biases through education and training can help investors recognize and address the effects of the availability heuristic. Behavioral finance training highlights common cognitive biases and their impact on decision-making can increase awareness and encourage more critical and reflective thinking. This can lead to better decision-making practices and a more balanced approach to evaluating investment opportunities. Finally, engaging in scenario planning and stress-testing can provide additional insights into potential risks and outcomes. By exploring different scenarios and assessing how various factors might impact investment performance, investors can gain a more nuanced understanding of potential risks and returns. This approach helps move beyond vivid but potentially unrepresentative examples and supports more robust risk management strategies. In conclusion, the availability heuristic significantly impacts Foreign Direct Investment by shaping how investors perceive opportunities, assess risks, and make decisions based on readily available or vivid information. This cognitive bias can lead to overestimation of potential gains, underestimation of risks, and reliance on anecdotal evidence rather than comprehensive analysis (Pedroni P. 2001).

Hindsight Bias and FDI: Learning from Past Investment Experiences

In the context of FDI, hindsight bias manifests when investors review past investments and retrospectively believe that the outcomes were more obvious or inevitable than they were at the time (Pedroni P. 2019). For example, an investor who faced losses on an investment might look back and conclude that the warning signs were clear and should have been acted upon, despite the fact that these signals were not apparent or were ambiguous at the time of decision-making. This skewed perception can lead to an overconfidence in predicting future outcomes and an undervaluation of the inherent uncertainties and complexities associated with international investments. The impact of hindsight bias extends to how investors evaluate their past performance and adjust their strategies. When investors look back on successful investments, they might attribute their success to their skill or foresight, rather than recognizing the role of favorable conditions or luck. Conversely, when investments fail, hindsight bias can lead them to blame themselves or their decision-making processes more harshly than is warranted, overlooking the role of unforeseen variables or systemic risks. This distorted self-assessment can influence how investors approach future opportunities, potentially leading to overconfidence in their predictive abilities or excessive caution based on past failures.

Hindsight bias can also affect how investors learn from their experiences. When reviewing past investments, investors influenced by hindsight bias might focus on what they should have done differently based on the outcome, rather than understanding the decision-making process and contextual factors that were present at the time. This can result in superficial learning and ineffective adjustments to their investment strategies (Sinha A., et al.,2021). For instance, if an investor attributes a failed investment to a single, obvious mistake they failed to see at the time, they may overlook the complex interplay of factors that contributed to the outcome. As a result, they may not address the underlying issues or systemic problems that could affect future investments. To mitigate the effects of hindsight bias, investors can adopt several strategies to enhance their decision-making processes and improve learning from past experiences. First, maintaining detailed records of investment decisions, including the rationale behind each decision and the information available at the time, can provide a more accurate and objective basis for reviewing past performance. By documenting the decision-making process, investors can better understand the context in which decisions were made and reduce the influence of hindsight bias on their evaluations. Implementing a structured review process that emphasizes objective analysis and critical reflection can also help address hindsight bias. Regularly reviewing investment decisions and outcomes using predefined criteria and performance metrics allows investors to assess their strategies based on empirical evidence rather than subjective perceptions. This approach encourages a more nuanced understanding of what worked, what didn't, and why, leading to more effective learning and adjustments to investment practices. Engaging in post-mortem analyses of both successful and unsuccessful investments can provide valuable (Swamy V., et al.,2018) insights into the decision-making process and the factors that influenced outcomes.

Behavioral Finance and FDI: A Framework for Understanding Investment Decisions

Behavioral finance, a field that integrates psychological insights into financial decision-making, offers a robust framework for understanding Foreign Direct Investment (FDI) decisions. By examining how cognitive biases, emotions, and social factors influence investors' choices, behavioral finance provides a more nuanced perspective on why investors might make decisions that deviate from traditional economic theories of rationality (Teal F., et al., 2010). This framework is particularly valuable in the context of FDI, where complex, uncertain, and high-stakes environments often challenge traditional investment models. Overconfidence bias is a prominent factor in FDI decision-making. Investors who are overconfident in their abilities may underestimate risks and overestimate their knowledge about foreign markets. This can lead to aggressive investment strategies and an underestimation of the complexities and challenges associated with entering new markets. For example, an investor with a high level of overconfidence might disregard crucial market data or ignore potential red flags, leading to poorly informed decisions. Behavioral finance suggests that addressing overconfidence involves adopting more rigorous due diligence processes, incorporating diverse perspectives, and employing systematic risk assessment techniques to counterbalance inflated self-assessments. Loss aversion, another key concept in behavioral finance, refers to the tendency for investors to prefer avoiding losses over acquiring equivalent gains. In the context of foreign investments, anchors such as initial market valuations or early financial forecasts can shape investors' subsequent judgments and decisions (Wang L., et al.,2018). For example, if an investor anchors their expectations based on optimistic initial reports, they may fail to adjust their assessments in light of new or conflicting information.

Bias Awareness and Education

Risk Management Strategies Developing robust risk management practices that account for biases like loss aversion can help investors make more balanced decisions. Techniques such as scenario planning, stress-testing, and diversification can mitigate the impact of perceived risks and enhance decision-making resilience (Westerlund J. 2005). Continuous Learning and Adaptation Encouraging a culture of continuous learning and adaptation can help investors refine their strategies and improve their decision-making processes. Regularly reviewing past investments, incorporating feedback, and staying informed about behavioral finance research can contribute to more effective FDI practices. In conclusion, integrating behavioral finance into the analysis of Foreign Direct Investment provides a comprehensive framework for understanding how cognitive biases, emotional factors, and social influences shape investment decisions. By addressing biases such as overconfidence, loss aversion, and anchoring, and by considering emotional and social dynamics, investors can develop more effective strategies for navigating the complexities of international markets. Adopting this framework enhances decision-making processes, improves risk management, and contributes to more successful investment outcomes in the diverse and evolving landscape of FDI.

Case Studies: Behavioral Factors in FDI Decisions in Emerging Markets

The Case of Overconfidence Bias in the Chinese Market One prominent example of overconfidence bias influencing FDI decisions can be seen in investments made by Western technology companies in China during the early 2000s. Many investors and companies, buoyed by China's rapid economic growth and the allure of its large consumer market, exhibited overconfidence in their ability to navigate the complexities of the Chinese business environment. For instance, major tech firms like Google and Yahoo invested heavily in China, assuming that their technological expertise and prior success in other markets would guarantee similar outcomes in

China. However, these investments were met with challenges that were underestimated or overlooked due to overconfidence (Westerlund J. 2007). The regulatory environment in China proved to be more restrictive than anticipated, with stringent government controls and censorship affecting operations. Additionally, cultural and market differences created obstacles that these companies had not fully accounted for. The eventual pullback of Google from China in 2010, driven by both operational difficulties and ethical concerns, illustrates how overconfidence in understanding a market can lead to costly mistakes. Loss Aversion in the Indian Retail Sector Loss aversion, the tendency to prefer avoiding losses over acquiring equivalent gains, has also influenced FDI decisions in emerging markets. A notable case is the entry and exit of several large retail chains in India.

Anchoring Bias in the Brazilian Energy Sector

Anchoring bias, where investors rely heavily on initial information, is evident in the Brazilian energy sector's investment landscape. In the early 2010s, Brazil was perceived as a high-growth market with promising returns in the energy sector, particularly in oil and gas. Initial investment decisions were often based on optimistic forecasts and initial positive indicators, such as high oil reserves and favorable government policies. However, as the market evolved, investors faced unforeseen challenges including political instability, economic downturns, and fluctuating commodity prices. The anchoring on initial positive projections led to substantial financial losses for many investors when reality diverged significantly from the early expectations. This case highlights the dangers of anchoring bias in dynamic and unpredictable markets, where initial impressions can skew long-term investment judgments. Emotional Influences in the South African Mining Industry Emotional responses, including fear and excitement, have significantly impacted FDI decisions in the South African mining industry (Yarba, I., et al.,2020). The excitement surrounding South Africa's mineral wealth and the potential for high returns attracted numerous foreign investors. However, this excitement often overshadowed critical considerations such as operational risks, political instability, and labor issues. The case of Vietnam’s rapid economic development and the influx of foreign investors provides a clear example. In the early 2010s, many foreign firms, observing the success of peers and influential market players, were drawn to Vietnam’s burgeoning market opportunities. Investors were often swayed by the perceived success of others rather than conducting independent and thorough market analyses. This social influence led to a wave of investments in sectors such as manufacturing and real estate, driven more by the desire to follow successful trends than by detailed assessments of local conditions. The subsequent market corrections and challenges faced by many of these investments underscore the impact of social dynamics on investment decisions. Conclusion These case studies illustrate how behavioral factors such as overconfidence, loss aversion, anchoring bias, emotional influences, and social pressures can significantly impact FDI decisions in emerging markets (Yao,Y., et al., 2019).

Mitigating Behavioral Biases in FDI: Strategies for Improved Decision-Making

This involves formalizing the investment evaluation procedure to reduce the impact of subjective judgments and cognitive biases. Structured decision-making includes creating clear criteria for evaluating investment opportunities, such as financial metrics, market potential, and regulatory risks. By adhering to predefined criteria, investors can minimize the influence of biases like overconfidence and anchoring, which might otherwise lead to hasty or poorly informed decisions. One effective method is to use decision matrices or scoring systems to objectively assess potential investments. These tools allow investors to systematically compare different opportunities based on quantifiable factors, thereby reducing the reliance on gut feelings or recent experiences (Xie, Z., et al., 2017). Additionally, incorporating checklists and decision frameworks ensures that all relevant factors are considered, helping to avoid the pitfalls of selective perception and biased assessments. Enhanced Due Diligence and Risk Assessment Enhanced due diligence and risk assessment are crucial for mitigating biases such as overconfidence and loss aversion. Comprehensive due diligence involves gathering extensive information about the investment opportunity, including market data, financial performance, regulatory environment, and competitive landscape. By conducting thorough research and analysis, investors can gain a more accurate and balanced understanding of the investment's potential and risks.

Bias Awareness and Training

Increasing awareness of cognitive biases through education and training is another effective strategy. Behavioral finance training programs can help investors recognize common biases, such as overconfidence, anchoring, and loss aversion, and understand their impact on decision-making. Training sessions that include case studies and practical exercises can enhance investors' ability to identify and address these biases in their own decision-making processes. Awareness campaigns and workshops can also promote a culture of critical thinking and reflective practice. Encouraging investors to question their assumptions, seek diverse perspectives, and engage in regular self-assessment can help mitigate the effects of cognitive biases and improve overall decision-making quality. Incorporating Diverse Perspectives Engaging with a diverse group of advisors, experts, and stakeholders can help counteract individual biases and broaden the scope of analysis (Zhou, C., et al.,2019. By consulting with professionals who have different backgrounds, experiences, and viewpoints, investors can gain a more comprehensive understanding of the investment opportunity. This approach reduces the risk of biased decision-making that may arise from relying solely on a narrow set of perspectives or personal experiences. For instance, involving local experts and industry specialists when considering investments in emerging markets can provide valuable insights into market conditions, regulatory challenges, and cultural nuances that may not be immediately apparent to external investors. Diverse perspectives can also help challenge entrenched biases and ensure a more balanced evaluation of potential investments.

Regular Review and Feedback Mechanisms

Feedback mechanisms, such as performance reviews and peer evaluations, can offer valuable insights into the impact of behavioral biases on investment outcomes (Selvakumar, P.,2023). By examining the results of past investments and assessing how biases may have influenced decisions, investors can refine their strategies and develop more effective approaches for future investments. Developing Emotional Regulation Techniques Developing emotional regulation techniques can help investors manage the impact of emotions such as fear, greed, and excitement, which can distort decision-making. Fostering a Culture of Rational Decision-Making Creating a culture that prioritizes rational decision-making, and critical thinking can help mitigate the influence of behavioral biases. Encouraging open discussions, promoting evidence-based decision-making, and rewarding objective analysis can foster an environment where biases are recognized and addressed proactively. Leadership within investment organizations can play a crucial role in setting the tone for rational decision-making. By promoting transparency, accountability, and a commitment to evidence-based practices, organizations can create a culture that supports sound investment decisions and minimizes the impact of cognitive biases. Addressing behavioral biases is essential for navigating the complexities of FDI and achieving successful outcomes in the dynamic and often unpredictable environments of emerging markets.

The Power of Behavioral Factors in Shaping FDI in Emerging Markets

Behavioral factors exert a profound influence on Foreign Direct Investment (FDI) decisions, particularly in emerging markets where uncertainties and complexities are pronounced. Understanding how cognitive biases, emotional responses, and social dynamics shape investment choices is crucial for navigating these markets effectively. These investors' overconfidence in their ability to navigate the complexities of the Chinese market led to costly misjudgments and, in some cases, exit strategies that were less profitable than anticipated (Paramasivam Selvakumar, et al., 2024). Loss aversion, another cognitive bias, impacts how investors perceive and react to potential losses versus gains. Investors in emerging markets often exhibit loss aversion by avoiding investments perceived as risky, even if the potential rewards are substantial. This tendency was highlighted during the 2014-2016 economic downturns in Brazil, where investors, fearing potential losses, withdrew from the market despite long-term growth prospects. The aversion to losses can result in missed opportunities and overly conservative investment strategies, which might stifle potential returns. However, as the market dynamics shifted due to political instability and operational challenges, these investors faced significant setbacks, demonstrating how anchoring can skew risk assessments and decision-making Emotional Responses and Investment Strategies Emotional factors also play a critical role in FDI (Vijayakumar G, et al., 2024). Emotions such as fear, greed, and excitement can significantly influence investment behavior.

Social Influences and Decision-Making

Social influences, including peer pressure and informational cascades, also impact FDI decisions. Social proof, where investors follow the lead of others, can drive investment trends in emerging markets. For instance, when influential investors or market leaders champion an emerging market, others may follow suit, sometimes without fully understanding the underlying risks. This was evident during the real estate boom in Vietnam, where the influx of foreign investments was partly driven by the observed success of early movers, leading to market overheating and subsequent corrections. Cultural and Social Norms further shape investment decisions. Investors from different cultural backgrounds may have varying attitudes toward risk, regulatory compliance, and investment strategies. Understanding these cultural nuances is crucial for tailoring investment approaches in emerging markets. For example, the preference for long-term relationships and gradual decision-making in many (Ramakrishnan T., et al.,2022) Asian cultures can impact the approach to market entry and partnerships. Failure to account for these cultural factors can result in misaligned strategies and suboptimal investment outcomes. Incorporating external viewpoints helps ensure a more comprehensive understanding of the investment environment and reduces the risk of following biased trends or social influences. Conclusion Behavioral factors, including cognitive biases, emotional responses, and social influences, play a significant role in shaping FDI in emerging markets (Sugumaran K. M, D., et al., 2024). These factors can both drive investment opportunities and introduce substantial risks. By recognizing and addressing these behavioral influences, investors can improve their decision-making processes, enhance risk management strategies, and navigate the complexities of emerging markets more effectively. Understanding the power of behavioral factors is essential for making informed, rational, and successful investment decisions in dynamic and uncertain environments.

CONCLUSION

Behavioral factors significantly drive Foreign Direct Investment (FDI) in emerging markets, impacting decision-making in profound and often unpredictable ways. As explored, cognitive biases, emotional responses, and social influences play crucial roles in shaping investment strategies, with implications for both opportunities and risks. Understanding these behavioral dynamics is essential for investors seeking to navigate the complexities and volatilities inherent in emerging markets. Cognitive Biases and Investment Decision Cognitive biases, such as overconfidence, loss aversion, and anchoring, can distort investors' perceptions and lead to suboptimal decisions. Overconfidence may lead investors to underestimate risks and overestimate their ability to navigate complex markets, resulting in potentially significant losses when unforeseen challenges arise. Developing emotional regulation techniques and promoting rational decision-making can help investors manage these emotional responses and make more measured investment choices. Social Influences and Investment Trends Social influences, including peer pressure and informational cascades, also shape FDI patterns. Investors often follow the lead of influential market players, which can drive investment trends and sometimes lead to herd behavior. Understanding the impact of social proof and cultural norms is essential for developing investment strategies that are both responsive to social dynamics and grounded in thorough market analysis. Engaging with a diverse range of advisors and experts can provide valuable perspectives and reduce the risk of biased decision-making. Mitigating Behavioral Biase Mitigating behavioral biases involves implementing a range of strategies. Structured decision-making frameworks, such as detailed due diligence and quantitative risk assessments, can help counteract cognitive distortions. Enhancing awareness of biases through training and education, coupled with regular reviews and feedback mechanisms, can improve decision-making processes. Incorporating diverse perspectives and leveraging data-driven analysis further support more rational and informed investment decisions. Strategic Implications for FDI Understanding and addressing behavioral factors is not only about avoiding pitfalls but also about harnessing potential advantages. By recognizing the impact of biases and emotional influences, investors can develop strategies that better align with market realities and reduce the likelihood of costly errors. This involves creating a culture of critical thinking, promoting evidence-based decision-making, and maintaining a disciplined approach to investment evaluation.

REFERENCES

Aharoni, Y. (2015). *The foreign investment decision process*. Routledge.

Arellano, M., & Bond, S. (1991). Some tests of specification for panel data: Monte Carlo evidence and an application to employment equations. *The Review of Economic Studies*, 58(2), 277–297. DOI: 10.2307/2297968

Asongu, S., Akpan, U. S., & Isihak, S. R. (2018). Determinants of foreign direct investment in fast-growing economies: Evidence from the BRICS and MINT countries. *Financial Innovation*, 4(1), 1–17. DOI: 10.1186/s40854-018-0114-0

Baker, S. R., Bloom, N., & Davis, S. J. (2016). Measuring economic policy uncertainty. *The Quarterly Journal of Economics*, 131(4), 1593–1636. DOI: 10.1093/qje/qjw024

Belke, A., & Volz, U. (2018). Capital flows to emerging market and developing economies. Global liquidity and uncertainty versus country–specific pull factors (Working Paper No. 23/2018). German Development Institute.

Bems, R., Catao, L., Koczan, Z., Lian, W., Poplawski-Ribeiro, M., Jiang, H., Liu, Y., & Yang, H. (2016). Understanding the slowdown in capital flows to emerging markets. In World economic.

Calvo, G. A., Leiderman, L., & Reinhart, C. M. (2011). Capital inflows and real exchange rate appreciation in Latin America: The role of external factors. *Staff Papers - International Monetary Fund. International Monetary Fund*, 40(1), 108–151. DOI: 10.2307/3867379

Carril-Caccia, F., & Pavlova, E. (2018). Foreign direct investment and its drivers: A global and EU perspective. *Economic Bulletin Articles*, 4, 60–78.

Cerutti, E., Claessens, S., & Rose, A. K. (2019). How important is the global financial cycle? Evidence from capital flows. *IMF Economic Review*, 67(1), 24–60. DOI: 10.1057/s41308-019-00073-5

De Vita, G., & Kyaw, K. S. (2008). Determinants of capital flows to developing countries: A structural VAR analysis. *Journal of Economic Studies (Glasgow, Scotland)*, 35(4), 304–322. DOI: 10.1108/01443580810895608

Dua, P., & Garg, R. (2015). Macroeconomic determinants of foreign direct investment: Evidence from India. *Journal of Developing Areas*, 49(1), 133–155. DOI: 10.1353/jda.2015.0025

Dumitrescu, E.-I., & Hurlin, C. (2012). Testing for granger non-causality in heterogeneous panels. *Economic Modelling*, 29(4), 1450–1460. DOI: 10.1016/j.econmod.2012.02.014

Eberhardt, M., & Bond, S. (2009). *Cross-section dependence in nonstationary panel models: A novel estimator (MPRA Paper 17692)*. University Library of Munich.

Edwards, S. (2001). Capital mobility and economic performance: Are emerging economies different? (Working Paper No. 8076). National Bureau of Economic Research.

Eissa, M. A., & Elgammal, M. M. (2020). Foreign direct investment determinants in oil exporting countries: Revisiting the role of natural resources. *Journal of Emerging Market Finance*, 19(1), 33–65. DOI: 10.1177/0972652719880153

Forbes, K. J., & Warnock, F. E. (2012). Capital flow waves: Surges, stops, flight, and retrenchment. *Journal of International Economics*, 88(2), 235–251. DOI: 10.1016/j.jinteco.2012.03.006

F¨orster, M., Jorra, M., & Tillmann, P. (2014). The dynamics of international capital flows: Results from a dynamic hierarchical factor model. *Journal of International Money and Finance*, 48, 101–124. DOI: 10.1016/j.jimonfin.2014.07.004

Fratzscher, M. (2012). Capital flows, push versus pull factors and the global financial crisis. *Journal of International Economics*, 88(2), 341–356. DOI: 10.1016/j.jinteco.2012.05.003

Hadri, K. (2000). Testing for stationarity in heterogeneous panel data. *The Econometrics Journal*, 3(2), 148–161. DOI: 10.1111/1368-423X.00043

Hannan, S. A. (2017). The drivers of capital flows in emerging markets post global financial crisis. Journal of International Commerce. *Economic Policy*, 8(02), 1750009.

Hannan, S. A. (2018). Revisiting the determinants of capital flows to emerging markets: A survey of the evolving literature (Working Paper No. 18/214). International Monetary Fund.

Im, K. S., Pesaran, M. H., & Shin, Y. (2003). Testing for unit roots in heterogeneous panels. *Journal of Econometrics*, 115(1), 53–74. DOI: 10.1016/S0304-4076(03)00092-7

Islam, M. A., Khan, M. A., Popp, J., Sroka, W., & Ol'ah, J. (2020). Financial development and foreign direct investment the moderating role of quality institutions. *Sustainability (Basel)*, 12(9), 3556. DOI: 10.3390/su12093556

Kao, C., & Chiang, M.-H. (2001). On the estimation and inference of a cointegrated regression in panel data. In Baltagi, B. H. (Ed.), *Nonstationary panels, panel cointegration, and dynamic panels*. Emerald Group Publishing Limited.

Koepke, R. (2019). What drives capital flows to emerging markets? A survey of the empirical literature. *Journal of Economic Surveys*, 33(2), 516–540. DOI: 10.1111/joes.12273

Kok, R., & Acikgoz Ersoy, B. (2009). Analyses of FDI determinants in developing countries. *International Journal of Social Economics*, 36(1/2), 105–123. DOI: 10.1108/03068290910921226

Mercado, R. V.Jr, & Park, C.-Y. (2011). What drives different types of capital flows and their volatilities in developing Asia? *International Economic Journal*, 25(4), 655–680. DOI: 10.1080/10168737.2011.636628

Moscone, F., & Tosetti, E. (2009). A review and comparison of tests of cross-section independence in panels. *Journal of Economic Surveys*, 23(3), 528–561. DOI: 10.1111/j.1467-6419.2008.00571.x

Nguyen, C. P., & Lee, G. S. (2021). Uncertainty, financial development, and FDI inflows: Global evidence. *Economic Modelling*, 99, 105473. DOI: 10.1016/j.econmod.2021.02.014

Pedroni, P. (2001). Fully modified OLS for heterogeneous cointegrated panels. In *Nonstationary panels, panel cointegration, and dynamic panels*. Emerald Group Publishing.

Pedroni, P. (2019). Panel cointegration techniques and open challenges. In Tsionas, M. (Ed.), *Panel data econometrics* (pp. 251–287). Elsevier. DOI: 10.1016/B978-0-12-814367-4.00010-1

Ramakrishnan, T., Mohan Gift, M. D., Chitradevi, S., Jegan, R., & Subha Hency Jose, P. Nagaraja, Rajneesh Sharma H.N., Selvakumar P., Sintayehu Mekuria Hailegiorgis, (2022). "Study of Numerous Resins Used in Polymer Matrix Composite Materials", Advances in Materials Science and Engineering, vol. 2022, Article ID 1088926, 8 pages, 2022. https://doi.org/DOI: 10.1155/2022/1088926

Selvakumar, P. (2023). Biomedical applications of polymers in biosensors, cancer vaccines and drug delivery systems. *Biopolimery i Kletka*, 39(4), 245–256. DOI: 10.7124/bc.000AA0

Selvakumar, P., Mariappan, P., Shunmugam, S., Paul, R., & Jabez, S. (2024). Removal of chemicals from effluent using photobioreactor technology to improve environmental and health impacts. *Zeitschrift für Physikalische Chemie*, 2024(7), 1295–1302. Advance online publication. DOI: 10.1515/zpch-2023-0450

Sinha, A., & Ghosh, T. (2021). Impact of economic policy uncertainty on FDI inflows: Evidence from India. In *Recent developments in Asian economics international symposia in economic theory and econometrics*. Emerald Publishing Limited. DOI: 10.1108/S1571-038620210000028009

Sugumaran, K. M. D., Pandiyarajan V., Y. B S, Selvakumar P. and M. S, (2024). "Analysis of Electromyography Signals for Control of Mechanical Prosthesis using Machine Learning Techniques," 2024 2nd International Conference on Intelligent Data Communication Technologies and Internet of Things (IDCIoT), Bengaluru, India, 2024, pp. 1059-1067, DOI: 10.1109/IDCIoT59759.2024.10467707

Swamy, V., & Narayanamurthy, V. (2018). What drives the capital flows into BRICS economies? *World Economy*, 41(2), 519–549. DOI: 10.1111/twec.12606

Teal, F., & Eberhardt, M. (2010). *Productivity analysis in global manufacturing production (Technical report)*. University of Oxford.

Vijayakumar, G., Rajkumar, M., Rajiv Chandar, N., Selvakumar, P., & Duraisamy, R. (2024). Muniyandi Rajkumar, Rajiv Chandar N, Selvakumar P and Ramesh Duraisamy, (2024). Environmentally friendly TDS removal from waste water by electrochemical ion exchange batch-type recirculation (EIR) technique. *Environmental Science. Water Research & Technology*, 10(4), 826–835. DOI: 10.1039/D3EW00793F

Wang, L., & Li, S. (2018). Determinants of foreign direct and indirect investments from the institutional perspective: A comparative analysis between emerging and mature markets. *International Journal of Emerging Markets*, 13(5), 1330–1347. DOI: 10.1108/IJoEM-01-2018-0038

Westerlund, J. (2005). New simple tests for panel cointegration. *Econometric Reviews*, 24(3), 297–316. DOI: 10.1080/07474930500243019

Westerlund, J. (2007). Testing for error correction in panel data. *Oxford Bulletin of Economics and Statistics*, 69(6), 709–748. DOI: 10.1111/j.1468-0084.2007.00477.x

Xie, Z., & Li, J. (2017). Export intensity, domestic competition, and product innovation in an emerging economy. *International Journal of Technology Management*, 74(1–4), 96–121. DOI: 10.1504/IJTM.2017.083612

Yao, Y., & Zhou, Y. (2019). Research on Outward Direct Investment in Emerging Economies. In 3rd International Seminar on Education Innovation and Economic Management (SEIEM 2018) (pp. 300–303). Atlantis Press. DOI: 10.2991/seiem-18.2019.78

Yarba, I., & Güner, Z. N. (2020). Uncertainty, macroprudential policies and corporate leverage: Firm-level evidence. *Central Bank Review*, 20(2), 33–42. DOI: 10.1016/j.cbrev.2020.03.005

Zhang, Y. A., Li, Y., & Li, H. (2014). FDI spillovers over time in an emerging market: The roles of entry tenure and barriers to imitation. *Academy of Management Journal*, 57(3), 698–722. DOI: 10.5465/amj.2011.0351

Chapter 3
Different Portfolio on Investment: A Practical Work to Reduce Risks

Junior Ntabanganyimana
https://orcid.org/0009-0007-8385-7446
Lovely Professional University, India

Amir Ahmad Dar
https://orcid.org/0000-0002-0379-2272
Lovely Professional University, India

Mohit Nain
https://orcid.org/0000-0002-9523-7179
Lovely Professional University, India

Mudassir Ahmad
https://orcid.org/0000-0002-5475-4428
Lovely Professional University, India

ABSTRACT

To understand the best strategy for the investment for the maximum return, one should accurately make a portfolio for the investment. It is a critical challenge to different investors to find the best path for investment. In this study, nine different companies are selected and the data collected from www.yahoo.finance. The 9 companies are divided into 3 categories such as high risk, moderate and low risk. The stock price on day one was recorded and on 30th day, the authors also recorded the close price of the stocks. Now, on the basis of the return of different companies, the authors will draw a conclusion regarding the investment strategy and will make the best strategy based on 9 companies for the maximum return. Now, the analysis part will provide

DOI: 10.4018/979-8-3693-9380-2.ch003

a good portfolio from future investment. Finally, the statistical tool will be used to check whether there is any significant difference between the portfolio or not.

1. INTRODUCTION

Investment can be defined as the activity of investing money or resources in different assets in the expectation of making a profit (Tyson, 2020). It is very important in individual finances, business development, and the economy. Those who invest either as individuals or organizations want to grow their wealth, achieve future ambitions and have financial security (Spuchľakova et al., 2015). It should be noted however that along with the profit comes the potential for loss, as any investment can be ditched by the market mood and other like factors.

Different types of investments include stocks, bonds, property, mutual funds, and even commodities. Each of the above categories of investments has its own risk and reward ratio. For example, stocks are high most of the time compared with the other classes of assets although they are very unstable and risky at the same time (Chou et al, 1992). On the other hand, bonds fall under low risk of investment, since the interest on the bonds is most of the time offered and it is not very high. Real property and merchandises create more diversification in the portfolio and help to protect the portfolio against the risk from economic downturns or inflation.

The risk and return relationship in investing is a very key concept. When an investor wants a bigger return, it then becomes expected that he should accept a higher risk. On the other hand, if the investment is in a lesser risk category, then the returns are either leaner or negligible (Ilmanen, 2003).

Taking risks and the risk of loss is a likely outcome of investing since external factors such as the market, the economy, and the performance of companies may influence the worth of investments made. Hence, it is imperative to state that risk management is an integral element in the successful investment process (Hopkin, 2018).

One of the quickest ways to eliminate the potential risk beyond a certain level for a single investment is through diversification of investments – this involves investing in different asset classes or geographical regions or targeting different sectors (Naqvi, et al, 2023). Hence, investors adopting a diversified portfolio can also minimize exposure to any adverse performance risks result from any single investment, thus the overall portfolio is safeguarded upside down. This works to moderate the risks versus returns for the expectations of investments in the longer term.

Investing in various portfolios is the main concern of this study due to their usefulness as effective risk management tools (Stulz., 2008). To consider those aspects, we struggle to analyze several sample portfolios for the situations, which help the investor to achieve their strategic goals by effectively diversifying risks and assets.

For instance, an investment in capital spread over stocks, bonds, real estate, will be more secure compared to a stockholder whose investment portfolio consists of just the stocks. In case of a fall in the general performance in the stock market, there is a high likelihood that losses registered in the stock portfolio are partly or completely compensated by stable and sometimes appreciating bond or real estate investments (Stout, 1995).

So, dive to take an example, the investor whose capital is divided between equities, bonds, real estate, and commodities is likely to have a better straight-line performance than the one who keeps his capital only in equities. If there is some correction in the stock market, the stable or even appreciated bond or real estate investment can compensate the losses he incurred in the equity portion of the portfolio. Diversification is thus a risk management practice that goes a long way in averting and smoothing volatilities that guard the portfolio from severe downturns.

The study mainly aims at providing an overview of investment in various portfolios as an actual world risk reduction technique. In this research paper, we would discuss a few sample portfolios and try to analyze how diversification can aid investors in achieving their financial goals without losses along the way. Various asset class combinations, sectoral allocations, and geographical diversifications will be analyzed to understand whether they work in terms of risk management and return enhancement. Through portfolio analyses, we can assist investors in making more prudent and quality investment decisions that stand in harmony with long-term strategy.

This research will also underscore the strategic importance of diversification in a globally changing economy. Economic shocks in one country are easily a ripple effect on global markets in today's dependent world. As such, knowing how to construct such resilient portfolios which are well equipped with respect to economic fluctuations is paramount for an investor. From this paper, we propose an effort to provide actionable insights on the construction of diversified portfolios that could yield an optimum risk-adjusted return.

In investment, the race is not on high yields but on mixing risk and reward by thought portfolios. Investors can increase the chances of investment for long-term success with investments in diversified ranges of assets and strategic management of risk. This paper will provide more in-depth analysis of diverse portfolios that give an investor a very practical insight of how one can optimize their investment strategy. Diversification serves as a risk management strategy that helps to smooth out volatility and safeguard the portfolio against significant downturns.

The core objective of this research is to explore the importance of investing in various portfolios as a practical tool for reducing risk. In this study, we will analyze several sample portfolios to examine how diversification can help investors achieve their financial goals while minimizing potential losses. Specifically, we will test the relative efficacy of different asset class combinations, sectoral allocation, and geographic diversification in managing risk and enhancing return. All this would be done through case studies of these portfolios to gain insights into how investors can make informed, well-aligned investment decisions about their long-term strategies.

2. CHALLENGE THAT INVESTORS FACE DURING INVESTMENT

Making investment decisions comes with many challenges for investors. One of the major challenges is market risk (Ojala & Hallikas, 2006). The efficient markets are very dynamic and depend upon varied factors such as economy, politics and performance of the company, among others (Bussy & Zheng, 2023). This lack of certainty can make investors make wrong policies, and buying and selling at wrong times may eventually lead to losses (Schoemaker, 2012). Another challenge comes through the amount of information that needs to be absorbed. Investors are also required to go through a lot of information including but not limited to trends in the market, history, and actual figures along with financial statements, news events and many others (Arnold., 2012). Due to lack of knowledge and information on how to read and understand this information some investors may make poor decisions. This information redeem has shortcomings especially in recruiting the right people for the job, making it a bother on time and decision making. Such emotions affect the investors in other ways such as making investment commits that are irrational like panic selling in the stock market or too much buying when the market is high due to fear and greed. Such emotional responses would make the investor act against the plan on how they would create assets over some time. Lastly, determination of risk against return in relation to individual investment objectives requires a lot of insight and tactics (Kahn, 2018). Overcoming such problems is critical in reducing losses and ensuring that wealth increases in size.

3. METHODS

In this study, we have selected 9 companies, divided into 3 distinct risk categories, to form a total of 27 unique combinations by taking one company from each category. The companies in Category R (R1, R2, R3) represent high-risk firms, Category A (A1, A2, A3) comprises moderate-risk firms, and Category L (L1, L2,

L3) includes low-risk firms, as shown in Table 1. The methodology aims to explore and analyze these combinations to determine the optimal portfolio. By selecting one company from each risk group, we will focus on creating a balanced portfolio that maximizes returns while minimizing risk. The optimization process will utilize various financial models to assess the trade-off between risk and return, considering the individual characteristics of the companies in different risk categories.

Table 1. Stock price of different firms

Companies	Price before 30 days	Price after 30 days
R1	14.13	10.65
R2	4.28	7.45
R3	6.69	5.99
A1	11.19	10.49
A2	72.47	70.87
A3	22.04	22.04
L1	40.28	21.25
L2	165.86	161.18
L3	77.23	77.45

Additionally, we will conduct descriptive statistics to analyze the behavior of the returns for the selected companies across different risk categories. This step will help us understand the distribution, central tendency, and variability of the returns in each category (high, moderate, and low risk). To further investigate the relationships between these categories, we will employ an ANOVA (Analysis of Variance) table. This statistical test will allow us to determine if there are any significant differences in the returns among the three distinct risk categories. Through this approach, we aim to uncover whether the risk classification meaningfully impacts the returns, thereby supporting or refuting the assumptions about risk-return dynamics in our optimization process.

3.1 Definitions

Mean

The mean, also referred to as the arithmetic mean, is simply the sum of all of the values in a dataset divided by the number of values in the dataset. It is one of the most commonly used measures of central tendency that can be used for the purpose of calculating the average value for a data set.

The formula for sample mean is:

$$\text{Mean} = \frac{\sum x}{n}$$

Where:

- $\sum X$: is the sum of all the values in the dataset.
- n is the number of values in the dataset.

It just so happens that when the values in a data set are normally distributed, then it is great to use the mean as a summary for that particular data set. However, it's really sensitive to outliers; thus, extreme values can easily pull the mean toward themselves.

The mean can be interpreted to give average income in a population, average score of students for an exam, and average time spent on a task. In many cases where the data are extreme outliers or skewed, using the median or mode might be the best measures to obtain a central tendency.

Standard Error

The standard error would be defined as the accuracy of the sample to be representative of the population from which it was obtained. It could be stated that the standard error is a measure of the standard deviation in the sampling distribution of any statistic, especially the mean.

The formula for standard error of the mean is:

$$\text{SE} = \frac{SD}{\sqrt{n}}$$

Where:

- **SD** is the standard deviation of the sample.
- **n** is the sample size.

The larger the sample size, the smaller is the standard error. The bigger the samples are, the more accurate estimates about a population parameter are obtained. Common uses of standard errors include the construction of confidence intervals and hypothesis testing.

For example, when you are trying to derive an estimate of the sample mean for a population regarding average height, the standard error will yield an impression of how far the sample mean is away from the actual population mean. The lower the standard error thus means that the mean of the sample is closer to the mean of the general population.

Standard Deviation

The standard deviation is a measure of the dispersal or spread of a dataset. It measures just how much the values in a dataset deviate from the mean. The lower the standard deviation of a dataset, the more its values cluster near the mean. The higher the standard deviation of a dataset, the further values scatter across a larger range.

The formula for standard deviation is:

$$\mathrm{SD} = \sqrt{\frac{(X - Mean)^2}{n}}$$

Where:

- X represents each value in the dataset.
- Mean is the mean of the dataset.
- n is the number of values in the dataset.

Standard deviation is widely used in finance to measure the risk of an investment's return, in quality control processes to assess variability, and in many other fields where understanding variability is important.

Sample Variance

Variance measures the average squared deviation of each number from the mean. The sample variance is used to estimate the population variance based on a sample of data.

The formula for sample variance is:

$$\text{Variance} = \frac{(X - Mean)^2}{n}$$

Where:

- X represents each value in the dataset.

• Mean is the mean of the dataset.

• n is the number of values in the sample.

Variance gives a good measure of how data points differ from the mean, but it is in squared units, which is why standard deviation is often used to interpret variability in the same units as the original data.

Range

The range is the difference between the maximum and minimum values in a dataset. It provides a measure of the spread of the data.

The formula for the range is:

Range = Maximum Value−Minimum Value

The range is easy to calculate but can be heavily influenced by outliers, making it a less reliable measure of spread for highly variable datasets.

Minimum

The minimum is the smallest value in a dataset. It is one of the key components of the range and is used to describe the lowest point in a set of data.

Maximum

The maximum is the largest value in a dataset. Similar to the minimum, it helps to define the range of the data and provides insights into the upper boundary of the dataset.

Each of these terms plays an important role in understanding and analyzing data. Together they explain datasets in terms of central tendency, variability, and shape of the distribution. For example, a mean provides us with a central value while the standard deviation and variance tell us about the variation that exists in the data around the mean. Skewness will give us an idea about the symmetry of data distribution, and kurtosis about its peakedness. Basic summary statistics that provide summarizing information of data include count, sum, range, minimum, and maximum. Sample variance, standard error, and the range are useful in understanding the broader characteristics of the dataset.

3.2 ANOVA

ANOVA (Analysis of Variance) A statistical method that tests whether means of three or more independent groups are significantly different can be said to be a strong tool through which researchers would be able to understand whether some of the differences that they obtain in the data are due to actual differences among the groups or maybe due to random variation.

Purpose of ANOVA

Generally, the objective behind ANOVA is to see whether a set of group means are equal, or if at least one of them is significantly different from others. It finds extensive application in experimental research and can be put into wide fields, ranging from biology to psychology, economics, and social sciences. It is particularly useful where there exist more than two groups for comparison. A t-test is well-suited for comparing two group means, but when making multiple t-tests over different groups, the probability of a Type I error - or false rejection of an actual null hypothesis- increases. ANOVA rectifies this problem by comparing the means of more than two groups in one single test.

Basic Principle

ANOVA works by partitioning the overall variance in the data into two components:

1. **Between-Group Variance**: This is the variation between the different groups. It represents the extent to which the group means differ from each other.
2. **Within-Group Variance**: This refers to the variation within each individual group. It reflects the natural variability among individual observations within the groups.

The F-statistic is then calculated as the ratio of between-group variance to within-group variance. If the between-group variance is significantly larger than the within-group variance, the F-statistic will be large, indicating that the differences between the groups are not likely to have occurred by chance. If the F-statistic is small, the differences between the groups are likely the result of random variation, and there is no significant difference between the group means.

If the ANOVA test reveals a significant F-statistic (typically, if the p-value is less than 0.05), this indicates that at least one group mean is significantly different from the others. However, ANOVA does not specify which groups are different. To identify specific differences, **post-hoc tests** such as Tukey's HSD (Honestly Significant Difference) or Bonferroni adjustments are performed. These tests control for the family-wise error rate and help pinpoint which group means are significantly different from each other. ANOVA is widely applied in different domains. For example, in medicine, it can be used to compare the effectiveness of different treatments on patient outcomes. In marketing, it can help assess the impact of different promotional strategies on sales. In agriculture, ANOVA is often used to compare the yields of different crop varieties under varying conditions. Its versatility and ability to handle complex experimental designs make ANOVA one of the most commonly used statistical techniques.

4. ANALYSIS

Initially, we selected 9 companies, each representing different levels of risk, as outlined above. The stock prices of these companies were recorded on Day 1, as presented in Table 2. After a 30-day period, we collected the stock prices of the same companies once again. Using this data, we calculated the returns for each company over the 30-day interval, also shown in Table 2. The returns were computed by analyzing the percentage change in stock prices, providing insights into the performance of each company in their respective risk categories. This approach enables us to assess the risk-return relationship for high, moderate, and low-risk companies over the specified time frame.

Table 2. Return of different combinations

S. No	Combinations	Comb. Before	Comb. After	Return
1	R1, A1, L1	65.6	42.39	-0.353810976
2	R2, A2, L2	242.61	239.5	-0.012818927
3	R3, A3, L3	105.96	105.88	-0.000755002
4	R1, A1, L2	191.18	182.32	-0.04634376
5	R1, A1, L3	102.55	98.59	-0.03861531
6	R1, A2, L1	126.88	102.77	-0.190022068
7	R1, A2, L2	252.46	242.7	-0.03865959
8	R1, A2, L3	163.83	158.97	-0.029664897
9	R1, A3, L1	76.45	54.34	-0.289208633
10	R1, A3, L2	202.03	194.27	-0.038410137
11	R1, A3, L3	113.4	110.54	-0.025220459
12	R2, A1, L1	55.75	39.19	-0.297040359
13	R2, A1, L2	181.33	179.12	-0.012187724
14	R2, A1, L3	92.7	95.39	0.029018339
15	R2, A2, L1	117.03	99.57	-0.149192515
16	R2, A2, L3	153.98	155.77	0.011624886
17	R2, A3, L1	66.6	51.14	-0.232132132

continued on following page

Table 2. Continued

S. No	Combinations	Comb. Before	Comb. After	Return
18	R2, A3, L2	192.18	191.07	-0.005775835
19	R2, A3, L3	103.55	107.34	0.036600676
20	R3, A1, L1	58.16	37.73	-0.351272352
21	R3, A1, L2	183.74	177.66	-0.033090236
22	R3, A1, L3	95.11	93.93	-0.012406687
23	R3, A2, L1	119.44	98.11	-0.178583389
24	R3, A2, L2	245.02	238.04	-0.02848747
25	R3, A2, L3	156.39	154.31	-0.013300083
26	R3, A3, L1	69.01	49.68	-0.280104333
27	R3, A3, L2	194.59	189.61	-0.025592271

Based on the analysis of the 27 company combinations, experiment 19, which consists of the combination R2 (high risk), A3 (moderate risk), and L3 (low risk), provides the best optimal result with a positive return of 0.0366. This combination delivers the maximum return among the selected portfolios, indicating that it effectively balances risk and return. The positive performance of this combination suggests that selecting companies with a mix of moderate and low risk, alongside carefully chosen high-risk companies, can lead to superior portfolio outcomes.

4.1 Descriptive Statistics

Descriptive statistics provide a summary of key features of the data, helping to understand the overall behavior of stock returns across different risk categories. In this study, we calculated descriptive statistics such as the mean, standard deviation, minimum, and maximum values for the stock returns of the selected companies. These metrics allow us to capture the central tendency, spread, and variability of returns for each risk group (high, moderate, and low). By examining these statistics, we can gain insights into the consistency and volatility of returns, and better understand the performance differences across the risk categories before further analysis (Alam et al., 2024; Mohammed et al., 2024; Jain et al., 2024; Dar and Anurdaha, 2018).

Table 3. Descriptive statistics

R		*A*		*L*	
Mean	0.129911974	Mean	-0.028211318	Mean	-0.16594
Standard Error	0.308096731	Standard Error	0.01831685	Standard Error	0.153515
Standard Deviation	0.533639191	Standard Deviation	0.031725715	Standard Deviation	0.265896
Sample Variance	0.284770786	Sample Variance	0.001006521	Sample Variance	0.070701
Kurtosis	#DIV/0!	Kurtosis	#DIV/0!	Kurtosis	#DIV/0!
Skewness	1.595767495	Skewness	-0.837428291	Skewness	-1.70549
Range	0.986938707	Range	0.062555853	Range	0.475292
Minimum	-0.246284501	Minimum	-0.062555853	Minimum	-0.47244
Maximum	0.740654206	Maximum	0	Maximum	0.002849

R begins at the average of its points at 0.1299, meaning R is netting up against the averages, while A and L come in down by -0.0282 and -0.1659 thus incurring a diminishment of value for their points, which suggests an average performing threshold for R above the other two. From Table 3, the standard error, a measure of accuracy of the sample mean, high for R at 0.3081, followed by L at 0.1535, while A has the least standard error at 0.0183. This in turn means that the sample mean for A highly stable and less variable as compared to the case of R and L. Measures of standard deviation, which measures the extent to which data are spread apart, R showed the highest value at 0.5336; it indicated that the values of this are very spread from the mean, meaning it has greater volatility. L then follows with a standard deviation value of 0.2659 while A has the smallest standard deviation with the value of 0.0317 in which the data points for this are bunched more closely around the mean. Similarly, the sample variance echoed the trend of the above table that with maximum variance has been that of R i.e. 0.2848 followed by L as 0.0707 and A as 0.0010 that stands in support of the fact that R has the largest variability and A has the smallest.

The skewness value reflects an asymmetric shape of the distribution of the datasets. Its skewness is 1.5958 and positive, so the data are skewed to the right since there are more values on the lower side with longer tails of the right side. The opposite applies for A with a skewness of -0.8374 and L with a skewness of -1.7055. There, the data are skewed to the left, since the right tails are longer than at the left. The range, or difference between max and min values, is largest for R at 0.9869, so R has the greatest spread of data points, L has a range of 0.4753, and A has the least range at 0.0626.

The minimum and maximum range supports this as well where the spread of R is between -0.2463 to 0.7407, A is between -0.0626 and 0.0000, and L ranges from -0.4724 to 0.0028. Again, R has the largest spread of minimum and maximum values, and A has the smallest that reflects its minimal spread. Lastly, the summation of all points is positive for R at 0.3897, whereas A and L show negative summations of -0.0846 and -0.4978, respectively. This further emphasizes that R has net positive performance while A and L establish negative results in general.

The highest variability combined with a net positive mean is seen in R. This variance suggests that this is the most volatile of the three datasets. A, on the other hand, is the most consistent and less variable with the range so narrow and deviations from the mean so minute. L falls somewhere in between and moderately variable, the negative skew being more pronounced in causing higher concentration of lower value.

4.2 ANOVA

To further analyze the differences in stock returns across the distinct risk categories, we employed Analysis of Variance (ANOVA). ANOVA helps determine whether there are statistically significant differences in the mean returns among the three risk categories: high, moderate, and low. By comparing the variability between groups and within groups, ANOVA tests the null hypothesis that the mean returns are equal across the categories. This analysis provides valuable insights into whether risk levels significantly influence stock returns, allowing us to assess the impact of risk classification (Alam et al., 2024; Mohammed et al., 2024; Jain et al., 2024; Dar and Anurdaha, 2018).

Table 4. ANOVA

Source of Variation	*SS*	*df*	*MS*	*F*	*P-value*	*F crit*
Between Groups	0.131498	2	0.065749	0.553321	0.601811	5.143253
Within Groups	0.712956	6	0.118826			
Total	0.844454	8				

Within Groups variance is the variation within each group itself, or, the individual data points of each group.

Sum of Squares (SS): Between Groups SS = 0.131498 This number presents the variability between the group means. The higher that the SS value is, the more the group means are spread out. Within Groups SS = 0.712956 This number represents the variability within each group. The higher that the SS value is, the more variability and spread can be found in each of the individual groups.

Mean Square (MS): Between Groups (MS = 0.065749): This is obtained by dividing the SS by the corresponding df, this is variation between groups average.

Within Groups (MS = 0.118826): The final step is to compute the mean square for the within-groups via the ratio that divides the sum of squares within groups with the respective degrees of freedom. This will give the average variation within each group.

For ANOVA, the test statistic is the F-value calculated as the ratio of the mean square between groups to the mean square within the groups. The larger F-value means that the means of the groups are farther apart than the variation within groups. The calculated F-value is very small at 0.5533. It may suggest that the group means are most likely not large enough to be significantly different as shown in Table 4.

The P-value is the probability that the differences among the groups that have been observed are due to chance. If the calculated P-value is smaller than a selected significance level, it would suggest that there is a statistically significant difference between the means of the groups.

In this scenario, P-value = 0.601811 is much higher compared to the typical value of 0.05. This may indicate that at a level of significance of 5%, there are no mean differences between the groups. This is the F critical value for the degrees of freedom obtained and the level of significance selected (usually 0.05). If the calculated F-value is larger than the F critical value, then the null hypothesis, which states that all group means are equal, must be rejected.

In this case, the F-value is at 0.553321, and it is way smaller compared to the F critical value, which is 5.143253. This simply implies that we fail to reject the null hypothesis.

Finally, we can conclude that the result of ANOVA did not find the any significance difference between means of the three groups under comparison. Now, with a P-value at 0.601811, it is way higher than the critical P-value of 0.05, and the value for F is far smaller than that of the F critical value. The group means which have a significantly large difference are likely an artefact of chance rather than revealing differences within the populations themselves. Thus, from this analysis, we cannot reject the null hypothesis of equality for the means of the groups.

4.3 Rate of Return

The rate of return refers to the amount of profit or loss that an investor will get from his investment. Computations, as this one, count on the amount placed in, very well known as an asset, capital, principal, or cost basis of the investment. Rate of return for an investor can be estimated through the consumption of both current data as well as projective for future investors. In most cases, the rate of return is represented in percentage form.

The rate of return(R) is calculated as follows:

R = (EMV – BMV) / BMV

where EMV – ending market value, BMV – beginning market value.

CONCLUSION

The study analyzed the data of selected nine companies categorized into high-risk, moderate-risk, and low-risk portfolios. It provides conclusions drawn from the study regarding investment strategies for maximizing the returns, thereby giving insight into how the company's stock performance, tracked over a period of 30th days, indicates how risk profiles can influence returns. Since closing prices on the 30th day were compared with the initial stock prices, each firm's return was considered in establishing that the class of risk with the largest gain, and the balance of risk versus return can be useful for an optimal investment strategy. It hints that diversified portfolio consisting of high-risk, moderate-risk, and low-risk stocks may offer even better returns if managed with respect to risk in an appropriate method.

The statistical analysis does reveal whether there is any significant difference between the return such portfolios include. If there is any significant difference, this would imply that an investor must strategically invest based on specified risk tolerance to optimize returns.

This research states the takeaway points where the full success of investment depends not only on the selection of risky companies but also on framing a balanced portfolio by taking into consideration the investor's financial goals and risk profile. Thus, the study has provided a basic framework for future investment that will illustrate the proper calculation and diversification method in managing a portfolio to obtain optimum returns.

REFERENCES

Alam, N., Khan, M. S., Azad, I., Shahid, F., & Dar, A. A. (2024). Identifying the approach to financial sustainability: Navigating the complexities of earning and spending. *Edelweiss Applied Science and Technology*, 8(4), 995–1006. DOI: 10.55214/25768484.v8i4.1477

Arnold, G. (2012). *The Financial Times Guide to Investing: The definitive companion to investment and the financial markets*. Pearson UK.

Bussy, A., & Zheng, H. (2023). Responses of FDI to geopolitical risks: The role of governance, information, and technology. *International Business Review*, 32(4), 102136. DOI: 10.1016/j.ibusrev.2023.102136

Chou, R., Engle, R. F., & Kane, A. (1992). Measuring risk aversion from excess returns on a stock index. *Journal of Econometrics*, 52(1-2), 201–224. DOI: 10.1016/0304-4076(92)90070-8

Dar, A., & Anuradha, N. (2018). Use of orthogonal arrays and design of experiment via Taguchi L9 method in probability of default. *Accounting*, 4(3), 113–122.

Hopkin, P. (2018). *Fundamentals of risk management: understanding, evaluating and implementing effective risk management*. Kogan Page Publishers.

Ilmanen, A. (2003). Expected returns on stocks and bonds. *Journal of Portfolio Management*, 29(2), 7–27. DOI: 10.3905/jpm.2003.319869

Jain, A., Hisam, M. W., Azad, I., Dar, A. A., Malhotra, M., & Khan, M. S. (2024). Digitalization's Revolutionary Effect on Education and Career Development. *Information Sciences Letters*, 13(1), 149–157. DOI: 10.18576/isl/130112

Kahn, R. N. (2018). *The future of investment management*. CFA Institute Research Foundation. DOI: 10.2139/ssrn.3474545

Mohammed, S., Dar, A. A., Khan, M. S., Azad, I., Jayaraman, G., & Albalawi, O. (2024). Goodwill Valuation Enhancement through Capitalization Method and Statistical Impact Analysis. *Journal of Risk and Financial Management*, 17(6), 226. DOI: 10.3390/jrfm17060226

Naqvi, B., Rizvi, S. K. A., Mirza, N., & Umar, M. (2023). Financial market development: A potentiating policy choice for the green transition in G7 economies. *International Review of Financial Analysis*, 87, 102577. DOI: 10.1016/j.irfa.2023.102577

Ojala, M., & Hallikas, J. (2006). Investment decision-making in supplier networks: Management of risk. *International Journal of Production Economics*, 104(1), 201–213. DOI: 10.1016/j.ijpe.2005.03.006

Schoemaker, P. (2012). *Profiting from uncertainty: Strategies for succeeding no matter what the future brings*. Simon and Schuster.

Spuchľakova, E., Michalikova, K. F., & Misankova, M. (2015). Risk of the collective investment and investment portfolio. *Procedia Economics and Finance*, 26, 167–173. DOI: 10.1016/S2212-5671(15)00910-7

Stout, L. A. (1995). Are stock markets costly casinos-disagreement, market failure, and securities regulation. *Virginia Law Review*, 81(3), 611. DOI: 10.2307/1073496

Stulz, R. M. (2008). Rethinking risk management. In *Corporate risk management* (pp. 87–120). Columbia University Press. DOI: 10.7312/chew14362-005

Tyson, E. (2020). *Investing for dummies*. John Wiley & Sons.

Chapter 4

Does the Bias Towards Under and Overconfidence Affect Investment Decisions?

Proof From India

Mayank Kumar
https://orcid.org/0000-0002-9643-5871
Christ University, India

Nirakarnath Pandey
https://orcid.org/0000-0003-0287-0969
Christ University, India

Abhinav P. Tripathi
https://orcid.org/0000-0002-5492-7616
Christ University, India

ABSTRACT

This article intends to understand the outcome of heuristic biases "overconfidence" and "underconfidence" in the short-term and long-term investment decision-making behaviour of investors in Indian market. Overconfidence and underconfidence biases have been measured through a well-structured questionnaire of various statements related to heuristic biases. SPSS 22 and the intuitive graphical user interface of PLS-SEM (SmartPLS) have been used to analyse the survey data. This article has found a positive relationship between the long-term and short-term investment decisions with overconfidence bias and a negative relationship between the short-term investment decisions and underconfidence bias. However, no relationship has

DOI: 10.4018/979-8-3693-9380-2.ch004

been identified between long-term investment decisions and underconfidence bias. This outcome is partially in sync with the findings of various studies related to overconfidence bias conducted in other countries. Whereas due to the unavailability of literature on underconfidence bias, results cannot be compared with the studies conducted in other countries

1. INTRODUCTION

1.1 Heuristic Biases

Conventional financial market theories make the assumptions that players are logical, that the market is ideal, and that they make logical decisions. Kubilay & Bayrakdaroglu (2016) recently demonstrated that even participants wished to choose investments sensibly. On the other hand, according to Shah et al. (2018), investors behave irrationally in the real world while making investment decisions. They never gave fundamental valuations any thought; instead, they liked to imitate their peers' tactics. They strive to hold onto loss-making stocks, but they book profits and sell them instead of holding the profitable equities. Rather than considering the future, their decisions are predicated on past performance. Stock market investor behaviour is complicated and frequently demonstrates both illogical and reasonable inclinations. Ideally, rational behaviour would entail investors responding logically to market fluctuations, seeking to maximize returns for a given degree of risk, and basing their judgments on all available information.

In reality, while some investors do behave rationally, a significant number of exhibit irrational behaviours influenced by various biases. This blend of rationality and irrationality can create inefficiencies in the market, sometimes leading to bubbles and crashes. Behavioural finance sheds light on these patterns and highlights methods to assist investors in reaching more unbiased, knowledgeable conclusions. Unlike economists, behavioral finance scholars have claimed that human investors act irrationally. Decisions are influenced by psychological feelings.

The market consists of investors with various levels of experience. Fear and greed often drive investor decisions. For example, during a market downturn, some investors may panic and sell their stocks to prevent losses, while in a bull market, they may buy overvalued stocks due to FOMO (fear of missing out). Even when it may not be in line with their risk tolerance or financial objectives, investors frequently follow the herd by purchasing popular stocks or selling when others do. Loss aversion is the tendency for investors to become "anchored" to particular prices, which causes them to hang onto losing companies even when their fundamentals are weak. Instead of carefully considering a stock's long-term potential, investors could place too much emphasis on current occurrences or easily accessible information.

Therefore, investors may decide in various ways from one another. Research reveals that investors use name-based heuristics or shortcuts, including alphabetical ordering (Itzkowitz et al., 2015) and name fluency (Anderson & Larkin, 2012); (Green & Jame, 2013) when trading stocks, resulting in irrational decisions. Nair & Shiva, (2023) found that "Overconfidence bias is an important predictor of retail investors' behaviour." Jain et al. (2022) finds that overconfidence bias influences investors' investment intentions. Raut *et al.* (2018) find that investors tend to be influenced by overconfidence biases. According to Fama (1970) and other scholars, conventional finance theories, markets are nearly perfectly efficient. Even with the efficient market theory, it is inferred that nobody can continually beat the market and make more money.

Simon (1956) asserts that humans are unable to act in an economically sensible manner because of their poor ability for handling knowledge. In order to overcome this dilemma, heuristics and shortcuts are utilized, which facilitate decision-making but result in the loss of previously used information (Tversky and Kahneman, 1973). This leads to systematic mistakes in judgment, which in turn causes investment decisions that, while initially reassuring, ultimately jeopardize the achievement of maximum utility. Any kind of bias that influences investment decision-making leads to incorrect decisions. This article focuses on one such bias "underconfidence." The confidence of an investor shakes the feeling that he is a new player in the field with limited knowledge or insufficient knowledge to make a correct decision. Such feelings lead to a sense of underconfidence in potential investors. Such feelings create a fear of downside risk in the minds of investors, who think that their decision will turn wrong and, in turn, will incur loss. They are unable to engage in the market actively because of this thinking. Reduced or non-existent market involvement will result in decreased liquidity and subpar price discovery. This lack of confidence spirals out of control and has a fatal knock-on effect in an unstable and unclear atmosphere.

Every investor, including fund managers, regulators, and current and potential investors, should be aware that any investment choice made while influenced by these biases would be flawed and have detrimental financial effects. This study attempts to measure investors' perceptions of underconfidence biases and various long-term and short-term investment decisions being taken by them and tries to determine the outcome to awaken potential and existing investors to avoid such biases in decision-making. Pikulina et al. (2017) find that heuristic biases, such as confidence, negatively influence investors' decisions. He stated that such investors overthink negative outcomes, leading to suboptimal portfolio management decisions and compromises in utility.

As was previously said, human behavior and psychological biases have a big influence on investment decisions, which are not solely determined by logical calculations. Among these, underconfidence and overconfidence are two cognitive tendencies that profoundly influence how investors perceive risks, evaluate opportunities, and allocate resources. According to behavioral finance theories, these biases frequently lead to departures from conventional economic models, which produce less than ideal investment results. This chapter aims to investigate the prevalence and impact of these biases on investment decisions in the Indian context, offering both theoretical insights and empirical evidence.

1.2 Overconfidence Bias

Investors who overestimate their expertise, forecasting skills, or control over events are prone to overconfidence bias, which can cause them to take unnecessary risks or trade excessively. They may trade frequently and get overexposed to volatile assets because they think they have better knowledge or insights than the general market. Conversely, underconfidence manifests as excessive caution or doubt, limiting an investor's ability to make timely decisions. Such investors may delay purchases, miss profitable opportunities, or rely heavily on external opinions, including financial advisors and market sentiment, leading to under-investment or conservative portfolios.

The delusion of knowing, the delusion of control, the delusion of improved comprehension, the delusion of validity, and the delusion of skill are some of the causes of overconfidence. The illusion of knowledge causes people to assume that their knowledge and forecasting accuracy increase with the amount of information they possess. However, more information does not always translate into more knowledge. The Investment industry seems to be addicted to information. As (Montier, 2009) put it, "The whole investment industry is obsessed with learning more and more about less and less, until we know absolutely everything about nothing." The factors that cause the illusion of control are choice, information, familiarity with the task, and outcome sequence. The illusion of better understanding comes from our illusion of a superior skill set. When people pick stocks, they study macroeconomic factors and forecasts, analyze industry growth rates, understand the competitive advantages of companies, examine financial statements, assess the quality of management, and arrive at estimates of value. Obviously, they believe that they are using high level skills, and this can induce illusions. As (Kahneman & Tversky, 2013) put it, "We know that people can maintain an unshakable faith in any proposition, however absurd, when they are sustained by a community of like-minded believers." The illusion of validity can be described in a better way with cognitive dissonance theory. Cognitive dissonance is the term used to describe the mental discomfort people typically experience when freshly learned knowledge contradicts their prior understanding. People naturally have a tendency to fabricate a compelling story under such circumstances and fall victim to the validity illusion.

Overconfidence is a pervasive phenomenon. The following are the implications of overconfidence for decision-making by investors and market participants:

a. Overconfidence leads to excessive trading.
b. Overconfidence causes investors to have under-diversified portfolios.
c. Analysts tend to be overly optimistic about the prospects of companies they follow.
d. Overconfident investors tend to underestimate risks and overestimate their ability to predict market movements.
e. Overconfident investors assume they have control over outcomes, leading to complacency.
f. Overconfident investors attribute successes to skill and downplay failures as external factors or bad luck.
g. Believing in their ability to beat the market, overconfident investors may follow trends without proper analysis.
h. They may assume that past performance trends will continue, ignoring potential disruptions.
i. Overconfident investors may rely heavily on personal forecasts or models, dismissing contrary data.
j. Overconfidence can heighten emotional attachment to investments, leading to impulsive actions.

Overconfidence can lead to excessive risk exposure, frequent trading, poor diversification, and emotional decision-making, all of which negatively impact investment outcomes. Is overconfidence not likely to get corrected in the wake of failures? It doesn't occur as frequently as it ought to. Why? Perhaps people tend to forget their failures and remember their victories, which keeps them overconfident in spite of setbacks. Langer (2016), a psychologist from Harvard, characterizes this tendency as "heads I win, tail it is chance." Self-attribution bias is the tendency for people to attribute their failure to bad luck and their success to skill. The human propensity to concentrate on plans for the future rather than on the past is another factor contributing to overconfidence and optimism. Investors must remain self-aware, disciplined, and receptive to feedback to mitigate these risks. Various researcher demonstrates that the impacts of availability, anchoring, overconfidence, and representativeness heuristics on investing decisions are not significantly mediated by financial literacy. Furthermore, risk tolerance and investing decisions are not influenced by financial knowledge. It has been established that in investment decisions, risk tolerance acts as a positive mediator between overconfidence, availability, anchoring, and representativeness heuristics. Kasoga (2021) found that financial literacy, availability, representativeness, risk tolerance, anchoring, and overconfidence have a greater impact on investing decisions than does overconfidence.

1.3 Underconfidence Bias

Underconfidence on the other hand is driven by a combination of cognitive biases, past experiences, social factors, and emotional tendencies. In the context of investment, an investor is classified as underconfident if they underestimate their subjective knowledge, as indicated by (Razmdoost et al., 2015). Underconfident investors often hesitate to make decisions, fearing failure or negative outcomes. They excessively seek advice or approval from others, doubting their own investment judgment. Underconfidence restricts their creativity and exploration, leading to limited investment avenues being considered. In nutshell underconfidence impairs decision-making by fostering hesitation, over-reliance on others, risk aversion, and missed opportunities. The following are some key contributors:

a. Insufficient understanding of investment concepts leads to doubt and hesitation.
b. Fear of making mistakes, especially financial ones, leads to risk aversion.
c. Negative past experiences create self-doubt and hesitation in investment decision-making.
d. Seeing others succeed can make individuals feel inferior, reducing their confidence.
e. Too much information can overwhelm individuals, leading to indecisiveness for investment.
f. Believing that one lacks the investment capability to succeed discourages effort.
g. Lack of encouragement or criticism from peers and family can undermine confidence.
h. Wanting perfect outcomes in investment decisions can lead to procrastination and reluctance to act unless conditions are ideal.
i. Difficulty in handling setbacks or criticism reduces the ability to take investment risks.
j. Negative news, sensational headlines, or market rumours can create fear and uncertainty.

Underconfidence is also a pervasive phenomenon. It can significantly impact investment decisions, leading to suboptimal outcomes. Following are the implications of underconfidence for decision-making by investors and market participants:

a. Investors may hesitate to act on time, fearing they lack the expertise to make sound decisions.
b. Underconfident individuals depend heavily on analysts, friends, or financial advisors.
c. Fear of making mistakes can lead investors to stick with familiar or low-risk assets.
d. Underconfident investors may panic at small market fluctuations and exit positions early.
e. Due to a lack of confidence in financial knowledge, investors may avoid defining clear goals and timelines.
f. Underconfident investors may avoid investing altogether, preferring to hold cash to avoid the risk of loss.

Underconfidence like overconfidence, can impair financial decisions, but with conscious effort, it can be managed effectively to achieve better outcomes.

Underconfidence and overconfidence biases are not unique to India, but the local socio-economic and cultural environment adds distinct layers of complexity. Factors such as limited financial literacy, evolving regulatory frameworks, and the prominence of retail investors influence how these biases operate within the Indian market. Additionally, herd mentality and family-driven financial decisions are common phenomena, intensifying the impact of psychological biases on individual and institutional investment behaviour. Various research has shown that Indian investors are predominantly myopic risk averse, which results in very little investment towards stocks. Indian stock market has often given negative returns in the short run, but in the long run, it has always delivered positive returns.

The Indian market offers a fertile ground to explore the influence of underconfidence and overconfidence, given the dynamic nature of its capital markets and the increasing participation of retail investors. The exponential increase in new DMAT Account shifts in the economy towards financialization, the rise of online trading platforms, financial apps, and easy access to information, have empowered investors but also exposed them to greater behavioural risks. Indian investors often demonstrate irrational enthusiasm during IPO booms. Recently, several IPOs have been oversubscribed despite questionable valuations, reflecting overconfidence in future gains. The abnormal surge in derivatives and margin trading reflects the overconfidence of Indian investors and underestimating risks. SEBI (Securities and Exchange Board of India) has come out with a report which narrates that 9 out of 10 traders in derivative segments are losing money. Disposition effect, herd behaviour, anchoring bias and narrow framing are common in Indian investors. As such, understanding how these cognitive biases affect investment outcomes in India is crucial for designing better financial products, improving investor education, and formulating effective policies.

In this chapter, we aim to explore the dual role of underconfidence and overconfidence in influencing key investment behaviors, such as stock selection, trading frequency, portfolio diversification, and risk tolerance. We also draw from relevant empirical studies to examine whether these biases lead to performance anomalies or irrational decision-making patterns in the Indian context. Lastly, the results will point to possible directions for behavioral training and legislative initiatives to lessen these biases and assist investors in achieving better financial results.

The research on behavioral finance emphasizes the importance of cognitive biases in affecting investing decisions, which are heavily influenced by investor psychology. Overconfidence and underconfidence stand out among these biases because they might result in less-than-ideal financial choices. While underconfidence might result in lost chances, overconfidence can lead to excessive risk-taking. Knowing how these biases affect investing choices is essential in the Indian context, where the number of regular investors participating in the equities market has grown dramatically in recent years. India's diverse market landscape, characterized by rapid economic growth, demographic changes, and increasing financial inclusion, provides a unique setting to examine the role of confidence biases. India's capital market is currently demonstrating strong momentum and growth, underpinned by both local and foreign investor interest. The Bombay Stock Exchange (BSE) and National Stock Exchange (NSE) have witnessed robust growth in market capitalization, with the indices reaching new highs due to increased investor participation. This surge is supported by favourable macroeconomic conditions and government-led investment initiatives. Domestic factors like monthly inflows into mutual funds, largely through Systematic Investment Plans (SIPs), have strengthened, and there is significant growth in the number of demat accounts, reflecting greater retail investor engagement. Global asset managers are optimistic about India’s market resilience, particularly in the equity sector, which remains attractive despite high valuations in small and mid-cap stocks. Additionally, with foreign portfolio investments (FPIs) reaching multi-year highs, the market is expected to remain buoyant as international investors continue to view India as a stable, growth-oriented economy. Overall, India’s capital market appears poised for continued expansion, supported by domestic demand, increased foreign investment, and a favourable regulatory environment aimed at enhancing financial inclusion and market accessibility.

1.4 Research Problem

This study aims to investigate the effect of under and overconfidence biases on investment decisions among Indian investors. By analysing primary and secondary data, this research seeks to answer the following questions:

1. Do Indian investors exhibit under or overconfidence biases in their investment decisions?
2. How do these biases influence investment choices, such as risk-taking and portfolio diversification?
3. Are there any demographic or psychological factors that contribute to the prevalence of these biases?

This study contributes to the existing literature by providing empirical evidence on the impact of confidence biases on investment decisions in the Indian context. The findings will have implications for investors, financial advisors, and policymakers seeking to promote informed investment decisions and improve market efficiency.

2 LITERATURE REVIEW

2.1 Investment Decision

Deposits and investments are the two terms being used interchangeably in common language. But the objectives of doing and risk perception are quite different. In the Indian context, The Securities and Exchange Board of India oversees investments, whereas the Reserve Bank of India controls deposits. Investment is about purchasing a financial asset, specifically a marketable instrument known as securities for a certain duration to reap the benefit of price appreciation. The duration or holding period defines the investment status as short-term or long-term. Any investment with a horizon of less than a year is known as a short-term investment. The other explanation of short-term investment can be buying and selling stock or asset in the same accounting period to make a quick return (Kenton, 2019).

Conversely, long-term investment is holding an asset for more than a year (Twin, 2019). Regardless of the investment duration, investors aim to optimize their investment decisions (Sharpe, 1964). Conventional finance functions on the presumption that investors are well-informed and can make logical decisions. It is generally accepted that sound financial knowledge serves as the basis for reasonable and optimal investment decisions (Merton, 1987).

According to researchers in the field of behavioural finance, investors' decisions about long- or short-term investments are typically irrational because of information gaps or incompleteness, limited rationality, illusional anomalies, fundamental heuristics, investor psychological biases, investor behavioural biases, or both (Bikhchandani et al., 1992)

2.2 Heuristic

According to Groner et al. (1983), the heuristic technique is a quick-cut manual for making difficult decisions that cannot be made using logic or the theory of probability. According to the traditional school of psychology, which included philosophers of the new generation such as Simon (1955) and psychologists such as Max Wertheimer, Wolfgang Kohler, and Karl Duncker, "heuristics are strategies that guide information search and modify the depiction of a problem to facilitate solutions."

Heuristics, according to Hertwig & Pachur (2009), are mental shortcuts or rules of thumb. By eliminating reasonable but unfeasible possibilities, it identifies a smaller number of viable options at the expense of some quality compromise, which lessens the complexity of problem-solving.

The heuristic method is defined as an intuitive process that solves a well-specified mathematical issue by interpreting and strategically using the problem's structure to derive a workable solution. The following topics are covered: (i) how to quantify a heuristic method's quality; (ii) various heuristic procedure kinds; (iii) the interactive participation of humans; and (iv) elements that may affect the selection or testing of heuristic methods. There are numerous references provided. (Silver et al., 1980, p. xx)

Taking a step back from any specific study program, Romanycia & Pelletier, (1985) in their paper explores the subject of what has traditionally been considered essential to the concept of a heuristic and which elements clash with each other. A synthesizing definition is offered following an analysis of the earlier definitions and a look at how the term is currently used. With this expanded definition of "heuristic," researchers should be able to make fuller use of other people's insights, even if those insights are expressed in a lexicon that may be unfamiliar to them.

In their work, Shah et al. (2018) provides an empirical explanation of the relationship among heuristic biases, perceived market efficiency, and investment choices. According to their findings, the perceived efficiency of the market and the investment choices made by individual traders are significantly harmed by the heuristic biases of overconfidence, representativeness, availability, and anchoring.

Because of the decision makers' cognitive biases, investment decisions can go wrong. Determining the decision's algorithm ahead of time and applying it objectively are two ways to stop cognitive biases from affecting judgments. When making decisions in a complicated setting where there is ambiguity, incomplete information, and limited rationality, heuristics are helpful, practical tools. We create a straightforward heuristic to help value investors decide which investments to make based on margin of safety, profitability, financial stability, and bankruptcy risk. This accomplishes two objectives. It helps the decision maker to avoid any cognitive bias issues in addition to streamlining the process without sacrificing quality. (Otuteye & Siddiquee, 2015)

2.3 Under Confidence Bias

Underconfidence bias, while less frequently discussed than overconfidence, is a significant cognitive bias in financial decision-making, where investors underestimate their knowledge, skills, or the accuracy of their judgments. This bias can result in excessive caution, missed investment opportunities, and overly conservative portfolio strategies, ultimately influencing investment performance and market dynamics.

Confidence bias is a sort of heuristic-driven prejudice that occurs when an individual or organization makes an investment decision based on the belief that they lack the necessary knowledge and abilities (Pikulina et al., 2017). Many individuals believe in their confidence, even when experiencing underconfidence bias. Many people tend to underestimate their abilities, resulting in a manifestation of underconfidence. Additionally, some individuals perceive themselves as having less knowledge than they possess, viewing themselves as inexperienced in decision-making—this behaviour indicates underconfidence. In the context of investment, an investor is classified as underconfident if they underestimate their subjective knowledge, as indicated by (Razmdoost et al., 2015)

2.4 Over Confidence Bias

Investors frequently overestimate their knowledge, abilities, and prediction accuracy due to overconfidence bias, a common cognitive error in financial decision-making. Investment results are eventually impacted by this tendency, which frequently results in excessive trading, risk-taking, and the underestimate of possible losses. Understanding how overconfidence bias affects investment decisions is essential for creating solutions to lessen its effects in the subject of behavioral finance.

Overconfidence causes investors to trade more frequently than is ideal because they think they have better information or predicting skills, according to research (Barber & Odean, 2012). Because of transaction costs and poor timing choices, frequent trading frequently yields inferior profits. Additionally, overconfident investors frequently undervalue risks, which can lead them to hold undiversified portfolios or make large investments in volatile assets, both of which raise the possibility of suffering big financial losses.

A growing body of literature indicates that demographic factors such as gender, age, and professional experience can influence the degree of overconfidence. The findings indicate that overconfidence is more common in males than in women and rises with education and investment experience. Education raises the degree of self-attribution. (Mishra & Metilda, 2015, p. xx). This demographic insight highlights the need for targeted interventions that address specific groups prone to overconfident behavior. On the other hand, overconfidence in one's abilities and judgment can occasionally result from having too much knowledge. Our limited knowledge puts a "dual burden" on us as we are unable to recognize what we do not know. It turns out that the less skilled financial professionals were actually more confident in their ability to manage their portfolios and make investments than their more capable competitors. (Cordell and others, 2011).

Current empirical research examines how overconfidence bias affects market dynamics and shows how it fuels events like market volatility and asset price bubbles. According to Daniel and Hirshleifer (2015), overconfident investors are more prone to follow trends and ignore basic analysis, which can result in herd mentality and speculative investments that drive asset values over their true value. Market crashes can result from abrupt sell-offs when reality deviates from these exaggerated expectations.

Scholars, legislators, and other interested parties have been paying close attention to financial literacy because of its ability to support investment decisions, enhance individual financial management, and boost overall financial health. This study looks at how financial knowledge affects investing choices while controlling for the overconfidence behavioural bias. It was discovered that investing decisions were positively and considerably influenced by financial literacy. Furthermore, the findings demonstrate that overconfidence had a beneficial impact on investment decisions and that overconfidence both favourably and significantly impacted the connection between financial literacy and investment decisions. (Alshebami & Seraj, 2022) Traders can leverage machine learning techniques to overcome the presence of behavioural biases in their decision-making. (Singh et al., 2022) For institutional investors, regular evaluations and independent audits of trading strategies may help in identifying and correcting overconfident tendencies.

2.5 Heuristic Bias and Investment decision

In their study, Ayaa et al. (2022) provides conceptual insights into how heuristic techniques and cognitive biases impact investing decision-making. According to the results of the conceptual study, investors have been employing a range of heuristics to try to reduce losses and maximize gains, which frequently leads to systemic mistakes in judgment.

Ahmad et al., (2022) in their paper shed more light on the connection between investment management practices and recognition-based, heuristic-driven biases. The findings imply that recognition-based, heuristic-driven biases have a negative impact on individual investors' investment performance while having a notably positive impact on investment decision-making. The findings also imply that the links between the recognition-based, heuristic-driven biases on the one hand and the investment management actions on the other are mediated by fundamental and technological irregularities.

Kasoga (2021) in their study demonstrates that the impacts of availability, anchoring, overconfidence, and representativeness heuristics on investing decisions are not significantly mediated by financial literacy. Furthermore, risk tolerance and investing decisions are not influenced by financial knowledge. It has been established that in investment decisions, risk tolerance acts as a positive mediator between overconfidence, availability, anchoring, and representativeness heuristics. Additionally, the study demonstrates that financial literacy, availability, representativeness, risk tolerance, anchoring, and overconfidence have a greater impact on investing decisions than does overconfidence. Kathpal et al., (2021) studied the responses of 290 stock investors in the National Capital Region (NCR) to evaluate a relationship between investors' perceptions of the severity of Covid-19 and heuristic biases. They found that Investor overconfidence is unaffected by COVID-19 in any way. Covid-19 and the other three heuristic biases like availability, anchoring, and representativeness have a strong positive correlation. This study looks at the connection between Covid-19 and the bias of some investors, although it does not prove causation. When making investments during the pandemic, the study might assist investors in recognizing their errors and learning how to fix them.

Ahmad, (2022) in their study found that cognitive heuristics are often used by investors to reduce the risk of losses in uncertain situations. But doing so results in poor judgment, which makes investors make irrational choices. The market may consequently overreact or underreact, leading to inefficiencies. Overall, the study demonstrates that there are currently differing views on the usefulness of cognitive heuristics in connection to investment management duties and market efficiency. Therefore, the lack of consensus on this topic suggests that additional research may contribute something worthwhile to the corpus of knowledge. Based on the gap analysis, three primary kinds of gaps—theoretical, methodological, and contextual—are found, highlighting areas that need more research.

Saeed, (2019) in their study demonstrates the significance of heuristic biases in pricing anchoring and mantel accounting on investor decision-making. This implies that price anchoring and mantel accounting biases have an impact on the investing decision-making process of individual investors.

Rohana Kumara & Kawshala, (2021) examined how heuristic biases affect the choices made by individual investors who trade regularly on the Colombo Stock Exchange (CSE). Their findings imply that the heuristic bias—anchoring and adjustment bias—created from the first piece of information has a major influence on how investments are made. However, other biases like availability, representativeness, and overconfidence bias have little to no effect on how individual investors in CSE decide which investments to make.

In the field of investment behavioural finance, one of the most intriguing study topics is thought to be the Behavioral Determinants (BD) of Perceived Investment Performance (PIP). Khan et al., (2023) examined the herding effects (HE) of PIP [Dependent Variable] as BD of confidence (OC), availability bias (OB), and representativeness (R) [Independent Variables] in the context of Pakistan Stock Exchange (PSX). Their findings of the regression analysis indicate that the perceived performance of investments is positively and significantly impacted by availability bias, herding effects, overconfidence, and representativeness.

Mathiyarasan & Krishnamoorthi, (2024) in their study looks at how heuristic biases affect investors' behaviour and decision-making both directly and indirectly (via how they perceive risk). The study also looks at the possible moderating effect of extraversion in investors' decisions, as well as the direct and indirect relationships between irrational behaviour and perceptual biases. The results of this study demonstrate that heuristic biases have an effect on investors' decision-making both directly and indirectly through risk perception.

Sherani et al., (2023) in their study investigated how prospect theory and heuristic biases affect Pakistani individual investors' portfolio management performance (PMP). The results showed that while availability bias and the gambler's fallacy have negligible effects, regret aversion, loss aversion, overconfidence, anchoring bias, and mental accounting all positively and significantly influence PMP. According to the study, employing mental accounting techniques may increase PMP, and investors with higher degrees of these biases are more likely to obtain better PMP. But in other situations, overconfidence can also result in taking undue risks and doing worse. In certain situations, regret aversion can result in less-than-ideal financial choices. The report advises investors to think about the possible dangers of overconfidence and regret aversion.

Yadav & Chaudhary, (2022) studied how heuristic biases affect the financial market investment decisions of certain investors. Additionally, try to determine whether or not the perception of danger mediates the relationship. The findings demonstrate the strong beneficial influence of heuristic bias on individual investors' illogical investing decision-making. A portion of the link is mediated by risk perception.

To measure the indicative parameters of overconfidence, information availability, anchoring, gambler's fallacy, representativeness, and hindsight, this study examined the impact of heuristic variables on the decision-making process of individual investors in Meru County. The greatest influence of information availability bias on investment decisions suggests that investors base their selections about which stocks to buy on easily obtainable and well-known information. Overconfidence and anchoring biases were two other heuristic biases that had a moderate influence on investor decision-making, whereas Gambler's fallacy and representativeness biases had minimal effects. Both positive and bad effects can be attributed to the factors influencing an individual investor. (Kirera F. K. & Mburugu, B. M., 2019)

Decision-making is distorted in a number of circumstances by cognitive biases, which are inadvertent mental errors brought on by streamlined information processing techniques. Serfas, (2011) shows that these biases also have a significant impact on judgments made in the context of capital investments, a field that has not yet received scholarly attention. They unequivocally demonstrate how cognitive biases brought on by anchoring consistently skew judgments and decision-making in relevant settings.

Gavrilakis & Floros (2021) discovered that the heuristic variable has a beneficial impact on the performance satisfaction level and portfolio construction of private investors. Investment behaviour during portfolio construction is impacted by heuristic and herding biases, according to a robustness test conducted on a second sample of experienced investors.

Ahmad & Wu (2023) in their findings demonstrates that heuristics are frequently used by investors, leading to a number of heuristic-driven biases when trading on the stock market. These include the use of cognitive heuristics like herding behaviour, disposition effect, anchoring and adjustment, repetitiveness, overconfidence, and availability biases, as well as recognition-based heuristics like alphabetical ordering of firm names, name memorability, and name fluency. This causes investors to decide on their investment management activities in less-than-ideal ways. Investors trade excessively in the stock market as a result of these heuristic-driven biases, which negatively impact their investment success.

The influence of unconscious thoughts and beliefs on investment decisions and their effect on market efficiency, as well as the part played by emotions like fear, greed, and expectancy. Sayrani et al., (2023) in their study look for significant effects. The greatest cognitive biases in finance, such as overconfidence, preconceptions, familiarity, and dependence on the judgments of individual investors and market efficiency, are prevalent in the Tehran Stock Exchange. The study's conclusions demonstrate that overconfidence biases and representation with the perceived efficiency of the market and investors' decisions have a positive and significant relationship, and that familiarity with market efficiency and investors' decisions has a negative and significant relationship. However, the significance of the relationship between these two variables and reliance bias is not confirmed.

2.6 Heuristic and Entrepreneurship

Ahmad et al. (2020) in their paper offer empirical insights into how heuristic-driven biases and strategic decision-making in entrepreneurship interact. The findings imply that heuristic-driven biases (representativeness, availability, overconfidence, and anchoring and adjustment) have a pronounced detrimental impact on the strategic choices that entrepreneurs in emerging markets make. It implies that the quality of the strategic decision-making process used in entrepreneurship might be harmed by biases motivated by heuristics.

2.7 Risk Heuristic Bias and Investment Decision

Jain et al. (2023) investigated how risk perception influences the link between heuristic biases and the decision-making of individual equities investors. It is discovered that risk perception fully mediates the relationship between representativeness bias and investment decision-making, but it only partially mediates the relationship between overconfidence bias and investment decision-making, availability bias and investment decision-making, gamblers' fallacy bias and investment decision-making, and anchoring bias and investment decision-making.

2.8 Other Biases and Investment Decisions

Khan et al., (2021) in their findings showed that representativeness and availability biases significantly and favourably affect investors' investment decisions. Moreover, a noteworthy moderating influence of long-term orientation is noted regarding the impact of representativeness bias on investment decisions. This implies that the impact of representativeness bias on investing decisions is mitigated by investors' long-term orientation. However, there was no discernible moderating influence for availability bias.

Hasan et al. (2023) in their study show that representativeness and anchoring biases have a substantial impact on how risk is perceived, which in turn has an indirect effect on investment decision-making. Nevertheless, through risk perception, the availability bias and the overconfidence bias did not show any appreciable indirect effects on investment decision-making.

2.9 Personality Traits, Heuristic Bias and Investment Decision

Chalissery et al. (2023) studied whether the moderating influence of the Big Five personality traits can reduce exposure to heuristic-driven biases, specifically availability bias, anchoring and adjustments bias, representativeness bias, and confirmation biases of individual investors operating in the Indian stock market. The study's findings demonstrate that heuristic bias susceptibility is not always mitigated by more trading expertise. Having more trading experience lessens an individual investor's vulnerability to availability, anchoring, and adjustment heuristics when they trade on the Indian stock market.

2.10 Other Factors and Investment Decisions

The funding policy and the dividend policy are the other two financial management policies, with the investment decision being the most significant. Fajri A. & Setiawati, E. (2023) studied to ascertain how beginner investors in Demak Regency make investment decisions in relation to overconfidence (X1), illusion of control (X2), availability (X3), anchoring bias (X4), and financial literacy (X5). The study's findings show that lack of availability, illusion of control, and overconfidence have little bearing on the choices people make about their investments. Investment decisions are influenced by financial knowledge and anchoring bias, in the meantime.

Based on the existing literature related to heuristics biases and long- and short-term investment decisions, the following hypothesis is expected and should be tested in the Indian scenario:

H1. Does underconfidence bias harm Indian investors' short-term investment decisions significantly?
H2. Does underconfidence bias harm Indian investors' long-term investment decisions significantly?
H3. Does overconfidence bias harm Indian investors' short-term investment decisions significantly?
H4. Does overconfidence bias harm Indian investors' long-term investment decisions significantly?

According to the literature, over confidence and underconfidence bias consistently affects both short- and long-term investment decisions. Furthermore, there is a notable deficiency in the study concerning the impact of biases generated by heuristics on investment choices made throughout a range of periods. This gap needs to be investigated in the context of nations such as India, which are moving from a developing to a developed status. Thus, in the context of India, which is considered an emerging country, this study aims to investigate the extent to which over and underconfidence heuristic-driven bias influences decision-making processes regarding both short- and long-term investments.

3. RESEARCH METHODOLOGY

3.1 Constructs

This study's primary objective is to look at how heuristic-driven biases, namely over and underconfidence, affect the decision-making processes for both short- and long-term investments. A survey approach was used to accomplish the research goal and a questionnaire based on pre-existing assessment tools from the literature was created (Ahmad, 2020). The author adjusted the scales to better suit the inter-relationships across heuristics and the context of Indian investors' decisions. For every multi-item concept, a 5-point Likert scale was used, where 1 meant "strongly disagree" and 5 meant "strongly agree." Techniques for reflection measuring were used to operationalize these ideas.

Four statements were used to gauge investment decisions: both short and long. One individual was dropped due to cross-loading, adapted from (Mayfield et al., 2008) and (Chaudary, 2019) also used the same measurement instrument to measure the variables of short-term and long-term investment decisions. To gauge short-term investment decisions, the author inquired about investors' agreement or disagreement with statements like "Your involvement in portfolio management activities at least twice per week" and "With the available investment opportunities, would you prefer to invest in the equity market rather than in the bond market," among others. In order to assess long-term investment decisions, investors were asked to indicate whether they agreed or disagreed with a number of assertions; your response did not include the specific remarks. This type of question includes things like "You have a portfolio that focuses on multiple asset classes (i.e., stocks, bonds, cash, real estate, etc.)" and "Do you invest some part of your money in long-term assets where your money will be blocked and illiquid for years." Underconfidence was assessed using the following three statements: These items were updated and adapted from Shedrake (2016) to better fit the investors' decisions and heuristics. To determine the respondents' level of underconfidence as investors, statements like "You feel nervous in your own investment opinions compared to opinions of your colleagues or friends" and "You underestimate about your abilities to outperform others in selecting stocks," among others, were presented. Next, participants were asked to rate their agreement or disagreement with these claims.

Overconfidence was assessed through nine items divided into two facets. Six statements were borrowed from Odean (1999), Barber and Odean (2000) and Ahmad & Shah, (2020) measuring facet one "Overestimation" by the statements like "You believe that your skills and knowledge of stock market can help you to outperform the market" "You are confident of your ability to do better than others in picking stocks" "You have control of your investment decisions" "The items for over placement include, "You have a better investment record as compared to others" "You earned higher returns than others" "You have planned to increase your investment in the stock market in next 12 months as compared to others". While the other facet is over-precision measured by three statements borrowed from Mouna and Anis (2015) and Kengatharan and Kengatharan (2014) like "You are actively involved in trade activity" "You make investments to make money quickly" "You make riskier investments for enjoyment"

3.2 Data Collecting Methods and Sampling Strategies

To achieve the research purpose, the study's sample consists of individual investors who trade actively on the National Stock Exchange or the Bombay Stock Exchange, or who are indirectly exposed to the share market. It is important to note that this study was carried out inside Indian borders, with a specific emphasis on examining the short- and long-term decision-making of individual investors; its findings may apply to similar markets worldwide. Of the 750 questionnaires distributed, the author received 316 were deemed suitable for analysis, resulting in an effective response rate of approximately 42%. Previous research on relevant themes by (Waweru et al., 2008) and (Shah et al., 2018), with sample sizes varying from 143 to 230, also revealed similar response patterns. According to (Hair et al., 2019), a sample size of 100 respondents or more is thought to be adequate for producing a dependable result in quantitative research. Because the Indian economy is still in its early stages of development and makes standardized data availability difficult, this study used the convenient purposive sampling technique for data collecting instead of random selection, which was judged problematic (Sekaran & Bougie, 1993).

There are several ways to gather data, including observations, group discussions, semi-structured and structured interviews, and unstructured interviews. Because it is a time- and money-efficient alternative to other data-gathering methods, such as brainstorming, video conferencing, and interviews, a self-reported questionnaire was used for this study (Bryman & Bell, 2011). In one-on-one interviews, investors typically avoid sharing information or expressing time constraints. This supports the use of questionnaires as a recommended technique for gathering data in this particular situation. Respondents could complete the questionnaire at their own pace, free from researchers' direct interference, thanks to its flexible style. A cover letter was attached to every questionnaire, clearly stating the author's dedication to maintaining the privacy and anonymity of respondents' responses. This assured the participants.

3.3 Data Analysis Methodology

SPSS 22 and the intuitive graphical user interface of PLS-SEM (SmartPLS) were used to analyse the survey data. In a pilot study with 75 individuals, the instrument's validity and reliability were initially assessed. Descriptive and reliability tests were performed on the data to prepare them for future research. Following that, the component structure was verified, the study constructs' convergent validity & discriminant validity were assessed, and items with low standardized outer loading were eliminated. Because of cross-loading from all dependent variables, this process excluded one variable. The study employed supplementary statistical techniques to accomplish its objectives, such as correlation analysis, structural equation modelling (SEM), and bootstrapping, a method for assessing hypotheses.

4 ANALYSIS IMPLICATIONS AND PERSPECTIVES

4.1 Analysis

4.1.1 Descriptive Statistics

The questionnaire was distributed online through personal networks using a purposive sampling method. Overall, we received 330 filled response sheets, and 14 were excluded from further analysis because of their non-experience with selected financial instrument investment. Therefore, the final sample was composed of 316 respondents. The primary attributes of the sample are enumerated in Table 1.

Table 1. Description of sample

Sr No	Classification	Category	Frequency	%
1	Gender	Male	172	54.4
		Female	126	39.9
		I prefer not to say	18	5.7
		Total	316	100
2	Age	Below 25	159	50.3

continued on following page

Table 1. Continued

Sr No	Classification	Category	Frequency	%
		25-30	31	9.8
		30-35	53	16.8
		35-40	42	13.3
		40 plus	31	9.8
		Total	316	100
3	Qualification	Up to 10th	2	0.6
		12th	11	3.5
		Bachelor	61	19.3
		Master	197	62.3
		PhD	45	14.2
		Total	316	100
4	Investment Experience	0-5 Years	214	67.7
		5 - 15 Years	65	20.6
		15+ Years	37	11.7
		Total	316	100
5	Marital Status	Single	199	63
		Married	95	30.1
		I prefer not to say	22	7
		Total	316	100
6	Employment Status	Private Sector	108	34.2
		Self Employed	37	11.7
		Not Employed	171	54.1
		Total	316	100

Constructs were modelled as reflected by the original scales. Multiple-item assessments for every concept derived from earlier research were included in the questionnaire and respondents were asked to rate it. Partial least squares structural equation modelling (PLS-SEM) was utilized for data analysis (Hair et al., 2019). The analysis was performed using the Programme SmartPLS 4. PLS-SEM is a nonparametric method compared to covariance-based SEM, which makes distributional assumptions. This method is effective for assessing a model's predictive power, which is the objective of this study.

4.1.2 Measurement Model for Overconfidence Bias (OCB) and Under Confidence Bias (UCB) and Reliability Analysis and Convergent Validity

To ensure the reliability of the constructs, a measuring model was included as an essential part of the research. The construct reliability in, Over Confidence Bias (OCB) and then in Under Confidence Bias (UCB), has been observed. It was found the Value of Cronback's alpha and Composite reliability is statistically significant as the values are > 0.7 (Hair et al., 2019). The convergent validity is assessed by analysing the correlation between the statement and latent variables. The indicative measure of the convergent validity is composite reliability (rho_c) and AVE i.e. Average variance extracted. The composite reliability (rho_c) for each construct >0.7 and the value of average variance extracted (AVE) for each construct is significant as the value of AVE for every construct is more than 0.50 (Hair et al., 2019).

Table 2. Overconfidence bias (OCB) and convergent validity

	Cronbach's alpha	Composite reliability (rho_a)	Composite reliability (rho_c)	Average variance extracted (AVE)
LTID	0.842	0.889	0.838	0.577
OCB	0.899	0.901	0.899	0.561
STID	0.864	0.865	0.864	0.614

Table 3. Under confidence bias (UCB) and convergent validity

	Cronbach's alpha	Composite reliability (rho_a)	Composite reliability (rho_c)	Average variance extracted (AVE)
LTID	0.842	0.881	0.838	0.577
STID	0.864	0.866	0.864	0.614
UCB	0.805	0.658	0.844	0.53

The term "AVE" (Average Variance Extracted) refers to the ratio of the variance accounted for by the latent construct (factor) to the variance resulting from measurement error. A value of more than 0.5 suggests strong convergent validity. The AVE values for LTID, STID, and UCB & OCB were 0.577, 0.614, and 0.530 & 0.561 respectively, suggesting a modest level of convergent validity. The composite reliability (CR) metric evaluates the dependability of the construct. Good reliability is often indicated by values > 0.7. Good dependability was indicated by the CR values of LTID, STID, and UCB & OCB which were 0.838, 0.864, and 0.844 & 0.899 respectively.

4.1.3 Measurement Model for Overconfidence Bias (OCB) and Under Confidence Bias (UCB) and Discriminant Validity

To ensure the discriminant validity of the constructs, the measuring model was included with the HTMT ratio and Fornell Larcker ratio. The value of HTMT ratio is less than 0.8 in every case whereas the Fornell Larcker ratio also met the necessary condition as the square root of AVE should be greater than all other correlations in the column (Hair et al., 2019).

Table 4. Overconfidence bias (OCB) and discriminant validity (HTMT ratio)

	Heterotrait-monotrait ratio (HTMT)
OCB <-> LTID	0.698
STID <-> LTID	0.624
STID <-> OCB	0.71

Table 5. Overconfidence bias (OCB) and discriminant validity (Fornell Larcker ratio)

	LTID	OCB	STID
LTID	0.76		
OCB	0.711	0.749	
STID	0.612	0.709	0.784

Table 6. Underconfidence bias (UCB) and discriminant validity (HTMT ratio)

	Heterotrait-monotrait ratio (HTMT)
STID <-> LTID	0.624
UCB <-> LTID	0.76
UCB <-> STID	0.718

Table 7. Underconfidence bias (UCB) and discriminant validity (Fornell Larcker ratio)

	LTID	STID	UCB
LTID	0.758		
STID	0.614	0.784	
UCB	0.769	0.761	0.574

4.1.4 Structural Model (Hypothesis Testing) for Overconfidence Bias (OCB) and Under Confidence Bias (UCB)

To test the significance of the cited relations (Hypothesis testing), we use the Bootstrapping module (re-sampling technique). Based on our objectives following hypotheses were suggested for testing under Overconfidence bias (OCB) & Underconfidence bias (UCB).

> H_1: Overconfidence bias (OCB) positively affects the Long-term Investment Decisions (LTID).
> H_2: Overconfidence bias (OCB) positively affects the Short-term Investment Decisions (STID).

The structural model (Fig 01) clearly states that overconfidence bias (OCB) positively affects Long-term Investment Decisions (LTID) as well as Short-term Investment Decisions (STID) as the path coefficient for the LTID is 0.636 and 0.626 for the STID. The value of r-square for LTID is 0.405 which means 40% of variations in LTID can be explained with an independent variable whereas 39% of the variations in STID can be explained with the dependent variable.

Figure 1. Structural model (hypothesis testing) for overconfidence bias (OCB))

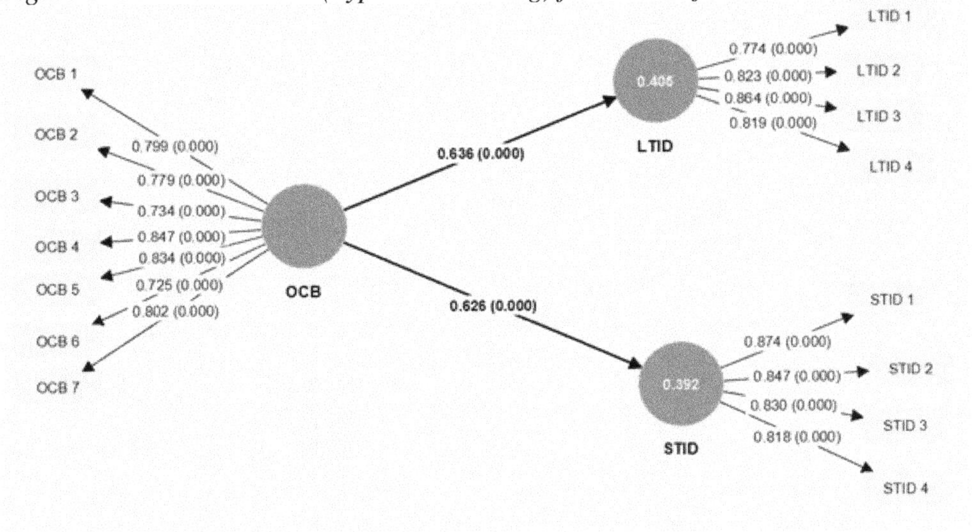

H_3: Underconfidence bias (UCB) positively affects the Long-term Investment Decisions (LTID).

H_4: Underconfidence bias (UCB) positively affects the Short-term Investment Decisions (STID).

The structural model (Fig 02) clearly states that underconfidence bias (UCB) does not affect Long-term Investment Decisions (LTID). In contrast, it negatively affects Short-term Investment Decisions (STID) as the path coefficient for the LTID is -0.093 and -0.166 for the STID. The value of r-square for LTID is 0.009 which means almost negligible variations in LTID can be explained with an independent variable. In contrast, only 3% of the variations in STID can be explained by the dependent variable. It is imperative to note that the underconfidence bias (UCB), negatively affects Short-term Investment Decisions (STID) as the p-value is less than .05 for the path, which means that a unit increase in the independent variable is associated with a decrease in the dependent variable, holding all other variables constant. The relationship between UCB and LTID is again negatively correlated but in that case, the path is not significant as the p-value is greater than 0.05.

Figure 2. Structural model (hypothesis testing) for under confidence bias (UCB)

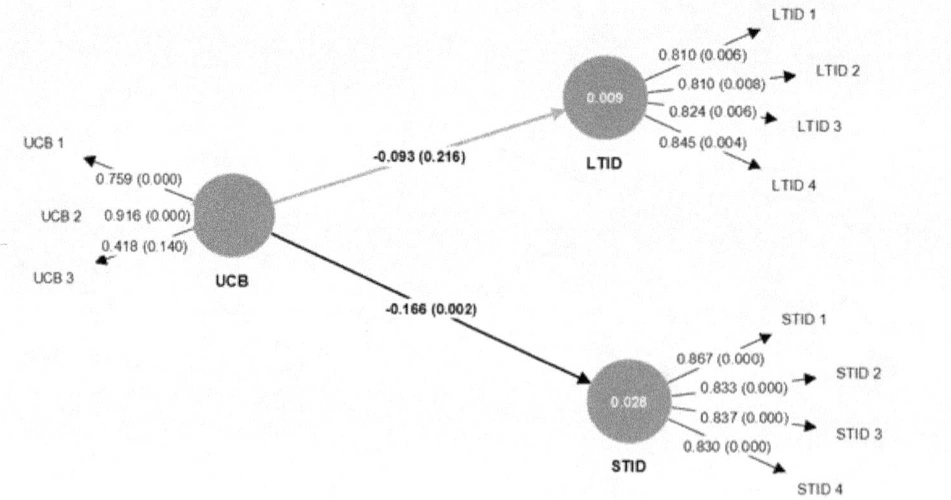

Based on the same, the following inferences can be summarised (Table 8)

Table 8. Inferential summary

S. No	Test Hypothesis	Decision
1.	H_1: Overconfidence bias (OCB) positively affects the Long-term Investment Decisions (LTID).	Accepted
2.	H_2: Overconfidence bias (OCB) positively affects the Short-term Investment Decisions (STID).	Accepted
3.	H_3: Underconfidence bias (UCB) positively affects the Long-term Investment Decisions (LTID).	Fails to accept
4.	H_4: Underconfidence bias (UCB) positively affects the Short-term Investment Decisions (STID).	Accept (Negative)

4.2 Implications

The study's results suggest that depending on fast and frugal rules in investment strategy may not lead to improved outcomes for finance practitioners. Given these findings, the researcher recommends that investors avoid relying solely on heuristics when formulating investment strategies for both short and long durations. Rather, a detailed examination of investment prospects, the establishment of quantitative standards for investments, and the definition of goals and limitations for investments are advised. Any decision should be made based on experience and financial holding capacity rather than only on feelings and cognitive heuristics. By adopting a more comprehensive approach, investors can enhance their ability to make informed and effective investment decisions and align themselves with appropriate investment opportunities.

While investing-related decisions, investors often consider both the negative and positive aspects of heuristic biases. (Otuteye & Siddiquee, 2015) advocate for mitigating the risk of succumbing to heuristic biases by the application of preset algorithms for investment management tasks in a detached manner. They argue that a disciplined approach considering such biases can overcome potential negative shortfalls. (Ahmad & Shah, 2020) highlight how financial literacy can mitigate the negative impacts of biases by implying that financial actions can serve as a buffer. (Jaiyeoba et al., 2018) propose that institutional investors can diminish the negative impact of biases by adhering to investment objectives, and board missions, maintaining self-discipline, and leveraging their professional expertise.

By obtaining more information from a variety of sources, including newspapers, articles, and research reports, as well as by consulting brokers and portfolio managers directly, individual investors can lessen the negative effects of emotions and psychological biases. This broader information-gathering approach can contribute to a more informed and rational decision-making process in the realm of investments.

In addition to that, this study provides an understanding for regulators and self-regulatory organizations like the National Stock Exchange and Bombay Stock Exchange to understand how such biases influence investor decision-making and develop appropriate action plans. (Spindler, 2011) emphasizes the importance of investors' protection for policymakers, advocating for mandatory awareness programs and allocated resources for investor protection. (Montier, 2002) and (Fromlet, 2001) caution investors about the serious consequences of neglecting behavioural biases in investment analysis. This study provides insightful information for investment managers by shedding light on the function and consequences of heuristic biases in the field.

4.3 Perspective

As per the above discussion, particularly in the Indian context, the study explores the impact of a certain heuristic-biased investment decision over the long and short terms. The researcher, found that overconfidence bias positively influences decision making however, did not discover a robust correlation between investment decisions and underconfidence bias. This may be due to the different investment environment prevailing in India in comparison to other countries operating at different levels of market maturity and different levels of regulatory compliance. So, this finding cannot be generalised to all developing countries. Further research is required to understand the impact in different countries. Further, there are several biases collectively impacting the investment decisions so more such biases should be considered at a time to understand the collective impact. So, more country-specific research based on more variable biases should be conducted to arrive at some generalised findings.

REFERENCES

Abhijith, R., & Bijulal, D. (2024). Heuristic biases influencing individual stock investment decisions: A hybrid fuzzy DELPHI-AHP-DEMATEL approach. *Journal of Advances in Management Research*, 21(4), 627–648. DOI: 10.1108/JAMR-03-2024-0093

Ahmad, M. (2020). Does underconfidence matter in short-term and long-term investment decisions? Evidence from an emerging market. *Management Decision*, 59(3), 692–709. DOI: 10.1108/MD-07-2019-0972

Ahmad, M. (2022). The role of cognitive heuristic-driven biases in investment management activities and market efficiency: A research synthesis. *International Journal of Emerging Markets*, 19(2), 273–321. DOI: 10.1108/IJOEM-07-2020-0749

Ahmad, M., & Shah, S. Z. (2020). Overconfidence heuristic-driven bias in investment decision-making and performance: Mediating effects of risk perception and moderating effects of financial literacy. *Journal of Economic and Administrative Sciences*, 38(1), 60–90. DOI: 10.1108/JEAS-07-2020-0116

Ahmad, M., Shah, S. Z., & Abbass, Y. (2020). The role of heuristic-driven biases in entrepreneurial strategic decision-making: Evidence from an emerging economy. *Management Decision*, 59(3), 669–691. DOI: 10.1108/MD-09-2019-1231

Ahmad, M., & Wu, Q. (2023). Heuristic-driven biases as mental shortcuts in investment management activities: A qualitative study. *Qualitative Research in Financial Markets*, 16(2), 291–309. DOI: 10.1108/QRFM-10-2022-0167

Ahmad, M., Wu, Q., & Abbass, Y. (2022). Probing the impact of recognition-based heuristic biases on investment decision-making and performance. *Kybernetes*, 52(10), 4229–4256. DOI: 10.1108/K-01-2022-0112

Alshebami, A. S., & Seraj, A. H. (2022). Investigating the impact of institutions on small business creation among Saudi entrepreneurs. *Frontiers in Psychology*, 13, 897787. Advance online publication. DOI: 10.3389/fpsyg.2022.897787 PMID: 35769726

Anderson, A. G., & Larkin, Y. (2012). Does non-informative text affect investor behavior? SSRN *Electronic Journal*. https://doi.org/DOI: 10.2139/ssrn.2181195

Ayaa, M. M., Peprah, W. K., Mensah, M. O., Owusu-Sekyere, A. B., & Daniel, B. (2022). Influence of heuristic techniques and biases in investment decision-making: A conceptual analysis and directions for future research. *International Journal of Academic Research in Business & Social Sciences*, 12(5). Advance online publication. DOI: 10.6007/IJARBSS/v12-i5/13339

Barber, B. M., & Odean, T. (2000). Trading is hazardous to your wealth: The common stock investment performance of individual investors. *The Journal of Finance*, 55(2), 773–806. DOI: 10.1111/0022-1082.00226

Barber, B. M., & Odean, T. (2011). The behavior of individual investors. SSRN *Electronic Journal*. https://doi.org/DOI: 10.2139/ssrn.1872211

Becker, J., Rai, A., Ringle, C. M., & Völckner, F. (2013). Discovering unobserved heterogeneity in structural equation models to avert validity threats. *Management Information Systems Quarterly*, 37(3), 665–694. DOI: 10.25300/MISQ/2013/37.3.01

Bikhchandani, S., Hirshleifer, D., & Welch, I. (1992). A theory of fads, fashion, custom, and cultural change as informational cascades. *Journal of Political Economy*, 100(5), 992–1026. DOI: 10.1086/261849

Bryman, A., & Bell, E. (2011). *Business research methods 3e*. Oxford University Press.

Chalissery, N., Tabash, M. I., Nishad, T. M., Aburezeq, I. M., & Daniel, L. N. (2023). Does the investor's trading experience reduce susceptibility to heuristic-driven biases? The moderating role of personality traits. *Journal of Risk and Financial Management*, 16(7), 325. DOI: 10.3390/jrfm16070325

Chaudary, S. (2019). Does salience matter in investment decision? *Kybernetes*, 48(8), 1894–1912. DOI: 10.1108/K-09-2018-0490

Cordell, D. M., Smith, R., & Terry, A. (2011). Overconfidence in financial planners. *Financial Services Review*, 20(4).

Daniel, K., & Hirshleifer, D. (2015). Overconfident investors, predictable returns, and excessive trading. *The Journal of Economic Perspectives*, 29(4), 61–88. DOI: 10.1257/jep.29.4.61

Fajri, A., & Setiawati, E. (2023). The Influence of Over Confidence, Illusion of Control, Availability, Anchoring Bias and Financial Literacy on Investment Decision Making in the Community of Demak District As Beginning Investors. *The International Journal of Business Management and Technology*, 7(4), 187–198.

Fama, E. F. (1970). Efficient capital markets: A review of theory and empirical work. *The Journal of Finance*, 25(2), 383. DOI: 10.2307/2325486

Fromlet, H. (2001). Behavioral finance – theory and practical application. *Business Economics (Cleveland, Ohio)*, 7(1), 63–69.

Gavrilakis, N., & Floros, C. (2021). The impact of heuristic and herding biases on portfolio construction and performance: The case of Greece. *Review of Behavioral Finance*, 14(3), 436–462. DOI: 10.1108/RBF-11-2020-0295

Gigerenzer, G., & Gaissmaier, W. (2011). Heuristic decision making. *Annual Review of Psychology*, 62(1), 451–482. DOI: 10.1146/annurev-psych-120709-145346 PMID: 21126183

Green, T. C., & Jame, R. (2013). Company name fluency, investor recognition, and firm value. *Journal of Financial Economics*, 109(3), 813–834. DOI: 10.1016/j.jfineco.2013.04.007

Groner, R., Groner, M., & Bischof, W. F. (1983). The role of heuristics in models of decision. *Advances in Psychology*, 16, 87–108. DOI: 10.1016/S0166-4115(08)62195-0

Hair, J. F., Risher, J. J., Sarstedt, M., & Ringle, C. M. (2019). When to use and how to report the results of PLS-SEM. *European Business Review*, 31(1), 2–24. DOI: 10.1108/EBR-11-2018-0203

Hasan, M., Ahmed, S. S., Mustafa, S., & Aziz, A. (2023). Risk perception as a mediator between heuristic biases and investment decision making: Case study of Pakistan stock exchange. *NICE Research Journal*, 16(4), 35–55. DOI: 10.51239/nrjss.v16i4.434

Hertwig, R., & Pachur, T. (2015). Heuristics, history of. *International Encyclopedia of the Social & Behavioral Sciences*, 829-835. https://doi.org/DOI: 10.1016/B978-0-08-097086-8.03221-9

Itzkowitz, J., Itzkowitz, J., & Rothbort, S. (2015). ABCs of trading: Behavioral biases affect stock turnover and value *. *Review of Finance*, 20(2), 663–692. DOI: 10.1093/rof/rfv012

Jain, J., Walia, N., Singla, H., Singh, S., Sood, K., & Grima, S. (2023). Heuristic biases as mental shortcuts to investment decision-making: A mediation analysis of risk perception. *Risks*, 11(4), 72. DOI: 10.3390/risks11040072

Jain, R., Sharma, D., Behl, A., & Tiwari, A. K. (2022). Investor personality as a predictor of investment intention – mediating role of overconfidence bias and financial literacy. *International Journal of Emerging Markets*, 18(12), 5680–5706. DOI: 10.1108/IJOEM-12-2021-1885

Jaiyeoba, H. B., Adewale, A. A., Haron, R., & Che Ismail, C. M. (2018). Investment decision behaviour of the Malaysian retail investors and fund managers. *Qualitative Research in Financial Markets*, 10(2), 134–151. DOI: 10.1108/QRFM-07-2017-0062

Kahneman, D., & Tversky, A. (2013). Prospect theory: An analysis of decision under risk. *World Scientific Handbook in Financial Economics Series*, 99-127. https://doi.org/DOI: 10.1142/9789814417358_0006

Kasoga, P. S. (2021). Heuristic biases and investment decisions: Multiple mediation mechanisms of risk tolerance and financial literacy—a survey at the Tanzania stock market. *Journal of Money and Business*, 1(2), 102–116. DOI: 10.1108/JMB-10-2021-0037

Kathpal, S., Akhtar, A., Zaheer, A., & Khan, M. N. (2021). COVID-19 and heuristic biases: Evidence from India. *Journal of Financial Services Marketing*, 26(4), 305–316. DOI: 10.1057/s41264-021-00116-x

Kengatharan, L., & Kengatharan, N. (2014). The influence of behavioral factors in making investment decisions and performance: Study on investors of Colombo stock exchange, Sri Lanka. *Asian Journal of Finance & Accounting*, 6(1), 1. DOI: 10.5296/ajfa.v6i1.4893

Kenton, W. (2019). *What are short-term investments?*https://www.investopedia.com/terms/s/shortterminvestments.asp

Khan, I., Afeef, M., Jan, S., & Ihsan, A. (2021). The impact of heuristic biases on investors' investment decision in Pakistan stock market: Moderating role of long term orientation. *Qualitative Research in Financial Markets*, 13(2), 252–274. DOI: 10.1108/QRFM-03-2020-0028

Khan, R., Awais, M., & Malik, Q. A. (2023). Innovation, Sentiment, Great Market Crash and Stock Market Value Reflection: A case of Over-confidence and Attribution Bias of Stock's Investors. [JTHS]. *Journal of Tourism, Hospitality, and Services Industries Research*, 3(2), 1–15.

Kirera, F. K., & Mburugu, B. M. (2019). IMPACT OF HEURISTIC BIASES ON INDIVIDUAL INVESTOR DECISION MAKING PROCESS AT NAIROBI SECURITIES EXCHANGE: A SURVEY OF INDIVIDUAL INVESTORS IN MERU COUNTY. *Journal of Environmental Sustainability Advancement Research, 5.*

Kubilay, B., & Bayrakdaroglu, A. (2016). An empirical research on investor biases in financial decision-making, financial risk tolerance and financial personality. *International Journal of Financial Research*, 7(2). Advance online publication. DOI: 10.5430/ijfr.v7n2p171

Langer, E. J. (2016). *The power of mindful learning*.

Mathiyarasan, M., & Krishnamoorthi, M. (2024). The role on heuristic biases over investor decision making—A risk perception as mediator. *Studies in Systems, Decision and Control*, 637-646. https://doi.org/DOI: 10.1007/978-3-031-50939-1_49

Mayfield, C., Perdue, G., & Wooten, K. (2008). Investment management and personality type. *Financial Services Review*, 17(3), 219–237.

Merton, R. C.MERTON. (1987). A simple model of capital market equilibrium with incomplete information. *The Journal of Finance*, 42(3), 483–510. DOI: 10.1111/j.1540-6261.1987.tb04565.x

Mishra, K., & Metilda, M. J. (2015). A study on the impact of investment experience, gender, and level of education on overconfidence and self-attribution bias. *IIMB Management Review*, 27(4), 228–239. DOI: 10.1016/j.iimb.2015.09.001

Montier, J. (2002). *Behavioural Finance: Insights into Irrational Minds and Markets*. John Wiley & Sons., DOI: 10.1057/9781137366290.0014

Montier, J. (2009). *Behavioural investing: A practitioner's guide to applying behavioural finance*. John Wiley & Sons.

Mouna, A., & Anis, J. (2015). A study on small investors' sentiment, financial literacy and stock returns: Evidence for emerging market. *International Journal of Accounting and Economics Studies*, 3(1), 10. DOI: 10.14419/ijaes.v3i1.4098

Nair, P. S., & Shiva, A. (2023). Specifying and validating overconfidence bias among retail investors: A formative index. *Managerial Finance*, 50(5), 1017–1036. DOI: 10.1108/MF-04-2023-0237

Odean, T. (1999). Do investors trade too much? *The American Economic Review*, 89(5), 1279–1298. DOI: 10.1257/aer.89.5.1279

Otuteye, E., & Siddiquee, M. (2015). Overcoming cognitive biases: A heuristic for making value investing decisions. *Journal of Behavioral Finance*, 16(2), 140–149. DOI: 10.1080/15427560.2015.1034859

Pikulina, E., Renneboog, L., & Tobler, P. N. (2017). Overconfidence and investment: An experimental approach. *Journal of Corporate Finance*, 43, 175–192. DOI: 10.1016/j.jcorpfin.2017.01.002

Raut, R. K., Das, N., & Mishra, R. (2018). Behaviour of individual investors in stock market trading: Evidence from India. *Global Business Review*, 21(3), 818–833. DOI: 10.1177/0972150918778915

Razmdoost, K., Dimitriu, R., & Macdonald, E. K. (2015). The effect of overconfidence and Underconfidence on consumer value. *Psychology and Marketing*, 32(4), 392–407. DOI: 10.1002/mar.20787

Research methods for business: A skill building approach. (1993). *Long Range Planning, 26*(2), 136. https://doi.org/DOI: 10.1016/0024-6301(93)90168-F

Ringle, C. M., Da Silva, D., & Bido, D. D. (2014). Modelagem de Equações Estruturais com Utilização do Smartpls. *Revista Brasileira de Marketing*, 13(2), 56–73. DOI: 10.5585/remark.v13i2.2717

Rohana Kumara, R. M., & Kawshala, B. A. (2021). The impact of heuristic biases on investors' investment decision making; Evidence from Colombo stock exchange. *Journal of Business and Technology*, 86-103. https://doi.org/DOI: 10.4038/jbt.v5i0.55

Romanycia, M. H., & Pelletier, F. J. (1985). What is a heuristic? *Computational Intelligence*, 1(1), 47–58. DOI: 10.1111/j.1467-8640.1985.tb00058.x

Saeed, K. (2019). Impact of heuristic biases on investment decision locus of control playing a moderating role. SSRN *Electronic Journal*. https://doi.org/DOI: 10.2139/ssrn.3499658

Sayrani, M., Razmjoy, & Samari, R. (2023). The Impact of Heuristic Biases in Investment Decision-Making and Perceived Market Efficiency a Survey at the Tehran Stock Exchange. *Financial and Behavioral Researches in Accounting*, 3(1), 1–16.

Serfas, S. (2011). The impact of cognitive biases on capital investments. *Zeitschrift für Planung & Unternehmenssteuerung*, 21(4), 427–446. DOI: 10.1007/s00187-011-0120-0

Shah, S. Z., Ahmad, M., & Mahmood, F. (2018). Heuristic biases in investment decision-making and perceived market efficiency. *Qualitative Research in Financial Markets*, 10(1), 85–110. DOI: 10.1108/QRFM-04-2017-0033

Sharpe, W. F. (1964). Capital asset prices: A theory of market equilibrium under conditions of risk. *The Journal of Finance*, 19(3), 425. DOI: 10.2307/2977928

Sheldrake, R. (2016). Students' intentions towards studying science at upper-secondary school: The differential effects of underconfidence and over-confidence. *International Journal of Science Education*, 38(8), 1256–1277. DOI: 10.1080/09500693.2016.1186854

Sherani, A. W., Naeem, A., & Shah, M. (2023). Following the crowd or making informed choices? the impact of heuristic and prospect biases on portfolio management and performance: Evidence from Pakistan's stock market downturn IN 2022. *International Journal of Business and Management Sciences*, 4(1), 203–221.

Silver, E. A., Victor, R., Vidal, V., & De Werra, D. (1980). A tutorial on heuristic methods. *European Journal of Operational Research*, 5(3), 153–162. DOI: 10.1016/0377-2217(80)90084-3

Simon, H. A. (1955). A behavioral model of rational choice. *The Quarterly Journal of Economics*, 69(1), 99. DOI: 10.2307/1884852

Simon, H. A. (1956). Rational choice and the structure of the environment. *Psychological Review*, 63(2), 129–138. DOI: 10.1037/h0042769 PMID: 13310708

Singh, H., Singh, A., & Nagpal, E. (2022). Demystifying behavioral biases of traders using machine learning. *EAI/Springer Innovations in Communication and Computing*, 179-188. https://doi.org/DOI: 10.1007/978-3-030-82763-2_16

Spindler, G. (2011). Behavioural finance and investor protection regulations. *Journal of Consumer Policy*, 34(3), 315–336. DOI: 10.1007/s10603-011-9165-6

The effect of optimism bias and over confidence on investment decisions in Aceh mediated by herding. (2023). *Quality-Access to Success, 25*(198). https://doi.org/DOI: 10.47750/QAS/25.198.19

Tversky, A., & Kahneman, D. (1973). Judgment under uncertainty: Heuristics and biases. https://doi.org/DOI: 10.21236/AD0767426

Twin, A. (2019). *What are long-term investments?*https://www.investopedia.com/terms/l/longterminvestments.asp

Waweru, N. M., Munyoki, E., & Uliana, E. (2008). The effects of behavioural factors in investment decision-making: A survey of institutional investors operating at the Nairobi stock exchange. *International Journal of Business and Emerging Markets*, 1(1), 24. DOI: 10.1504/IJBEM.2008.019243

Yadav, K., & Chaudhary, R. (2022). Impact of heuristic-driven biases on investment decision-making of individual investors: The mediating role of risk perception. *Orissa Journal of Commerce*, 127-143. https://doi.org/DOI: 10.1504/IJBEM.2008.019243

Chapter 5
Investment Decision-Making and Intricate Role of Behavioral Biases:
Delhi-NCR Study

Rohit Kaushik
https://orcid.org/0000-0002-4929-5247
Jagannath International Management School, New Delhi, India

ABSTRACT

The paper is an attempt to study the relationship between different biases and the investment decision-making of the investors, in this study three biases were selected namely Over-confidence bias, disposition bias and Home bias. To achieve the objectives this study gathered data from a sample of 400 respondents and the data analysis took place with the help of SPSS and Warp-PLS. Findings of the study suggested overconfidence bias does not share a significant relationship with investment decision-making but on the other hand disposition and home bias share a significant relationship with investment decision-making.

INTRODUCTION

The stock market has been covered by the traditionalists in the recent decades and the movements of the stock market were seen through the prism of traditional finance theories (Lintner, 1965). These theories emphasized upon the risk and return aspects of the investments. Framework of these theories were based on rationality of the human mind while making investment decisions. But the basic flaw of these theories lies in the assumption of rationality in behavior of individual investors

DOI: 10.4018/979-8-3693-9380-2.ch005

while making investments (Sharpe, 1964; Lintner, 1965; Fama, 1970). Therefore, traditionalists were unable to decode the mystery behind the stock market movements and irrational behavior exhibited by individuals during trading. With these a new study or a new branch of finance evolved known as behavioral finance which emphasized upon the behavioral factors of the investors and the consequences of those decisions taken under undue influence of biases. In other words, emotions, feelings and instincts play a pivotal role in the emergence of irrational decisions taken by investors. Behavioral finance ultimately leads to decoding of mystery behind stock market movements and irrational behavior of investors (Kahneman & Tversky, 1979).

In studies on financial markets institutional investors are found to be smarter with respect to their trading behavior but on the other hand individual investors are termed as noise traders

With the passage of time the behavioral finance theorists found one more important aspect that behavioral biases change their magnitude in different countries. Asian investors have exhibited the traits of herding bias during their trading activities.

Home bias is another bias which plays a pivotal role in shaping the decisions of investors as under the influence of this bias investors tend to stick to their obvious choices and they don't try to experiment to increase their returns. On the other hand, over-confidence bias makes investors place extra-ordinary confidence in their decisions with respect to investment. Disposition bias points to the inclination of the retail investors to sell their profit-making positions as soon as possible while holding on to loss making positions in hope of squaring them off in profit.

In the present study an attempt has been made to understand the linkages between Overconfidence, Disposition and Home biases with Investment Decision Making.

LITERATURE REVIEW

Home Bias

Beracha et al. (2014) considered home bias as closely related to affinity with culture. He found that HNI investors and mutual fund managers tend to trade frequently in those countries which are culturally are quite similar to their home country. Fedenia et al. (2013) examined the language aspect in the home bias and the resultant effect on the investment decision making, as according to this study investors coming from English speaking countries tend to exhibit less home bias during trading activities. Anderson et al. (2011) suggested that cultural closeness between the countries of institutional investors and target countries leads to the preference given to the similar country. Suh (2005) in his study showcased evidence of prevalence of home bias in the investment of financial institutions of global level and showcasing that home assets have been preferred over foreign assets. Hamburg (2013) studied the impact of different accounting practices in different countries on home bias and concluded that it results in the weakening of home bias after steps like IFRS accounting system as practices became uniform. Oehler et al. (2008) studied the investment pattern of German mutual funds and found that German portfolios are heavily invested in domestic stocks, but it also concluded that investment pattern of German mutual funds are shaped by home biased investors of Germany. Lütje and Menkhoff (2007) conducted study to understand home bias exhibited by mutual funds and concluded that for gaining information advantage they prefer to stay invested in the domestic stocks. Menkhoff et al. (2010) carried out research on Home bias in Germany and divided the respondents into three categories namely individual investors, institutional investors and investment advisors and concluded that institutional investors exhibited home bias during trading activities.

Disposition Effect

Barber et al. (2007) carried out research in the stock market of Taiwan and disposition effect was seen among the retail investors' behavior but institutional investors did not exhibit this bias. It is closely linked to the patience and belief in one's positions. Talpsepp (2011) carried out study in Estonia to understand the impact of Disposition effect, divided the sample population in the category of domestic and foreign investors and observed that institutional investors did not exhibit disposition in the trading behavior. Cici (2012) stated that when mutual funds are desperate to earn profits and when managed by a team tend to showcase effects of disposition. Choe and Eom (2009) examined the impact of disposition effect on futures trading and concluded that impact of disposition effect has weakened over the period of time with the advent of superior technology and experience of dealing in stock market.

OVER-CONFIDENCE BIAS

Mishra and Metilda (2005) have suggested in their study that more experienced and sophisticated investors usually exhibit traits of over-confidence during trading in comparison to less educated and less experienced retail investors. Barber and Odean (2001) have studied the prevalence of over-confidence in context of gender and concluded that Men are more confident as compared to their female counterparts. Odean (1998) suggested in his study that over-confidence bias leads to the muted response to a verified piece of information about any particular stock and resulting in unexpected losses. Baker and Nofsinger (2002) examined the impact of over-confidence bias among retail investors and concluded that it generally leads to a tendency among investors to control events, underestimating risks and over-estimating their knowledge during trading and leading to losses or below average return. Cooper, Folta and Woo (1995) examined various aspects of over-confidence bias that affect retail investors and concluded that investors do not seek help during decision-making process and end-up making wrong decisions.

Objective of the Study

- Primary purpose of the study is to comprehend the linkages between over-confidence, disposition and home bias with the investment decision making of the retail investors in Delhi-NCR.
- Objective of the study is to cover the Home Bias which is less-covered in relation to investment decision making.

Methodology of the Study

By perusing the available literature in the public domain structured questionnaire was designed which was divided into two parts. First part was carrying questions related to personal details of the respondents and Second part was dealing with questions related to behavioral biases and investment decision making using with the help of a Likert Scale.

The study involved a sample size of 400 respondents belonging to the Delhi-NCR area as Delhi-NCR is the most important part of India in terms of politics and financial activities, as people are more flexible in sharing their beliefs and thought process while making investment decisions. Data collection took place with the help of Google form.

Data Analysis and Hypothesis Development

Data-analysis in this study was conducted with the help of SPSS 23. As the key variables to be studied were clear from the onset their linkages or relationships with the investment decision making needed to be studied from a different perspective and the linkages were tested with the help of WARP-PLS 7.0 so that every factor can be analyzed in isolation with each other. Following Hypothesis were formed to simplify the research process:

H01: over-confidence bias does not share a significant relationship with investment decision making of investors.

H02: home bias does not share a significant relationship with investment decision making of investors.
H03: disposition bias does not share a significant relationship with investment decision making of investors

Demographic Profile

Table 1. Demographic profile

Gender	Frequency	Percent
Male	203	50.75
Female	197	49.25

Table 2. Age

Age Group	Frequency	Percent
18-30	227	56.75
31-45	148	37
46-60	23	5.75
More than 60	2	0.5

Table 3. Marital status

Status	Frequency	Percent
Married	171	42.75
Unmarried	229	57.25

Table 4. Educational qualification

Education	Frequency	Percent
Graduation	214	53.5
Post-Graduate	148	37
Doctorate	16	4
Others	**22**	**5.5**

Table 5. Occupation

Occupation	Frequency	Percent
Private Sector Employee	107	26.75
Public Sector Employee	44	11
Self-Employed	71	17.75
Retired	1	0.25
Others	177	44.25

Table 6. Income

Income	Frequency	Percent
Less than 03 Lakhs	272	68
3-6 Lakhs	42	10.5
>6-10 Lakhs	42	10.5
>10 Lakhs	44	11

Table 7. Investment experience

Experience	Frequency	Percent
Less than 02 Years	282	70.5
2-5 Years	77	19.25
>5-10 Years	18	4.50
>10 Years	23	5.75

RESULTS

Research Framework

Figure 1. Research framework

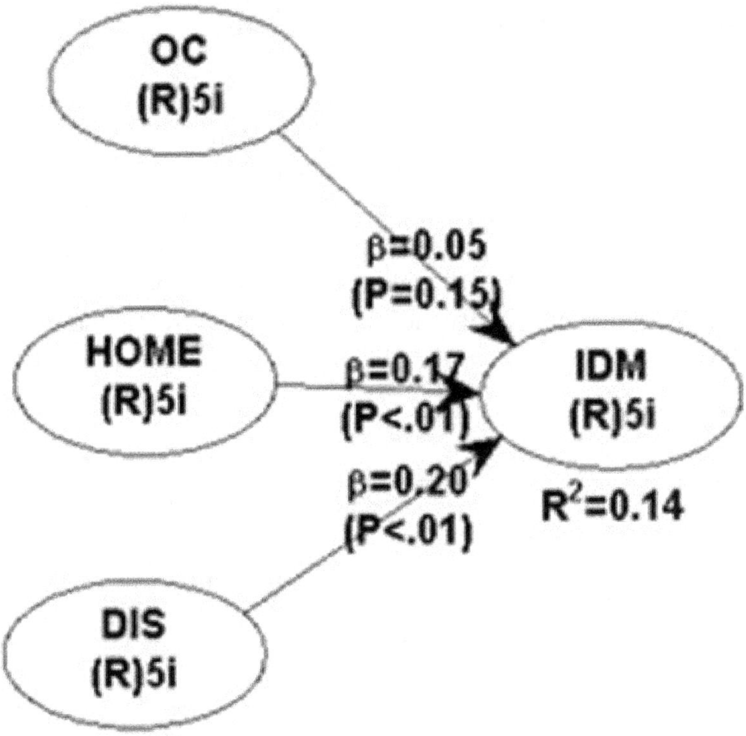

Reliability

Cronbach's alpha is the most widely used method to analyze the reliability of a construct in the questionnaire, as it measures the inter-item reliability. Cronbach's alpha is usually acceptable when the construct value is more than 0.70. Each construct in this study has measured more than 0.70 showing high correlation.

Table 8. Reliability

Construct	No. of Items	Alpha (α)
OC	5	0.775
DIS	5	0.809
HOME	5	0.808

Measurement Model (Convergent Validity)

For analyzing the statistical aspects of the model in the case of reflective items can be done by testing construct validity. In addition to this various other aspects were examined like AVE, Convergent Validity, and Discriminant Validity. Composite reliability is relied upon mainly to assess the internal consistency of the variable and the factor loadings are expected to more than 0.70, in the present study all the factor loading are more than 0.70 whereas AVEs are higher than 0.50. In the case of assessing discriminant validity the AVE value of construct should be more than inter construct correlation.

Table 9. Construct correlation

Items	Factor Loadings
OC1	0.712
OC2	0.734
OC3	0.758
OC4	0.721
OC5	0.706
Home1	0.777
Home2	0.733
Home3	0.749
Home4	0.782
Home5	0.721
DIS1	0.708
DIS2	0.773
DIS3	0.753
DIS4	0.784
DIS5	0.746
IDM1	0.778

continued on following page

Table 9. Continued

Items	Factor Loadings
IDM2	0.744
IDM3	0.740
IDM4	0.752
IDM5	0.757

Table 10. Confirmatory factor analysis

Items	Overconfidence	Disposition	Home Bias	Investment Decision Making
AVE	0.528	0.567	0.567	0.569
Composite Reliability	0.848	0.867	0.867	0.868

Table 11 Full collinearity VIF

Overconfidence	Home	Disposition	Investment Decision Making
1.195	1.107	1.239	1.122

Table 12. Discriminant validity

Constructs	Overconfidence		Disposition		Home Bias		Investment Decision Making	
	FLC	HTMT	FLC	HTMT	FLC	HTMT	FLC	HTMT
Overconfidence	0.727		0.370		0.215		0.214	
Disposition	0.370	0.468	0.753		0.240	0.298	0.273	
Home Bias	0.215	0.270	0.240		0.753		0.218	
Investment Decision Making	0.214	0.270	0.273	0.337	0.218	0.269	0.754	

Table 13. Hypothesis results

Relationship	Path Coefficient	P-Value	Hypothesis Supported
Overconfidence → Investment Decision Making Behavior	0.052	0.150	Supported
Home → Investment Decision Making Behavior	0.169	<0.01	Not Supported
Disposition→ Investment Decision Making Behavior	0.201	<0.01	Not Supported

DISCUSSION AND CONCLUSION

The study analyses the impact of Overconfidence bias, Disposition Bias and Home Bias on the Investment Decision Making of the retail investors in Delhi-NCR area. In a fast-growing economy like India people are rapidly expanding their area of operation in terms of investment and in pursuit of earning high return on their investment, they try to explore new investment avenues like stock market (shares and mutual funds). As stock market is known for its unpredictability and daily volatility, an investors is expected to behave diligently. The findings of the study reveal that disposition bias has a significant relation with investment decision making, in other words people in Delhi-NCR are suffering from disposition bias during investment decision making which is consistent with the previous studies like Frazzini (2006), which found that disposition affects the investment behavior to a great extent, due to which retail investors sell their profit making shares very soon and holding on to loss making stocks far longer than they should.

Whereas overconfidence bias is not significantly related with investment decision making as people with achieving maturity and with the help of using other tools can overcome the problem of overconfidence during investment decision making but our findings in relation to overconfidence bias is partly consistent with previous studies like Kurniawati D. et al. (2019), which found that overconfidence leaves a positive impact on the outlook of investors. But on the contrary Home bias was found to be sharing a significant relation with investment decision making, which is quite similar to the findings of the previous studies like Kang (1997) which found that foreign investors also wish to place more importance to those shares where they enjoy informational advantage. This brought to the fore a critical aspect of the retail investor's personality that due to easy availability of data they prefer to invest in domestic companies rather than going global for earning higher rate of return as it is not possible for them in case of global companies to gather credible piece of information about their financial health due to which sometimes they are not able to take advantage of many lucrative opportunities in the foreign markets and this hampers growth as an investor. By taking stock of the thought process of the investors with the help of this research regulators and mutual funds can formulate policies which can help them train retail investors to invest properly in the stock market in a balanced way and will also help financial advisors to advice investors in an even-handed manner, in the context of various biases affecting their decision making.

REFERENCES

Anderson, C. W., Fedenia, M., Hirschey, M., & Skiba, H. (2011). Cultural influences on home bias and international diversification by institutional investors. *Journal of Banking & Finance*, 35(4), 916–934. DOI: 10.1016/j.jbankfin.2010.09.006

Baker, H. K., & Nofsinger, J. R. (2002). Psychological biases of investors. *Financial Services Review*, 11(2), 97–116.

Barber, B. M., Lee, Y. T., Liu, Y. J., & Odean, T. (2007). Is the aggregate investor reluctant to realise losses? evidence from Taiwan. *European Financial Management*, 13(3), 423–447. DOI: 10.1111/j.1468-036X.2007.00367.x

Beracha, E., Fedenia, M., & Skiba, H. (2014). Culture's impact on institutional investors' trading frequency. *International Review of Financial Analysis*, 31, 34–47. DOI: 10.1016/j.irfa.2013.10.002

Choe, H., & Eom, Y. (2009). The disposition effect and investment performance in the futures market. *Journal of Futures Markets*, 29(6), 496–522. DOI: 10.1002/fut.20398

Cici, G. (2012). The prevalence of the disposition effect in mutual funds' trades. *Journal of Financial and Quantitative Analysis*, 47(4), 795–820. DOI: 10.1017/S0022109012000348

Cooper, A. C., Folta, T. B., & Woo, C. (1995). Entrepreneurial information search. *Journal of Business Venturing*, 10(2), 107–120. DOI: 10.1016/0883-9026(94)00022-M

Fedenia, M., Shafer, S., & Skiba, H. (2013). Information immobility, industry concentration and institutional investors' performance. *Journal of Banking & Finance*, 37(6), 2140–2159. DOI: 10.1016/j.jbankfin.2013.01.034

Frazzini, A. (2006). The disposition effect and underreaction to news. *The Journal of Finance*, 61(4), 2017–2046. DOI: 10.1111/j.1540-6261.2006.00896.x

Kang, J. K., & Stulz, R´. M. (1997). Why is there a home bias? An analysis of foreign portfolio equity ownership in Japan. *Journal of Financial Economics*, 46(1), 3–28. DOI: 10.1016/S0304-405X(97)00023-8

Kurniawati, D., & Sutrisno, S. (2019). The Benchmark of Investor Decisions to Invest In the Initial Public Offering (IPO). Riset Akuntansi dan Keuangan Indonesia, 4(2), 166-176.

Lütje, T., & Menkhoff, L. (2007). What drives home bias? evidence from fund managers' views. *International Journal of Finance & Economics*, 12(1), 21–35. DOI: 10.1002/ijfe.309

Menkhoff, L., Schmeling, M., & Schmidt, U. (2010). Are All Professional Investors Sophisticated? *German Economic Review*, 11(4), 418–440. DOI: 10.1111/j.1468-0475.2009.00497.x

Mishra, K. C., & Metilda, M. J. (2015). A study on the impact of investment experience, gender, and level of education on overconfidence and self-attribution bias. *IIMB Management Review*, 27(4), 228–239. DOI: 10.1016/j.iimb.2015.09.001

Oehler, A., Rummer, M., & Wendt, S. (2008). Portfolio selection of german investors: On the causes of home-biased investment decisions. *Journal of Behavioral Finance*, 9(3), 149–162. DOI: 10.1080/15427560802341434

Suh, J. (2005). Home bias among institutional investors: A study of the economist quarterly portfolio poll. *Journal of the Japanese and International Economies*, 19(1), 72–95. DOI: 10.1016/j.jjie.2003.12.003

Talpsepp, T. (2011). Reverse disposition effect of foreign investors. *Journal of Behavioral Finance*, 12(4), 183–200. DOI: 10.1080/15427560.2011.606387

Chapter 6
Investor Behavior and Market Efficiency in Emerging Markets:
An Empirical Study on Retail Investors

Palak Srivastava
https://orcid.org/0009-0007-7591-7218
Christ University, India

Puja Chopra
Christ University, India

ABSTRACT

In this chapter, we focus on the interaction between the behavior of investors and the efficiency of the market in the conditions of emerging markets. It bears merit that many investments can be made in these markets. However, they are distinctive by those challenges that change how they invest. How the markets operate is doubtful, emerging markets have quickly become an essential part of global finance and resolving conflicts (Chauhan, Ahmad, Aggarwal, & Chandra, 2019b). As these forms of investment are becoming more popular and extend into new territories the need to comprehend the contact patterns associated with the investor behavior retakes its significance.

DOI: 10.4018/979-8-3693-9380-2.ch006

INTRODUCTION

Global markets that comprise the emerging markets are those experiencing a relatively high growth rate and high financial risk, they are currently the center of attraction for consumers and researchers. These markets seem to hold a lot of potential for penetration and the generation of more sales revenues and, as such, are inherently volatile and unstable. Such a comparison of the opportunity against the possible loss shows that investing in emerging markets is not a simple affair. Analyzing the intricacies of emerging markets requires going beyond basic financial theories that underlie classical approaches rooted in the efficiency of markets. This implies that there is probably a need to question current theories used to explain these special financial contexts. As highlighted previously, investor biases are essential in determining market behavior in these regions (Chauhan, Ahmad, Aggarwal, & Chandra, 2019b). The study's premise is based on the assumption that an investment's cognitive, emotional, and social aspects are the core determinants, which can significantly help in understanding the effective working of the overall structure of the market in the emerging economy. This point of view shifts the focus in analyzing market behavior from rationality and efficiency, which is somewhat limiting, to considering the research on behavior. Some Investor biases, such as overconfidence, herding, loss aversion, and others, are some of the major driving forces of the emerging financial market (Elangovan, Irudayasamy, & Parayitam, 2022b). These biases cause deviations from the rationality model of efficiency standards of the market and hence can cause inefficiency. For instance, overconfidence, which sees investors trading too often and underestimating risks, will lead to more losses (Hussain, Korkeamäki, Xu, & Khan, 2015b). This chapter focuses on the objective of understanding the mechanisms that link the behavior of the investors and their cognitive biases to the behavioral outcomes in the emerging market, thus, disentangling the psychological perspective of the investors' decisions. Investor behavior is critical in determining market outcomes such as enhancing economies. It is, therefore, essential to note that the sale or purchase of any form of securities by an investment individual thus, whether institutional or individual is likely to impact on prices of the assets, trading volume, or even the state of the entire market (Elangovan, Irudayasamy, & Parayitam, 2022b). Nevertheless, often they have such decision-making influenced by cognitive and behavioral biases that affect how and what factors lead to distortions of the markets. This chapter systematically seeks to investigate how these biases affect the capital market's efficiency by examining the extent to which they are present among the investors of the emerging processes market. Cognitive biases discussing overconfidence, anchoring, or, more broadly, availability heuristics can cause the investor to misinterpret the available market information, resulting in investments being made poorly (Hussain, Korkeamäki,

Xu, & Khan, 2015b). Investing behavioral biases, like loss aversion, herding, or confirmation bias, induce fundamental investors' behavior and irrational reactions to market events (Chauhan, Ahmad, Aggarwal, & Chandra, 2019b). This chapter reviews the existing literature examine the biases of investors in studying the emerging equity markets and the consequences this has on asset valuation, investment behavior, and stability of the financial markets. To holistically explain the mental processes leading to uninformed investing in emerging markets, this chapter combines behavioral finance perspectives with existing research on various emerging markets. Bringing forward the results of the previously conducted studies and presenting new empirical data, this chapter highlights the controversial relationship between investor behavior and market efficiency concerning emerging economies (Hussain, Korkeamäki, Xu, & Khan, 2015b). The lessons from this chapter also bring strength to the efficiency of the market and the determination of portfolio strategies in the case of investment in the markets which are in evolution. Knowing the logic and biases that cause confident investors to behave in a certain way would help policymakers, regulators, and market players develop specific policies and investment opportunities to alleviate the negative effects of such biases. This chapter puts forth some of the recommendations that can be undertaken in future research to address some of the gaps that were observed and also discuss the opportunities and challenges of further incorporation of behavioral finance into investment decision processes such as asset allocation. At the same time, herding is likely to cause a boom or a bust due to shifts in investors' sentiments. Such phenomena prove that the financial markets in emerging economies are multilayered and cannot be fully understood using conventional economic theories.

Cognitive Bias

The understanding of the Indian investors therefore means the systematic violation of rationality in judgment and decision making that may influence investment decisions. It is even more relevant today as India's financial markets advance and become more complex for both ordinary and sophisticated shareholders (Kumari, Nidhi & Sar, Ashok. (2017). Like their counterparts across the world, Indian investors also tend to fall prey to several cognitive biases that have their seeds in psychological aspects, culture, beliefs, and market characteristics that exist in India. Some of the biases that were evident are herd effect, over confidence, home bias, recency effect and loss aversive bias. Said biases can result in poor investment decisions that include copying other investors, failure to do one's research and analysis, overconfidence in market movement forecasts, domestic blinders, recency bias, and reluctance to cut losses(Syed Zain ul Abdin, Fiza Qureshi, Jawad Iqbal,Sayema Sultana,2022). This paper aims to identify some of the more common cognitive biases affecting the decision making of Indian investors and suggest ways on how these biases could be managed to increase the likelihood of the investors making better decisions that will therefore augment the efficiency of the Indian stock markets.

Financial Literacy

Indian investors even today lack adequate financial literacy that has deeper implications for their financial and overall welfare and the nation's progress. Literacy research indicates that mere 27% of the adult India population is formally financially included which is considerably low compared to many developed countries. This lack of financial literacy results in negative financial behaviors and consequences inclusive of; poor financial styles, excessive debt, low retirement savings, and insufficient insurances. Lack of financial education and knowledge refers to the inability of these people to manage their finances better, avoid fraudsters and unfair loans, and avoid easy fall for fraudulent investment scams. In this regard, different approaches or methodologies have been developed. The youth can take help from various web-based systems launched by some of the Indian startups like MoneyTree, FinEdu, Piggy and Chalo Paisa to plan your financial future (Agarwal et al., 2015). Currently both the government and different regulatory authorities such as the RBI and SEBI are playing an active role in increasing financial literacy. The NSE has to date organized more than 3800 investor awareness programs all over the country targeting investors across the regions through a variety of media. Nevertheless, a large gap persists, and it steadily grows even between the urban and rural populations. The implementation of financial education is highly active in tier 1 cities, schools than in tier-2/3 cities. The government and financial institutions understand the importance of proper financial literacy as the approach to the management of resources and decision making (Agarwal et al., 2015). In view of this there is need to enhance the level of financial literacy in Indian investors for their own welfare and that of the country as startups, government and other regulatory bodies try to make efforts to give an appropriate financial education to people, efforts that are still likely to be called for in future.

Behavioural Bias

The literature revealed that Indian investors are also overwhelmed by behavioral biasses that affect their investment choices and therefore the market trends. Research has long demonstrated that different cognitive and emotional biases influencing the decision-making process produce negative consequences for Indians, including inefficient investment returns. Among others, overconfidence bias that leads investors to overestimate their knowledge of the security values is highly evident in the Indian market especially in the pre-crash epoch. Other biases include herding, in which a number of investors party-term by the band, and the disposition effect, which involves selling off winners too soon and holding on to losers for inordinate lengths of time, and so on (Mokoaleli-Mokoteli et al., 2009). These biases are typically compounded by conditions in the market where time, during good earnest bull periods conjures lots of joy and trading activity and vice versa, during the bad bear periods people feel less than happy and more careful. Optimism and pessimism biases, and the representativeness bias in which an individual sorts through an event based on the typical case as opposed to the likelihood of the occurrence can result to poor financial decision making during up and down turns in the market. Scholars have earlier studies the antecedents of investment biases in North India and structural equation modeling has also revealed that overconfidence, representativeness and herding bias matters a lot about the investment decisions and it has impact on individual investors as well as market level factors such as trading volume and returns (Kumari, Nidhi & Sar, Ashok. (2017). The examination of these bias therefore raises the question of the client's psychological aspect, therefore an important part of the advisor building a portfolio for the client. Managing an investment portfolio by using robo-advisors is suggested as one of the possible ways for getting almost unbiased advice since it relies on the input of data. Conclusively, behavioural biases including overconfidence, herding, disposition effect, and representativeness explain Indian investors' behaviours. These biases are with market conditions that are not always the best for the financial environment existing at the time. It is crucial to rise up to these biases in providing better financial education and advisory services and through new forms such as robo advisors to investors in India and, in turn, the equity market in India.

Market Efficiency

For purposes of this analysis it is useful to define some important characteristics of 'market efficiency' when referring to Indian investors. In view of this, it is apparent that although growing at a fast pace, the efficiency of the Indian stock market in the past has been in the semi strong form of efficiency whereby the prices of stocks adjust to all the available public information. These surveys also demonstrated that the Indian investors on an average were not able to achieve market beating performance consistently with the help of fundamental or technical analysis therefore implying high level of info efficiency (Martin & Nagel, 2022). This is partly attributed to the expansion of the depth and coverage of the capital markets in India and improvement in information access among institutional and retail investors as well as more research coverage (Tuyon & Ahmad, 2016). However, the Indian market is also not devoid of imperfections and inefficient market characterised by the anomalies emerging from what is found as the January effect and the size effect to mean that there are some parts of the market that are inefficient. In addition, the psychological factors of Investors includes overconfidence, herding and loss aversion, which hinders the development of efficient markets in India (Martin & Nagel, 2022). Ex ante regulating authorities at India have taken many steps for the increased market efficiency, controlling the amount of information asymmetry, focused on making an appropriate flow of information to the share market investors; to minimize the level of information asymmetry, the regulating bodies like SEBI has taken following actions. An appreciation of the degrees of efficiency in the context of the Indian financial markets and the impact there of are critical to understanding the dynamics of the constantly changing markets and to the investment decision making of the various stakeholders in the markets (Thathaiah, Mallikarjunappa & Dsouza, Janet. (2013).

2. LITERATURE REVIEW

This section provides some background information regarding the subject by presenting an analysis of the current body of knowledge on behavioral finance, exhibiting investor biases and market efficiency. Literature that questions the rationality postulate and efficient markets hypothesis and seminal theories underpinning behavioral finance will be discussed.

Investor Biases in Emerging Markets: This section examines various cognitive and behavioral biases of investors in emerging markets. We will explore the biases such as overconfidence, herding, loss aversion, and disposition effects (Chauhan, Ahmad, Aggarwal, & Chandra, 2019b). Field studies on emerging markets will provide an understanding of the common manifestations of these biases across the various market settings.

2.1. Cognitive Bias (Overconfidence,Anchoring)

Overconfidence bias: is a distortion that makes investors' beliefs that they know a lot and are capable of predicting a lot than what is actually possible. This leads to both higher proportion trading, higher cost of trading, and therefore, lower portfolio returns (Barber & Odean, 2001). Investors with overconfidence often lack appreciation of risks, ultimately experiencing negative effects such as a loss of money. Overconfidence has been established to be highest in India among young investors using little information when markets are good. Mishra and Metilda (2015) observed that overconfidence for the Indian retail investor rose particularly during the upward market trends which in turn resulted in increased trading yet lower returns. They established that although this bias was caused by customers making the wrong decisions and as a result poor portfolios, a lack of financial literacy put clients at the mercy of volatile markets.

Anchoring bias comes from investors fixing themselves to certain numbers say the price of a firm's stock or any other figure they initially fix their sight on. Tversky and Kahneman (1974) showed that people are overbound to such reference points, thus distorting their judgement even in consequence of the receipt of new data. The paper provided evidence of how anchoring influences Indian investors' capacity to adjust to new information. Sehgal and Tripathi (2009) said that Indian investors tend to rely upon historical prices while investing and thus the actual prices take a longer time to reflect and take its own inefficiencies. Jain et al. (2023) also argue that the presence of anchoring bias is more so found active with the Indian investors who have low level of financial literacy since such investors give preference to outdated information instead of updating their judgments with current information.

2.2. Behavioral Biase (Herding, Loss Aversion)

Herding: takes place when investors copy what others do without considering investing time to find out the truth. Such actions might lead to their stock prices moving far from their true value, group decisions overriding the analysis of every single person. Similar with herding theory, Bikhchandani and Sharma (2000) pointed out that herding is most likely to happen in emerging markets due to the limitation on information for retail investors. In India, the herding behavior is caused in high volatility periods that leads to formation of market bubbles and crashes. It has been ascertained by Batra (2003) that herding rises during bull markets because people prefer copying others instead of undergoing personal evaluations. The increased availability of the social media networks and trading forums has only contributed to such increase as it gives an inexperienced investor a chance to mimic the moves of others, thereby taking advantage of market inefficiencies.

Loss aversion: is another behavioral bias by investors who naturally abhor losing more than they appreciate gaining of the same amount of money (Kahneman and Tversky, 1979). This bias inspires investors to spend more time hoping that the stocks they invested in will go up instead of buying better stocks to put their money in. Research evidence on the effect of loss aversion in the context of Indian investors has been identified in several studies. Sahi et al., (2013) mentioned that due to this, portfolio management in India suffers due to a lack of willingness of investors to accept their losses and sell off unfavorable securities. It therefore results in wasted resources and decreased rates of return on investment for the entire business. In the same vein, Bhattacharya et al. (2020 established that; Financial literacy decreases loss aversion, meaning investors are able to let go of their losing stock instead of 'holding a losing stock'.

2.3. Financial Literacy

To this end, the current paper investigates the moderating role of financial literacy levels in the relationship between financial inclusion and economic development. This knowledge defined as financial literacy, the set of skills that enable a person to make correct financial choices. A majority of people in India, especially the retail shareholders busy in small towns and rural areas, still remain financially illiterate. Only 27% Indian adults are financially literate, as stated by the OECD data and it has for lower than the world average according to the data obtained in year 2020. Lusardi & Mitchell (2014) said that financial literacy is crucial for reducing the bias because in a financially literate world, people get tools to make sound decision using the data. In India also, the effects of general improvement in financial literacy appear to have had positive impacts on self-control biases such as overconfidence and herding. For example, Agarwal et al. (2021) noticed that investors from India who had higher financial literacy levels were significantly less likely to herd or overconfident, thus, they used analysis. SEBI and RBI along with many non-governmental organizations in India have also launched financial education program across the country. Examples include SEBI which have organized many Investor Awareness Programmes (IAP) to increase understanding of Investment, with thrust on logical instrumental use and on the meta-cognition of self-bias. Jain et al. (2023) note that those programs helped investors to mitigate biases such as loss aversion, for example, diminishing their reluctance to sell underperforming assets.

2.4 Impact on Market Efficiency

Working through the angle of market efficiency, a loss to India was found to have been occasioned by the operation of biases. The compound nature of biases and financial literacy is important to the efficiency of markets in India. Cognitive and behavioral biases like overconfidence, anchoring, herding, and loss aversion disrupt market efficiency by causing prices to deviate from intrinsic values. Overconfidence and Market Efficiency, Self-confident traders take way in less worth but engage in more trading which otherwise results in more volatility. Some surveys revealed that the Indian markets are more volatile where these trades took place because random investors invest in such higher risk securities assets which, on average, reduces the overall returns. "Herding" distorts the market by creating a self-fulfilling positive feedback mechanism of price increase or decrease based on the activity of the herding individuals and not on the merit of their investment." According to Bikhchandani and Sharma 2000, herding is much more damaging to a marketplace such as the one in India because people there seem to look for visible benchmarks rather than actual financial parameters. Naresh & Thiyagarajan (2019) highlighted that herding behavior was most relevant concerning newly established Indian investors, increasing during economic volatility. Loss Aversion and Market Efficiency: In a loss aversion regime investors do not correctly allocate capital because instead of selling poorly performing stocks and investing in better performing ones they hold to the former. It is argued that such behaviour slows down the market processes and keeps the assets stranded in inefficient configurations.

2.5 Bridging the Gap

Policy Recommendations: In order to foster market efficiency, the regulatory authorities in India have this year shifted their concentration to increase the financial literacy. Financial literacy education should focus on behavioural finance to ensure that the investors identify the biases. Technological application, for instance, the robo-advisor' also held potential to overcome cognitive biases. These platforms can then offer third-party, data-led advice, thus lessening the impact of overconfidence, the anchoring effect, and similar Conversely, there has been a rise in usage of fin-tech solutions as well as mobile apps among young investors in India with those tools being bias-free strategies as identified by Chakraborty and Gupta (2022). Thus, robo-advisors assist with diversification and go too far in reducing biases, so investors do not overly rely on judgmental decisions. Policymakers can learn about these cognitive and non-cognitive biases, they can then craft the right policies that will improve investor knowledge and information. Such programs would address some practice biases like being overconfident or following others. This could mean general investment literacy programs, which will help investors decrease all these risks related to subsuming and ignorance of behavioral finance.

Research Objective

- To find out the relationship between Emerging Markets and the Complex Dynamics of Investor Behavior
- To provide a comparative analysis between Cognitive and Behavioral Biases in Emerging Markets
- To provide theoretical Insights and Empirical Research

This chapter considers the impact of these factors on the theory of the rational investor and the efficiency of the markets in which they operate. In doing this, the Cognitive framework employed in the thesis is extended to explain why and how their decisions were made, hence putting investment behavior in the context of the economic development of emerging markets. The Global scene while emerging economies have risks and prospects within the financial markets. This chapter explores the interplay between investor behavior and market efficiency in emerging markets. Through understanding the nature of the cognitive and behavioral biases present in these regions, we hope to provide an understanding of how the respective biases affect the process of asset pricing and trading strategies as well as the general stability of the market.

Policy Implications: Based on the findings, there are practical solutions that may be adopted in order to reduce the effects of cognitive and behavioural biases on investment decisions and improve the efficiency of the emerging markets, such as India. First of all, the improvement of financial literacy by undertaking first specific training aimed at its participants will have a positive effect in enhancing their awareness of overconfidence, anchoring, herding, and loss aversion biases. The good news is, these programs can be adapted to the needs and realities of different target populations. In addition, the digital learning platforms can present the information that may help to improve financial literacy and avoid the impact of cognitive biases among investors. Investment platforms should also integrate bias-finding tools that can be used to warn its users of biased information that is in the market to help users make better decisions. For example, investment apps could incorporate nudges that may put a warning message that read 'Hello, don't fall into the trap of the bandwagon mentality or holding on to the stocks that are not performing well.' Furthermore, there should be education of the bias for the financial advisors themselves that require them to take considerable efforts to avoid biases in the client; there should be methods used to prevent and avoid biased decisions from the client. This can be resolved by the creation of robo-advisors that are designed to identify bias to help investors remain impartial on their investment decisions. Disclosure requirements are also important; SEBI or other similar authorities could require disclosures which would decrease the extent of reliance on stale information, while restrictions on risky trades might solve problems originating from overconfidence and loss aversion. Moreover, the granting of tax incentives to long-term investments can stabilize irrational economic behavior and focus people on long-term future results. Conducted policy measures, as well as further scientific research on the effectiveness of applied intercessions, will contribute to the subsequent improvements of these approaches. Finally, the efforts made through media advertisements and community sensitization drives can also increase general financial literacies with references to rural communities that are likely to be neglected. With such effective solutions, the current and future policymakers, regulators, and the financial institutions shall approach more of an educated and rational investor in the organization which in result creates efficient and controlled markets for the provision of investment.

3. CONCEPTUAL FRAMEWORK (MODEL)

In this chapter, patients will be presented with direct models that explain investor biases and their impact on asset pricing. To further build a conceptual framework for the suggested variables, it can be the sequence of welcomed people's views and emotions, their Financial Literacy, and market efficiency. This is the framework in the discourse:

Dependent Variable

1. Market Condition

Independent Variable

1. Cognitive Bias (Overconfidence, anchoring)
2. Financial Literacy
3. Behavioural Bias (Loss Aversion, Herding)

3.1 Survey Analysis From 100 Participants

Enduring the results of the analysis of the survey data regarding the relationship between cognitive biases, financial literacy, behavioral biases and efficiency of the market some crucial outcomes came into view which show interdependence that influences investment behavior and the performance of the market. The questionnaire was developed in a manner that aimed at getting quantitative responses from diverse people regarding their investments and about their knowledge about financial concepts for evaluating the data collected; correlation as well as regression analysis were used to evaluate the data. The primary technique that was used was the use of Pearson's correlation – this provided the level of the correlation between variables. This statistical method enhanced the understanding of how confidence levels in investment decisions, understanding in inflation and effects of behavioral aspects like herd behavior affect the efficiency of the market. The findings showed that confidence in investment decisions was positively correlated with market efficiency above any other correlation figure at 0.99. This co-relation thus gives credence to the psychological angle of investing: voters who are confident are generally knowledgeable and experienced to deal with the knotty issues of the market. In addition, the knowledge of inflation was also highly and positively correlated with market efficiency; efficiency = 0.83 Therefore, the efficient investors who possess strong analytical skills in terms of understanding inflation are likely to adapt actively their investment behavior to the economic forces, including inflation, at play in the economy. This type of financial literacy is important in that it enables the investors to forecast variations in purchasing power and the value of assets that improves market efficiency. However, the survey revealed that herd behavior, normally seen as a negative social influence on investment strategy, has a moderate positive correlation (0.74) with Market Efficiency. This outcome shows that although the environment needed for gearing independent analysis as the supreme tool in investment decision making prevails, there emerge some settings where 'follow the herd's principle brings profit, especially in dynamic settings where timely decisions are pivotal. However, this could also serve to point to a potential flaw; herd mentality can cause investors to become lazy and disorderly, in other words, investors can cease to do their own research and simply follow the market trend. The correlation of the extent of financial literacy to the score in the financial concepts test (= 0·61) further supports posited notion of the role of certain level of financial literacy in improving the decision-making processes resulting to improved market interactions. Investment knowledgeable people will be in a position to estimate risks and returns well and in the same manner as how professionals in managing investments are supposed to. On the other hand, Loss aversion correlated minimally positively with market efficiency with correlation coefficient of 0.18; while risk aversion is a good thing to some extent, extreme fear of loss may inhibit the necessary risks to extract maximum gains. This aspect is a pure psychological reflection of investors and stresses the indispensability of balance between the risk aversion and the risk-tolerant measures. The results also showed that the 'home bias' had a moderate but negative (.23) relationship with efficiency suggesting that preference for domestic stocks inhibits diversification. This limitation may lead to investors having higher risk which is peculiar to the sectors familiar to it; this tends to decrease market efficiency. This finding is in line with the general notion that efficient investing depends on diversification beyond so called safe and known securities to have a sound and diversified portfolio. Furthermore, reliance on personal knowledge demonstrated a weak negative relationship (-0.34) with market efficiency translating into situations whereby investors who rely only on their knowledge may lose critical market data and analytical perception that may improve their returns. The highest negative correlation coefficient was recorded on the risk sensitivity (-0.63); the findings reveal that sensitivity to risks means that awareness of such exposures would keep an investor from seeking high risk opportunities that would yield high returns. This outcome highlights a paradox within the investment community: although risk appreciation is highly important an obsession with a downside often results in a failure to recognize the steep potential for great benefits. Thus, this survey has shown the multi- faceted relationship between cognitive biases, financial literacy and market efficiency to reveal the psychologic and educational factors that impact investment decisions. As the correlation obtained through the statistical data are in one hand depicts the plus and minuses of one investment approach while gothic on the other hand points out the commonality of mass market actions. Finally, this research points to the need for investors to learn how to be confident and at the same time manage to understand the fundamental concepts that are governing the markets, in equal measure, the risks posed by self-inflicted mental bias and behaviors. As the financial world expands with ever-evolving products and services, the results of this survey can be used in improving the number of educational programs aimed at developing the rationality of the people in investing their money to increase market efficiency. Thus, by accepting the idea of the interaction of these factors, the investor will be able to build less vulnerable but more effective investment measures that would help to accomplish successful results in investments in the long term.

3.2 Implications of the Survey

Cognitive and behavioural aspects, which contribute to the efficiency of Market, or within the context of empirical research regarding emerging markets, does constitute another major dimension of behaviour finance. Market efficiency as proffered by the Efficient Market Hypothesis (EMH) holds the opinion that prices in Security markets capture all available relevant information and therefore there is hardly anywhere investors can go looking for superior performance. But increasingly, the evidence available also suggests that this hypothesis is tested most frequently by biases; more so in the emergent markets such as India where investors are reflected to be under cognitive and behavioral bias. These include overconfidence, the self-herding effect and heuristics like anchoring that complicated decision making resulting to wrong interpretations of new information leading to trade effecting market prices. Another cognitive bias that has been highlighted earlier is overconfidence. This arises from an investor's overestimate of his/her knowledge or skills leading to over trading and high volatility in the market. Barber and Odean (2001) argue that overconfident traders trade more frequently and add little value in markets and thereby cause changes in price and create an imbalance in the markets. Chuang and Lee (2006) also maintain that overconfident investors make decisions based on fallacious information hence leading to the imbalances in assets' prices and a deterioration of efficiency in financial markets. Still, on cognitive biases, anchoring means that people rely extensively on the first information received, without paying much attention to other information received. A noted tendency observed by Kaustia, Alho, and Puttonen (2008) is that it may result in underreaction to new information getting in the way of much needed and efficient price revisions. Other behavioral inefficiencies include herding and loss aversion, where herding takes investors away from rationality since investors copy the decisions of others. Bikhchandani and Sharma (2000) have pointed out that herding is most dangerous in emerging markets since investors here are looking for visibility not value and generating positive or negative feedback which move up or pull down prices far away from their real worth based on the actions of others rather on merits of assets. It induces short-term national and global price fluctuations that do not reflect inherent values of products, which aggravates deterioration of market efficiency. Investors suffer from the phenomenon called loss aversion, revealed by Kahneman and Tversky (1979), which makes portfolio capital reallocation impossible. On the same note, this inclination to hang on to undesirable assets than sell them with their superior performing substitutes fuels the inefficient resourcing as capital locking-up dampens the market hence contributing to inefficiency. It has been ascertained that this bias prevails with the retail investor class of investors in India; this could delay the selling of assets at a lower price due to the reluctance to recognize losses and might impede the speed at which the market's price discovery mechanism functions. Education is now viewed as a controlling factor to these biases since well informed investors are endued with the ability to avoid biases. Lusardi and Mitchell (2014) research indicate that there exists a positive correlation between financial literacy and mitigated bias such as overconfidence, meaning that by raising the content information of the investors, efficiency of the decisions and the overall market would improve. Specifically for the India situation, Agarwal (2020) underlines the need for financial literacy efforts, particularly where there is ever increasing activity especially from new and hence relatively inexperienced investors. The suggested educational programs for investors may minimize herding and the fear of loss, and restore the rationality of the stock market. The problem of biases can be solved with the help of technology, and, for instance, robo-advisors exclude such negative heuristics as overconfidence and anchoring. D'Acunto et al. (2019) also opine that robo-advisors for investors can make portfolio performance better by avoiding economically distorting decisions, and boost the portfolio diversification, thereby making market more efficient. Chakraborty and Gupta (2022) opine that this has been made possible by the emergence of fin-tech solutions for young investors in India; unlike traditional human assisted services, biological predispositions towards bias and irrationality are eliminated by digital platforms, through providing direction and specific information on the best investment opportunities to pursue. Analyzing cognitive and behavioral biases as two separate and distinct categories of biases, the research notes that they both have different impact on markets. Cognitive biases promote more trading and fluctuations, whereas self-generated biases like herd behaviour produce large fluctuations during uncertainty. Using time-varying CAPM by designated dating the cross-sectional data, Thiyagarajan and Naresh (2019) reaffirm that herding behaviour of neophyte Indian investor amplify volatility during the economic cycle. Understanding these dynamics, policy suggestions have shifted over time to becoming less biased to enhance the market environment. The implementation of a new financial literacy program that connects with those modern biases can inform investors about the costs of overconfidence, herding, and loss aversion. Lusardi and Mitchell also note that fine-tuning such programs has proven effective, with the authors recommending an age, experience, or socio-economic position-based chunking of the investors. Some financial platforms are adding bias-checking features; firms receive real-time notifications to avoid knowing pitfalls. For example, in the form of so-called 'nudge' elements, which may provide investors with signals of herd behavior or to avoid stocks which they own for a long time and thus improve the general efficiency of the stock market. Robo-advisors, which provide automatic revalidation of portfolios help an investor to avoid overconfidence bias and Anchoring effect while disclosure rules and further tax preferences are bound to long-term investments. These interventions target to build the stakeholders into more rational investors that ultimately lead to efficient markets. However, the findings of this paper have a striking policy implication of constant policy making to remove the market irrationalities, which are caused by biases. As such, the policymakers and the regulators can play their part of reaching out to these masses, ensure that they spread the right knowledge, improve access to financial literacy and include efforts that enhance technology so that, collectively, we can reduce on the possibility of people making perpetual cycles of irrational investment decisions. With all these strategies, the emerging markets such as India are in a position to attaining a more efficient and sustaining financial markets within attracting both domestic and foreign investors improving the markers; volume of sustainable economic development.

4. RELATED CASE STUDY INTERPRETATIONS

Both Anglo American and Indian investors elucidate concrete expressions of these discriminations. For instance, in 2020 investments, as the market declined due to COVID-19 shocks, everyone mimicked the herd and funds' investments followed the increasing market indices despite the fact that most companies' operations were badly affected. Consequently, the stock prices rose, not because of some good reason but people chasing a fast buck, which is another form of herding behavior. Naresh and Thiyagarajan (2019) explained that begin investors who blindly copied others contributed to this run which was followed by corrections and heavy losses for those who invested without any deeper research. These investors displayed a carry-on loss aversion where they could not sell their deteriorated assets with the hope of being able to retrieve their money. A similar example is overconfident investors during the bull run of 2021 where overconfident traders made the wrong trades in erratic stocks, expecting quick financial returns. Not only did this inflate the risk in the market but to further heights was the propensity to sell their stocks within a short time when their expected gains failed to materialize. Analyses show that such fluctuations would have been dampened had these investors acted prudently or invested in diversified investment asset portfolios. Such examples show that these biases are not only distorting price signals but the wider costs associated with volatility that biases create. Another important example could be observed with the appearance of robot advisors, which are popular among young people and those having technological tools as their investing robots. According to Chakraborty and Gupta's (2022) study, the investor that engaged robo-advisors defeated bias-related behaviors than those who did not engage the services and further incurred high diversification. Robo-advisors reduce the impact of the two tested biases by providing consumers with personalised advice given certain data on them, and hence, promoting a correct pricing for the assets. This shows how technology together with financial literacy can function as voice to rebalance the biased self-dealing by investors to make markets more stable and efficient.

5. THEORETICAL DISCUSSIONS

5.1 The efficiency of financial markets

The degree to which the prevailing price accurately incorporates all public information, has been a major part of the received wisdom for many years. However, subsequently using efficient market hypothesis, the assumption is challenged often in contexts that exist in emerging markets like India where investor behavior is time and again acting in accordance with cognitive and behavioral biases. Complexity economics, unlike earlier models such as the perfect market model, the efficient market hypothesis, which asserts that markets are rational and self-contained, are inadequate in explaining price dynamics and institutional investors' behaviors in these economies. Instead, all these matters suggest that inefficiencies peculiar to the emerging markets ensue from a host of factors including economic insecurity, asymmetry of information, and demography. Overconfidence, self-anchoring, and confirmation bias of the preparers/experts, herding and loss aversion behavioral traits cause investment decisions to be distorted and may also cause mis-pricing and excessive volatility. Provided model implies, Relationship between Financial Literacy, Biases and Market efficiency or inefficiency arrows up or down as Financial Literacy levels rise or sink, therefore, Herd bias, and overconfidence bias all feedback and interact to determine market-level efficiency. These and related issues are examined in this chapter, where we provide an overview of investor psychology and its interaction with fast growing markets and offer ideas regarding how financial literacy campaigns and related policy changes might help close the gap between efficient markets. Overconfidence is one of the most discussed biases affecting market efficiency. Confidence in the market is the factor that makes some investors invest more than others due to the feeling that one has better knowledge, or better ways to predict the market. This behavior is especially rife amongst India's new and young traders as they are buoyed by new advances in application trading and opening of markets to retail trade, they are overconfident of their ability to beat the market. Such overconfidence leads to reckless trading, and not only becomes costly given that the number of trades increases the transaction costs, but also intensifies the volatility of the market because market prices change as a result of individual trades by the small investor. This is especially so given that to some extent their market is volatile due to lacking a strong institutional backbone to shield them from market fluctuations; the turbulences thus caused may cause prices that are more erratic than any reflection on value (erratic here denotes the fact that they are random and abrupt). Programs designed to combat overconfidence may help solve this problem and provide investors with better long-term diversified strategies and knowledge about the risks of excessive trading. However, attaining these objectives is not easy because when people desire high yield investments, the principles that financial literacy advocates in terms of risk diversification often lose appeal. Another important bias that distorts market efficiency is the herding where people make decision in the market following other people decisions instead of evaluating the market by their own. Herding is especially strong in emerging markets where information about equity prices is possibly costly to acquire, inconclusive, or ambiguous, thus standard triggers are followed from other investors. In India due to influence of collective culture and social validation herding leads to formation of bubbles and crashes emerge as investors tend to follow trends rather than analyzing capabilities of a company to earn profits. For instance, it is perceived that in periods of increased macroeconomic risk, investors may buy certain stocks or in specific industries merely because everyone else appears to have done so. This enables a loop to be created whereby everybody is attracted to investment the more by high prices making asset prices ever higher until the bubble busts. In this regard, Naresh and Thiyagarajan (2019) establish that herding behaviour is worst among the inexperienced investors especially those with low financial literacy skills. Of course, addressing herding, it is not sufficient to seek to increase access to high-quality information, but also to promote an investment environment encouraging nonconformity with peer opinion or trend. This may be done through the policy changes that include requiring disclosures that convey the risk associated with investing based on herd followed by educative campaigns that enable investors appraise market trends. Another cognitive bias associated with investing in emerging markets is the anchoring bias, whereby investors attach excessive importance to first information, including past data –like a stock or index's performance – with which they develop their opinions. This works out to cause biases because the information is fixed with investors considered as 'anchored,' even if other information suggests otherwise. In India for example many a retail investors rely on one or two sources of information, which are greatly influenced by what they read in newspapers or hear from friends or relatives and such ethics such as anchoring leads them astray by making them ignore the changing fundamentals in the market. For example, a certain firm might continue to invest in a particular stock whose performance has been declining, mainly because their brains are wired to expect that the stock will perform as well as it did in the past. This bias leads to market mispriced or delayed and thus leads to inefficient capital structure and capital continues to circulate in assets that are generating suboptimal returns. Education interventions that included skills-training along with intellectual-accumulation might assist investors to learn and apply countermeasures against anchoring bias, although this anticipation suggests more and different education paradigms. Both cognitive training and targeted skills training could be acted out through the use of practical tools like simulations that render investors potential decision-making tasks in fluctuating market environments. Another behavioral bias familiar to every trader is the loss aversion, where a trader would avoid a loss more than hunt equal gains. This bias makes the investors continue to hold poorly performing securities for fear of crystallizing the reported losses as the firms' actual losses are not physical losses that can be locked in. In India, where individuals save and invest in family-based businesses or conventional instruments, because of the disposition to avoid loss and risk, they are willing to re-allocate resources even where there are better returns available. For example, an investor might choose to continue investing in a stock whose price is in a continuous decline, in an expectation that it will bounce back, instead of liquidating their portfolio and investing in a high growth industry. This behavior hampers the speed at which new information is processed and mispriced assets continue to prevail in the market. The culture of loss aversion might be greatly reduced if the general public kept up to date on financial opportunities and potential risks, focusing better on concepts of loss such as opportunity costs, assets/stocks portfolios. In addition, digital investment platforms can include 'defaults' which are used as prompts to make investors reconsider and rebalance their portfolio more often than experiencing a "loss aversion". Hence, the moderating effects which financial literacy plays cannot be underestimated. Here, financial literacy acts as a mediator and enhances the investor's cognition to rescue them from cognitive and behavioral bias. Unfortunately, the level of financial literacy in India is still low, particularly among the population investing in the retail segment, obviously, there is a demand for educational programs that include not only the rules of investing but also the psychological component affecting the decision-making process. Such programs can help investors develop a particular behavioral attitude towards financing and investing and avoid showing various biases. For instance, sessions, which could fit into community sensitisation programmes, can be developed around the topics such as overconfidence, herding and thinking about the loss could be conducted in collaboration with the local banks or fintech firms. Also, financial literacy could be accompanied by simulations or real-life experience of feeling how investors make rational decisions in different conditions in the financial market. This practical involvement could be more efficient than conventional lessons, also known as classroom learning, because it involves the investors in the decision-making process at SA. Existing technologies like robo-advisors pose as a perfect example that can indirectly curb biases affecting efficiency within the market. Robo-advisors help their clients make investment decisions by using computer algorithms and therefore take out most of the factors such as emotions and reasoning from the decisions they recommend. That is especially true for the Indian market, where the use of fintech is rapidly growing and robo-advisors might contribute significantly to the efficiency of the market. The robo-advisors can address the issues such as overconfidence, herding and anchoring by providing clients with diversity unbiased recommendations. For example, instead of such parameters as market trends of the recent period, robo-advisors deal with a number of factors such as risk profile, time horizon, and diversification levels. The underlying strategy of this approach is also coherent with the principles of rational investment yet holds the ability of extending professional financial advisory services to retail investors who cannot afford, or are unable, to find conventional financial consultants. The problem, however, is how investors, especially in rural or underbanked areas can afford robo-advisors. The role of policy intervention in increasing efficiency in the market is another area that cannot be overemphasized because it targets structural causes of market bias. Regulators like SEBI could prescribe rule mandates that enlighten investors on risk and return profiles to help overcome the incidences of herd behavior as well as anchoring. For instance, demanding that critical elements of financial statements and business risks be presented in a set pattern may help customers make better comparisons, and not merely rely on the tip-line figures or signs of a trend. Also, rules that constrain short selling, particularly by neophyte traders—may also prevent 'overconfidence effect' trading styles Donaldson and Kim argue. Similarly, provision of tax credit for long term investments might equally lead to more serious approaches to investment hence creating a bigger link between investors and market. However, this kind of concept of financial literacy should also incorporate strategies of financial education that are directed at the specific groups of the population. Rural people especially are excluded from typical financial literacy interventions due to lack of access to formal financial trappings and structures, and hence need culturally sensitive intervention. For example, in areas where earning from agriculture is a major source of wealth, financial literacy can be targeted at ways of managing cyclical income. Likewise, more educational programs that could be directed towards young tech – savvy young investors specially in big urban cities could be the dangers of doing high frequency trades and the advantages of portfolio diversification. In light of the above, this paper posited that through offering differentiated programs skewed by investor type, financial literacy programs should increase market efficiency through all titular classes in society.

Last but not least, the media and financial influences influence investor behavior; and this has a positive or negative impact on the market efficiency. In India alone social media and financial influencers plays a significant role so the potential to transform this platform to be positive. Most financial influencers when operating under certain ethical benchmarks enable customers to gain understanding of various financial concepts and rational saving strategies. This has largely been compounded by the recent advances in influencer-led trading, where big social media followers push certain stocks or certain strategies, thereby encouraging herding and speculation. Those concerns could be resolved if the policymakers prescribe possible regulating rules that make the influencers responsible for information provided, which may need some or all travel warnings or recommendations of specific risks referring to investments to be labeled or banned.

Last but not the least, this study reveals that market efficiency in emerging economies like India is contingent upon cognitive and behavioral biases, shareholder's financial knowledge, technology intervention and extent of regulation. In conclusion, a large interaction exists between the cognitive and behavioral biases and financial literacy regarding, efficiency of the emerging Indian market. In overconfidence, herding, anchoring or loss aversion has led to inefficient asset prices, high risk and poor capital structure decisions. However, there are indications that these biases are gradually being eliminated either by financial literacy and drive towards turning the investor population into more reasonable one, or by technological solutions connected with the appearance of robo-advisors. In a nutshell policymakers should continue to promote such tools for and to fund directed and specific Financial Literacy Campaigns so as to reach all the stakeholders in the process. Conversely, specific actions that can form part of an enhancement are laws that require firms to state their solvency and measures that prohibit reckless selling that do not even take financial reality into consideration. For a sound unbiased and fair financial environment to be set up and to support economic growth as the EM's go on to mature there will still be need to eliminate bias and develop portfolio literacy. Der the prices that reflect the actual economic conditions. As the EMs go on to mature, elimination of bias and development of literacy will remain critical if a sound and fair financial environment that will support economic growth is to be established.

6.CONCLUSION

To conclude, this chapter has stressed the various reasons why understanding of investor behavior in emerging markets is essential if the objective is to glean information regarding market efficiency. We intend to fill the gap between traditional finance and empirical studies while synthesizing the field. The literature points out cognitive biases which includes overconfidence bias and anchoring bias as well as behavioral biases, such as herding bias that significantly influences investment decisions and market efficiency in India. Such bias is compounded by low financial literacy which results to non-rational behaviour and thus deviation from intrinsic values. Solving these problems implies using not only financial literacy, state programs, and improvements but also the integration of technology. Thus, the authorities of the country can increase the degree of financial literacy and encourage investors to overcome prejudices, which will eventually lead to the occurrence of more efficient markets in the Indian state for individual investors and other related economic subjects. However, there are indications that these biases are gradually being eliminated either by financial literacy and drive towards turning the investor population into more reasonable one, or by technological solutions connected with the appearance of robo-advisors. In a nutshell policymakers should continue to promote such tools for and to fund directed and specific Financial Literacy Campaigns so as to reach all the stakeholders in the process. Conversely, specific actions that can form part of an enhancement are laws that require firms to state their solvency and measures that prohibit reckless selling that does not even take financial reality into consideration. For a sound unbiased and fair financial environment to be set and to support economic growth as the EM's go on to mature there will still be need to eliminate bias and develop portfolio literacy. Der the prices that reflect the actual economic conditions. As the EMs go on to mature, elimination of bias and development of literacy will remain critical if a sound and fair financial environment that will support economic growth is to be established.

REFERENCES

A, C., & R, K. (2016). IMPACT OF SELECTED BEHAVIOURAL BIAS FACTORS ON INVESTMENT DECISIONS OF EQUITY INVESTORS. *ICTACT Journal on Management Studies, 2*(2), 297–311. https://doi.org/DOI: 10.1016/j.jhe.2015.02.003

Agarwal, S., Amromin, G., Ben-David, I., Chomsisengphet, S., & Evanoff, D. D. (2015). Financial literacy and financial planning: Evidence from India. *Journal of Housing Economics*, 27, 4–21. DOI: 10.1016/j.jhe.2015.02.003

Agarwal, S., Amromin, G., Ben-David, I., Chomsisengphet, S., & Evanoff, D. D. (2015). Financial literacy and financial planning: Evidence from India. *Journal of Housing Economics*, 27, 4–21. DOI: 10.1016/j.jhe.2015.02.003

Chauhan, Y., Ahmad, N., Aggarwal, V., & Chandra, A. (2019). Herd behaviour and asset pricing in the Indian stock market. *IIMB Management Review*, 32(2), 143–152. DOI: 10.1016/j.iimb.2019.10.008

Elangovan, R., Irudayasamy, F. G., & Parayitam, S. (2022). Testing the market efficiency in Indian stock market: Evidence from Bombay Stock Exchange broad market indices. *Journal of Economics, Finance and Administrative Science*, 27(54), 313–327. DOI: 10.1108/JEFAS-04-2021-0040

Hussain, S. M., Korkeamäki, T., Xu, D., & Khan, A. H. (2015). What drives stock market growth? a case of a volatile emerging economy. *Emerging Markets Finance & Trade*, 51(1), 209–223. DOI: 10.1080/1540496X.2015.1011533

Mokoaleli-Mokoteli, T., Taffler, R. J., & Agarwal, V. (2009). Behavioural bias and conflicts of interest in analyst stock recommendations. *Journal of Business Finance & Accounting*, 36(3–4), 384–418. DOI: 10.1111/j.1468-5957.2009.02125.x

Pathak, D. D., & Thapa, B. S. (2024). Beyond market anomalies: How heuristics and perceived efficiency shape investor behavior in developing markets. *Investment Management and Financial Innovations*, 21(3), 1–14. DOI: 10.21511/imfi.21(3).2024.01

Results - OpenURL Connection - EBSCO. (n.d.). https://search.ebscohost.com/login.aspx?direct=true&profile=ehost&scope=site&authtype=crawler&jrnl=22494561&AN=119728965&h=V%2BVpbk08dKwQWZsrOFly0%2Br1EiAFTltLQCCqvJjhaceQ0krgFQPbQ3q7vD5TZWfNYp80StbJ1Q4cNse46hQL8g%3D%3D&crl=c

APPENDIX

Questionnaire

Section A (Demographics)

1. Name
2. Age
3. Educational level
4. Profession
5. Investment experience

Section B (Cognitive Bias)

6. Are you confident in my ability to make profitable investment decisions
7. Do you end up trusting my investment knowledge more than external advice
8. Do you rely heavily on initial decisions when making financial decisions, even after more data is available
9. Do you see a familiar stock price, I feel more comfortable investing in it
10. Do you often base my on recent events or market trends
11. If the stock has recently performed well, do you believe it will continue to do so?

Section C (Financial Literacy)

12. Do you understand critical concepts like inflation, risk diversification, and compound interest.
13. Can you correctly interpret financial statements or annual reports of companies.
14. Do you understand different types of investment options and their risk levels
15. Can you calculate expected returns on investment using available information
16. Do you know how to assess the risk level of an investment accurately
17. Can you evaluate how market conditions impact my investments

Section D (Behavioural Bias)

18. Do you avoid investments that I think have a high chance of loss, even if they have high potential returns.
19. Losses have a stronger impact on Your decisions than equivalent gains?
20. Do you tend to invest in stocks that others around you tend to invest in
21. Are you more comfortable with investments popular in the market

22. Do you allocate specific funds to specific types of investments (e.g. One account for retirement, another for emergencies)
23. Do you treat money earned from investments differently than regular income

Section E (Market Condition)

24. Do you monitor economic indicators (GDP growth, inflation, interest rates) before making investment decisions.
25. Do you believe market conditions simply impact my investment choices and outcomes?
26. Do you feel confident in, my investment approach regardless of market volatility?

Chapter 7
Mental Accounting: Shaping Financial Choices and Behaviors

Razia Nagina
https://orcid.org/0000-0002-0305-8393
Lovely Professional University, India

ABSTRACT

This chapter explores the concept of "mental accounting," first introduced by Richard Thaler, and its influence on financial behaviors. It aims to understand how mental categorization of finances affects decisions related to spending, saving, and debt management. Through both theoretical insights and empirical data, the chapter reveals how biases arising from mental accounting often lead to irrational financial decisions, such as overspending on windfalls and inefficient debt management. Using primary and secondary data, the chapter highlights potential implications for long-term financial well-being and recommends strategies for individuals and institutions to mitigate these biases and promote better financial outcomes.

1. INTRODUCTION

The idea of "mental accounting," first proposed by behavioral economist Richard Thaler, highlights how people mentally organize, assess, and manage their financial resources, posing a major challenge to conventional economic theory (Silva et al., 2013; Thaler, 2016). In contrast to the conventional economic paradigm, which views money as fungible that is, as being equal to any other dollar, mental accounting shows that people mentally assign varying values to money depending on arbitrary elements like its source, timing, or intended use. These mental models frequently

DOI: 10.4018/979-8-3693-9380-2.ch007

cause people to make financial decisions that are not in line with reason, which leads to inefficiencies and worse than ideal financial results (Becker et al., 2020).

The theory of mental accounting offers a framework for comprehending why people could perceive lottery winnings or tax refunds as "extra" money, which encourages more extravagant spending, while treating regular paychecks with more caution (Garduno, 2022). In a similar vein, even though the interest rates and financial gains imply otherwise, people may classify funds set aside for savings and expenses in separate categories. For instance, a person may continue to make high-interest credit card debt while retaining savings in a low-yield bank account. This division of labor is not always advantageous and might make money problems worse (Mitchell & Lusardi, 2020).

Mental accounting is useful in institutional contexts in addition to personal money. When designing products or treatments meant to enhance financial decision-making, financial institutions and legislators need to take mental accounting into account (Gajewski et al., 2024). Modern financial methods are greatly influenced by behavioral economics, which includes mental accounting. This includes how people save for retirement and react to marketing campaigns that present financing or discount choices (Bogunjoko, 2021). Organizations may be able to develop financial solutions that better suit consumer behavior by taking these cognitive biases into account. This might lead to increased financial well-being for both individuals and society as a whole.

Though mental accounting plays a crucial role in behavioral economics, its practical ramifications are still largely unexplored, especially when it comes to long-term financial well-being, demographic variations, and ways to reduce the biases that result from this cognitive phenomenon (Hon et al., 2021). Moreover, much of the available material tends to focus on Western contexts, with relatively less emphasis paid to how these biases operate across other cultural and socioeconomic settings. Furthermore, there is a dearth of studies directly connecting mental accounting to its possible effects on long-term financial stability. Therefore, it's still crucial to comprehend the particular situations in which mental accounting can support or undermine sound financial judgment (Hans et al., 2024).

The influence of mental accounting on debt management is one of the primary challenges it raises. Because people have a propensity to psychologically separate their finances, they may find themselves with savings in one account and high-interest debt in another (Silva et al., 2023). Mental accounting biases that put the satisfaction of saves ahead of the sensible choice to pay off expensive debt are directly responsible for this behavior (Sattar et al., 2020). This chapter attempts to show how these cognitive biases are not only present but also perpetuated by societal conventions and standard financial procedures, underscoring the importance of devising counter strategies.

The impact of mental accounting on consuming behaviors is another significant aspect of the phenomenon (Weixiang et al., 20200). Individuals frequently make irrational decisions because they divide their income and expenses into discrete mental accounts for things like housing, entertainment, transportation, etc. (Shukla et al., 2020). For instance, even though the person's overall financial status could call for the money to be used for debt repayment or savings, a bonus at work might be viewed as a "windfall" and used toward discretionary spending (West, 2021). Over time, these spending habits may compound and put a heavy burden on finances. Moreover, people's emotional connections to certain spending categories, such as perceiving holidays or celebrations as exceptional, add further complexity to their financial behavior and planning (Sinnewe & Nicholson, 2023).

Furthermore, it is impossible to overestimate the significance of mental accounting in saving behavior. Studies reveal that people frequently keep different mental accounts for savings that might not be the best ones financially (Skwara, 2023). For example, they may place more importance on setting aside money for an emergency fund than they do on paying off high-interest loans or credit card debt, even though doing so will increase their total savings. The psychological benefits of knowing that money is set away are satisfied by this conceptual division of finances, but it might be at the expense of making more calculated financial decisions (Sobkow et al., 2020).

The application of mental accounting concepts is not limited to individuals but extends to financial institutions as well. Businesses and financial institutions that are conscious of these prejudices can create products that either enhance or lessen the effects of mental accounting (Nanda & Banerjee, 2021). To combat people's propensity to leave money in low-interest accounts out of inertia, banks may, for instance, provide savings accounts that automatically move money into higher-interest accounts. Financial products that are built around mental accounting, on the other hand, can also result in manipulative tactics (Puaschunder, 2020). For example, they may encourage consumers to overspend by providing credit alternatives that appeal to their mental classification of "small monthly payments," despite the fact that these options have a higher long-term financial impact.

Policy-wise, a deeper understanding of how mental accounting affects consumer behavior might result in more thoughtfully crafted financial legislation and instructional initiatives. For example, financial literacy initiatives that educate people about the myths surrounding mental accounting may facilitate better reasoned choices on investing, saving, and spending. Reducing the financial stress that arises from poor decision-making due to mental accounting biases is another way that such interventions may have wider social repercussions (Adil et al., 2022; de Mello Ferreira, 2021).

Therefore, although the idea of mental accounting offers insightful understandings into human financial behavior, there is still a large body of research to be done to determine how these biases vary among populations, how they affect long-term financial health, and what kinds of interventions can effectively lessen their effects. Previous studies frequently draw attention to the cognitive biases connected to mental accounting, but they don't thoroughly examine the methods that people and organizations might use to mitigate these errors. Moreover, a large portion of the extant literature focuses on certain geographical areas, creating a knowledge vacuum on the functioning of mental accounting across various cultural and economic contexts.

1.1 Research Gap and Contribution

This chapter addresses the gap by examining the implications of mental accounting on financial decision-making across diverse demographic groups. Through both secondary and primary data analysis, the chapter aims to provide a more comprehensive understanding of how mental accounting affects financial behaviors and long-term financial well-being. By integrating real-world examples, case studies, and empirical findings, this chapter contributes to the broader field of behavioral economics, offering both theoretical insights and practical recommendations for individuals and financial institutions alike. The objectives outlined within this chapter aim to fill the gaps in current knowledge by not only identifying the biases inherent in mental accounting but also proposing actionable strategies to overcome these biases and improve financial outcomes.

2. MENTAL ACCOUNTING AND ITS THEORETICAL FOUNDATIONS IN BEHAVIORAL ECONOMICS

The term "mental accounting" refers to a psychological framework developed in the 1980s by Nobel winner Richard Thaler, which describes how people mentally organize and manage their finances. The premise that money is interchangeable and identical, as per the classical economic theory, is challenged by this concept, which emphasizes the reality that people handle money differently based on criteria such as its source, intended purpose, or other subjective considerations. Behavioral economics benefits greatly from mental accounting since it demonstrates how cognitive biases affect financial decision-making and result in illogical behavior.

2.1 Theoretical Foundations of Mental Accounting

The study of behavioral economics combines economics and psychology to shed light on the mental processes that influence decisions made in the real world, which frequently deviate from logical economic models. According to the precepts of classical economics, people always behave rationally, aiming to maximize utility and make the best financial decisions (Corr & Plagnol, 2023). However, behavioral economics acknowledges that emotions, cognitive biases, and mental shortcuts can impact human behavior and lead to less-than-ideal outcomes. A good illustration of how psychological influences cause people's financial decisions to diverge from rational models is mental accounting (Rikberg, 2023).

The mental accounting framework is built on a few key principles that explain how people mentally segregate money into different "accounts" and how that affects their decision-making process:

1. **Segregation of Funds:** People separate their money into various mental accounts, frequently based on the money's origin (pay vs bonus), its intended use (savings vs daily needs), or its timing (present vs. future income) (Skwara, 2023). Irrational decisions, such spending a bonus money carelessly while saving money on a regular basis, might result from this mental dissociation. The mental accounts generate psychological obstacles that lead to less-than-ideal financial decisions, even though all money should ideally be regarded equally (Mahapatra & Mishra, 2020).
2. **The Endowment Effect and Loss Aversion:** Mental accounting is associated with psychological phenomena like loss aversion, which is the preference for avoiding losses over achieving comparable benefits, and the endowment effect, which leads people to overvalue the money they own. Due to this bias, even in situations where spending from specific mental accounts (like savings) might result in a better financial outcome (like paying off high-interest debt), people are hesitant to do so (Helmina et al., 2023).
3. **Choice Bracketing:** Choice bracketing, in which individuals make decisions in discrete silos as opposed to adopting a comprehensive perspective of their financial circumstances, is another fundamental component. For instance, if someone has mentally allocated resources to a certain future goal, they might refrain from utilizing them to settle costly debt. Mental accounting in this situation results in disjointed decision-making that ignores total financial optimization (Ellis & Freeman, 2024; Read et al., 2020).
4. **Sunk Cost Fallacy:** The sunk cost fallacy, which is connected to mental accounting, occurs when people keep putting money, time, or effort into a project or account because they have already invested it rather than considering its

potential return. This fallacy has the potential to legitimize illogical spending habits, such as keeping up with a subscription or service that is no longer required just because money has previously been paid for it (Ülkü et al., 2020).

2.2 Real-World Examples of Mental Accounting

1. **Tax Refunds and Bonuses:** The way people handle bonuses or tax refunds is a typical illustration of mental accounting. These sources of income are generally seen as "extra" or "windfall" money, and thus are more likely to be spent on discretionary items like holidays, electronics, or dining out. This is not the case with regular income, which is typically used for bills, groceries, and rent. Although people manage both sources of income differently due to mental accounting, in reality, they should be regarded equally when it comes to financial planning.

For example, a study conducted by Thaler discovered that a lot of people would rather perceive windfalls, like tax refunds or year-end bonuses, as "found money," which they then use for leisure or luxuries rather than for needs like paying off debt. Different spending behaviors result from the mental separation of these sources, even when it would be financially sensible to invest or conserve these assets (Pompian, 2021).

2. **Credit Card Debt vs. Savings:** Mental accounting also helps to explain why people frequently have funds in low-interest savings accounts and high-interest credit card debt. According to a purely rational model, people would save money on interest if they prioritized paying off high-interest debt before starting savings. They behave in an unproductive manner financially as a result of treating debt and savings as distinct entities due to mental accounting (Nteso, 2021; Shukla, 2020).

People might, for instance, have an emergency savings account and yet be paying off credit card debt at a rate of interest that is far greater than their savings rate. Even though paying off the debt would have greater financial results, this conduct is motivated by the psychological stability of keeping a savings balance.

3. **Spending from Different Mental Accounts:** People also allocate spending depending on categories such as essentials, entertainment, or emergency. In a traditional behavioral economics experiment, participants are given a certain amount of money and asked to allocate it among several categories of expenditure. The results demonstrate that people typically make different spending

decisions dependent on how they identify the money. If branded as "savings," people are likely to resist spending it, but if labeled as "entertainment," they are more willing to spend it on non-essential products (Fuster et al., 2021; Pillay, 2021; Shefrin & Thaler, 1992).

Thaler also provided an example in his research of how individuals budget for vacation spending separately from their regular monthly expenses (Thaler, 1990). They may allocate a large amount of money for a trip and spend lavishly, even if they are struggling with other financial obligations at home, because they have mentally separated their vacation funds from their regular budget. This separation allows for indulgent spending without guilt, even though it might not align with overall financial health.

2.3 Theoretical Frameworks Supporting Mental Accounting

Mental accounting draws from several key behavioral economics theories:

1. **Prospect Theory:** Prospect theory, which was developed by Daniel Kahneman and Amos Tversky, is essential to understanding how people make decisions when faced with risk. It emphasizes how they balance possible advantages and losses. This theory and mental accounting are closely related because mental accounting describes how people treat potential losses in various mental accounts with greater seriousness than they do potential profits. For example, even in situations where it makes financial sense to sell depreciating assets (like stocks) at a loss, people could choose to cling onto them in a mental "investment" account (Kahneman & Tversky, 2013).
2. **Behavioral Life-Cycle Hypothesis:** The behavioural life-cycle hypothesis, which postulates that people mentally split their wealth into present income, current assets, and future income and treat these categories differently, lends further credence to the idea of mental accounting. People might, for instance, be more inclined to spend from their present income than from savings or an expected inheritance, which are current assets and future income sources. This split influences how they save and spend money, which leads to the poor financial management that is often observed in personal finances (Russell, 2024; Sui et al., 2021).

2.4 Implications for Personal Finance and Institutions

The implications of mental accounting are significant for financial organizations as well as for people. Individuals can become more conscious of their cognitive biases and make more logical financial judgments by having a better understanding of mental accounting. By recognizing how they cognitively organize their money, individuals can adopt techniques to limit splurging on discretionary things, optimize savings, and pay down high-interest debt more effectively.

Financial organizations can benefit from using mental accounting insights to guide their marketing and product design. In order to take advantage of consumers' propensity to view these offers as "cheap money" or future liabilities—even though they ultimately result in higher long-term costs—banks and credit card companies, for example, frequently offer products like low-interest promotional rates or "deferred payment" options. Likewise, businesses that provide automated savings programs—that is, systems that round up purchases and deposit the difference into a savings account—adopt mental accounting concepts to promote responsible financial practices.

In addition, financial institutions have the ability to create resources that assist customers in better mental account management. The detrimental effects of compartmentalization might be lessened by, for instance, offering integrated views of checking, savings, and investment accounts. This would enable people to see their entire financial situation and make better decisions.

Through the lens of mental accounting, a deeper understanding of financial decision-making can be gained by identifying the cognitive biases that lead to illogical behaviors. People frequently make judgments that are not in their best financial interests when they mentally divide money into several accounts. Mental accounting shows how psychological variables affect economic conduct. Examples of this behavior include interpreting a tax rebate as extra spending money, keeping credit card debt while hoarding savings, and making strict budgets for various categories of expenses.

Better financial results can result from individuals and institutions making better decisions by being aware of and taking steps to remove the biases that are inherent in mental accounting. While mental accounting might ease planning and spending for people, it also offers substantial concerns when it leads to inefficiencies and financial mismanagement. By making people aware of these cognitive biases and offering techniques to overcome them, both personal money management and the design of financial products can be improved.

3. EXAMINING HOW MENTAL ACCOUNTING SHAPES INDIVIDUAL FINANCIAL DECISIONS IN AREAS SUCH AS SPENDING, SAVING, DEBT MANAGEMENT, AND INVESTING

According to Richard Thaler, mental accounting is a psychological framework that affects how people organize and manage their money resources in their minds (Shukla, 2020; Thaler, 1990). Because humans perceive money differently depending on its source, purpose, or time, this compartmentalization frequently results in decision-making that deviates from conventional economic theory. This chapter tries to study how mental accounting impacts individual financial decisions in crucial areas such as spending, saving, debt management, and investing. 200 working respondents participated in a primary survey aimed at shedding light on real-world actions and the consequences of mental accounting.

Demographic Characteristics of Respondents

The survey was conducted through an online intercept questionnaire using Google Forms, with 200 working respondents participating. The demographic breakdown is as follows:

Table 1. Demographics

Gender:	**Age:**	**Income Slabs**: (Per month)	**Financial Literacy:**
Male: 55% Female: 45%	18–25 years: 35% 26–35 years: 40% 36–45 years: 15% Above 45 years: 10%	Below 20,000: 15% 20,000– 50,000: 35% 50,000– 1,00,000: 30% Above 1,00,000: 20%	High: 35% Moderate: 45% Low: 20%

(Source: Author work)

Table 1 displays A wide range of age groups and income levels were represented among the respondents, offering insight into the ways in which mental accounting influences financial decision-making.

3.1 Survey Design and Frequency Analysis

The questionnaire was developed with questions arranged to highlight the influence of mental accounting biases in order to gather information about respondents' approaches to investing, debt management, saving, and spending. The main queries and the frequency of answers are listed below.

3.1.1 Spending Behavior

Even though all income should be seen as fungible from an economic standpoint, mental accounting reveals that people frequently handle money from diverse sources—such as salaries, bonuses, or windfalls—differently.

Table 2. Do you treat bonuses or windfalls (e.g., tax refunds) differently from regular income?

Options	Percentage of Responses
Yes	75%
No	25%

(Source: Author work)

Table 3. What do you primarily use bonus or windfall money for?

Options	Percentage of Responses
Luxury/Discretionary spending (e.g., vacations, electronics, Any other unplanned shopping	45%
Savings	30%
Paying off debt	15%
Investments	10%

(Source: Author work)

Inferences on Spending Behavior as per results of Table 2 and Table 3:

The majority of respondents (75%) confessed that they regard bonuses and windfalls differently from their regular income, with 45% of them admitting that they put such money toward luxury or discretionary spending. This behavior is consistent with the mental accounting hypothesis, which holds that "extra" money is frequently handled less carefully than regular income, which is normally set aside for necessities. The cognitive bias where bonuses or unexpected profits are mentally labeled as separate and consequently less constrained is reflected in the inclination to spend windfall money on non-essential products.

3.1.2 Saving Patterns

Mental accounting often leads individuals to maintain separate mental accounts for savings, categorizing funds for specific purposes like emergency funds, vacations, or future investments.

Table 4. Do you maintain separate savings for different purposes?

Options	Percentage of Responses
Yes	70%
No	30%

(Source: Author work)

Table 5. Do you prioritize saving even if you have debt to repay?

Options	Percentage of Responses
Yes	50%
No	50%

(Source: Author work)

Inferences on Saving Patterns:

Notably, 70% of respondents said they kept separate accounts for various purposes, which shows mental accounting causes them to group savings according to certain objectives as per survey results shown in Table 4 and Table 5. Even though it offers psychological clarity, this compartmentalization can occasionally result in wasteful financial outcomes. As an illustration of the mental division of savings and debt, 50% of respondents said they prioritize saving even when they have outstanding debt. Rationally speaking, paying off high-interest debt should come first before concentrating on savings.

3.1.3 Debt Management

Mental accounting is also a major factor in how people approach paying off debt. Individuals who treat debt and savings as distinct mental accounts are more likely to make poor financial decisions, such continuing to save while holding high-interest debt.

Table 6.How do you prioritize debt repayment in relation to saving?

Options	Percentage of Responses
Pay off debt first	45%
Balance both equally	40%
Prioritize savings	15%

(Source: Author work)

Table 7. Do you hold savings in a low-interest account while carrying high-interest debt?

Options	Percentage of Responses
Yes	65%
No	35%

(Source: Author work)

Inferences on Debt Management:

According to the statistics shown in Table 6 and Table 7, just 45% of participants prioritize saving over paying off debt, and 65% acknowledged that they carried high-interest debt yet kept their savings in low-interest accounts. This conduct exemplifies a typical mental accounting trap in which people mistakenly divide their debt commitments and savings, creating inefficiencies in their finances. Although paying off high-interest debt with savings might make more sense in theory, people are often prevented from doing so by mental accounting fallacies.

3.1.4 Investment Behavior

The survey additionally examined the impact of mental accounting on investing choices, specifically how people divide money in their minds into short- and long-term investments and how they handle windfall profits or incomes.

Table 8. How do you approach investing money from bonuses or windfalls?

Options	Percentage of Responses
I invest a portion of it	40%
I do not invest windfalls	60%

(Source: Author work)

Table 9. Do you mentally separate short-term and long-term investment funds?

Options	Percentage of Responses
Yes	55%
No	45%

(Source: Author work)

Inferences on Investment Behavior:

Table 8 and Table 9 show that a sizeable percentage of participants (60%) expressed their preference to allocate windfalls or bonuses to spending or saving categories rather than investing them. This bolsters the hypothesis of mental accounting, which holds that these types of funds are handled differently than normal income and are frequently seen as expendable. Furthermore, according to 55% of respondents, their investment methods may be influenced by their mental distinction between short-term and long-term investments. While this division may help with goal-setting, it can also cause imbalances in one's overall financial planning because people may start prioritizing one account over another without taking the big picture into account.

Managerial Implications

The survey's findings have a number of managerial implications for how people make financial decisions, including both individuals and financial advisors.:

Addressing Mental Accounting Biases: Programs for financial education should educate people about mental accounting biases and how they impact decisions about debt management, saving, and spending. People can make more sensible financial decisions by realizing how they psychologically divide up their money. For example, they can pay off high-interest debt before saving, or they can invest windfalls instead of squandering it.

Debt Repayment Strategies: The necessity for improved debt management techniques is one of the survey's most important ramifications. When carrying high-interest debts, financial advisors should advise customers to put debt payments ahead of savings. People who keep savings while accruing costly debt may be able to overcome mental accounting biases with the use of strategies like debt consolidation or automatic debt payback.

Investment Planning: When people treat windfalls differently or divide short-term and long-term funds differently, mental accounting might result in inadequate investment strategies. Financial planners can assist people in adopting a more holistic view of their financial resources and in making investment decisions that are consistent with their long-term objectives, as opposed to concentrating on isolated mental accounts.

Financial Product Design: Financial companies can create tools that assist customers in managing their money more skillfully by taking mental accounting into consideration. For instance, combining savings and debt accounts into one platform can persuade users to prioritize their overall financial well-being over discrete accounts. Products that assist customers in automatically directing windfalls toward investments or savings could also lessen the propensity for them to spend this money on frivolous things.

The survey's findings show that people's judgments about how much to spend, save, invest, and manage their debt are greatly influenced by their mental accounting. Even though mental accounting can be helpful in helping people manage their money, it frequently results in inefficient and illogical actions like hoarding funds while carrying debt or dividing investments into short- and long-term categories. People can enhance their overall financial well-being and make better decisions by addressing these biases and offering tailored financial education and planning solutions.

4. ANALYZING THE EFFECTS OF MENTAL ACCOUNTING ON FINANCIAL BEHAVIORS ACROSS DEMOGRAPHIC GROUPS

Understanding how people approach their financial decisions based on criteria like age, income, and financial literacy requires examining the effects of mental accounting on financial habits across various demographic groups (Van Raajj, 2016). Due to varying priorities, levels of experience, and expertise, mental accounting—a term that refers to the cognitive processes by which people arrange, assess, and manage their finances—often varies across demographic lines (Kumar at al., 2023). In order to investigate this, respondents were surveyed from a range of demographic backgrounds on their financial habits, methods for mental accounting, and the influence of financial literacy on their financial judgments.

4.1 Defining and Assessing Financial Literacy

Definition of Financial Literacy for Respondents: Financial literacy was defined for respondents as the knowledge and understanding of financial concepts such as budgeting, savings, investment, debt management, and the ability to make informed financial decisions. Based on their knowledge with these concepts and the ability to use them in real-world contexts, respondents were asked to rate their own financial literacy.

Assessment of Financial Literacy: Respondents were categorized into three levels based on their self-assessment and their responses to specific financial literacy questions:

Highly Financially Literate: Individuals who demonstrated a strong understanding of complex financial concepts and actively applied them to their financial management.

Moderately Financially Literate: Individuals who had a basic understanding of financial concepts and applied them occasionally but lacked a comprehensive grasp of more advanced financial strategies.

Low Financial Literacy: Individuals who had limited understanding of financial concepts and struggled to apply financial knowledge effectively in managing their finances.

Table 10. How do you categorize your monthly income?

Demographic Group	Separate categories for bills, savings, discretionary spending (%)	Treat all income as one lump sum (%)
Gender		
Male	65%	35%
Female	60%	40%
Age		
18–25 years	55%	45%
26–35 years	65%	35%
36–45 years	70%	30%
Above 45 years	75%	25%
Income Level		
Below 20,000	45%	55%
20,000– 50,000	60%	40%
50,000– 1,00,000	70%	30%
Above 1,00,000	75%	25%
Financial Literacy		
Highly Literate	80%	20%
Moderately Literate	60%	40%
Low Literacy	30%	70%

(Source: Author work)

Table 10 shows how different demographic groups manage their income, either by categorizing it into separate funds (bills, savings, discretionary spending) or by treating it as a single lump sum. Here are the key insights and implications:

Gender Differences: Males are more likely to categorize their income (65%), while females show a slightly lower tendency (60%). This suggests that men may be marginally more structured in managing their money.

Age Groups: The older the age group, the more likely they are to categorize their income. For instance, 75% of people over 45 categorize their income, compared to just 55% of those aged 18–25. Younger individuals are less likely to adopt structured financial habits, possibly due to lower income or fewer financial obligations.

Income Levels: Higher income levels strongly correlate with more organized financial management. 75% of those earning above 1,00,000 categorize their income, while only 45% of those earning below 20,000 do the same. This could imply that lower-income individuals may not have enough surplus income to justify separate categories for spending.

Financial Literacy: Financial literacy is a significant predictor of income categorization. 80% of highly literate individuals categorize their income, while only 30% of low literacy individuals do so. This shows that those with more financial knowledge are better at managing their money, while those with less knowledge tend to treat their income as a lump sum.

Implications: The findings suggest that financial education initiatives should primarily target women, younger individuals, and those with lower financial literacy, as these groups are less inclined to organize their income. Tailored programs can help them develop better money management skills by teaching them to allocate resources more efficiently, even at lower income levels, where income is often treated as a lump sum. Age-specific financial literacy programs are also essential, with younger individuals (18–25) needing guidance on building good financial habits early, while older individuals can benefit from more advanced strategies. Across all demographics, promoting structured budgeting—dividing income into categories like bills, savings, and discretionary spending—can significantly enhance financial stability by improving expense management and reducing financial stress.

Table 11. How do you allocate unexpected income (bonuses, gifts)?

Demographic Group	Save it entirely (%)	Spend it entirely (%)	Spend part and save part (%)
Gender			
Male	55%	15%	30%
Female	60%	10%	30%
Age			

continued on following page

Table 11. Continued

Demographic Group	Save it entirely (%)	Spend it entirely (%)	Spend part and save part (%)
18–25 years	45%	25%	30%
26–35 years	55%	15%	30%
36–45 years	65%	10%	25%
Above 45 years	75%	5%	20%
Income Level			
Below 20,000	35%	35%	30%
20,000– 50,000	45%	25%	30%
50,000– 1,00,000	55%	15%	30%
Above 1,00,000	70%	5%	25%
Financial Literacy			
Highly Literate	65%	5%	30%
Moderately Literate	45%	15%	40%
Low Literacy	15%	35%	50%

(Source: Author work)

The results of Table 11 indicate clear trends in how different demographic groups allocate unexpected income such as bonuses or gifts. Older individuals, particularly those above 45 years (75%), are more likely to save the entire amount, compared to younger individuals, with only 45% of 18–25-year-olds opting to save everything. Similarly, those with higher financial literacy (65%) and higher income levels (70%) are also more inclined to save entirely, compared to people with low literacy or those earning below 20,000, who are equally likely to spend the entire amount (35%) as they are to save it.

Gender differences show that women (60%) are slightly more likely than men (55%) to save unexpected income, while both groups exhibit the same tendency to split the income between saving and spending (30%). Individuals with low financial literacy have the lowest savings rate, with only 15% saving entirely and 35% spending entirely, indicating their lack of financial planning and foresight.

Implications: These results underscore the need for financial literacy programs, especially targeting younger individuals and lower-income groups, to stress the importance of saving unexpected income. Encouraging a habit of saving for unforeseen expenses or future needs can help create a financial safety net, improving long-term financial resilience. For people with lower incomes, teaching the importance of balancing saving and spending could promote better financial stability. Additionally, strategies aimed at enhancing financial literacy in these vulnerable groups will ensure they make more informed and prudent financial decisions.

Table 12. How do you prioritize expenses when managing mental accounts?

Demographic Group	Essentials first, then discretionary spending (%)	Mix of both essentials and discretionary (%)	Focus on discretionary spending (%)
Gender			
Male	60%	30%	10%
Female	65%	25%	10%
Age			
18–25 years	50%	35%	15%
26–35 years	60%	30%	10%
36–45 years	70%	25%	5%
Above 45 years	75%	20%	5%
Income Level			
Below 20,000	45%	40%	15%
20,000– 50,000	55%	35%	10%
50,000– 1,00,000	70%	25%	5%
Above 1,00,000	75%	20%	5%
Financial Literacy			
Highly Literate	75%	20%	5%
Moderately Literate	55%	35%	10%
Low Literacy	35%	45%	20%

(Source: Author work)

Table 12 provides insights into how different demographic groups prioritize their expenses when managing their financial accounts, revealing clear distinctions based on age, income level, and financial literacy. The data shows that older individuals (particularly those above 45 years) and those with higher financial literacy are more likely to prioritize essential expenses before discretionary spending. For instance, 75% of respondents over 45 and 75% of highly literate individuals focus on essentials first, whereas only 50% of 18–25-year-olds and 35% of people with low literacy do the same.

Income also plays a significant role, with 70% of people earning 50,000– 1,00,000 prioritizing essential expenses, compared to 45% of those earning below 20,000, who are more inclined to mix essentials and discretionary spending (40%). Lower-income groups also show a higher tendency to focus solely on discretionary spending (15%), while only 5% of higher-income individuals do the same.

Gender-wise, women (65%) slightly outperform men (60%) in prioritizing essential expenses, but both genders have similar proportions when it comes to focusing solely on discretionary spending (10%).

Implications: The results highlight the need for financial literacy programs, particularly for younger people, lower-income groups, and those with low financial literacy. These groups are more prone to focusing on discretionary spending or mixing essential and non-essential expenses, increasing the risk of financial instability and debt accumulation. Teaching the importance of prioritizing essential expenses—such as housing, food, and healthcare—before spending on non-essentials could improve financial discipline and long-term financial stability. Focusing on budgeting and expense management can help vulnerable groups better manage their resources, avoid unnecessary debt, and plan for the future effectively. Financial literacy education that emphasizes responsible budgeting practices would be especially beneficial for these demographics, improving overall financial health and resilience.

Managerial Implications

The survey results show that mental accounting practices differ significantly throughout demographic groups, especially when examining financial literacy, age, gender, and income levels. More financially literate and well-off individuals are inclined to follow disciplined financial behaviors, like classifying their income, setting aside unforeseen cash, and giving priority to necessities. Individuals who lack financial literacy or income, on the other hand, are more likely to participate in unstructured financial practices, which may lead to long-term instability in their finances. The survey's findings have a number of managerial implications that are given ahead.

Targeted Financial Education: Financial literacy programs should focus on younger individuals, women, and those with lower financial literacy levels to promote better income management. Educational initiatives can teach structured financial organization, encouraging improved financial stability across these demographics.

Emphasizing Saving: Financial literacy programs should emphasize the importance of saving unexpected income, particularly for younger individuals and those with lower income. This practice will foster long-term financial security and create a buffer for future uncertainties.

Prioritization of Essentials: Programs targeting younger individuals and lower-income groups should stress the importance of prioritizing essential expenses. By developing better financial habits in these areas, participants can prevent debt accumulation and achieve better long-term financial health.

In summary, this analysis underscores the critical role of financial literacy in shaping financial behaviors across various demographic groups. The data suggest that targeted financial education and practical strategies can significantly improve the financial management practices of individuals, particularly those with lower financial literacy and income levels. By addressing these educational gaps and promoting disciplined financial behaviors, it is possible to enhance overall financial stability and well-being across diverse populations.

5. EXPLORING THE POTENTIAL CONSEQUENCES OF MENTAL ACCOUNTING ON LONG-TERM FINANCIAL WELL-BEING

The concept of "mental accounting" describes how people treat and classify money differently depending on where it comes from or what it will be used for. This cognitive approach has consequences that may have a major impact on long-term financial well-being, even though it occasionally helps people manage their money more effectively. The present investigation aims to examine the possible ramifications of mental accounting, uncovering both favorable and unfavorable outcomes for an individual's economic development and stability.

5.1 Positive Consequences of Mental Accounting(Iram et al., 2024; Bai, 2023; Ozkan & Ozkan, 2020)

1. **Promotion of Saving Behavior:** The potential of mental accounting to encourage saving behavior is among its most advantageous features. People can better manage their resources if they establish distinct mental accounts for each type of savings objective, such as emergency funds, retirement savings, and vacation funds. This classification pushes for a more methodical approach to saving.

Example: Consider a thirty-year-old professional who sets aside ten percent of his or her paycheck each month for a "Vacation Fund." Such persons are encouraged to save and fight the urge to spend these resources on frivolous things since they are treating these saves differently from their normal expenses. They are able to afford their vacation as a result, demonstrating how mental accounting may result in reaching financial objectives.

2. **Enhanced Budgeting Discipline:** Mental accounting fosters improved budgeting discipline. Organizing their spending allows people to see exactly where their money is going, which helps them make wise decisions. It is easier to avoid needless spending when finances are clearly visualized.

For instance, a couple uses a budgeting app to divide their monthly income into categories such as housing, food, entertainment, and savings. By sticking to these categories, they can ensure that essential expenses are prioritized. Over time, they develop a habit of living within their means, contributing to long-term financial security.

3. **Psychological Comfort and Reduced Financial Stress:** Another positive outcome of mental accounting is the psychological comfort it provides. People feel more in control of their money when they mentally allocate money for particular goals, which lowers anxiety associated with money management. Many Researchers have found that individuals who practiced mental accounting reported lower levels of financial stress. The act of separating funds for different purposes created a sense of security, contributing to overall well-being.

5.2 Negative Consequences of Mental Accounting (Leković, 2020)

1. **Overspending in Designated Categories:** Mental accounting has benefits, but it can also result in overspending in some areas. When people see money as distinct from other uses, they could rationalize excessive spending, which puts a pressure on their finances.

Example: People frequently set aside money for festivities and gifts around the holidays. But the sentimental connection to the festive season may cause them to splurge and go over their allocated spending limit. Financial stability may be at risk if this leads to months-long credit card debt repayment.

2. **Neglecting Long-Term Financial Goals:** Mental accounting can lead to a narrow-sighted viewpoint where people put short-term spending above long-term financial objectives. This kind of behavior can impede the accumulation of money and future financial readiness.

Example: Young professionals often see entertainment and dining out as distinct categories when allocating their budget. They can forget to invest for retirement while savoring instant delight. Financial difficulty in later life may result from this disregard over time and insufficient retirement funds.

3. **Inconsistent Financial Decision-Making:** Inconsistent decision-making may occasionally result from mental accounting. People could apply distinct guidelines to different financial categories, which could result in disparities in their total financial plan.

Example of Inconsistency: While adhering to a strict budget for groceries, a student may indulge in overspending when dining out. The inconsistency may result in unforeseen costs that exacerbate their financial circumstances and may increase their debt.

5.3 The Role of Financial Literacy

Financial literacy plays a significant role in shaping the consequences of mental accounting. Individuals with a higher understanding of financial concepts tend to navigate the complexities of mental accounting more effectively.

1. **Improved Financial Decision-Making:** Financially literate individuals are better equipped to make informed choices that balance short-term needs with long-term goals. They understand the interplay between different financial categories and can manage their resources more effectively.

Example: Financially literate people make sure they contribute to a retirement account in addition to setting aside money for necessities. This balanced approach helps them maintain a healthy financial status throughout their life.

2. **Effective Use of Mental Accounts:** Mental accounting might be advantageous for those with high levels of financial literacy. Long-term financial health can be promoted by creating realistic budgets that take into account both current demands and future goals.

Example: A young adult who has taken financial literacy courses understands the importance of setting up mental accounts for emergency savings, discretionary spending, and retirement. This structured approach not only assists in managing current expenses but also prepares them for future financial challenges.

5.4 Practical Strategies for Long-Term Financial Well-Being

To optimize the benefits of mental accounting while minimizing its drawbacks, individuals can implement several practical strategies:

1. **Develop Comprehensive Budgets:** Creating an all-inclusive budget that takes into consideration savings, investments, and discretionary spending helps people see the overall picture of their finances. This strategy discourages overspending in particular areas and promotes balanced allocation.

Implementation: A family could divide their monthly income into fixed costs, savings targets, and discretionary expenditures using a spreadsheet. They can ensure that financial objectives continue to be a top priority by routinely assessing and adjusting this budget.

2. **Set Specific Financial Goals:** Financial goals that are specific and quantifiable enable people to align their saving and spending habits. They can make better informed judgments that support overall financial stability by concentrating on long-term goals.

Example: A person who wants to buy a house can decide to set aside 20% of their savings for a down payment. They can see their progress and maintain motivation if they set aside a certain percentage of their monthly income for this purpose.

3. **Regular Review of Financial Accounts:** People can determine whether their mental accounting methods serve their long-term interests by periodically analyzing their financial accounts and spending patterns. Ongoing financial balance is ensured by adjustments made in response to evolving conditions.

Implementation: Finding patterns in spending and saving might be facilitated by setting aside time each month to evaluate financial statements. By enabling proactive modifications, this practice guarantees that budgetary objectives be fulfilled.

4. **Utilize Financial Management Tools:** Financial management can be improved by utilizing personal finance applications. These tools make it easier for users to track their income and expenses, which enables them to better categorize and evaluate their financial habits.

Example: Users can track spending in different categories, set financial objectives, and get alerts when their budget is about to be exceeded with the use of a budgeting app. This instantaneous feedback promotes financial responsibility and accountability.

5.5 Implications for Financial Education and Policy

The consequences of mental accounting highlight the importance of financial education initiatives. Programs aimed at improving financial literacy can empower individuals to recognize the implications of their mental accounting practices and make informed choices.

1. **Targeted Financial Literacy Programs:** The core concepts of saving, investing, and budgeting should be taught in educational programs. People can utilize mental accounting to assist their long-term financial well-being more effectively by improving their comprehension.

Example: Community-based organizations can provide workshops that teach participants how to create an effective budget and why it's important to set aside money for certain uses. These courses can give participants useful tools to improve their money management.

2. **Promotion of Holistic Financial Planning:** Promoting a holistic approach to financial planning can assist people in understanding the relationships between various financial categories. This viewpoint promotes consistent decision-making and a more comprehensive grasp of personal finances.

Implementation: In order to develop complete financial plans that take into account income, expenses, savings, and investments, financial advisors can collaborate with their clients. This approach makes sure that every facet of a person's financial life is focused on reaching their objectives.

The exploration of mental accounting's consequences on long-term financial well-being reveals its multifaceted nature. Mental accounting entails dangers including overpaying, ignoring long-term goals, and making inconsistent decisions, but it can also promote savings, enhance budgeting discipline, and lessen financial stress. Being financially literate is essential to assisting people in successfully navigating these complexities. People can develop better financial habits that support long-term stability and security by using doable tactics for goal-setting, budgeting, and regular financial reviews. In the end, encouraging wise financial practices and attaining long-term financial well-being depend on comprehending and managing the effects of mental accounting.

6. UNDERSTANDING HOW MENTAL ACCOUNTING LEADS TO SUBOPTIMAL FINANCIAL DECISIONS

The term "mental accounting" describes the thought process people use to classify and assess financial results. This idea, which was first put forth by Richard Thaler, describes how people view and handle money differently according on where it comes from or what it will be used for. Although mental accounting has some organizational advantages, it frequently results in less-than-ideal financial choices (Huang et al., 2020). This section looks at the causes of mental accounting biases, how they affect financial behavior, and how to counteract them.

6.1 Mechanisms Behind Mental Accounting Biases

1. **Segregation of Gains and Losses:** A fundamental feature of mental accounting is the propensity to divide profits and losses. A windfall, such a bonus or tax refund, is frequently treated differently by people than their normal income, which results in the "house money effect." Due to this tendency, people may spend unexpected profits more carelessly and frequently fail to consider the long-term effects of their decisions.

Example: A person who receives a year-end bonus could consider this money to be different from their regular salary and use it to treat themselves to upscale purchases or trips. This choice may make it more difficult for them to save money for investments or other necessities, which would ultimately jeopardize their financial stability.

2. **Misplaced Emphasis on Sunk Costs:** Individuals sometimes make the mistake of considering prior investments in their decision-making, even when those expenses cannot be recovered. This is known as the "sunk cost fallacy." Due to this bias, people may continue to invest in unsuccessful projects just because they have already made an investment in them, which can result in irrational financial decisions.

Example: Instead of cutting losses and reinvesting the money in more potential ventures, someone may choose to keep funding a failed firm due to the money already wasted. This behavior not only wastes resources but can also delay recovery from financial setbacks.

3. **Inconsistent Valuation of Money:** People who engage in mental accounting may value money differently depending on where it comes from or how it will be used. For example, people may consider money obtained as a windfall or gift to be "free money," which makes them more likely to spend it carelessly than money gained through work.

Research Evidence: Studies have shown that individuals are less likely to save or invest unexpected income, such as lottery winnings, compared to their regular paycheck. This behavior results from the mental categorization of these funds, leading to potential long-term financial detriment.

6.2 Consequences of Suboptimal Financial Decisions

The biases stemming from mental accounting can lead to various negative financial outcomes, including:

1. **Inadequate Savings and Investments:** When people handle their income sources differently, they might not set aside enough money for investments and savings. Over time, this conduct may impede the building of wealth.

Case Study: According to a survey, people who often divide their money up are less likely to put money into retirement accounts because they value short-term spending above long-term savings objectives. This underinvestment may lead to insufficient retirement savings, endangering future financial stability.

2. **Increased Debt Levels:** The propensity to spend excessive amounts of unexpected cash could increase debt levels. When people think of some money as disposable, they could use credit to cover daily costs, which puts them in debt over time.

For instance, a customer who views tax returns as "extra cash" would spend it on impulsive items rather than paying off debt that already exists. They might therefore have to pay increasing interest rates, which would put them in a vicious circle of debt.

3. **Failure to Optimize Resource Allocation:** Decision-making can be distorted by mental accounting, which keeps people from allocating resources as efficiently as possible. People who compartmentalize their finances run the risk of missing out on opportunities to make better use of their resources.

Example: A person with credit card debt that has a significantly higher interest rate may have a sizable amount of money in a low-interest savings account. Due to mental accounting biases, people decide to keep their savings intact rather than reallocating cash to pay off debt, which increases their financial difficulties.

6.3 Strategies for Overcoming Mental Accounting Biases

To mitigate the detrimental effects of mental accounting on financial decisions, individuals can adopt several strategies:

1. **Emphasize Holistic Financial Management:** Using a holistic approach to financial management—treating all finances as belonging to a single financial pool—is one successful tactic. People are better equipped to save, invest, and spend their money when they see it as replaceable.

Implementation: By encouraging clients to view their entire income and expenses as a whole, financial advisor can assist clients in consolidating their finances. This viewpoint assists in prioritizing debt reduction and savings while fostering a better knowledge of cash flow.

2. **Create a Comprehensive Budget:** The impacts of mental accounting can be mitigated by creating a thorough budget that accounts for all financial actions. People can organize their income and expenses into categories and still have a clear picture of their overall financial health, which helps them make decisions that will help them reach their long-term objectives.

For instance, a family could make a thorough budget that lists fixed costs, discretionary expenditures, monthly income, and savings targets. They may keep focused on long-term financial goals and make any required adjustments by often evaluating this budget.

3. **Educate on Financial Literacy:** Recognizing and correcting mental accounting biases requires improving financial literacy. People who comprehend the fundamentals of sound money management can recognize the situations in which their mental accounting techniques could result in less-than-ideal choices.

Program Implementation: Workshops and courses on budgeting, saving, investing, and comprehending the psychological biases that affect financial decision-making can be provided by community organizations and financial institutions. Giving people mental accounting knowledge can enable them to make wiser financial decisions.

4. **Encourage Reflective Decision-Making:** Mental accounting biases can be mitigated by encouraging people to approach financial decisions thoughtfully. People can make more sane financial decisions if they take the time to consider the possible long-term effects of their decisions.

Strategy: People should consider if a big purchase or other financial commitment is in line with their overall financial objectives before making it. By reflecting on it, one might avoid making snap conclusions that result from thinking in silos.

5. **Utilize Financial Tools and Apps:** By using financial management software and tools, people may track their money more efficiently, giving them better visibility and control over their spending. Users can monitor spending, create budgets, and examine their financial habits with a variety of tools.

For instance, personal finance applications such as Mint or YNAB (You Need A Budget) assist users in organizing their spending and offer a comprehensive summary of their financial status. This all-encompassing perspective might lessen the possibility of making mistakes when mentally accounting.

Mental accounting presents both benefits and challenges in the realm of personal finance. Even though it can help people become more organized and disciplined with their money, it frequently results in less-than-ideal financial decisions, like insufficient savings, higher debt levels, and inefficient resource allocation. Recognizing the effects of mental accounting biases on financial behavior requires an understanding of the mechanisms underlying these biases.

People can lessen the consequences of mental accounting biases by putting measures like holistic financial management, thorough budgeting, financial literacy education, introspective decision-making, and using financial instruments into practice. In the end, encouraging a more integrated approach to financial decision-making will improve long-term financial well-being and provide people the ability to make decisions that are in line with their objectives.

7. IMPLICATIONS FOR STAKEHOLDERS

There are important ramifications of mental accounting for a variety of stakeholders, including people, financial institutions, legislators, and educators.

- *Individuals* can see how cognitive biases result in inefficient financial activities by having a basic understanding of mental accounting. People often spend bonuses or windfalls, for example, more freely than they would on normal income, which can impede long-term financial objectives like saving and paying off debt. By being more conscious of their mental accounting biases, people can adopt more beneficial behaviors, such treating all sources of income equally and creating detailed budgets that put paying off debt before frivolous savings.

- *Financial institutions* can create products that either minimize or take advantage of these biases by using mental accounting. Credit card firms and banks might create promotional offers or low-interest loans that play on consumers' propensity to group money, which would encourage more spending. Positively, they can implement mechanisms that automatically transfer money from low-yield accounts to higher-yielding investments, promoting wiser financial practices.

    Policymakers can use insights from mental accounting to inform the development of financial literacy programs that teach the public how to overcome these cognitive biases. By promoting greater awareness and understanding of financial behaviors, policies can foster a more financially responsible society, reduce debt accumulation, and improve overall economic stability.
- *Educators and financial advisors* have a crucial role in addressing mental accounting biases through targeted financial literacy programs. These programs can teach individuals to adopt holistic approaches to money management, focusing on comprehensive financial strategies that incorporate debt repayment, savings, and investments. The integration of mental accounting awareness into financial education is essential to improving long-term financial well-being across various demographics.

8. CONCLUSION

The concept of mental accounting, while a useful cognitive framework for organizing finances, often leads to suboptimal financial behaviors such as irrational spending, inefficient savings, and poor debt management. This chapter highlights how individuals mentally separate funds into distinct categories, treating them differently based on their source or intended use. These mental distinctions may result in behaviors that contradict rational economic principles, like overspending windfalls or maintaining savings while carrying high-interest debt. Understanding the influence of mental accounting is crucial for both individuals and financial institutions. Individuals must recognize their cognitive biases to make more rational financial decisions, such as prioritizing debt repayment over unnecessary savings.

Financial institutions, on the other hand, should design products that encourage better financial practices without exploiting consumer biases.

Overall, mental accounting has both positive and negative impacts on financial decision-making. When managed properly, it can foster disciplined budgeting and savings. However, if left unchecked, it can exacerbate financial inefficiencies. Therefore, financial education programs that address these biases can significantly improve long-term financial well-being, enabling individuals to make more informed, rational decisions aligned with their overall financial goals.

9. REFERENCES

Adil, M., Singh, Y., & Ansari, M. S. (2022). How financial literacy moderate the association between behaviour biases and investment decision? *Asian Journal of Accounting Research*, 7(1), 17–30. DOI: 10.1108/AJAR-09-2020-0086

Bai, R. (2023). Impact of financial literacy, mental budgeting and self control on financial wellbeing: Mediating impact of investment decision making. *PLoS One*, 18(11), e0294466. DOI: 10.1371/journal.pone.0294466 PMID: 37963159

Becker, J., Hopp, D., & Kriebel, M. (2020). Mental accounting of public funds–The flypaper effect in the lab. *Journal of Economic Behavior & Organization*, 176, 321–336. DOI: 10.1016/j.jebo.2020.04.026

Bogunjoko, A. (2021). *Impact of Behavioral Finance on Investment decisions Investigation in to how psychological factors affect Investment decisions among millennial Investors in Nigeria* (Doctoral dissertation, Dublin, National College of Ireland).

Corr, P., & Plagnol, A. (2023). *Behavioral economics: The basics*. Routledge. DOI: 10.4324/9781003166900

de Mello Ferreira, V. R. (2021). Financial literacy and behavioral economics: Knowledge, nudging, and the psychology of decision-making. In *The Routledge Handbook of Financial Literacy* (pp. 489–504). Routledge. DOI: 10.4324/9781003025221-37

Ellis, A., & Freeman, D. J. (2024). Revealing choice bracketing. *The American Economic Review*, 114(9), 2668–2700. DOI: 10.1257/aer.20210877

Fuster, A., Kaplan, G., & Zafar, B. (2021). What would you do with $500? Spending responses to gains, losses, news, and loans. *The Review of Economic Studies*, 88(4), 1760–1795. DOI: 10.1093/restud/rdaa076

Gajewski, J. F., Heimann, M., Meunier, L., & Ohadi, S. (2024). Nudges for responsible finance? A survey of interventions targeted at financial decision making. *Corporate Social Responsibility and Environmental Management*, 31(2), 1203–1219. DOI: 10.1002/csr.2625

Garduno, J. C. (2022). *Financial Advisor Decisions and Behavioral Biases*. California Baptist University.

Hans, A., Choudhary, F. S., & Sudan, T. (2024). Behavioral determinants of investment decisions: evidence from Indian retail equity investors in the wake of COVID-19 induced financial risks. *International Journal of Accounting & Information Management*.

Helmina, M. R. A., Rosari, N., Yusniar, M. W., & Utaminingsih, N. S. (2023). Mind Matters in Investments: Unveiling the Psychological Forces Shaping Decision Making Behavior. [Jurnal Dinamika Manajemen]. *Journal of Database Management*, 14(2), 273–285.

Hon, T. Y., Moslehpour, M., & Woo, K. Y. (2021). Review on behavioral finance with empirical evidence. *Advances in Decision Sciences*, 25(4), 1–30.

Huang, J., Antonides, G., & Nie, F. (2020). Is mental accounting of farm produce associated with more consumption of own-produced food? *Journal of Behavioral and Experimental Economics*, 88, 101594. DOI: 10.1016/j.socec.2020.101594

Iram, T., Bilal, A. R., & Latif, S. (2024). Is awareness that powerful? Women's financial literacy support to prospects behaviour in prudent decision-making. *Global Business Review*, 25(5), 1356–1381. DOI: 10.1177/0972150921996185

Kahneman, D., & Tversky, A. (2013). Prospect theory: An analysis of decision under risk. In *Handbook of the fundamentals of financial decision making: Part I* (pp. 99-127).

Kumar, P., Islam, M. A., Pillai, R., & Sharif, T. (2023). Analysing the behavioural, psychological, and demographic determinants of financial decision making of household investors. *Heliyon*, 9(2), e13085. DOI: 10.1016/j.heliyon.2023.e13085 PMID: 36793953

Leković, M. (2020). Cognitive biases as an integral part of behavioral finance. *Economic Themes*, 58(1), 75–96. DOI: 10.2478/ethemes-2020-0005

Mahapatra, M. S., & Mishra, R. (2020). Behavioral influence and financial decision of individuals: A study on mental accounting process among Indian households. *Cogent Economics & Finance*, 8(1), 1827762. DOI: 10.1080/23322039.2020.1827762

Mitchell, O., & Lusardi, A. (Eds.). (2020). *Remaking Retirement: Debt in an Aging Economy*. Oxford University Press. DOI: 10.1093/oso/9780198867524.001.0001

Nanda, A. P., & Banerjee, R. (2021). Consumer's subjective financial well-being: A systematic review and research agenda. *International Journal of Consumer Studies*, 45(4), 750–776. DOI: 10.1111/ijcs.12668

Nteso, D. C. (2021). *Mental accounting of saving and debt in South Africa*. University of Johannesburg.

Ozkan, M., & Ozkan, O. (2020). Financial evaluation of mental accounting.

Pillay, P. (2021). *Households' Review of their Budgets to Deal with the Paradox of Covid-19 Financial Disruptions and Increased Health-Related Expenses: A Mental Accounting Approach* (Master's thesis, University of Pretoria (South Africa)).

Pompian, M. M. (2021). *Behavioral Finance and Your Portfolio: A Navigation Guide for Building Wealth*. John Wiley & Sons.

Puaschunder, J. (2020). *Behavioral economics and finance leadership*. Springer Books. DOI: 10.1007/978-3-030-54330-3

Read, D., Loewenstein, G., Rabin, M., Keren, G., & Laibson, D. (2000). Choice bracketing. *Elicitation of preferences*, 171-202.

Rikberg, O. (2023). The Impact of Behavioural Biases on Individual Investors' Decision-Making: An Analysis of Cognitive and Emotional Biases in Investment Choices.

Russell, C. (2024). *The aging experience*. Taylor & Francis. DOI: 10.4324/9781032683720

Sattar, M. A., Toseef, M., & Sattar, M. F. (2020). Behavioral finance biases in investment decision making. *International Journal of Accounting. Finance and Risk Management*, 5(2), 69.

Shefrin, H. M., & Thaler, R. H. (1992). Mental accounting, saving, and self-control. *Choice over time*, 287-330.

Shukla, A., Rushdi, D. N. J., & Katiyar, D. R. C. (2020). Impact of behavioral biases on investment decisions 'a systematic review'. *International Journal of Management*, 11(4).

Silva, E. M., de Lacerda Moreira, R., & Bortolon, P. M. (2023). Mental Accounting and Decision Making: A systematic review of the literature. *Journal of Behavioral and Experimental Economics*, 107, 102092. DOI: 10.1016/j.socec.2023.102092

Sinnewe, E., & Nicholson, G. (2023). Healthy financial habits in young adults: An exploratory study of the relationship between subjective financial literacy, engagement with finances, and financial decision-making. *The Journal of Consumer Affairs*, 57(1), 564–592. DOI: 10.1111/joca.12512

Skwara, F. (2023). Effects of mental accounting on purchase decision processes: A systematic review and research agenda. *Journal of Consumer Behaviour*, 22(5), 1265–1281. DOI: 10.1002/cb.2193

Sobkow, A., Garrido, D., & Garcia-Retamero, R. (2020). Cognitive abilities and financial decision making. *Psychological perspectives on financial decision making*, 71-87.

Sui, L., Sun, L., & Geyfman, V. (2021). An assessment of the effects of mental accounting on overspending behaviour: An empirical study. *International Journal of Consumer Studies*, 45(2), 221–234. DOI: 10.1111/ijcs.12613

Thaler, R. H. (1990). Anomalies: Saving, fungibility, and mental accounts. *The Journal of Economic Perspectives*, 4(1), 193–205. DOI: 10.1257/jep.4.1.193

Thaler, R. H. (2016). Behavioral economics: Past, present, and future. *The American Economic Review*, 106(7), 1577–1600. DOI: 10.1257/aer.106.7.1577

Ülkü, S., Hydock, C., & Cui, S. (2020). Making the wait worthwhile: Experiments on the effect of queueing on consumption. *Management Science*, 66(3), 1149–1171. DOI: 10.1287/mnsc.2018.3277

Van Raaij, W. F. (2016). *Understanding consumer financial behavior: Money management in an age of financial illiteracy*. Springer. DOI: 10.1057/9781137544254

Weixiang, S., Qamruzzaman, M., Rui, W., & Kler, R. (2022). An empirical assessment of financial literacy and behavioral biases on investment decision: Fresh evidence from small investor perception. *Frontiers in Psychology*, 13, 977444. DOI: 10.3389/fpsyg.2022.977444 PMID: 36225674

West, C. R. (2021). *Windfalls of Time and Money: Effects on Wellbeing and Decision-Making*. University of California.

Chapter 8
Overconfidence and Its Consequences in Financial Markets

Ishaan Gupta
https://orcid.org/0009-0003-5282-1062
Christ University, India

Vikas Garg
Christ University, India

ABSTRACT

This chapter is about overconfidence in financial markets. This occurs when individuals and institutions exaggerate their knowledge and capabilities, leading to over-trading, greater risks, and market volatility. Overconfidence can fuel asset bubbles, bad decisions, and costly mergers with ramifications for market liquidity and investor confidence. Remedies are proposed, including investor education, AI-driven analytics, regulatory adjustments, and ethical awareness. It emphasizes humility and accountability among financial institutions, working toward mitigating overconfidence so as to enhance stability and efficiency in the markets.

INTRODUCTION

Overconfidence is one of the most pervasive and well-studied biases in behavioral finance, manifested through an investor's unjustified belief that he or she is more knowledgeable and confident about judgments and predictive skills than other investors. This cognitive bias implies that investors believe they have better insight or a special gift that would allow them to make better decisions in markets than

DOI: 10.4018/979-8-3693-9380-2.ch008

others do and more returns with regularity. Overconfidence tends to distort rational judgment and is often directly responsible for excessive trading, overinflated expectations, and, ultimately, suboptimal returns. This means that overconfidence will tend to lead to enormous distortions in market dynamics not only among individual investors but also in broader economic systems owing to the unpredictable nature and complexity of financial markets.

In this respect, the traditional finance models, which include the Efficient Market Hypothesis and rational actor theory, hold that investors make decisions based on the information available to them, processing the same in such a way as to reach logical and optimal outcomes. These models are based on the idea that market participants operate on rationality grounds, in which prices reflect all known information, and assets are traded at their intrinsic value. Despite these often-conflicting theories, the coming of behavioral finance as a field challenged all this by forcing psychological factors that can cause distortion in judgment. Overconfidence is one of the more powerful and prevailing biases for explaining why markets stray from rationality and efficiency as well.

Behavioral finance, the study of how psychological factors influence financial decision-making, has placed overconfidence at the center as an explanatory mechanism for anomalies that would otherwise remain unexplained within the rational paradigm. Overconfident investors trade more than others because they believe better than the average investor to pick winners. It usually leads to underperformance due to the cost of transactions, miscalculation of risk estimates, and poor diversification. Overconfidence is also part of underlying psychology, which generates some side effects including market bubbles where collective gullibility of investors propels asset prices significantly beyond their inherent values.

Technological advancement and fintech innovation in the recent financial world only also added flavor to overconfidence. Robinhood, and others offering zero-commission trading, makes market participation easier than ever. Although democratization of finance is very positive in many aspects, it also allows overconfident investors to make more frequent trades and be speculative. This real-time availability of data, the complexity of analytical tools, and the algorithmic trading system itself are fertile ground for overconfidence to germinate from the perspective of a retail investor who does not possess formal education in finance but feels confident about having gained control over his or her trading strategy.

Overconfidence introduced by digital trading platforms is another layer. These sites may unintentionally encourage more trading activity in the way of making the experience more gamified, providing instant access to a large number of available assets. Some investors mistake the ease of using the platform and the high availability of information as signals of their own expertise. This leads to what's often called the "illusion of control." This creates the risk of investors accepting more risk than they have the capacity to bear-an especially worrisome consequence given the volatility and sophistication of modern financial instruments, such as options and leveraged ETFs.

In addition, overconfidence is not exclusive to individual retail investors. Institutional investors, fund managers, and corporate executives are also affected by this bias. Even experts with the most advanced data analytics, financial models, and special training may experience this. For example, research has concluded that overconfident managers trade more frequently than relatively more modestly confident peers for the simple reason that overconfident managers tend to lose money for their customers. Overconfident CEOs are also more likely to pursue hostile acquisitions and mergers, believing that their firm will reap more than it realizes from such a deal. Therefore, these managers could overlook significant risks or overhype potential synergies as a result of which a great loss and diluted shareholders' value is incurred.

Beyond trading behavior, overconfidence has implications in broader market volatility and economic stability. Overconfident investors who invest their capital into overvalued assets may create speculative bubbles, such as the late 1990s dot-com bubble or the housing market leading to the 2008 global financial crisis. In these cases, asset prices were driven way beyond their sustainable levels by a generalized overconfidence among market participants, creating an unsustainable environment. As the overvaluation became a reality, these bubbles burst with steep falls in asset prices and extensive financial losses and economic downturns. Overconfidence thus plays a critical role in both boom and bust cycles and forms the more macroeconomic environment.

The pervasiveness and influence of overconfidence make it essential to understand its mechanisms and consequences for investors, policymakers, and financial professionals. Recognition of overconfidence can help investors make better decisions, potentially avoiding pitfalls of excessive trading and undue risk-taking. For financial advisors and fund managers, understanding their overconfidence allows them to better make sensible decisions on the behalf of their clients for a better responsible approach at wealth management. Regulators can be equally benefited as they look to design appropriate frameworks, which temper speculation, ensure more transparency and lead toward a more stable financial framework.

This book will endeavor to provide a comprehensive exploration of overconfidence and what it means to financial markets. We consider overconfidence in its various dimensions: over-precision, over-placement, and over-optimism. We explain how each form of overconfidence uniquely affects investor behavior and market dynamics and illustrate through case studies the potential for widespread market disruption due to this bias-from historical financial events like the 2008 financial crisis to the GameStop short squeeze. Furthermore, through comparative analysis, it will be seen how overconfidence manifests in different ways across asset classes, whether it is in stocks, real estate, or cryptocurrencies.

The paper will also explore the ethical implications of overconfidence, especially within the realm of financial professionals. Overconfidence might push the fiduciary obligations of a fund manager or corporate leader or analyst to supplant their fiduciary duty to clients and shareholders, instead using ego rather than financial prudence to make decisions. Ethical lapses stemming from overconfidence harm the individual client but also derail public trust in financial institutions and markets at large. This chapter will point out why humility, accountability, and self-awareness are what are needed to counter this risk of overconfidence.

The final section of this chapter discusses the use of advanced technologies like AI/ML in real time. This can help detect the onset of overconfidence along with managing it in real-time. AI and ML-based algorithms will be able to analyse vast datasets that will actually reveal the patterns leading up to overconfident trading behavior. Using these tools, financial institutions can predict overconfidence and prevent its amplification to the point of more systemic disruption. Nevertheless, higher algorithmic trading raises more questions on ethical and practical concerns of AI as algorithms can inadvertently further the culture of overconfidence by encouraging high-frequency trading and speculative investment.

TYPES OF OVERCONFIDENCE IN FINANCIAL MARKETS

Over-Precision: Misplaced Confidence in Data Accuracy

The propensity to overestimate the correctness of one's own knowledge, analysis, or forecasts is known as over-precision. When investors think their forecasts, predictions, or analyses of market data are more accurate than they actually are, this is known as over-precision in financial contexts. Riskier choices, including less diversification or larger-than-justified investments in particular assets, might result from this misguided faith in the accuracy of one's understanding.

Impact on Financial Decisions

Over-precision investors frequently undervalue the possible downside risk by concentrating their portfolios in a small number of assets they think will perform extraordinarily well. They may ignore or minimise contradicting information that contradicts their viewpoint, which can result in "tunnel vision," where they only pay attention to facts that support their opinions. Because investors could overlook more general economic indications or neglect to account for unanticipated disruptions, this behaviour is particularly dangerous in volatile markets.

Case Study: The Dot-Com Bubble

The dot-com boom of the late 1990s is a prime example of over-precision. Optimistic predictions of internet-based businesses, many of which were start-ups with untested business strategies, gave investors excessive optimism. Both private investors and analysts thought that these companies would be profitable because to the rapid developments in technology. Many investors poured money into tech stocks without critically evaluating their fundamentals since it was widely believed that the industry would continue to develop at an exponential rate.

For instance, a study found that investors during the dot-com boom exhibited high levels of over-precision, with some assuming near-perfect accuracy in the anticipated growth rates of tech companies. As the bubble expanded, so did investor confidence in the projected earnings of these companies. When the bubble burst, those who were heavily invested in these companies suffered severe financial losses, as they had overestimated the precision of their knowledge and the reliability of market predictions.

Over-Placement: Comparative Superiority and the "Better-Than-Average" Effect

The idea that one's abilities, expertise, or performance would continuously surpass those of others is known as over-placement. This is frequently referred to as the "better-than-average" effect, in which people believe they are more capable than the average person. The belief that one can outperform the market or make superior investment choices than peers is one way that this bias appears in the finance industry..

Impact on Financial Decisions

Over-placement-influenced investors are more inclined to trade frequently, presuming they have the ability to consistently "beat the market." Transaction fees, possible tax repercussions, and the possibility of ill-timed trades might make this behaviour expensive. In financial strategies, over-placement can sometimes result in hubris, as investors take on excessive risk without sufficient hedging.

Research Findings and Empirical Evidence

One of the most important research on over-placement in trading behaviour was carried out by Barber and Odean (2000). Their findings showed that overconfident investors often engage in excessive trading, with men trading 67% more than women because of a greater propensity for over-placement. Due to transaction costs and lost chances for long-term gains, their research revealed a direct correlation between higher trading frequency and worse returns.

Case Study: Rise of Day Trading Culture in the 1990s and Early 2000s

One of the best examples of over-placement among retail investors was the emergence of day trading in the late 1990s. Thousands of inexperienced traders thought they could compete with seasoned Wall Street traders after the introduction of internet trading platforms. Many believed that they would regularly profit from short-term price fluctuations if they traded often and kept a careful eye on equities. However, research indicates that day traders generally did worse than the overall market, with many suffering large losses as a result of costly transaction fees and poorly timed trades.

These results frequently did not deter day traders since their "better-than-average" bias made them blame losses on other forces rather than admitting their own shortcomings. After experiencing repeated financial losses, many day traders eventually left the market, realising the cost of over-placement.

Over-Optimism: Excessive Expectation of Favorable Outcomes

The propensity to overestimate the possibility of favourable outcomes and underestimate possible risks is known as overoptimism. Overly optimistic investors in the financial sector tend to minimise the likelihood of losses or unfavourable market conditions because they think their investments will perform very well. During market booms, when mood is generally positive and investors believe that the current favourable conditions will last forever, this bias is especially strong.

Impact on Financial Decisions

Investors that are overly optimistic are likely to take on excessive risk because they believe that great profits are almost a given. Due to this tendency, investors allocate a sizable amount of their wealth to a limited number of high-risk assets, which results in under-diversification. An extended exposure to failed assets can result from overoptimism, which can also lead investors to disregard warning signs or bad news about their investments.

Case Study: The Cryptocurrency Boom and Bitcoin's Boom-and-Bust Cycles

A good example of an over-optimistic instance is the cryptocurrency market, such as Bitcoin. When, in 2017, and then again in 2021, Bitcoin recorded a very fast price acceleration, many investors entered that market believing that the coin would just keep growing perpetually. Hyped about by social media and online platforms, retail investors were led to believe that Bitcoin possessed limitless potential, and this led some to predict a future where Bitcoin would overthrow traditional currency.

This over-optimism led many people to invest significant amounts in Bitcoin and other digital assets without much thought towards the possibility of price volatility. As one can guess, the over 80% plunge of Bitcoin's value in 2018 meant a very high loss for those investors who had entered at its peak. Over-optimism is a recurrent factor in cryptocurrency markets as the next wave of investors seems to assume that price rallies mean permanently high returns.

LITERATURE REVIEW

One of the most important topics in behavioral finance is overconfidence, which has been analyzed in depth for its deep impact on investor behavior, asset pricing, and market dynamics. Overconfidence is defined as the tendency of an individual to overestimate knowledge, skills, or predictive accuracy. It is one of the major deviations from rationality. Classical financial theories, especially the Efficient Market Hypothesis, claim that investors are rational and that markets efficiently process all available information. This concept, however, challenges show the contrary as demonstrated the manner in which overconfidence among others can actually produce suboptimal investment decision making through psychological biases often resulting in negative consequences for investors. Cognitive biases first conceived of in groundbreaking studies by Tversky and Kahneman in 1974 introduced this important concept as one challenging the rational actor model of economics and therefore it served to lay foundational studies to focus on the phenomenon of overconfidence in core issues concerning finance. In particular, Kahneman and Tversky's Prospect Theory (1979) brought attention to the fact that people tend to evaluate gains and losses asymmetrically, overestimate their ability in such matters, and thus end up trading too much, with poor risk management and thus assets get mispriced. These contributions formed a platform for further research. For example, Barberis and Thaler (2003) proposed that the reason for biases like overconfidence causing irrationality in investment behavior is because rationality concerning financial decisions, based on classical assumptions, cannot be sustained in such situations.

In behavioral finance, there are three types of overconfidence: over-precision, over-placement, and over-optimism. Each of them has different implications on the decision-making processes within finances, as argued by Moore and Healy (2008), in that investors tend to miscalculate risk due to over-precision, mainly through diversifying their portfolio based on an incorrect assumption that the knowledge is accurate. Hilary and Menzly (2006) discovered that over-accurate investors disregard diversification to focus on concentrated bets and are sometimes financially hurt once market conditions change in unpredictable ways. Over-placement, or the tendency to feel that one is better than others, compels excessive trading by investors who think they can beat the market every time. As found in the foundational study on the topic by Barber and Odean in 2000, men investors that place over-invest far outstrip the number of transaction of females with big differences in the costs they are incurred in transactions besides losing money through lower returns in their accounts. Conversely, over-optimism leads to a higher belief on better prospects that forms one of the causes leading speculative bubbles. During the dot-com bubble, Shiller (2000) investigated overestimation bias where overstated optimism made investors assume exponential returns from holding of tech stocks. The categorization explains why there is an importance of realizing the different types of overconfidence as each uniquely influences the behavior of an investor, the acceptable level of risk undertaken in trades, and the stability of a market.

Barber and Odean (2001) discovered that overconfidence in trading leads to excessive trading, increased expenses, and decreased returns. As demonstrated by the 2008 housing catastrophe and the 2021 GameStop boom, overconfident investors frequently herd, escalating asset bubbles and volatility. Retail and institutional investors are both impacted by this behaviour; for example, CEOs who are overconfident tend to undertake hazardous purchases (Malmendier and Tate, 2005). According to Shiller (2000) and De Bondt and Thaler (1985), these traders cause bubbles to burst by pushing prices away from fundamentals. Additionally, Baker and Wurgler (2006) connected rising volatility with investor sentiment, which resulted in capital misallocation and poor economic performance.

An instance in which speculative bubbles facilitate analysis of overconfidence from the perspective of macroeconomy, where individual biases pose as a source of risk on the systemic level. One instance is Shiller (2000) research work done on the dot-com bubble, which indicated excessive capital flows due to group overconfidence in technology stock investment. Brunnermeier's (2009) study on the cause of the 2008 financial crisis showed that group overconfidence in mortgage-based securities made banks and other investors ignore the systemic risk existing in the housing sector. These events illustrate the harmful consequences of overconfidence since speculative bubbles tend to experience sudden, drastic corrections affecting global markets. The latest studies on cryptocurrency markets reveal that overconfidence endures in new asset classes. For example, Hasso, Pelster, and Breitmayer (2020) demonstrate the following: The overconfidence of retail investors is one key characteristic that fuels speculation and extreme volatility in these markets. They believe the price of assets such as Bitcoin will never fall; it will just keep growing.

Researchers have proposed several interventions to mitigate the adverse effects of overconfidence. Thaler and Sunstein's 2008 work on "nudging" further shows that behavioral interventions, such as financial education programs, may aid investors in identifying and eliminating biases. Advocates of behavioral finance argue that financial education programs that address cognitive biases minimize excessive trading and result in more balanced investment strategies. Besides, regulatory policies that foster greater transparency and accountability among financial institutions have also been proposed as mechanisms of controlling the institutional effects of overconfidence, especially within corporate executives and fund managers. In summary, all these studies show that despite the persistence of overconfidence in finance, behavioral understanding and regulatory approaches can limit its influence on financial markets.

CASE STUDIES:EXAMPLES OF OVERCONFIDENCE IN FINANCIAL CRISES

The 2008 Global Financial Crisis

The 2008 Global Financial Crisis, for instance, is considered the most profound financial meltdown within recent years, and excessive overconfidence played a role in how it unfolded. In fact, within those years just before the meltdown, overconfidentness in regards to banks' and institutions' perception in the housing market and Mortgage-Backed Securities was largely dependent on the conviction that there would never be any decline of house prices. This assumption was institutional overconfidence, because senior executives, analysts, and risk managers in the industry assumed that they had a relatively good understanding of the market while ignoring early warning signals about a potential downturn.

Development of Overconfidence

The roots of the crisis lay in the complex financial innovations of MBSs and CDOs that enabled banks to package together home loans, including very risky subprime mortgages, and sell them as investment opportunities. Executives and analysts at

Wall Street were too sanguine about the models that led to low predicted default rates for even the borrowers with histories of poor credit. The reliance on these models, developed by quantitative analysts who believed they had precisely measured risk, created an illusion of security. Managers trusted that these sophisticated financial products would yield consistent returns with minimal risk, assuming that the prices of houses would always go up. This false confidence in risk assessment was followed by significant financial exposure to subprime mortgages.

The Role of Rating Agencies

Rating agencies were among those that fueled this overconfidence through their high credit ratings on MBS and CDOs, reflecting their overconfidence in the housing market. The high rating further spur demand among the investors due to institutional investors' dependence on assessments of rating agencies through pension funds, hedge funds, and insurance companies. The assumption was so deeply ingrained that few questioned the models or the validity of these ratings. The collective overconfidence led to a cascade of investments in increasingly risky mortgage securities.

Consequences of Overconfidence

When housing prices started to decline and mortgage defaults rose, the fragility of these securities became evident. Thus, the overconfident notion of market stability and this new financial innovation masked the true risk that led to massive loss in the entire financial sector. In such a scenario, big institutions like Lehman Brothers crashed, while others such as AIG and Citigroup ran into a liquidity crisis. They were eventually rescued by the government. In the end, it finally culminated into the kind of unemployment unprecedented along with the loss of household wealth and a very long world recession. This case emphasizes how overconfidence at the institutional level, amplified by reliance on complex financial models and trusted ratings, can have catastrophic implications for the financial system and the general economy.

The GameStop Stock Surge

This phenomenon is more recently typified by the stock price ramp at GameStop that appeared at the start of 2021, clearly indicating how overconfidence driven through social media among individual investors can drive great volatility in the market. Discussion threads at Reddit's "WallStreetBets" prompted mostly individual investors to force a price of a collapsing video game retailer GameStop to levels much higher than their intrinsic value. This was spurred on by a mix of reasons, including mutual animus toward institutional investors, excessive confidence in the group's ability to bring about change, and the attraction of making money from a "short squeeze" against Wall Street hedge funds.

The Mechanism of Overconfidence

The retail investors who found themselves on the GameStop surge believed they could somehow outsmart large hedge funds who had shorted the stock. This was rooted in the over-placement bias--investors perceived themselves superior to institutional traders, that by banding together they could influence market dynamics and their way. Retailers' collective overconfidence fuelled by the belief of being able to "beat" Wall Street at their own game, ignoring all risks involved in highly speculative, volatile trading.

Amplification on Social Media

Social media came in handy for the influencers on Reddit and Twitter to amplify such overconfidence. From this commotion, supporters emerged to back GameStop; they even crafted a narrative that described the trade as an act of symbolic triumph over the institutional investors. Comments even encouraged retail investors to stay put and thus have "diamond hands," as the community describes it – holding stocks at fluctuating prices. This led to a sort of herd mentality, a self-reinforcing cycle, as the traders' beliefs were increasingly reinforced as prices continued to advance; more participants joined this movement.

Market Impact and Takeaways

GameStop stock rose from under $20 to over $400 in weeks, thus resulting in many hedge funds taking the worst financial hits as they had shorted the same while some retail investors stood to gain highly. However, when the price eventually collapsed, the late entrants were all but washed away by a wave of heavy losses since the speculative bubble had burst. What happened with GameStop indicated how overconfidence in the abilities of the retail investors and social influence could powerfully be in one direction, but the phenomenon equally highlighted the risks of sentiment-driven speculative trading as against fundamental-based trade. This reminds us all that overconfidence, particularly in the aftermath of social media, creates unsustainable market conditions that eventually erupt into great volatility.

Dot-Com Bubble and Cryptocurrency Surges

Recent evidence includes the spectacular blowout of the late 1990s dot-com bubble and more current surges in cryptocurrencies: these incidents clearly highlight that investor overconfidence driven by trust in revolutionising technologies leads inevitably to the un-sustainability of inflation of asset prices accompanied by nasty market corrections later.

Dot-Com Bubble (1995–2000)

Massive investor confidence regarding Internet-based companies catapulted fuelled the speculative rise in the dot com bubble. Investors thought the Internet would change industries. It was going to be one of those things that is going to grow companies exponentially and give you extraordinary returns. Over-optimism then led to capital pouring into tech stocks-many of them had little revenue, no proven business models, and high cash burn rates. Others such as Pets.com and Webvan were able to attract millions of dollars in investments because they were not profitable, given that investors were ignoring the traditional metrics of financial soundness, imagining that these companies would win their markets.

As it inflated, the stock of tech companies became unsustainable and reached the stratospheric levels. By 2000, the Nasdaq Composite index, which comprises lots of tech stocks, increased more than threefold in some years. However, when it was realized that most of these companies were not going to be profitable, investor confidence collapsed. The bubble burst, and there was a sharp market decline, wiping out about $5 trillion in market value. The dot-com bubble is an example of over-optimism, whereby investors overestimated the near-term prospects of new technologies, throwing caution to the wind for speculative gains.

Cryptocurrency Soars (2017 and 2021)

Above all, Bitcoin and other cryptocurrencies have experienced numerous speculative peaks. In 2017, the price of Bitcoin started from below $1,000 and soared to about $20,000. The surge was due to universal expectation that it would turn out to be “digital gold” and an alternative for the financial system in place. But again, like with the dot-com bubble, there was much hype and even speculation into the Bitcoin bubble since most investors did not know what Bitcoin was nor what it could and couldn't do, so investors poured in speculatively mainly on hype and over-exuberance of its value into the future. It thus hit a rock-bottom at about

$3,000 in 2018 following price correction on issues of regulation and profit taking from the early investors that gave a heavy loss for the latecomers.

The boom occurred in 2021, where Bitcoin peaked over $60,000 for the first time in its history. Again, the boom was led by retail investors who believed that Bitcoins and other digital assets were going to revolutionize the financial system. Social media influences and online forums fueled it further. Many retail investors, often not understanding any technology and not being keen on risks, invested hundreds of millions in different cryptocurrencies.

The dangers of collective over-confidence are now very evident when prices in the crypto market, just like the real ones, plummet just as readily as they surge. Exposed, naive investors feel the pain.

Lessons from Both Bubbles

Dot-com and cryptocurrency bubbles are some of the best examples of overconfidence in speculative markets, especially for new technologies. Typically, investors believe they are on the forefront of revolutionary change, so much so that they end up overvaluing their investment and paying little heed to traditional valuation metrics. Sharp corrections when the expected growth fails to materialize end up financially devastating investors who entered at the peak. Such cases illustrate the dangers of group over-optimism, especially in speculative asset classes in which fundamentals are vague or hard to evaluate.

MACRO-ECONOMIC RAMIFICATIONS OF OVERCONFIDENCE

Formation of Asset Bubbles

At the heart of asset bubbles is overconfidence: price crosses the level above and beyond intrinsic or fundamental value. Assets such as stocks, real estate, or commodities are then overpriced. This often occurs in a scenario where investors start expecting that an asset's price will continue rising eternally, eliminating all the possible risks brought about by optimistic and positive feedback through increased prices. A stage like this can make collective overconfidence run into a feedback loop where, high asset prices continue to fuel that overconfidence even further, thus increasing even more demand which, in turn, pushes the prices up and up. And, as investors continue to bet on returns that are unrealistically high, prices are driven to levels that no longer make sense.

One such classic case of the same dynamics is the U.S. housing market boom that occurred in early 2000. Overconfident views regarding the stability and rise in housing prices made all financial institutions, individual investors, and even the regulators collectively ignore such fundamental risks. Housing price increases never ended, but the investors took it for granted; therefore, giving birth to high-risk mortgage products like subprime loans. In view of this low risk perception for the high-risk mortgages, the financial institutions began to overstretch themselves in the making and selling of these mortgages as securities in the market. Thus, the amplification of the housing bubble.

Distortion of Economic Indicators and Investor Expectations

One of the most severe macroeconomic consequences arising from these overconfidence-driven bubbles is through distorting the economic metrics. With the mushrooming asset prices, those traditional measures attributed to the economy will turn unrepresentative in situations where the P/E ratios shoot up too high, property prices too high, and the LTVs sky rocketing, thereby making the economy look good on paper, but wrong decisions for the investors and wrong policy choices by authorities for the economy.

At the peak of the bubble, there will exist the "wealth effect" phenomenon in that people and businesses are getting wealthy as a result of escalating asset prices and hence may be compelled to spend more. Inflated spending increases seemingly misleading economic growth numbers, such as GDP even if the actual value is supported by no real economic productivity. As more consumer spending could be supported by the supposed increased wealth temporarily buoying up figures for economic growth, mainly proved unsustainable, being far more speculative than any real fundamental.

Consequences of Bubble Bursts: Liquidity, Capital Costs, and Economic Downturns

The inevitable bursting of a bubble driven by overconfidence would have severe and widespread consequences. A chain reaction of financial crises has been initiated by a sharp decline in asset prices triggered by the sudden evaporation of market liquidity. That is to say, liquid assets can be bought and sold with little or no drastic movement in price when liquidity dries up with investors getting rid of their devaluing assets. This massive sell-off causes a sharp fall in the asset values while, in most cases, the investors do not get willing buyers and hence leads to a market freeze. Without liquidity, financial institutions face dilemmas when they have to meet their obligations, and this ultimately leads to broader market disruptions.

Another aspect of a bursting asset price bubble is the dramatic rise in the cost of capital. Given the falling asset prices and growing financial uncertainty, lenders grow more timid and squeeze credit with interest rates that will more than pay for the risks perceived to be greater now, which they are assuming. The borrowers who had been particularly reliant on low-cost debt during the bubble were no longer able to acquire capital at favorable rates. Higher capital costs amount to a direct consequence on business and consumption life, which reflects on investments hence slowing down economic growth and loan defaults.

This regarding the most representative case of the one witnessed in the year 2008 as a result of the financial crisis over overconfidence about the liquidity and the costs of capital. A credit crunch resulted upon bursting the housing bubble from when mortgage-backed securities lost values and all other allied financial products. Severely indebted, those financial institutions which were facing bankruptcies experienced huge liquidity shocks that went to massive bankruptcy situations and bailouts, in return tightening credit became pretty expensive and increased heavily raising the cost of borrowings, huddling the spending of business investments. The impact of both liquidity shortages as well as increased capital costs led to prolonged economic recession, hence generalizing the wide ramification of over-confidence on macroeconomic stability.

The Need for Macro-Prudential Measures to Address Overconfidence

Thus, systemic risk through overconfidence should also be addressed with appropriate measures of macro-prudentiality that can dampen this risk. The regulators and financial policymakers can take the critical monitoring role of the indicators for the speculative bubbles such as steep asset price rises and extremely high leverage, then interfere in the case of severe risk-taking. Measures include strict capital requirements for financial institutions, higher risk disclosures for investments perceived to carry higher risks, and stricter leverage ratios in the context of asset price inflation.

Financial institutions can also apply risk assessment tools based on data analytics to detect overconfident trading patterns. Predictive models based on historical data can alert regulators and institutions to emerging bubbles, thus allowing them to take preventive action before systemic risks escalate. When combined with investor education programs that focus on cognitive biases, policymakers can encourage more responsible behavior and reduce the likelihood of overconfidence-driven economic disruptions.

CONCEPTUAL DEVELOPMENT

1. Overconfidence Bias and Trading Behavior
    - **Argument**: Overconfidence bias leads investors to overestimate their predictive abilities and underestimate associated risks, often resulting in increased trading frequency and suboptimal financial performance.
    - **Explanation**: Overconfidence bias is particularly pervasive among retail investors who frequently overvalue their stock-picking abilities. The seminal study by Barber and Odean (2000) demonstrates that overconfident investors tend to engage in excessive trading, erroneously believing they possess insights superior to the market. This behavior, however, yields higher transaction costs, poorer returns, and often disregards diversification principles—exposing portfolios to greater risk.
    - **Example**: Barber and Odean's study on trading behavior using data from a large brokerage firm (1991–1997) revealed that frequent traders underperformed less active investors by 6.5% annually. Investors often fell into a cycle of "success-reinforced" confidence where initial profitable trades increased self-assurance, driving more frequent, riskier trades. The study highlighted that while these investors believed they could "beat the market," their overall returns declined due to cumulative transaction costs and increased exposure to volatility.
    - **Implications**: Financial advisors could apply these insights to discourage clients from excessive trading by educating them on the financial costs of frequent trades and the inherent unpredictability of market trends. Advisors might recommend structured, long-term strategies that focus on diversification and risk management rather than trying to consistently outperform the market.
2. Impact of Overconfidence on Market Volatility
    - **Argument**: Overconfidence contributes significantly to market volatility by fueling speculative bubbles and price distortions, often leading to market corrections with widespread financial consequences.
    - **Explanation**: When overconfidence permeates market sentiment, speculative bubbles emerge as asset prices soar beyond fundamental values, driven by collective optimism rather than rational investment principles. Robert Shiller's concept of "irrational exuberance" (2000) addresses how overconfident expectations can inflate asset bubbles, heightening volatility and making markets susceptible to abrupt corrections once prices realign with intrinsic values.
    - **Example**: The dot-com bubble in the late 1990s illustrates how overconfidence in the tech sector fueled price escalation well above sus-

tainable levels. Investors, influenced by high valuations and optimistic media narratives, overlooked traditional valuation metrics, leading to unprecedented price-to-earnings (P/E) ratios among tech stocks. When reality undercut expectations in 2000, the bubble burst, leading to a 78% drop in the NASDAQ index over two years, erasing trillions in market value.

- **Implications**: Understanding overconfidence's role in volatility can guide policymakers and financial institutions to adopt regulatory measures aimed at tempering speculative excesses. For instance, circuit breakers or margin limitations can prevent extreme swings in trading, fostering a more stable environment by slowing down the feedback loop of overconfidence-driven speculation.

3. Professional Overconfidence Among Fund Managers and Executives
   - **Argument**: Even experienced professionals, including fund managers and corporate executives, are vulnerable to overconfidence, which can lead to value-destructive investment and strategic decisions.
   - **Explanation**: Overconfidence is not confined to retail investors; it also impacts seasoned professionals whose decisions carry significant financial implications. Malmendier and Tate (2005) examined how overconfident CEOs are more likely to pursue mergers and acquisitions (M&As) at a premium, often to the detriment of shareholder value. This behavior stems from the conviction that their judgment can create synergies or market advantages, despite evidence that many acquisitions fail to meet anticipated outcomes.
   - **Example**: The acquisition of ABN AMRO by the Royal Bank of Scotland (RBS) in 2007 exemplifies executive overconfidence. Sir Fred Goodwin, then CEO of RBS, led a consortium to acquire ABN AMRO for $100 billion, largely financed by debt, confident of the merger's synergistic potential. The financial crisis hit soon after, rendering ABN's assets liabilities and leaving RBS on the brink of collapse, necessitating a £45 billion government bailout. The miscalculation, fueled by Goodwin's overconfidence, is often cited as one of the most value-destructive acquisitions in corporate history.
   - **Implications**: Recognizing overconfidence among corporate executives can lead to enhanced governance practices. Corporate boards could implement more rigorous oversight and encourage independent evaluations of major strategic decisions. Emphasizing data-driven analyses over individual intuition may help mitigate the risks associated with executive overconfidence in high-stakes corporate ventures.
4. Macro-Economic Ramifications of Overconfidence

- **Argument**: At a macro level, widespread overconfidence among investors contributes to systemic financial risks, especially during speculative bubbles and subsequent crashes.
- **Explanation**: When overconfidence becomes widespread, it can contribute to financial instability, potentially triggering economic downturns. Brunnermeier and Nagel (2004) explain that excessive optimism across financial markets creates systemic risks as overconfident investors pour capital into speculative assets. The 2007–2008 financial crisis, for example, demonstrated how collective overconfidence in housing markets and complex financial instruments increased asset valuations and liquidity in the short term but led to a severe economic contraction once the bubble burst.
- **Example**: The U.S. housing bubble preceding the 2008 crisis epitomizes systemic overconfidence. Lenders, investors, and consumers alike bought into the belief that housing prices would perpetually rise. Mortgage-backed securities (MBS) and collateralized debt obligations (CDOs) became wildly popular investment vehicles. However, once housing prices fell, these instruments became worthless, triggering massive defaults. The ensuing liquidity crisis brought about a near-global recession.
- **Implications**: To reduce systemic risks stemming from overconfidence, regulators could institute macroprudential measures such as stress testing, countercyclical capital buffers, and enhanced risk disclosures. These practices could identify potential vulnerabilities in financial institutions and prevent the unchecked expansion of speculative bubbles, thereby stabilizing the broader economic environment.

5. Role of Technology in Managing Overconfidence
    - **Argument**: Advanced technologies like AI and machine learning (ML) present opportunities to identify and mitigate overconfidence in real time, improving market stability.
    - **Explanation**: AI and machine learning (ML) can analyze massive datasets and detect patterns indicative of overconfidence, offering tools for preemptively identifying risky behavior. By evaluating factors like trade volume spikes, optimistic earnings forecasts, and aggressive investment behaviors, AI can provide actionable insights to regulators and financial firms. Studies in behavioral finance support AI's utility in flagging irrational patterns, allowing institutions to temper speculative tendencies before they escalate.
    - **Example**: JP Morgan employs AI algorithms in monitoring trading activity and generating real-time risk assessments. The bank's AI systems

help assess when trades deviate from standard risk parameters, acting as a safeguard against the influence of cognitive biases. Through early identification of risk patterns, JP Morgan aims to limit excessive trading and encourage more informed, rational decisions by its traders.

- **Implications**: Integrating AI and ML tools in trading and regulatory oversight can significantly mitigate the impact of overconfidence in financial markets. By preemptively identifying speculative excesses, AI-driven monitoring can enable more rational market behavior and prompt regulatory responses, potentially reducing the frequency of asset bubbles and the severity of corrections.

6. Ethical Considerations in Financial Decision-Making
    - **Argument**: Addressing overconfidence is crucial not only for economic stability but also for upholding ethical standards in the financial profession.
    - **Explanation**: Overconfidence bias can cause financial professionals to act contrary to their fiduciary duties, exposing clients to unnecessary risks and potentially leading to conflicts of interest. Ethical training, combined with self-awareness practices, can help professionals recognize and mitigate overconfidence, ensuring that they prioritize client interests and uphold ethical standards. Behavioral finance research underscores the need for ethical education to foster accountability and humility within financial institutions.
    - **Example**: The Wells Fargo cross-selling scandal (2016) highlights how unchecked overconfidence can lead to unethical behavior. Executives, overconfident in their growth projections and the soundness of their aggressive sales tactics, pressured employees to meet unattainable sales targets. This led to the creation of millions of unauthorized customer accounts, resulting in a significant ethical breach and reputational damage for the bank.
    - **Implications**: Embedding a culture of accountability, transparency, and ethical responsibility within financial institutions can counterbalance overconfidence and its associated risks. Regular ethical training and emphasizing client-centric decision-making are essential steps in building trust within the financial sector and ensuring that professional conduct aligns with fiduciary responsibilities.

COMPARATIVE ANALYSIS OF OVERCONFIDENCE ACROSS FINANCIAL MARKETS

Stock Markets: Overconfidence and Trading Frequency

In stock markets, overconfidence is frequently observed among individual and institutional investors alike. Overconfident investors often overestimate their abilities to forecast market movements, leading to excessive trading and insufficient attention to broader economic indicators or long-term strategies. This behavior intensifies volatility, particularly in bull and bear markets, where overconfident investors may overreact to short-term information and ignore signals that would encourage caution or restraint.

Explanation: Overconfidence in stock markets typically arises when investors experience short-term success, reinforcing their belief in superior predictive skills. This bias encourages frequent trading as investors become more willing to make riskier bets, assuming their insights will yield profitable outcomes. Barber and Odean's (2000) research illustrates that overconfident traders engage in higher trading volumes, accruing transaction costs that erode net returns. The cost of these transactions, coupled with a lack of diversification, often results in underperformance compared to investors who adopt more disciplined, long-term approaches.

Case Study: The dot-com bubble of the late 1990s exemplifies how overconfidence drove market behavior. Many investors believed they could identify "winning" internet stocks and overlooked fundamental valuations, leading to inflated prices across the tech sector. When reality eventually contradicted expectations, markets corrected sharply, eroding investor confidence and wiping out billions in market value. This instance highlights how overconfidence-driven trading can amplify bubbles and subsequent busts in stock markets, particularly when driven by speculative enthusiasm rather than intrinsic valuation.

Implications: Recognizing overconfidence in stock markets calls for a more cautious, structured approach to trading and investment decisions. Financial advisors and institutional investors may benefit from incorporating behavioral insights into investment strategies, emphasizing diversification and a long-term focus to counteract the propensity for overtrading. Additionally, educating retail investors on the risks associated with frequent trading could mitigate some of the adverse effects of overconfidence in stock markets.

Cryptocurrency Markets: Overconfidence and Speculative Bubbles

Cryptocurrency markets are particularly susceptible to overconfidence due to their novelty, minimal regulatory oversight, and extreme volatility. The allure of rapid wealth creation in cryptocurrencies often attracts a specific type of investor—one who is highly optimistic about quick returns and willing to take on substantial risks. This environment cultivates overconfidence, where investors frequently underestimate potential downsides and ignore the intrinsic uncertainties associated with unregulated digital assets.

Explanation: Cryptocurrency investors are often driven by a blend of enthusiasm and a "fear of missing out" (FOMO), spurred by media hype and anecdotes of significant returns. Many lack comprehensive knowledge of cryptocurrency mechanics and are swayed by price trends rather than intrinsic value, leading them to overestimate their understanding of the market. Overconfident investors in cryptocurrencies may believe they can time market entry and exits, making speculative investments without a sound understanding of blockchain technology or the regulatory risks involved. This dynamic is reinforced by the relative youth and lack of formal structure in the market, where valuations can be driven more by hype cycles than by fundamentals.

Case Study: The 2017 Bitcoin bubble is a prime example of overconfidence in cryptocurrency markets. Bitcoin's price increased by nearly 2,000% within the year, fueled largely by optimistic projections and media coverage. Many new, unseasoned investors entered the market, confident that Bitcoin's value would continue rising indefinitely. When demand stalled and regulatory concerns intensified, Bitcoin's price fell dramatically, resulting in steep losses for many retail investors. This bubble underscores how overconfidence in cryptocurrency markets can create volatility and significant financial harm, particularly for less-informed investors who enter during periods of intense market enthusiasm.

Implications: To address the effects of overconfidence in cryptocurrency markets, regulators could introduce frameworks to enhance investor protection, such as mandatory risk disclosures and educational requirements for new investors. Financial institutions might also develop valuation models for cryptocurrencies that can inform investor decision-making, helping them understand the risks inherent in these assets. Additionally, platforms could provide real-time risk assessments to caution investors against overexposure to highly volatile assets, fostering a more balanced approach to crypto trading.

Real Estate Markets: Overconfidence and Housing Booms

In real estate markets, overconfidence often surfaces during housing booms, as investors and homeowners assume property values will continue to rise indefinitely. This belief can lead to over-leveraging and speculative purchases, as well as a general underestimation of the risks associated with real estate investment. The tangible nature of real estate as an asset, combined with a perception of stability, often fuels a belief that it is immune to the volatility seen in other financial markets.

Explanation: In real estate, overconfidence is closely linked with the concept of "price momentum"—the idea that asset prices will continue their current trajectory. This belief leads to speculative purchases, where investors buy properties with the sole intention of selling at a profit as prices rise. During housing booms, overconfident investors frequently rely on accessible credit and low interest rates to leverage their investments, often assuming they will be able to refinance or sell the property at a higher price. When investors rely too heavily on borrowed funds and expect perpetual price appreciation, they expose themselves to substantial risk. This overconfidence also affects banks and lenders, who may become overly optimistic in their lending practices, assuming property values will cover the risks of default.

Case Study: The 2008 U.S. housing bubble exemplifies the dangers of overconfidence in real estate. Leading up to the crisis, both individual investors and institutional lenders believed that housing prices would continue to appreciate, even as lending standards loosened. Financial products like mortgage-backed securities (MBS) and collateralized debt obligations (CDOs) proliferated, enabling and fueling speculative investments by allowing subprime borrowers to access credit. When housing prices declined, defaults increased, exposing the fragility of the financial system. The crisis had severe economic impacts globally, illustrating how overconfidence-driven lending and investment in real estate can trigger widespread financial instability.

Implications: Addressing overconfidence in real estate markets requires stricter lending standards, particularly during periods of rapid price appreciation. Regulators can implement measures such as "stress testing" for banks and higher capital requirements for mortgage lending to reduce the risk of systemic overconfidence. Financial education initiatives that emphasize the risks of leveraged investments in real estate can also help individual investors make more informed decisions. Policymakers might also consider cyclical adjustments to loan-to-value (LTV) ratios and interest rates to prevent over-leveraging during housing booms.

IMPLICATION AND FUTURE RESEARCH

1. Implications for Financial Stability

Investor Education Programs and Financial Stability

The pervasive nature of the impact of overconfidence on trading behavior calls for measures of financial stability, including focused education of investors. Overconfident investors will more often than not engage in excessive trading, speculation, and overleveraging-the very behaviors that are most pronounced when market bubbles are brewing. Education programs that teach the need for investor education regarding their own cognitive biases, such as overconfidence, will foster more restrained long-term investment styles.

Through structured learning, investors can be enlightened on the risks of excessive trading and speculative practices. For example, these courses may include modules on the costs of high trading volumes, pitfalls of inadequate diversification, and how overconfident decision-making leads to poor outcomes because it neglects market fundamentals. Illustrate the potential consequences of overconfidence in practice using case studies of historical financial bubbles, such as the dot-com bubble or cryptocurrency surges. Expose investors to data on transaction costs and portfolio performance in illustrations showing how overconfident trading behaviors can lose money directly for a manager.

Institutional Measures and Policy Initiatives

Beyond education for individual investors, institutions can play a more significant role in promoting market stability by using detecting and assessing overconfident trading patterns. Institutions would possibly use data analytics tools to detect high-risk overconfidence behaviors such as the rate of speculative trades as well as concentrated investment behavior. Such monitoring systems provide instant feedback to investors as they are able to self-correct before major loss or market disruption occurs.

Policy measures could also support this by creating regulatory standards, which discourage excessive speculation, for example. Regulatory agencies may consider putting limits to high-frequency trading or setting mandatory risk disclosures on particularly volatile or unregulated asset classes. These frameworks are believed to protect both retail and institutional investors by reducing collective overconfidence from driving the markets into unstable territory. By such means, regulators can hope for stability in financial markets, checking excessive overconfidence and dubious behavior, thus reducing volatility as well as investment losses for stakeholders.

2. Directions for Future Research

Exploring Technology-Driven Solutions for Overconfidence Mitigation

As technology continues to change financial markets, future research may be on how technological interventions, especially AI and ML, can reduce overconfidence. These technologies can analyze vast data streams to identify patterns indicative of overconfident behavior, such as unusually optimistic trading strategies or consistent risk-taking. The research in this area can focus on the effectiveness of AI-driven systems in identifying early warning signs of market speculation and overconfident trading patterns.

Another area of research could be to test the AI and ML capabilities in high-frequency trading environments. High frequency trading platforms are typically attracting overconfident traders who depend on algorithms for quick returns. Real-time alerts on AI systems can cut down the number of impulsive, high-risk trades and lead to more planned decisions. It is feasible to research the effectiveness of such AI-based solutions in curbing market bubbles and creating a safer environment in HFT, thereby perhaps changing the dynamics of markets so that cognitive biases have as small an impact as possible.

Long-Term Impact of Educational Programs on Investor Behavior

Future work could further explore long-term impacts of investor education programs on awareness of cognitive biases, especially overconfidence. For instance, researchers might ask if training investors in recognition and reduction of overconfidence imparts permanent changes in trading behavior-including lower volumes of trades, increased diversification, and improved portfolio outcomes. Questions like these could be answered through longitudinal studies which would track investors over time after exposure to these programs comparing the decision-making patterns of those investors to a control group.

These may potentially provide insight into the depth at which the bias-awareness training holds a lasting influence on moderating excessive confident trading; this particularly extends to such high-risk trading environments such as day trading and other speculative asset markets. Long-term studies regarding retention of bias-specific information, its interaction with behavior and other behavioral changes might even help indicate the optimal ways in formats, contents, and also delivery systems in such teaching programs. These findings would serve to improve investor education programs, hence contributing to the adoption of more careful and informed approaches toward complicated financial markets by investors.

Governance Frameworks and Overconfidence in Professional Settings

Overconfidence is not limited to the individual retail investor but plays a significant role in professional settings as well, influencing the decisions of fund managers, corporate executives, and financial analysts. Future research could explore how robust governance frameworks can counterbalance overconfidence among these professionals whose decisions have far-reaching implications for organizations and shareholders. For instance, governance measures such as board oversight, periodic performance reviews, and independent risk assessments can provide checks and balances to mitigate overconfident decision-making.

Studies in this field could explore how various oversight practices impact major strategic choices, such as mergers and acquisitions, capital distribution, and financial projections. Future research on how, for instance, governance structures require additional approvals for significant transactions can affect overconfidence-driven actions can inform best practices for boards and management teams. These insights could help a company lead to a better-balanced decision-making culture, thereby reducing the chances of an overconfident leadership ending up destroying values.

Developing Predictive Models for Market-Wide Overconfidence Detection

Understanding collective overconfidence at the macroeconomic level is important for identifying early signs of market-wide speculative bubbles. Future research can be oriented toward developing predictive models to analyze investor sentiment, trading volumes, and asset valuations to detect signs of collective overconfidence. These models can be calibrated to provide early warnings when asset prices are driven more by sentiment and speculation than by intrinsic value, thereby allowing for timely regulatory intervention.

Predictive models might actually use the market's metrics, such as trading frequency and leverage ratios and price/earnings multiples, among many other things, to ascertain just how far into the overconfident territory that level swings. These will be of enormous value not only for policymakers but even for central banks since these will then be taken on board as they make a decision with regard to interest rate policies and so on and so forth, liquidity provisions or a regulatory response to deflate overheated markets. Development and improvement in these predictive instruments during the course of further research might add to the ability to check the emergence and influence of overconfidence-based market bubbles.

Ethical Standards and Overconfidence in Financial Decision-Making

Overconfidence raises crucial ethical concerns in the financial sector. The fiduciary responsibilities of fund managers, financial advisors, and corporate heads are to exercise prudent decisions that protect the interests of clients, stakeholders, and the larger market. This study can focus on how ethics training might affect overconfident decisions, particularly in the financial sector, which makes such high-risk decisions. Personal biases may be developed through ethics training to foster a culture of responsibility and accountability in financial organizations.

Further research could expand on the variations in the ethical framework—such as humility, client-centric or fiduciary-based—and how such differences influence the overconfidence in professional practices. The study would prove to be particularly relevant whenever professionals have to make choices that entail a high amount of risk, such as leveraged investments, significant mergers, or aggressive growth policies. Training in ethics can neutralize the overconfident tendencies of individuals by influencing responsible decisions and a climate of prudence and accountability in finance.

CONCLUSION

This chapter has undertaken a comprehensive review of overconfidence in financial markets and how the same cognitive bias impacts individual behavior, professional decision-making, and the economy at large. Overconfidence is that attitude where an individual has an overconfidence belief in their own skills for predicting and deciding matters. Overconfidence has been found to be one of the most influential behavioral factors shaping market activity. Despite the general awareness of potential pitfalls, overconfidence remains a deeply rooted and pervasive bias at the level of low as well as high-level investors. Through empirical studies, case studies, and technological interventions, this chapter throws emphasis on the multi-dimensional approach that will help the incidence of overconfidence at the advantage of more sustainable and stable financial systems.

Overconfidence is manifested primarily through excessive trading and risk-taking by individual investors. As discussed, overconfident investors tend to trade frequently, mistakenly believing in their ability to "beat the market." Consistent research has shown that frequent trading often results in lower net returns, increased transaction costs, and higher exposure to market volatility. This pattern of behavior is particularly worrisome in the context of asset bubbles, where collective overconfidence among individual and institutional investors can inflate asset prices far beyond their intrinsic values. There is several historical examples of bubbles-including the dot-com one that led to the recent housing market bubble precipitating the 2008 financial crisis-overconfidence plays central role in driving unsustainable dynamics leading to sharp corrections in economies.

Over and above individual investors, over-confidence impacts professional actors in finance markets including fund managers and their analysts as well as other corporate executives. These professionals are not immune to the cognitive bias of overconfidence, despite their availability of advanced analytical tools and data. Overconfident fund managers often engage in aggressive trading strategies, making concentrated bets and underestimating the associated risks. In a similar manner, an overconfident CEO can pursue ambitious mergers and acquisitions, believing in the ability to generate synergies and create shareholder value. However, research has indicated that these decisions often are disappointing, including unsuccessful M&As and overly leveraged positions that negatively affect shareholder interests. The chapter highlighted the importance of governance structures that would have oversight and accountability to counteract overconfidence in professional decision-making, with data-driven assessments and more robust board oversight as effective measures.

At a macroeconomic level, overconfidence introduces systemic risks with far-reaching consequences. Widespread overconfidence sentiment helps fuel the formation of speculative bubbles that destabilize entire financial systems. Several actors, including the individual, the financial institution, and the regulator, came to converge in overconfidence that culminated in the collapse of housing markets followed by a global recession during 2008. This crisis depth underlined the interdependence of financial markets and the economy, showing how unchecked overconfidence can create ripple effects in employment, consumer confidence, and economic growth. Therefore, overconfidence is not only an improvement in individual decision-making but also a key component of macro-prudential stability.

The chapter further underlined the importance of ethical considerations in dealing with overconfidence within financial institutions. Professionals in finance, such as fund managers, advisors, and corporate executives, are expected to act responsibly in the best interest of the clients and stakeholders. Overconfidence blurs judgment and may lead to decisions that weigh short-term gains over long-term stability, usually against the interests of the client and the health of the market. The development of a culture of humility, accountability, and ethical responsibility is important in reducing the impact of overconfidence. Regular programs of ethical training may help professionals recognize their biases and become more prudent, client-centered professionals. Such insights are not only valuable but this chapter also provides several directions for future research that can lead to further investigation of the impact of overconfidence and more effective interventions that can be developed. Future research could be based on long-term impacts of investor education programs related to cognitive biases, changes that these programs induce in trading behavior, risk acceptance, and portfolio performance. In a similar way, the study on AI and ML applications could be carried out on the further development of algorithms identifying and countering overconfidence in various trading conditions, their effectiveness, and ethical considerations. Researches into governance frameworks and professional ethical standards may shed light on the role of oversight mechanisms and organizational culture in reducing the incidence of overconfident decision-making.

REFERENCES

Barber, B. M., & Odean, T. (2000). Trading is hazardous to your wealth: The common stock investment performance of individual investors. *The Journal of Finance*, 55(2), 773–806. DOI: 10.1111/0022-1082.00226

Barber, B. M., & Odean, T. (2001). Boys will be boys: Gender, overconfidence, and common stock investment. *The Quarterly Journal of Economics*, 116(1), 261–292. DOI: 10.1162/003355301556400

Barberis, N., & Thaler, R. (2003). A survey of behavioral finance. In *Handbook of the Economics of Finance* (pp. 1053–1128). Elsevier.

Biais, B., Hilton, D., Mazurier, K., & Pouget, S. (2005). Judgmental overconfidence, self-monitoring, and trading performance in an experimental financial market. *The Review of Economic Studies*, 72(2), 287–312. DOI: 10.1111/j.1467-937X.2005.00333.x

Brunnermeier, M. K. (2009). Deciphering the liquidity and credit crunch 2007-2008. *The Journal of Economic Perspectives*, 23(1), 77–100. DOI: 10.1257/jep.23.1.77

De Bondt, W. F., & Thaler, R. H. (1985). Does the stock market overreact? *The Journal of Finance*, 40(3), 793–805. DOI: 10.1111/j.1540-6261.1985.tb05004.x

Hasso, T., Pelster, M., & Breitmayer, B. (2020). Who trades cryptocurrencies, how do they trade it, and how do their trades affect the cryptocurrency market? *Journal of International Financial Markets, Institutions and Money*, 65, 101–141.

Hilary, G., & Menzly, L. (2006). Does past success lead analysts to become overconfident? *Management Science*, 52(4), 489–500. DOI: 10.1287/mnsc.1050.0485

Kahneman, D., & Tversky, A. (1979). Prospect theory: An analysis of decision under risk. *Econometrica*, 47(2), 263–291. DOI: 10.2307/1914185

Malmendier, U., & Tate, G. (2005). CEO overconfidence and corporate investment. *The Journal of Finance*, 60(6), 2661–2700. DOI: 10.1111/j.1540-6261.2005.00813.x

Moore, D. A., & Healy, P. J. (2008). The trouble with overconfidence. *Psychological Review*, 115(2), 502–517. DOI: 10.1037/0033-295X.115.2.502 PMID: 18426301

Shiller, R. J. (2000). *Irrational exuberance*. Princeton University Press.

Thaler, R. H., & Sunstein, C. R. (2008). *Nudge: Improving decisions about health, wealth, and happiness*. Yale University Press.

Chapter 9
Social Media Influence on Market Sentiment

P. Selvakumar
https://orcid.org/0000-0002-3650-4548
Department of Science and Humanities, Nehru Institute of Technology, Coimbatore, India

Raj Kumar Mishra
https://orcid.org/0000-0002-6912-6694
University of Lucknow, India

Ankur Budhiraja
JIMS Engineering Management Technical Campus, Greater Noida, India

Parihar Suresh Dahake
https://orcid.org/0000-0002-2286-4120
Ramdeobaba University, Nagpur, India

Pankaj Singh Chandel
https://orcid.org/0000-0002-4135-8194
Dev Sanskriti Vishwavidyalaya, India

Chirayu Vats
https://orcid.org/0009-0008-1703-6292
Dev Sanskriti Vishwavidyalaya, India

ABSTRACT

Social media has profoundly transformed the landscape of market sentiment, playing a pivotal role in how investors, companies, and consumers interact and influence financial markets. The integration of platforms such as Twitter, Facebook, LinkedIn, and Reddit into daily life has created a new realm of information dissemination and opinion formation that was previously non-existent. Social media's immediacy and reach enable rapid sharing of news, opinions, and market analyses, making it an influential factor in shaping market perceptions and behaviors. Traditional media outlets, such as newspapers and television, often have a delay in reporting news, which can lead to a lag in market reactions. In contrast, social media allows for real-time updates, providing investors with immediate access to news, rumors, and opinions. This immediacy can lead to swift market movements, as traders and investors react to information as it becomes available, often before it reaches more

DOI: 10.4018/979-8-3693-9380-2.ch009

traditional media channels.

INTRODUCTION TO SOCIAL MEDIA'S IMPACT ON MARKET SENTIMENT

Social media has profoundly transformed the landscape of market sentiment, playing a pivotal role in how investors, companies, and consumers interact and influence financial markets. The integration of platforms such as Twitter, Facebook, LinkedIn, and Reddit into daily life has created a new realm of information dissemination and opinion formation that was previously non-existent. Social media's immediacy and reach enable rapid sharing of news, opinions, and market analyses, making it an influential factor in shaping market perceptions and behaviors. Traditional media outlets, such as newspapers and television, often have a delay in reporting news, which can lead to a lag in market reactions. In contrast, social media allows for real-time updates, providing investors with immediate access to news, rumors, and opinions. This immediacy can lead to swift market movements, as traders and investors react to information as it becomes available, often before it reaches more traditional media channels. For instance, a single tweet from a high-profile individual or a viral post about a company's earnings can cause significant fluctuations in stock prices. Social media also democratizes information by giving a platform to a wider range of voices and perspectives. Previously, market insights and analyses were predominantly available through institutional sources such as financial analysts and brokerage firms. Today, social media enables individual investors and amateur analysts to share their views and predictions, often creating a diverse array of opinions that can influence market sentiment. This democratization can lead to a more varied and dynamic market environment, where sentiment is shaped by a broader spectrum of voices. Furthermore, social media platforms are increasingly used by companies and financial institutions to manage their public relations and investor relations strategies. Companies often use social media to communicate directly with their stakeholders, share updates, and address concerns.

This direct communication can help shape investor perceptions and market sentiment, as companies are able to control the narrative and engage with their audience in real-time. Influencers and online personalities, with their large followings and perceived expertise, can sway public opinion and drive market trends. For example, a popular influencer endorsing a particular stock or cryptocurrency can generate significant interest and investment, sometimes leading to dramatic price movements. Similarly, online communities, such as those found on Reddit's WallStreetBets, have shown how collective sentiment and coordinated actions can impact stock prices, often leading to phenomena like short squeezes and market volatility. The rapid spread of misinformation and rumors can lead to market manipulation and volatility. The ease with which false information can be disseminated on social media can create confusion and drive market behaviors based on inaccurate or misleading information (Akhtar S., et al., 2011). This has led to increased scrutiny from regulators and the need for investors to be more discerning about the sources of information they rely on. Moreover, the psychological aspects of social media also play a role in shaping market sentiment. The constant flow of information and the visibility of others' opinions can lead to herd behavior, where individuals make investment decisions based on what others are doing rather than on fundamental analysis. This can amplify market trends, leading to bubbles and crashes driven by collective behavior rather than underlying economic conditions. The dynamic interplay between social media and market sentiment underscores the need for a nuanced understanding of this influential medium and its role in the modern financial landscape.

Understanding Market Sentiment: Definition, Measurement, and Importance

It is often seen as a reflection of the collective mood or psychology of market participants, encompassing their general outlook on the market's direction (Aljanabi A. R. A. 2023). This sentiment is pivotal because it can influence investment decisions, drive market trends, and contribute to the overall volatility observed in financial markets. Sentiment analysis extends beyond traditional financial metrics to incorporate data from alternative sources, including social media, news sentiment, and economic reports. Social media platforms offer real-time insights into public opinion and can reflect shifts in sentiment quickly. The importance of market sentiment cannot be overstated. It serves as a leading indicator of potential market movements, often providing early signals of changes in market trends before they become apparent through traditional financial metrics (Al-Shabi M. 2020). For example, a sudden shift from bullish to bearish sentiment can precede a market correction or downturn, offering investors an opportunity to adjust their strategies accordingly. Conversely, a shift from bearish to bullish sentiment can signal the potential for market recovery or growth, influencing investment decisions. Market sentiment also plays a crucial role in shaping investor behavior and market dynamics. During periods of high market sentiment, investor confidence can drive increased buying activity, leading to rising asset prices and market expansion. Conversely, negative sentiment can result in selling pressure, reduced market activity, and potential declines in asset values. Understanding sentiment trends helps investors anticipate market movements, manage risk, and make informed decisions based on prevailing attitudes (Baumeister R. F., et al.,2001).For instance, excessive optimism during a market bubble can lead to overvalued assets and subsequent corrections, while pervasive pessimism during a downturn can result in undervaluation and missed opportunities. As financial markets continue to grow and evolve, the role of market sentiment will remain a critical factor in shaping investment strategies and market outcomes.

Social Media Platforms: Channels for Market Sentiment Expression

Social media platforms have become pivotal channels for expressing and shaping market sentiment, offering a dynamic space where investors, analysts, and the general public can share opinions, insights, and forecasts. These platforms, including Twitter, Facebook, Reddit, LinkedIn, and specialized forums, have transformed how market sentiment is communicated and analyzed, providing both opportunities and challenges for market participants and analysts. Twitter, known for its real-time information flow, is a major conduit for market sentiment expression (Barrie C., et al., 2021). The platform's brevity and immediacy allow users to quickly share news, opinions, and market observations. High-profile investors, financial analysts, and industry leaders use Twitter to broadcast their views, which can significantly influence market perceptions (Berger J., et al., 2012). For instance, a tweet from a prominent investor or a news outlet can rapidly spread across the platform, impacting stock prices or triggering market reactions. Twitter's use of hashtags and trending topics further amplifies the reach of sentiment-driven discussions, making it a powerful tool for gauging market mood. Facebook, with its broader demographic reach, serves as a platform for more in-depth discussions and community engagement. Users share articles, personal opinions, and analyses within groups and pages dedicated to finance and investing (Cepoi C.-O. 2020). This platform facilitates longer-form content and detailed discussions, allowing for a more nuanced expression of market sentiment. Financial groups and investor communities on Facebook often debate market trends, share insights, and provide a platform for collective sentiment that can influence market behavior. The platform's integration of multimedia content, such as videos and infographics, also enhances the depth of sentiment expression and information sharing. Reddit has emerged as a unique social media channel for market sentiment, particularly through

Subreddits like WallStreetBets. This platform's forum-style structure allows users to post and discuss detailed analyses, stock picks, and investment strategies. Reddit's community-driven approach means that sentiment is often expressed through collective actions and discussions, leading to significant market movements. The viral nature of Reddit content can drive large-scale buying or selling, as seen with the GameStop short squeeze episode, where coordinated actions by Reddit users led to dramatic price increases. Reddit's upvote and downvote system also enables the community to highlight popular or contentious sentiment, providing insight into prevailing market attitudes. LinkedIn, a professional networking platform, offers a space for more formal expressions of market sentiment. Industry experts, financial analysts, and corporate leaders use LinkedIn to publish articles, share research, and discuss market trends. This platform's professional focus allows for the dissemination of in-depth analyses and strategic insights, contributing to a more refined understanding of market sentiment. LinkedIn's network of professionals also facilitates connections and discussions that can influence market perceptions and investment strategies. Specialized financial forums and platforms, such as StockTwits and Seeking Alpha, provide targeted channels for market sentiment expression. StockTwits, for example, integrates Twitter-like functionality with a focus on financial markets, allowing users to share short messages about stocks and trading strategies. The platform uses sentiment analysis tools to aggregate and interpret market sentiment from its user base, providing valuable insights for traders and investors. Seeking Alpha offers a space for detailed investment analysis and opinion articles, contributing to a broader understanding of market sentiment through expert and user-generated content. The influence of social media on market sentiment extends beyond direct communication to include the analysis of sentiment data. Advanced sentiment analysis tools and algorithms are employed to aggregate and interpret vast amounts of social media content, extracting insights into prevailing market moods and trends. However, the role of social media in expression market sentiment also presents challenges.

Text Analysis and Natural Language Processing: Tools for Sentiment Analysis

Text analysis and natural language processing (NLP) are pivotal tools in sentiment analysis, providing sophisticated methods for extracting insights from textual data. These technologies enable the automated analysis of vast amounts of text, transforming qualitative information into quantifiable metrics that help understand and interpret sentiment (Cevik E. et al., 2022). The integration of text analysis and NLP into sentiment analysis has revolutionized how organizations, researchers, and analysts approach the interpretation of public opinions, market sentiment, and consumer feedback. Part-of-speech tagging helps determine the grammatical structure of sentences, aiding in the understanding of sentiment-bearing phrases. Dependency parsing analyzes the grammatical relationships between words, which can further refine sentiment interpretation. The application of text analysis and NLP in sentiment analysis spans various domains, including market research, social media monitoring, customer feedback, and financial analysis (Deng C., et al.,2023). In financial analysis, sentiment analysis of news articles, financial reports, and social media can provide insights into market sentiment and potential investment opportunities. Despite its advancements, sentiment analysis faces several challenges. Ambiguity in language, such as homonyms and polysemy, can complicate sentiment interpretation. Sarcasm, irony, and complex emotional expressions are particularly challenging for automated systems to detect accurately. Additionally, sentiment analysis models can be biased if trained on unrepresentative datasets, potentially leading to skewed results. Addressing these challenges requires ongoing refinement of models, diverse training data, and continuous evaluation to ensure accuracy and reliability. In conclusion, text analysis and natural language processing are powerful tools for sentiment analysis, offering advanced methods for extracting and interpreting sentiment from textual data(Chang E. C., et al.,2000). Through techniques such as lexicon-based analysis, machine learning, deep learning, and feature extraction, sentiment analysis has become a critical component of modern data analytics. The integration of these tools into various applications provides valuable insights across domains, enhancing decision-making and strategic planning. As NLP technologies continue to evolve, sentiment analysis will likely become even more sophisticated, addressing current limitations and offering deeper understanding of human emotions and opinions expressed through text.

Social Media Sentiment and Stock Market Performance: Correlation and Causality

The interplay between social media sentiment and stock market performance has garnered substantial attention in recent years, reflecting a growing interest in understanding how online public opinion influences financial markets (Dhar S., et al.,2020). This relationship is multifaceted, involving the exploration of both correlation and causality to discern how social media sentiment impacts stock prices and market behavior. Correlation between social media sentiment and stock market performance is often explored through empirical studies that analyze the statistical relationships between online sentiment metrics and market indicators. Researchers use various methodologies to quantify sentiment from social media platforms, such as sentiment analysis of tweets, posts, and comments. For instance, platforms like Twitter and Reddit are analyzed for the frequency and tone of mentions related to specific stocks or market sectors. These sentiment scores are then compared with stock price movements and trading volumes to identify potential correlations. However, correlation does not necessarily imply causality. To establish causality, researchers employ more sophisticated techniques, including causal inference models and event studies. Causal inference models attempt to determine whether changes in social media sentiment directly cause changes in stock prices, rather than merely being associated with them. For example, Granger causality tests can be used to analyze whether changes in social media sentiment precede changes in stock prices, suggesting a causal relationship (Dhawan D. et al.,2021). Event studies, on the other hand, examine specific events or announcements and their impact on stock prices, considering how sentiment on social media before and after the event influences market outcomes. One notable example of causality is the impact of social media-driven events on stock performance.

The GameStop short squeeze of early 2021 provides a clear illustration of how social media sentiment can lead to significant stock price movements. Coordinated buying activity driven by positive sentiment on Reddit's WallStreetBets forum led to a dramatic increase in GameStop's stock price, which in turn caused significant losses for short sellers and heightened market volatility. This event highlights how social media sentiment can not only correlate with but also directly drive substantial changes in stock prices. Despite these insights, establishing causality remains challenging due to the complex nature of financial markets and the myriad factors influencing stock prices. Social media sentiment is one of many variables that can impact market performance, including economic indicators, company fundamentals, geopolitical events, and broader market trends. Disentangling the specific effects of social media sentiment from these other factors requires careful consideration and robust analytical methods. Moreover, the impact of social media sentiment on stock market performance is subject to varying degrees of influence depending on the context and platform. For example, sentiment expressed on platforms like Twitter may have different implications compared to sentiment on Reddit or financial news websites. The volume and nature of sentiment, as well as the credibility of sources, play a crucial role in determining how sentiment translates into market behavior. The role of sentiment amplification and feedback loops also complicates the relationship between social media sentiment and stock market performance (Evanega S., et al., 2020).

Influencers and Market Sentiment: The Role of Opinion Leaders

Influencers and opinion leaders play a pivotal role in shaping market sentiment, leveraging their substantial reach and perceived authority to impact investor perceptions and financial markets. These individuals, who often command large followings on social media platforms like Twitter, Instagram, LinkedIn, and YouTube, wield significant influence over public opinion and investment behavior (Filip A. M., et al., 2023). Understanding their role involves examining how their opinions, endorsements, and analyses affect market dynamics and sentiment. Influencers, defined as individuals with the ability to affect the purchasing decisions and opinions of their followers through their expertise or personal brand, have become key figures in modern financial markets. Their influence stems from their perceived credibility, expertise, and the trust they have built with their audience. This credibility allows influencers to sway public opinion and investor sentiment, often amplifying their impact on market performance. One of the primary ways influencers affect market sentiment is through their endorsements and recommendations. When a well-known influencer endorses a stock, cryptocurrency, or investment strategy, it can lead to increased interest and investment in that asset (Fukasawa M., et al., 2021). For example, a prominent figure in the finance community sharing positive news or predictions about a stock can drive significant buying activity, pushing up its price. Conversely, negative commentary from a respected influencer can lead to selling pressure and declines in asset prices. This effect is particularly pronounced when influencers have large and engaged audiences, as their opinions can quickly reach and resonate with a broad group of investors. The impact of influencers on market sentiment is also evident in the realm of social media-driven phenomena. Platforms like Twitter and Reddit, where influencers frequently share their views, can amplify sentiment through their vast networks. Influencers often act as trendsetters, shaping the narrative around specific stocks or market trends. For instance, during the GameStop short squeeze in early 2021, influencers and key opinion leaders on Reddit's WallStreetBets played a crucial role in driving the narrative and rallying retail investors to buy the stock, leading to a dramatic increase in its price (Garfin D. R.,et al., 2020). This phenomenon underscores the power of influencer-driven sentiment to create market movements and influence investor behavior.

In addition to their direct influence, opinion leaders often contribute to shaping broader market trends through their ability to set agendas and frame discussions. They have the power to highlight specific issues or trends, thereby influencing the focus of market participants and media coverage. By steering the conversation around certain stocks, sectors, or economic indicators, opinion leaders can indirectly shape market sentiment and drive investment decisions. The influence of opinion leaders and influencers is not without its challenges and potential drawbacks. The credibility of influencers can be questioned, particularly if they have conflicts of interest or if their recommendations are perceived as self-serving (Gilardi F., et al., 2022). For example, influencers who promote stocks they hold can face scrutiny for potential conflicts of interest, raising questions about the reliability of their endorsements. Additionally, the rapid spread of misinformation and hype on social media platforms can lead to inflated or misleading sentiment, resulting in volatile market reactions and investor losses. Moreover, the impact of influencers on market sentiment highlights the importance of critical thinking and due diligence among investors(Haroon O., et al., 2020). While influencers can provide valuable insights and perspectives, relying solely on their opinions without conducting independent research can be risky. Investors must assess the credibility and expertise of influencers and integrate their insights with other sources of information to make informed investment decisions. Regulatory bodies have also begun to address the role of influencers in financial markets, particularly concerning disclosure and transparency. Ensuring that influencers disclose any financial interests or affiliations related to their endorsements is crucial for maintaining market integrity and protecting investors from potential conflicts of interest. As the influence of social media and digital platforms continues to grow, regulators are working to establish guidelines and frameworks to address these issues and safeguard market participants. In conclusion, influencers and opinion leaders play a significant role in shaping market sentiment, leveraging their reach and credibility to impact investor perceptions and market behavior. Their endorsements, analyses, and ability to set agendas contribute to the dynamics of financial markets, influencing stock prices and investment trends (Hayes A. F. 2013). While their impact can be profound, it is essential for investors to approach influencer-driven sentiment with critical thinking and conduct thorough research to make informed decisions. As the role of influencers in financial markets continues to evolve, ongoing attention to transparency, credibility, and regulatory oversight will be crucial in managing their influence and ensuring market integrity.

Social Media Sentiment and Consumer Behavior: Predicting Demand and Preferences

Social media sentiment has become a vital tool for understanding and predicting consumer behavior, offering insights into demand and preferences that drive market dynamics. The integration of social media data into market analysis provides businesses and researchers with a powerful mechanism for gauging consumer attitudes, predicting trends, and tailoring strategies to meet evolving demands (Khan R., et al., 2021). This analysis helps in identifying consumer sentiment patterns, which are crucial for predicting how public opinion may influence purchasing decisions and market demand. One significant application of social media sentiment analysis is in forecasting consumer demand. Predicting consumer preferences through social media sentiment also involves understanding emerging trends and shifts in consumer behavior (Lavazza A., et al.,2020). Social media platforms are often the first places where new trends and preferences emerge, making them valuable for trend forecasting. By analyzing sentiment around specific topics, hashtags, or influencers, companies can identify rising trends and adapt their product development and marketing strategies accordingly. For instance, if social media sentiment around sustainable and eco-friendly products is predominantly positive, businesses can capitalize on this trend by offering green alternatives and promoting their commitment to sustainability. Sentiment analysis also helps companies personalize their marketing efforts by providing insights into consumer preferences and attitudes. By understanding the sentiments expressed by different demographic groups, businesses can tailor their marketing messages to resonate with specific audiences.

Market Sentiment and Social Media During Economic Crises: Lessons from History

In earlier economic crises, such as the Great Depression of the 1930s, information spread primarily through newspapers, radio broadcasts, and face-to-face communication. The impact of market sentiment was somewhat slower to manifest due to the limited speed of these information channels. The media of the time played a crucial role in shaping public perception, but the reach and immediacy were constrained compared to today's standards (Lekkas D., et al., 2022). For example, during the Great Depression, the widespread media coverage of bank failures and stock market crashes contributed to growing pessimism and a loss of confidence, exacerbating the economic downturn. With the advent of television and later the internet, the speed at which information could influence market sentiment increased significantly. The 2008 global financial crisis demonstrated the profound effect of instant information dissemination on market behavior.

Social media platforms such as Twitter and Facebook became vital channels for spreading news and opinions. During the crisis, rapid dissemination of information—whether accurate or not—led to increased market volatility (Maia V. M., et al., 2021). Rumors, speculative trading, and emotional responses spread quickly, often exacerbating market swings and contributing to a more chaotic economic environment. The role of social media in shaping market sentiment during economic crises extends beyond mere information dissemination. Social media platforms enable real-time interaction and the viral spread of ideas, which can amplify both positive and negative sentiments (Mazur M., et al., 2021). For instance, during the COVID-19 pandemic, social media played a critical role in shaping public perception of economic impact. Market participants and the general public used these platforms to share personal experiences, economic forecasts, and political opinions, all of which influenced market behavior.

The speed and breadth of social media communication allowed for rapid shifts in sentiment, as seen in the dramatic fluctuations in stock prices driven by viral posts and news stories. Additionally, social media has introduced a new dimension to market sentiment through the phenomenon of "crowdsourced" opinions. Platforms like Reddit, particularly with forums such as r/WallStreetBets, demonstrated how collective sentiment and coordinated actions could influence financial markets. During the GameStop short squeeze of early 2021, the power of social media to rally individual investors against institutional players highlighted the significant impact of collective sentiment on market dynamics. This event underscored how social media can amplify market movements and contribute to volatility, as coordinated trading efforts and viral narratives can drive dramatic price swings. The evolution of market sentiment and social media during economic crises reveals a complex relationship where each influences the other. Social media has transformed market dynamics by providing a platform for the rapid dissemination and amplification of information, which can both stabilize and destabilize markets. On one hand, social media can facilitate timely information sharing, potentially improving market efficiency and allowing for better-informed decisions.

Sentiment Analysis in Cryptocurrency Markets: A Social Media Perspective

Sentiment analysis in cryptocurrency markets, particularly from a social media perspective, represents a burgeoning field of study that reflects the unique dynamics of digital finance and investor behavior (Naeem S. B., et al., 2020). Unlike traditional financial markets, cryptocurrency markets are characterized by high volatility, rapid innovation, and a strong influence from social media discourse. Sentiment analysis, which involves evaluating public opinions and emotional tones expressed in text data, has become a crucial tool for understanding market movements and predicting price trends in this highly speculative and decentralized sector. Social media platforms such as Twitter, Reddit, and Telegram have become pivotal in shaping and reflecting market sentiment within the cryptocurrency space. These platforms provide real-time communication channels for millions of users who share their opinions, forecasts, and trading strategies. The decentralized nature of cryptocurrency markets means that traditional financial news sources and institutional analyses are often supplemented—or even overshadowed—by social media discourse (Naseem U., et al., 2021). As such, sentiment analysis of social media data has emerged as a valuable method for gauging investor sentiment and predicting market trends. One prominent example of the impact of social media on cryptocurrency markets is the phenomenon of "pump and dump" schemes, where coordinated social media campaigns can drive up the price of a cryptocurrency before a large-scale sell-off. Platforms like Reddit's r/WallStreetBets have demonstrated how collective sentiment can lead to significant price movements. In the case of Dogecoin, social media hype and endorsements from celebrities like Elon Musk have resulted in dramatic price surges, reflecting the power of social media-driven sentiment (Ozili P. K. et al.,2023). Sentiment analysis tools, which analyze user-generated content for positive or negative emotional cues, can detect these trends and provide insights into potential market movements before they fully materialize.

The methods employed in sentiment analysis for cryptocurrency markets often involve natural language processing (NLP) techniques to assess the tone and context of social media posts. Advanced algorithms can parse vast amounts of textual data, identify key themes, and quantify sentiment into actionable insights. These insights can then be used to predict price changes and market sentiment shifts. For example, an increase in positive sentiment regarding a particular cryptocurrency might precede a rise in its price, while a surge in negative sentiment could signal a potential downturn. However, sentiment analysis in cryptocurrency markets is not without its challenges. The highly speculative nature of cryptocurrencies means that social media sentiment can be both highly influential and highly volatile. Sentiments expressed on social media can be influenced by misinformation, pump-and-dump schemes, and coordinated social media campaigns, which can skew sentiment analysis results. Additionally, the anonymity and pseudonymity of many cryptocurrency users on social media platforms can complicate the verification and interpretation of sentiment data. Moreover, the rapid pace of social media interactions and the sheer volume of data generated pose significant challenges for sentiment analysis. Unlike traditional financial markets, where information dissemination is relatively controlled and predictable, cryptocurrency markets are influenced by a constant stream of social media activity. This requires sophisticated analytical tools capable of real-time processing and sentiment assessment to keep pace with market dynamics.

Social Media Sentiment and IPO Performance: Initial Public Offering Success

Social media sentiment refers to the collective attitudes and emotional responses expressed by users in online platforms regarding a particular topic—in this case, an IPO. This sentiment can manifest through various forms of content, including news articles, opinion pieces, tweets, posts, and comments. The sheer volume and speed at which information spreads on social media mean that sentiment can rapidly shift, affecting investor behavior and, consequently, the performance of an IPO (Pang A. 2013). Empirical studies have shown that positive social media sentiment can be a significant predictor of strong IPO performance. When potential investors express enthusiasm and optimism about a forthcoming IPO, it can create a buzz that drives interest and demand. This heightened interest can lead to oversubscription, where the demand for shares exceeds the supply, ultimately resulting in a higher initial trading price. For instance, high-profile IPOs like those of tech giants such as Uber and Airbnb have seen significant social media attention, which has, in many cases, contributed to a strong debut in the stock market. Conversely, negative sentiment on social media can have detrimental effects on IPO performance. Criticism, skepticism, and negative reviews can dampen investor confidence and lead to weaker demand (RavenPack. 2023).

This can manifest as lower subscription rates and a reduced initial trading price. For example, if a company facing an IPO encounters substantial criticism or concerns raised on social media platforms regarding its business model, financial health, or market potential, this can result in a less favorable reception when the stock is listed. The influence of social media sentiment on IPO performance is amplified by the speed and volume of information flow. Social media platforms facilitate real-time updates and discussions, allowing for rapid dissemination of both positive and negative sentiments. This can lead to swift shifts in market sentiment and investor behavior, making it crucial for companies and underwriters to monitor social media closely and respond proactively (Sadhu S., et al., 2022). For instance, companies often engage in social media campaigns and public relations efforts to shape positive sentiment and address potential concerns before an IPO. By managing the narrative and engaging with potential investors, they aim to foster a favorable perception and mitigate negative impacts. The authenticity and accuracy of social media information can vary, with the presence of misinformation, hype, and speculative comments potentially distorting sentiment analysis results. Additionally, social media sentiment can be influenced by coordinated campaigns, where groups of users may deliberately promote or undermine an IPO for strategic reasons. This necessitates a cautious approach to interpreting sentiment data and an understanding of the broader context in which social media discussions occur. Furthermore, the impact of social media sentiment on IPO performance can be context-specific, varying across different sectors, industries, and market conditions (Tiwari A. K. et al., 2022). For example, technology and consumer-facing companies may experience more pronounced effects of social media sentiment compared to companies in less visible or more niche sectors. Investors' familiarity with and engagement in specific industries can influence how social media sentiment translates into market performance.

The Impact of Fake News and Disinformation on Market Sentiment

The impact of fake news and disinformation on market sentiment is a critical and increasingly relevant issue in today's financial markets, where the rapid spread of information can have profound effects on investor behavior and market dynamics (Valle-Cruz D., et al., 2022). In an era of digital communication and social media proliferation, the speed and scale at which misinformation can circulate pose significant challenges for maintaining market integrity and investor confidence. The mechanisms through which fake news and disinformation influence market sentiment are multifaceted (van Dijck J., et al., 2020). Firstly, misinformation can create uncertainty and confusion among investors. When market participants are exposed to conflicting or erroneous information, they may struggle to make informed decisions, leading to increased volatility and erratic market behavior. This uncertainty can be particularly pronounced during periods of market stress or when the information pertains to high-profile companies or sectors. Secondly, the rapid dissemination of fake news via social media amplifies its impact. Social media platforms, characterized by their real-time nature and wide reach, enable misinformation to spread quickly and widely. Algorithms designed to prioritize engaging or sensational content can exacerbate this issue by promoting misleading news to a larger audience (Weimann G., et al., 2017). As a result, fake news can rapidly shift market sentiment by generating unwarranted fear, optimism, or skepticism among investors. The effects of fake news and disinformation on market sentiment can be observed in various ways. During the 2016 U.S. presidential election, for instance, misinformation and fake news campaigns were shown to have influenced public opinion and behavior. Similarly, in financial markets, instances such as the false reports of a company's bankruptcy or regulatory violations have led to significant stock price movements, highlighting how misinformation can distort market perception and investor behavior. Addressing the impact of fake news and disinformation on market sentiment involves a multifaceted approach. One key strategy is improving the quality and accuracy of information. Financial news outlets and social media platforms are increasingly focusing on fact-checking and verification processes to combat misinformation (Yang A., 2019).

Educational initiatives that emphasize critical thinking, media literacy, and the importance of verifying sources can help investors make more informed decisions and reduce the susceptibility to fake news. Additionally, regulatory measures and policy interventions can play a role in mitigating the impact of disinformation. Governments and regulatory bodies are increasingly considering frameworks to address misinformation and enhance market transparency. For example, some jurisdictions are exploring regulations that require greater disclosure of the sources of information and the intent behind financial communications. Such measures aim to increase accountability and reduce the spread of misleading or fraudulent information. The rapid spread of misleading information through social media and other digital channels can distort market sentiment, leading to increased volatility and irrational investor reactions. Addressing this challenge requires a comprehensive approach that includes improving information accuracy, enhancing investor education, implementing regulatory measures, and leveraging technological advancements. By continuing to develop and refine strategies to combat misinformation, financial markets can better safeguard against the disruptive effects of fake news and disinformation, promoting greater stability and investor confidence.

Regulatory Environment and Social Media's Influence on Market Sentiment

The regulatory environment and the influence of social media on market sentiment intersect in increasingly significant ways, reflecting the evolving dynamics of information dissemination and investor behavior in modern financial markets (Zainuri Z., et al., 2021). As social media platforms become central to how investors receive and share information, regulators are grappling with how to address the challenges and risks posed by this digital transformation. Understanding this interaction involves exploring how social media impacts market sentiment, the regulatory measures in place to manage these effects, and the ongoing debate about the appropriate balance between market transparency and information control. Social media has revolutionized the way market sentiment is formed and expressed. Platforms like Twitter, Reddit, LinkedIn, and Facebook enable real-time communication and widespread sharing of opinions, forecasts, and news. This immediacy can amplify sentiment, both positively and negatively, potentially influencing market prices and investor decisions. For instance, social media discussions can rapidly escalate into large-scale trading movements, as seen with the phenomenon of "meme stocks" where coordinated online activity leads to dramatic stock price fluctuations (Zargar F. N., 2023). The power of social media to shape market sentiment underscores the need for effective regulatory oversight to ensure market stability and protect investors from manipulation and misinformation.

Regulators have begun to address the challenges posed by social media through a range of measures aimed at maintaining market integrity and transparency. In the United States, the Securities and Exchange Commission (SEC) has taken steps to adapt existing regulations to the digital age. For example, the SEC has issued guidelines clarifying how social media communications by public companies should comply with disclosure requirements, ensuring that material information is shared in a manner that does not unfairly advantage or disadvantage certain investors. The global nature of social media means that regulatory approaches must often be harmonized across jurisdictions to effectively manage cross-border market activities and ensure consistent standards. The balance between regulation and the free flow of information is a key consideration in the debate over social media's role in financial markets. On one hand, robust regulatory measures are necessary to prevent manipulation and protect investors. On the other hand, excessive regulation could stifle legitimate market discourse and hinder transparency. Regulators face the challenge of crafting policies that safeguard market integrity while allowing for the open exchange of information that is fundamental to efficient and fair markets. This balance is crucial for fostering an environment where investors can make informed decisions based on accurate and timely information without undue influence from manipulated or misleading content. Technological advancements also play a role in shaping the regulatory landscape. The use of artificial intelligence (AI) and machine learning tools to monitor and analyze social media activity is becoming increasingly prevalent.

Social Media Sentiment and Market Anomalies: Identifying Investment Opportunities

The intersection of social media sentiment and market anomalies presents a rich field for identifying investment opportunities, as the rapid dissemination of information and collective investor behavior can reveal patterns not immediately evident through traditional financial analysis. Social media platforms like Twitter, Reddit, LinkedIn, and financial forums have become vital sources for gauging market sentiment, which can in turn influence market anomalies—irregularities or deviations from expected market behavior. Understanding how social media sentiment interacts with these anomalies can offer investors unique insights and potential advantages in identifying lucrative investment opportunities. Market anomalies often manifest as deviations from expected asset pricing, including phenomena such as price bubbles, market inefficiencies, or unexpected shifts in asset values (Ramakrishnan T., et al.,2022). Social media sentiment can both reflect and drive these anomalies by amplifying or dampening investor reactions. For instance, when social media platforms buzz with positive sentiment about a particular stock or sector, it can lead to overvaluation as hype drives demand beyond intrinsic value. Conversely, negative sentiment can precipitate undervaluation, creating potential buying opportunities when the market overreacts to unfavorable news or speculation. One well-documented example is the role of social media in the emergence of "meme stocks," where stocks like GameStop and AMC saw dramatic price increases driven largely by online communities. These instances illustrate how collective sentiment on social media can create market anomalies that diverge significantly from traditional valuation metrics. The social media-driven surge in these stocks was fueled by a combination of user-generated hype, coordinated trading strategies, and the viral spread of content.

The identification of market anomalies through social media sentiment also involves understanding the dynamics of investor behavior and the impact of information dissemination. Social media can amplify the effects of news, rumors, and market speculation, leading to rapid price movements that may not align with fundamental valuations. However, while social media sentiment offers valuable insights, it also comes with risks and limitations. The accuracy of sentiment analysis can be affected by the prevalence of misinformation, hype, and manipulation (Sugumaran K. M, D., et al., 2024). Coordinated efforts to drive market behavior, such as pump-and-dump schemes or artificial sentiment creation, can distort analysis and lead to misguided investment decisions. Investors must therefore exercise caution and combine sentiment analysis with traditional financial metrics and thorough due diligence.

Visual and Multimedia Content: Impact on Market Sentiment and Engagement

Visual and multimedia content has become a powerful force in shaping market sentiment and driving engagement in financial markets, reflecting the increasing role of digital media in influencing investor behavior and market dynamics (Selvakumar, P.,2023). In an era where information is consumed rapidly and visually, the impact of images, videos, infographics, and interactive content on market sentiment is profound. This evolution highlights how visual and multimedia elements can enhance, distort, or shift investor perceptions, ultimately affecting market trends and engagement levels. Visual content, such as charts, graphs, and infographics, plays a crucial role in simplifying complex financial information and making it more accessible to a broader audience. For instance, well-designed infographics can distill intricate financial data into digestible visuals, helping investors quickly grasp key insights and trends. This simplification not only aids in understanding but also enhances the ability of investors to make informed decisions based on visualized data. For example, a clear and compelling chart illustrating a company's revenue growth can attract positive sentiment and boost investor confidence, while a negative trend depicted through a graph might prompt caution or selling. Videos and interactive multimedia content further amplify this effect by providing dynamic and engaging ways to convey information. Financial news networks, investment analysts, and market commentators use videos to deliver real-time updates, analyses, and expert opinions. The immediacy and visual engagement of video content can significantly influence market sentiment by providing timely insights and emotional cues that textual content alone might lack. For instance, a video interview with a company's CEO discussing positive earnings projections can generate optimism and drive stock prices up, while a dramatic news video covering a corporate scandal might lead to negative sentiment and a drop in stock value. Social media platforms have become central to the dissemination and impact of visual and multimedia content. Platforms like Twitter, Instagram, YouTube, and TikTok enable rapid sharing of visual content that can quickly influence market sentiment. Memes, short videos, and infographics that go viral can create or amplify market trends, as seen with the rise of "meme stocks" where social media-driven visuals played a significant role in driving stock price volatility (Vijayakumar G, et al., 2024). The ability of visual content to capture attention and spread rapidly through social networks means that market sentiment can shift quickly, sometimes based on the viral nature of content rather than fundamental analysis. Interactive content, including live streams, webinars, and interactive charts, adds another layer engagement by allowing users to interact with information in real-time.

Harnessing Social Media's Power for Market Sentiment Analysis and Prediction

Harnessing social media's power for market sentiment analysis and prediction represents a transformative approach in understanding and forecasting financial markets, leveraging the vast and dynamic pool of user-generated content available online. By effectively analyzing social media content, investors and analysts can gain a competitive edge in predicting market movements and making informed decisions. The sheer volume and diversity of data generated on social media offer a rich reservoir for sentiment analysis (Paramasivam Selvakumar, et al.,2024). Users on these platforms frequently share their opinions, predictions, and reactions to market events, which can collectively reflect broader market sentiment. For instance, positive or negative sentiment expressed in tweets about a company can provide early indicators of market reactions, potentially influencing trading strategies and investment decisions. This immediacy enables analysts to detect shifts in sentiment and market trends almost as they occur. For example, a sudden surge in positive sentiment about a company's upcoming product launch can signal increased investor confidence and potential price appreciation, while a wave of negative posts about a regulatory issue may indicate forthcoming challenges and possible price declines. The predictive power of social media sentiment analysis extends beyond immediate market reactions. Historical data and advanced analytical techniques can reveal correlations between sentiment trends and future market movements. For instance, longitudinal studies have shown that sustained positive sentiment on social media can correlate with longer-term stock price increases, while prolonged negative sentiment often precedes declines. By integrating social media sentiment with traditional financial indicators, analysts can develop more robust predictive models and enhance their forecasting accuracy. Despite its advantages, social media sentiment analysis faces challenges and limitations. The accuracy of sentiment analysis can be affected by the prevalence of misinformation, biased opinions, and manipulative tactics, such as coordinated campaigns to influence market sentiment. For example, "pump and dump" schemes, where misleading positive sentiment is generated to inflate a stock's price before a sell-off, can distort the analysis and lead to erroneous predictions. Analysts must, therefore, be vigilant and incorporate additional validation measures to ensure the reliability of their insights. Another challenge is the dynamic and fast-paced nature of social media interactions. The volume of data and the rapidity of sentiment shifts can make it difficult to maintain real-time accuracy and relevance.

CONCLUSION

In conclusion, the influence of social media on market sentiment represents a profound and multifaceted evolution in the dynamics of financial markets, reshaping how information is disseminated, perceived, and acted upon by investors. The pervasive reach of platforms like Twitter, Reddit, LinkedIn, and others has transformed social media into a powerful force in shaping investor behavior and market trends. By facilitating real-time communication and providing a space for the rapid exchange of opinions, predictions, and reactions, social media has become a critical determinant of market sentiment, capable of driving substantial price movements and creating both opportunities and risks for market participants. The immediacy and breadth of social media enable it to act as both a barometer and a catalyst for market sentiment. Positive or negative sentiment expressed through social media can quickly influence investor perceptions and market behavior. For example, a surge in positive sentiment about a company's prospects, driven by enthusiastic user discussions or viral content, can lead to heightened investor interest and increased stock prices. Conversely, negative sentiment, whether stemming from criticism, rumors, or backlash, can result in declines and market volatility. The ability of social media to amplify sentiment and disseminate information at unprecedented speeds underscores its significant impact on market dynamics. Despite its advantages, the influence of social media on market sentiment is accompanied by challenges and risks. The potential for misinformation, manipulation, and sensationalism can distort sentiment and lead to irrational market behavior. Instances of coordinated campaigns to spread false information or artificially inflate sentiment highlight the need for vigilance and critical evaluation of social media content. Investors and analysts must navigate these risks by employing robust sentiment analysis techniques, incorporating additional sources of information, and maintaining a balanced perspective on the data. The regulatory landscape also plays a crucial role in managing the impact of social media on market sentiment. As social media's influence grows, regulators are increasingly focused on ensuring market integrity and transparency. Measures to address misinformation, prevent market manipulation, and enforce disclosure requirements are essential for maintaining fair and orderly markets. At the same time, regulators must balance these concerns with the need to support the free flow of information and innovation in digital communication. This balance is critical for fostering an environment where social media can contribute positively to market transparency and investor engagement without compromising market stability. Technological advancements, including the development of sophisticated sentiment analysis tools and machine learning algorithms, have enhanced the ability to harness social media data for market insights. These technologies enable the extraction of valuable information from vast volumes of social media content, providing real-time sentiment tracking and trend analysis.

REFERENCES

Akhtar, S., Faff, R., Oliver, B., & Subrahmanyam, A. (2011). The power of bad: The negativity bias in Australian consumer sentiment announcements on stock returns. *Journal of Banking & Finance*, 35(5), 1239–1249. DOI: 10.1016/j.jbankfin.2010.10.014

Al-Shabi, M. (2020). Evaluating the performance of the most important lexicons used to sentiment analysis and opinions mining. IJCSNS - International Journal of Computer Science and Network Security, 20(1), 1. DOI: 10.1016/j.jbankfin.2010.10.014

Aljanabi, A. R. A. (2023). The impact of economic policy uncertainty, news framing and information overload on panic buying behavior in the time of COVID-19: A conceptual exploration. *International Journal of Emerging Markets*, 18(7), 1614–1631. DOI: 10.1108/IJOEM-10-2020-1181

Barrie, C., & Ho, J. C. T. (2021). academictwitteR: An R package to access the Twitter academic research product track v2 API endpoint. *Journal of Open Source Software*, 6(62), 3272. DOI: 10.21105/joss.03272

Baumeister, R. F., Bratslavsky, E., Finkenauer, C., & Vohs, K. D. (2001). Bad is stronger than good. *Review of General Psychology*, 5(4), 323–370. DOI: 10.1037/1089-2680.5.4.323

Berger, J., & Milkman, K. L. (2012). What makes online content viral? *JMR, Journal of Marketing Research*, 49(2), 192–205. DOI: 10.1509/jmr.10.0353

Cepoi, C.-O. (2020). Asymmetric dependence between stock market returns and news during COVID-19 financial turmoil. *Finance Research Letters*, 36, 101658. DOI: 10.1016/j.frl.2020.101658 PMID: 32837370

Cevik, E., Kirci Altinkeski, B., Cevik, E. I., & Dibooglu, S. (2022). Investor sentiments and stock markets during the COVID-19 pandemic. *Financial Innovation*, 8(1), 69. DOI: 10.1186/s40854-022-00375-0 PMID: 35814528

Chang, E. C., Cheng, J. W., & Khorana, A. (2000). An examination of herd behavior in equity markets: An international perspective. *Journal of Banking & Finance*, 24(10), 1651–1679. DOI: 10.1016/S0378-4266(99)00096-5

Deng, C., Liang, C., Hong, Y., & Jiang, Y. (2023). CCTV news' asymmetric impact on the Chinese stock market during COVID-19: A combination analysis based on the SVAR and NARDL models. *Emerging Markets Finance & Trade*, 59(4), 1232–1246. DOI: 10.1080/1540496X.2022.2123219

Dhar, S., & Bose, I. (2020). Emotions in Twitter communication and stock prices of firms: The impact of Covid-19 pandemic. *Decision (Washington, D.C.)*, 47(4), 385–399. DOI: 10.1007/s40622-020-00264-4

Dhawan, D., Bekalu, M., Pinnamaneni, R., McCloud, R., & Viswanath, K. (2021). COVID-19 news and misinformation: Do they matter for public health prevention? *Journal of Health Communication*, 26(11), 799–808. DOI: 10.1080/10810730.2021.2010841 PMID: 34865604

Evanega, S., Lynas, M., Adams, J., Smolenyak, K., & Insights, C. G. (2020). Coronavirus misinformation: Quantifying sources and themes in the COVID-19 'infodemic'. *JMIR Preprints*, 19(10), 2020. DOI: 10.2196/preprints.25143

Filip, A. M., & Pochea, M. M. (2023). Intentional and spurious herding behavior: A sentiment driven analysis. *Journal of Behavioral and Experimental Finance*, 38, 100810. DOI: 10.1016/j.jbef.2023.100810

Fukasawa, M., Kawakami, N., Nakayama, C., & Yasumura, S. (2021). Relationship between use of media and radiation anxiety among the residents of Fukushima 5.5 years after the nuclear power plant accident. *Disaster Medicine and Public Health Preparedness*, 15(1), 42–49. DOI: 10.1017/dmp.2019.132 PMID: 31779727

Garfin, D. R., Silver, R. C., & Holman, E. A. (2020). The novel coronavirus (COVID-2019)outbreak: Amplification of public health consequences by media exposure. *Health Psychology*, 39(5), 355–357. DOI: 10.1037/hea0000875 PMID: 32202824

Gilardi, F., Gessler, T., Kubli, M., & Müller, S. (2022). Social media and political agenda setting. *Political Communication*, 39(1), 39–60. DOI: 10.1080/10584609.2021.1910390

Haroon, O., & Rizvi, S. A. R. (2020). COVID-19: Media coverage and financial markets behavior–A sectoral inquiry. *Journal of Behavioral and Experimental Finance*, 27, 100343. DOI: 10.1016/j.jbef.2020.100343 PMID: 32427152

Hayes, A. F. (2013). *Introduction to mediation, moderation, and conditional process analysis: A regression-based approach*. Guilford Press.

Khan, R., Rustam, F., Kanwal, K., Mehmood, A., & Choi, G. S. (2021). US based COVID-19 tweets sentiment analysis using TextBlob and supervised machine learning algorithms [Conference session]. International Conference on Artificial Intelligence (ICAI), Islamabad, Pakistan, IEEE, pp. 1–8. DOI: 10.1109/ICAI52203.2021.9445207

Lavazza, A., & Farina, M. (2020). The role of experts in the Covid-19 pandemic and the limits of their epistemic authority in democracy. *Frontiers in Public Health*, 8, 356. https://www.frontiersin.org/articles/10.3389/fpubh.2020.00356. DOI: 10.3389/fpubh.2020.00356 PMID: 32760690

Lekkas, D., Gyorda, J. A., Price, G. D., Wortzman, Z., & Jacobson, N. C. (2022). Using the COVID-19 pandemic to assess the influence of news affect on online mental health-related search behavior across the United States: Integrated sentiment analysis and the circumplex model of affect. *Journal of Medical Internet Research*, 24(1), e32731. DOI: 10.2196/32731 PMID: 34932494

Maia, V. M., Tommasetti, R., & da Silva Macedo, M. A. (2021). Australian market response to COVID-19 as moderated by social media. *Pacific Accounting Review*, 33(5), 625–635. DOI: 10.1108/PAR-09-2020-0138

Mazur, M., Dang, M., & Vega, M. (2021). COVID-19 and the March 2020 stock market crash. Evidence from S&P1500. *Finance Research Letters*, 38, 101690. DOI: 10.1016/j.frl.2020.101690 PMID: 32837377

Naeem, S. B., & Bhatti, R. (2020). The Covid-19 'infodemic': A new front for information professionals. *Health Information and Libraries Journal*, 37(3), 233–239. DOI: 10.1111/hir.12311 PMID: 32533803

Naseem, U., Razzak, I., Khushi, M., Eklund, P. W., & Kim, J. (2021). COVIDSenti: A large-scale benchmark Twitter data set for COVID-19 sentiment analysis. *IEEE Transactions on Computational Social Systems*, 8(4), 1003–1015. DOI: 10.1109/TCSS.2021.3051189 PMID: 35783149

Ozili, P. K., & Arun, T. (2023). Spillover of COVID-19: Impact on the global economy. In *Managing inflation and supply chain disruptions in the global economy* (pp. 41–61). IGI Global., DOI: 10.4018/978-1-6684-5876-1.ch004

Pang, A. (2013). Social media hype in times of crises: Nature, characteristics and impact on organizations. *Asia Pacific Media Educator*, 23(2), 309–336. DOI: 10.1177/1326365X13517189

Ramakrishnan, T., Mohan Gift, M. D., Chitradevi, S., Jegan, R., & Subha Hency Jose, P. Nagaraja, Rajneesh Sharma H.N., Selvakumar P., Sintayehu Mekuria Hailegiorgis, (2022). "Study of Numerous Resins Used in Polymer Matrix Composite Materials", Advances in Materials Science and Engineering, vol. 2022, Article ID 1088926, 8 pages, 2022. DOI: 10.1155/2022/1088926

RavenPack. (2023). Coronavirus media monitor [dataset]. https://coronavirus.ravenpack.com/

Sadhu, S., Poddar, V., Paul, P., Hansda, S., Saha, R., Chakraborty, A., Paul, T., & Mondal, . (2022). Sentiment analysis on COVID-19 Twitter data. *American Journal of Electronics & Communication*, 3(2), 21–29. DOI: 10.15864/ajec.3205

Selvakumar, P. (2023). Biomedical applications of polymers in biosensors, cancer vaccines and drug delivery systems. *Biopolimery i Kletka*, 39(4), 245–256. DOI: 10.7124/bc.000AA0

Selvakumar, P., Mariappan, P., Shunmugam, S., Paul, R., & Jabez, S. (2024). Removal of chemicals from effluent using photobioreactor technology to improve environmental and health impacts. *Zeitschrift für Physikalische Chemie*, 2024(7), 1295–1302. Advance online publication. DOI: 10.1515/zpch-2023-0450

Sugumaran, K. M. D., Pandiyarajan V., Y. B S, Selvakumar P. and M. S, (2024). "Analysis of Electromyography Signals for Control of Mechanical Prosthesis using Machine Learning Techniques," 2024 2nd International Conference on Intelligent Data Communication Technologies and Internet of Things (IDCIoT), Bengaluru, India, 2024, pp. 1059-1067, DOI: 10.1109/IDCIoT59759.2024.10467707

Tiwari, A. K., Abakah, E. J. A., Bonsu, C. O., Karikari, N. K., & Hammoudeh, S. (2022). The effects of public sentiments and feelings on stock market behavior: Evidence from Australia. *Journal of Economic Behavior & Organization*, 193, 443–472. DOI: 10.1016/j.jebo.2021.11.026

Valle-Cruz, D., Fernandez-Cortez, V., López-Chau, A., & Sandoval-Almazán, R. (2022). Does Twitter affect stock market decisions? Financial sentiment analysis during pandemics: A comparative study of the H1N1 and the COVID-19 periods. *Cognitive Computation*, 14(1), 372–387. DOI: 10.1007/s12559-021-09819-8 PMID: 33520006

van Dijck, J., & Alinejad, D. (2020). Social media and trust in scientific expertise: Debating the Covid-19 pandemic in The Netherlands. *Social Media + Society*, 6(4), 2056305120981057. DOI: 10.1177/2056305120981057

Vijayakumar, G., Rajkumar, M., Rajiv Chandar, N., Selvakumar, P., & Duraisamy, R. (2024). Muniyandi Rajkumar, Rajiv Chandar N, Selvakumar P and Ramesh Duraisamy, (2024). Environmentally friendly TDS removal from waste water by electrochemical ion exchange batch-type recirculation (EIR) technique. *Environmental Science. Water Research & Technology*, 10(4), 826–835. DOI: 10.1039/D3EW00793F

Weimann, G., & Brosius, H.-B. (2017). Redirecting the agenda: Agenda-setting in the online Era. *The Agenda Setting Journal*, 1(1), 63–102. DOI: 10.1075/asj.1.1.06wei

Yang, A., & Saffer, A. J. (2019). Embracing a network perspective in the network society: The dawn of a new paradigm in strategic public relations. *Public Relations Review*, 45(4), 101843. DOI: 10.1016/j.pubrev.2019.101843

Zainuri, Z., Viphindrartin, S., & Wilantari, R. N. (2021). The impacts of the COVID-19 pandemic on the movement of composite stock price index in Indonesia. The Journal of Asian Finance. *Economics and Business*, 8(3), 1113–1119. DOI: 10.13106/jafeb.2021.vol8.no3.1113

Zargar, F. N., & Kumar, D. (2023). Market fear, investor mood, sentiment, economic uncertainty and tourism sector in the United States amid COVID-19 pandemic: A spillover analysis. *Tourism Economics*, 29(2), 551–558. DOI: 10.1177/13548166211052803

Chapter 10
Strategic Flexibility in Investment Portfolios:
Adapting to Technological Advancements and Market Volatility in Emerging Economies

Yang Ze
Universiti Malaya, Malaysia

Ooi Kok Loang
https://orcid.org/0000-0003-0412-8899
Universiti Malaya, Malaysia

ABSTRACT

This study examines the importance of strategic flexibility in managing investment portfolios, particularly in emerging markets characterized by rapid technological advancements and heightened market volatility. By focusing on key factors such as portfolio diversification, technological adaptability, and regulatory changes, the research highlights how investors can navigate uncertainties and capitalize on opportunities in volatile economies. Strategic flexibility is presented as a dynamic tool that enables investors to adjust their strategies in real-time, ensuring resilience and optimizing returns. The study underscores the need for a proactive approach to managing risk and seizing growth opportunities in rapidly evolving markets

DOI: 10.4018/979-8-3693-9380-2.ch010

INTRODUCTION

The swift transformation of global markets, especially in emerging economies, has compelled investors to reevaluate conventional portfolio methods, highlighting the necessity for enhanced strategic adaptability (Zahoor & Lew, 2023). In a globalised investing environment, marked by rapid technological progress and constant market volatility, conventional investment models may be inadequate. Emerging markets, frequently regarded as high-risk yet high-reward regions, provide both opportunity and problems. These markets exhibit significant development potential but are also prone to heightened volatility, regulatory concerns, and technology changes, necessitating a flexible and adaptive strategy for investors.

Portfolio diversification is frequently seen as a fundamental element of investment strategy in turbulent markets. It functions as a risk reduction instrument, enabling investors to diversify their capital over many asset classes and geographical areas, thus diminishing exposure to the hazards linked to a singular market or industry. In emerging markets, where market dynamics are ever evolving, diversification methods require greater sophistication. These markets frequently demonstrate elevated levels of uncertainty attributable to economic volatility, political fluctuations, and regulatory unpredictability. Diversification must go beyond merely distributing risk; it must also be guided by a comprehensive grasp of the unique hazards associated with each market.

Alongside market volatility, technical adaptability is essential in influencing investment performance. Emerging economies, albeit occasionally trailing in technological infrastructure, are swiftly advancing and, in numerous instances, are surpassing outdated technologies. This has significant ramifications for investment portfolios. Technological innovation can serve as a catalyst for growth or disruption, contingent upon an investor's ability to foresee and adapt to these changes. Companies or investors that exhibit flexibility to technological innovations—either by directly investing in technology-oriented sectors or by integrating technical tools into their investment evaluations—are more likely to attain superior profits. Strategic flexibility must, therefore, encompass a profound understanding of how technological changes might impact market trajectories in emerging economies.

Regulatory alterations provide a considerable hurdle for investors in emerging markets. These markets frequently see swift policy alterations, resulting in an unpredictable investment landscape. Regulatory frameworks in emerging nations are generally less stable than those in developed markets, resulting in possible risks such as abrupt policy changes, modifications in trade agreements, or unforeseen adjustments in tax regimes. Investors must stay alert and flexible to these developments, adjusting their portfolios as needed to reduce regulatory risks while seizing chances from advantageous policy modifications (Loang, 2023).

The dependent variable, investment performance, is influenced by the interaction of five factors: portfolio diversification, market volatility, technological adaptability, and regulatory changes. Strategic flexibility is crucial for enhancing investment performance in this context, enabling investors to adeptly manoeuvre through the intricacies of emerging markets with a more agile and anticipatory strategy (FaXing & Loang, 2024). By persistently modifying their tactics in reaction to changing market conditions, investors can enhance their ability to capitalise on opportunities while reducing possible losses. Notwithstanding the expanding literature on strategic flexibility in investment portfolios, considerable gaps persist, especially on its implementation in emerging markets. Much of the current research predominantly concentrates on investment strategies within developed economies, characterised by more stable and predictable economic situations, legal frameworks, and technical infrastructures. The distinctive traits of developing markets, such as their volatility, swift economic expansion, and vulnerability to political and regulatory changes, pose issues inadequately addressed in conventional finance research. This gap requires a thorough examination of how investors might proactively navigate these unique risks while optimising returns in these volatile contexts.

A significant deficiency in existing research is the insufficient representation of empirical studies that specifically investigate the significance of technology flexibility in investment strategies within emerging economies. Despite the increasing acknowledgement that technological improvements can both disrupt and improve market performance, there is a paucity of understanding regarding how investors should systematically integrate technological flexibility into their portfolio management strategies. Most studies primarily concentrate on the effects of technology on specific enterprises or industries, rather than examining its influence on overarching market dynamics and investment results across many sectors and geographies. This oversight allows for more extensive study that incorporates technological adaptation as a fundamental element of strategic flexibility in developing market ventures (Prelipcean & Boscoianu, 2020).

Moreover, although portfolio diversity is broadly recognised as a risk management strategy, the complexities of diversification in emerging markets remain inadequately examined. Emerging markets frequently encounter greater market fragmentation, currency volatility, and sectoral disparities, necessitating more advanced diversification methods compared to those utilised in industrialised nations. Nonetheless, the current literature inadequately explores the necessity of adapting diversification techniques to accommodate these challenges. Furthermore, the majority of studies concentrate on conventional asset classes, such as shares and bonds, while neglecting alternative investments like venture capital, private equity, or digital assets, which are becoming increasingly pertinent in developing market scenarios. Rectifying this deficiency may yield significant insights into the optimisation of diversification within these high-risk contexts (Suresh & Loang, 2024).

A notable gap pertains to the influence of regulatory alterations on investment performance in emerging markets. Despite the established understanding that regulatory environments in these markets are more dynamic and unpredictable than in developed economies, there is a paucity of research on how investors can proactively modify their portfolios in response to these fluctuations. Contemporary literature frequently analyses regulatory risks in isolation, neglecting the interplay between these risks and other elements, including market volatility and technological disruptions. A comprehensive understanding of how regulatory changes affect portfolio performance, especially in conjunction with other variables, is crucial for formulating robust investment strategies that withstand the uncertainties of emerging markets.

Moreover, the notion of strategic flexibility is inadequately theorised within the realm of investment management. Although there is widespread agreement on the significance of flexibility in managing volatile markets, there is a lack of consensus regarding its implementation and measurement. Numerous studies provide qualitative insights into the advantages of flexibility yet lack definitive frameworks or metrics for assessing the extent of flexibility in a portfolio. The absence of a standardised methodology hinders investors from executing strategic flexibility in a systematic and measurable manner. Rectifying this deficiency could improve the practical utility of strategic flexibility, allowing investors to more effectively evaluate and modify their portfolios in real-time according to changing market conditions (Loang, 2024a).

There is a dearth of longitudinal studies that monitor the long-term performance of portfolios emphasising strategic flexibility in emerging markets. Much research primarily emphasises short-term outcomes, potentially overlooking the advantages of flexibility over prolonged durations. This gap is especially significant due to the cyclical characteristics of market volatility and technological advancements in emerging economies (Loang, 2024b). Prolonged studies may yield more substantial evidence regarding the enduring significance of strategic flexibility, elucidating the performance of adaptable portfolios throughout various economic cycles, technological transitions, and regulatory contexts.

LITERATURE REVIEW

Underlying Theory: Strategic Flexibility Theory

Theory of strategic flexibility emerges from the extensive domain of strategic management and has been utilised in other disciplines, including finance, to elucidate how organisations and investors adapt to fluctuating external circumstances. Strategic flexibility fundamentally denotes an entity's ability to adapt, pivot, and reorganise its resources in reaction to environmental uncertainties and dynamic changes. This idea emphasises the necessity of flexible solutions in investment management that can withstand shocks, leverage new possibilities, and reduce risks linked to market fluctuations, regulatory alterations, and technology upheavals (Tang & Loang, 2024).

The core principle of strategic flexibility theory is based on the notion that uncertainty is an intrinsic characteristic of any decision-making context (Fu & Loang, 2024). Investors, especially in emerging economies, encounter uncertainty through economic volatility, political changes, technology progress, and regulatory modifications. Consequently, strategic flexibility emerges as a crucial differentiator between individuals capable of navigating uncertainties and those who are not. It allows investors to circumvent the inflexibility of fixed investing methods, which may succeed in calm conditions but generally underperform in turbulent markets. Flexibility facilitates prompt modifications to portfolios, ensuring that investors stay aligned with ever-changing market conditions.

A fundamental component of strategic flexibility theory is the capacity to develop and sustain "real options" within a portfolio. Derived from corporate finance, real options denote the strategic alternatives available to investors that enable them to postpone, enlarge, reduce, or forgo investments in response to changing market conditions. Theory of strategic flexibility posits that investors gain advantages by maintaining choices in uncertain situations, allowing them to exploit favourable conditions while reducing vulnerability to unfavourable ones. In a swiftly changing technological environment, investors who integrate flexibility into their portfolios may direct funds towards rising tech industries while maintaining the agility to divest if a disruptive technology renders these investments obsolete. This method differs from conventional investment methods that may confine investors to fixed asset allocations, restricting their capacity to adapt to emerging trends (Prelipcean & Boscoianu, 2020).

Strategic flexibility theory underscores the distinct difficulties and opportunities inherent in emerging markets. These markets exhibit significant volatility, substantial development potential, and frequent regulatory alterations, rendering them less predictable than mature markets. Strategic flexibility in this context entails not only modifying portfolio compositions in reaction to market fluctuations but also forecasting and preparing for changes in the regulatory and technology environment. Flexibility is essential in unpredictable regulatory environments, commonly found in emerging countries where governments regularly introduce new rules that may impede or enhance investment prospects (Iriani et al., 2024). Investors who can swiftly adjust to these changes are more likely to maintain performance and safeguard their wealth.

Technological innovations further complicate the financial landscape, necessitating a significant level of adaptation. Theory of strategic flexibility underscores the necessity of adopting a proactive perspective that accounts for possible technology disruptions. Investors with adaptable portfolios are more strategically positioned to direct resources towards innovation-centric sectors and companies that may yield substantial profits owing to technological progress (Zahoor & Lew, 2023). Simultaneously, they can mitigate exposure to sectors that may be negatively impacted by these alterations. Strategic flexibility allows an investor to reallocate capital from conventional energy sectors to renewable energy technologies when market conditions and regulatory incentives support environmentally sustainable alternatives. The hypothesis posits that individuals exhibiting this degree of adaptability are more inclined to attain sustained success, since they can effectively address the dangers and possibilities associated with technological advancement.

A fundamental aspect of strategic flexibility theory is its acknowledgement of the relationship between long-term planning and short-term adaptability (Vrontis et al., 2023). Although long-term planning is crucial for establishing broad investment objectives, it frequently proves inadequate amid swiftly evolving markets. Theory of strategic flexibility promotes a dynamic methodology that reconciles long-term goals with the necessity for short-term tactical adjustments. Investors must implement adaptable techniques that facilitate the reconfiguration of their portfolios in response to emerging knowledge. This entails not only modifying asset allocations but also refining risk management measures, including the utilisation of hedging techniques or the application of financial instruments to safeguard against downside risks. In emerging markets, characterised by heightened volatility, the ability to implement short-term modifications while maintaining long-term objectives is a defining feature of effective portfolio management.

The idea also encompasses organisational structures and decision-making processes within investment organisations. Strategic flexibility involves not just the reallocation of money but also the cultivation of an adaptable culture within investment teams. Organisations that promote flexibility are more apt to provide an atmosphere in which decision-makers are empowered to respond rapidly to evolving circumstances. This entails decentralising decision-making, promoting continual learning, and enhancing the ability to adapt as required. Theory of strategic flexibility posits that organisations with more adaptable structures are more adept at navigating the intricacies of investment in uncertain and volatile markets.

Portfolio diversification is among the most thoroughly examined concepts in investment literature. Diversification, grounded in Modern Portfolio Theory (MPT) formulated by Harry Markowitz, is regarded as an essential strategy for risk management through the distribution of investments across diverse asset classes, sectors, and geographical areas. Multiple studies have shown that diversification mitigates unsystematic risk—the risk associated with particular assets—thereby stabilising portfolio results. Elton and Gruber (1997) emphasise the risk-mitigating advantages of diversification, especially in volatile markets, when the probability of significant price fluctuations in a single asset is elevated. Nevertheless, the literature on diversification within emerging economies reveals a more intricate scenario. Emerging markets demonstrate elevated market inefficiencies, currency risk, and sectoral concentration, potentially constraining the efficacy of conventional diversification techniques. Bekaert and Harvey (1995) propose that diversification in emerging economies necessitates more sophisticated strategies, frequently integrating alternative assets like commodities or private equity to mitigate region-specific risks. Emerging markets, marked by significant volatility and swift development potential, necessitate diversification to balance risk with prospects for substantial rewards, a balance essential for strategic flexibility (Ahammad et al., 2021).

The second component, market volatility, has been a subject of financial research for decades, especially about its effects on investment performance. Market volatility denotes the extent of fluctuation in asset prices over time and is frequently regarded as an indicator of market risk. The Capital Asset Pricing Model (CAPM) posits that volatility is a critical factor in determining the risk premium required by investors, as heightened volatility generally correlates with higher projected returns, while simultaneously heightening the chance of losses. Research conducted by French, Schwert, and Stambaugh (1987) indicates that heightened market volatility correlates with diminished average returns, as investors demand compensation for assuming additional risk. In emerging markets, volatility is frequently exacerbated by political instability, economic uncertainty, and underdeveloped financial institutions. Researchers such as Hwang and Salmon (2004) have examined the increased volatility in these markets, indicating that it necessitates greater agility in portfolio management for investors. Strategic flexibility is essential, enabling investors to swiftly adapt to abrupt market changes. Literature increasingly acknowledges that conventional volatility management techniques, often tailored for developed markets, may be insufficient for tackling the high oscillations observed in emerging nations.

Technology adaptation, the third variable, has lately gained relevance in investment literature due to the rapid pace of technology innovation across all sectors. The capacity to adjust to technology advancements is widely regarded as a crucial factor in achieving competitive advantage, both for individual companies and for investors overseeing portfolios. Research conducted by Brynjolfsson and McAfee (2014) on the "Second Machine Age" underscores the capacity of technical breakthroughs to significantly transform market dynamics, rendering adaptation crucial for seizing growth possibilities. In investment, technological adaptation entails identifying and investing in sectors anticipated to experience disruption while concurrently mitigating risks associated with obsolescence in adversely affected industries. Research has examined the significance of technical foresight in portfolio design, indicating that investors who include technological trends into their strategies frequently surpass those who depend exclusively on conventional financial measurements. In emerging markets, where technology infrastructure is sometimes inadequate yet swiftly advancing, adaptation is paramount (Shahzad & Jasińska, 2024). Technological developments in these regions may facilitate substantial leapfrogging, enabling markets to circumvent conventional growth phases and embrace the latest innovations, hence generating new investment opportunities and hazards. The literature on the systematic integration of technological flexibility into portfolio strategies for investors is weak, indicating a vacuum for future study to explore.

The last element, regulatory changes, significantly influences investment environments, particularly in emerging markets. Regulatory systems in these places are generally more variable and unpredictable than in established markets, typically attributable to political instability, economic shifts, or institutional deficiencies. Research on regulatory risk, including the work of La Porta, Lopez-de-Silanes, Shleifer, and Vishny (1998), highlights that inadequate legal protections and erratic enforcement of rules might dissuade foreign investment and elevate capital costs. Regulatory changes can also present possibilities, since governments in emerging markets frequently implement reforms to attract foreign investment, liberalise essential industries, or promote technological innovation. Investors exhibiting strategic flexibility by remaining aware of regulatory changes are typically more adept at leveraging advantageous policy modifications while minimising potential dangers. Literature indicates that regulatory risk is generally addressed via political risk analysis; nevertheless, the interplay between regulatory alterations and other elements, such as market volatility and technology disruption, remains underexplored. This signifies an additional domain where strategic flexibility theory may be further refined, providing insights into how investors might navigate the complex risks associated with regulatory instability in emerging nations.

The research on portfolio diversity, market volatility, technological adaptation, and regulatory changes offers a robust framework for comprehending their distinct effects on investment performance. Nonetheless, the interrelation of these factors, especially within the framework of rising markets, necessitates additional investigation. The notion of strategic flexibility connects these elements, providing a framework that enables investors to adjust to the uncertainties present in various contexts. Subsequent study may expand upon this literature by investigating the interactions of these variables within a more extensive strategic flexibility framework, so providing investors with enhanced tools for navigating the many issues associated with emerging market investments (Saeed et al., 2021).

RESEARCH METHODOLOGY

The research methodology for examining strategic flexibility in investment portfolios, especially within emerging markets, requires a mixed-method approach that integrates both qualitative and quantitative methodologies. The intricate nature of the topic, encompassing various interconnected factors like market volatility, technological adaptation, and regulatory changes, is enhanced by a thorough methodological framework. The integration of qualitative and quantitative methodologies for a comprehensive examination of both the subjective and objective aspects of strategic flexibility, enhancing the knowledge of how investors might adjust to fluctuating market conditions.

The qualitative component of the study will concentrate on elucidating the intricate views and decision-making processes of investors and financial managers in emerging markets. Qualitative methodologies, including semi-structured interviews, focus groups, and case studies, are especially appropriate for this objective. This study examines how investors interpret market volatility, regulatory changes, and technology upheavals, and how they integrate strategic flexibility into their decision-making processes. Semi-structured interviews with portfolio managers and institutional investors would yield insights into their risk and opportunity assessments, the criteria employed for portfolio adjustments, and their experiences with regulatory and technological changes in specific emerging markets. The adaptability of qualitative approaches facilitates comprehensive examination of intricate phenomena, allowing researchers to elucidate the complexities of strategic flexibility that may be challenging to quantify.

Furthermore, case studies of particular investment firms or portfolios in emerging economies would offer valuable real-world illustrations of the application of strategic flexibility. This analysis will investigate how companies have managed market fluctuations or regulatory alterations, providing specific instances of effective and ineffective solutions. A case study demonstrating how a specific investment firm adjusted its portfolio in reaction to an abrupt technology disruption in an emerging market would exemplify the practical application of strategic flexibility. The qualitative data obtained through these methodologies would be essential for comprehending the contextual aspects that affect strategic flexibility, as well as the obstacles investors have in executing flexible strategies.

The quantitative aspect of the study will concentrate on measuring and analysing the correlations among the important variables that affect investment performance in emerging markets. Quantitative tools, including statistical analysis, econometric modelling, and surveys, will be utilised to evaluate the influence of factors such as market volatility, portfolio diversification, technological adaptation, and regulatory changes on investment results. This method facilitates the detection of patterns, correlations, and causal linkages among various factors, yielding a more objective evaluation of the impact of strategic flexibility on investment performance.

An essential component of the quantitative analysis entails the development of econometric models that measure the impact of the independent variables—portfolio diversification, market volatility, technological adaptation, and regulatory changes—on the dependent variable, investment performance. The study could utilise historical market data from emerging nations to do regression analysis and ascertain the statistical significance of each variable. The model could analyse the degree to which enhanced diversification mitigates risk in unpredictable markets, or how adaptability to technology advancements influences long-term returns. Time-series data analysis can be employed to evaluate the effects of regulatory changes over time on portfolio performance, especially during periods of political or economic upheaval. Employing econometric models offers a systematic, data-informed methodology for comprehending the intricate relationships among variables, providing empirical evidence to corroborate or disprove claims concerning strategic flexibility.

Surveys and questionnaires would enhance this quantitative research by collecting extensive data from investors, portfolio managers, and financial institutions in emerging markets. These surveys may assess attitudes towards strategic flexibility, perceptions of market risk, and the degree to which technological advances and legislative changes influence investment decisions. Investors may be requested to evaluate their adaptability to technology improvements using a Likert scale or to disclose the frequency with which they modify their portfolios in reaction to market volatility. The survey data could subsequently be analysed via statistical approaches such as factor analysis or structural equation modelling to discern underlying patterns and relationships. This approach offers a quantitative assessment of subjective elements, enabling the research to incorporate both objective market data and investor perspectives into its analysis.

The amalgamation of qualitative and quantitative methodologies, referred to as a mixed-methods approach, enhances the research by facilitating triangulation. Triangulation denotes the employment of various methods or data sources to corroborate conclusions, hence augmenting the validity and trustworthiness of the research. This study will cross-reference qualitative insights from interviews and case studies with quantitative data from surveys and econometric models to ensure a full knowledge of strategic flexibility in investment portfolios. Qualitative studies regarding investor perceptions of technology adaptability may be juxtaposed with quantitative data illustrating the actual effects of technological developments on portfolio performance. This methodological combination allows the study to encompass both the subjective experiences of investors and the objective market outcomes, offering a comprehensive perspective on strategic flexibility in emerging countries.

Figure 1. Conceptual framework

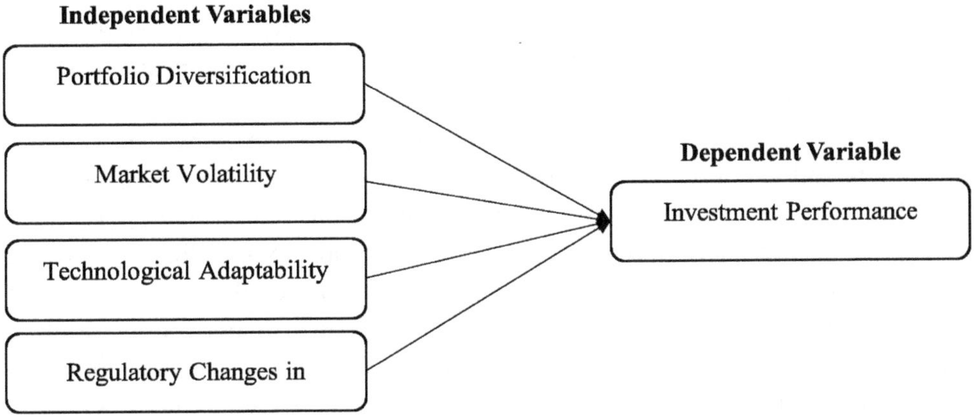

This study's conceptual framework on strategic flexibility in investment portfolios within emerging countries is based on the interaction of several key elements that affect investment performance. The framework fundamentally aims to elucidate how investors might navigate and adjust to the uncertainty intrinsic to emerging markets by employing adaptable techniques. It synthesises essential theoretical principles from finance, strategic management, and technological innovation to analyse the intricate interplay among portfolio diversification, market volatility, technological adaptability, and regulatory changes, and how these elements collectively influence investment results (Anand et al., 2021).

The dependent variable in the framework is investment performance, signifying the primary goal for investors in emerging markets (Sony et al., 2023). In this context, investment performance pertains to the financial returns and risk management results that investors want to attain. Performance can be assessed using conventional metrics like return on investment (ROI), risk-adjusted returns, and portfolio volatility, with more sophisticated indicators such as long-term growth potential and resilience to market disruptions. The dependent variable is directly affected by the independent variables, each representing a distinct facet of the investment landscape and the strategic choices investors must undertake.

Portfolio diversification is a crucial independent variable inside the framework. Diversification, entailing the allocation of investments across many asset classes, industries, or geographic locations, is fundamental to mitigating unsystematic risk—risks inherent to certain assets or sectors. In emerging markets, diversification is increasingly essential due to elevated market inefficiencies and volatility. The conceptual framework asserts that diversification strategies must be more refined and customised to the distinct risks and opportunities presented by emerging markets.

Investors may need to incorporate alternative asset classes, such as private equity, commodities, or digital assets, to mitigate the risks associated with traditional investments like equities and bonds. The framework posits that effective diversification, when implemented with adaptability, enhances portfolio stability and alleviates the negative impacts of market disruptions.

Market volatility, a significant independent variable, indicates the extent of uncertainty and variation in asset prices, especially evident in emerging markets. Volatility increases risk for investors while simultaneously offering opportunities for those who can swiftly adjust to market fluctuations. Within this framework, market volatility is regarded not merely as a risk factor but also as a catalyst for strategic flexibility. Investors who retain flexibility in their portfolios are more adept at reacting to abrupt fluctuations in market conditions, including significant drops in asset prices or unforeseen economic disturbances. The framework asserts that increased flexibility in modifying portfolio allocations in reaction to volatility will improve investment performance, enabling investors to seize opportunities during market downturns and safeguard their capital during times of elevated risk (Bilyay-Erdogan, 2020).

Technological adaptability, the third independent variable, denotes an investor's capacity to identify, foresee, and react to technological innovations that could disrupt or alter markets. The swift advancement of technology, especially in emerging markets, presents both opportunities and challenges for investors. Emerging economies frequently undergo technological leapfrogging, adopting advanced technologies that circumvent older, established systems. This may create new investment opportunities in sectors like fintech, renewable energy, and e-commerce, while concurrently making other industries obsolete. The conceptual framework highlights the significance of technological adaptability as a means of strategic flexibility. Investors who are cognisant of technological trends and can adjust their portfolios towards innovative sectors are more likely to attain superior returns (Vrontis et al., 2023). The framework posits that technological adaptability improves portfolio performance and fosters resilience against disruptions from technological change.

The final independent variable, regulatory changes, reflects the impact of governmental policies, legal structures, and institutional stability on investment results. The regulatory landscapes in emerging markets tend to be more dynamic and uncertain compared to developed economies, presenting both risks and opportunities for investors. Abrupt alterations in tax policies, trade rules, or sector-specific legislation can profoundly affect investment profitability. The framework conceptualizes regulatory changes as a significant issue that needs strategic flexibility. Investors that are able to quickly modify their portfolios in reaction to regulatory shifts—whether by reallocating capital, divesting from high-risk businesses, or capitalizing on new government incentives—are better positioned to manage risks and grab opportunities.

The framework emphasises that legislative changes do not operate in isolation but combine with other elements such as market volatility and technological improvements, hence emphasising the need for a flexible and adaptive strategy.

In this conceptual framework, strategic flexibility works as a mediating variable that links the independent variables—portfolio diversification, market volatility, technological adaptability, and regulatory changes—with the dependent variable, investment success. Strategic flexibility refers to the ability of investors to alter their plans in reaction to changing market conditions, making it a dynamic and continuous process rather than a static decision. Flexibility can show in numerous ways, such as modifying portfolio allocations, adjusting risk management strategies, or adopting new financial technologies (Prelipcean & Boscoianu, 2020). The theory claims that strategic flexibility enables investors to better negotiate the risks and complexities of emerging economies, leading to higher investment performance. Flexibility functions as a buffer against negative shocks, allowing investors to remain agile and sensitive to new information, and it provides a mechanism for capitalizing on possibilities in fast-growing, but turbulent, markets.

The interplay between these variables are key to understanding the dynamics of the conceptual framework. For instance, market volatility and regulatory changes are often interrelated; in times of political instability, regulatory changes can aggravate market volatility, thus elevating risk. Likewise, technical adaptation and regulatory changes may interact in ways that provide new investment opportunities, such as when governments introduce incentives for investments in innovative industries like green technology or digital infrastructure. Strategic flexibility serves as the method via which investors can manage these interactions, allowing them to alter their portfolios in real-time based on shifting market conditions.

Moreover, the approach underscores the iterative character of strategic flexibility. Investors must regularly examine and analyse their portfolios, not only in response to external shocks but also as part of a proactive effort to anticipate future trends. In this respect, flexibility is not only a reactive measure but also a forward-looking approach that blends foresight and adaptability into the investment process. The framework identifies strategic flexibility as a crucial element for investment success in emerging markets, characterised by more volatility and unpredictability compared to developed economies (Zahoor & Lew, 2023).

This study's conceptual framework incorporates several interrelated variables—portfolio diversification, market volatility, technological adaptability, and regulatory changes—to elucidate how strategic flexibility improves investment performance in emerging markets. Strategic flexibility is the crucial mediating element that permits investors to manoeuvre through market uncertainty, enabling them to address risks, seize opportunities, and sustain portfolio resilience amid dynamic fluctuations (Loang, 2024b). The interplay among these variables and the function of flexibility as an ongoing, iterative process offer a thorough framework for comprehending the intricacies of investing in emerging economies. This approach establishes the basis for additional empirical research and offers a theoretical perspective to analyse the influence of strategic flexibility on investment results.

CONCLUSION

The research on strategic flexibility in investment portfolios in developing economies offers an extensive examination of the elements affecting investment performance in dynamic and volatile conditions. This study emphasises the necessity of implementing adaptable investment strategies that provide rapid modifications in reaction to changing market conditions, through an in-depth examination of portfolio diversification, market volatility, technological adaptation, and regulatory changes. Strategic flexibility is essential for investors seeking to manoeuvre through the difficulties of emerging economies, where conventional investment models may fail amid increased unpredictability and swift changes in economic and technical environments.

The primary result of this study is that strategic flexibility is essential for attaining sustainable investment performance in emerging economies. Due to the susceptibility of these markets to elevated volatility caused by political instability, regulatory uncertainty, and technological change, investors must remain vigilant and consistently adjust their portfolios. Inflexible, rigid investment strategies that may be effective in stable, industrialised markets are improbable to thrive in the dynamic contexts of emerging economies. Investors that integrate strategic flexibility into their decision-making are more adept at mitigating risks and seizing opportunities presented by the dynamic character of these markets.

This study indicates that portfolio diversity, albeit a fundamental risk management strategy, requires a more nuanced application in emerging markets. Conventional diversification methods that distribute risk among asset classes or geographic areas are inadequate for addressing the distinct hazards presented by these markets. Investors should implement more sophisticated diversification strategies that include other asset classes and consider region-specific risks, such as currency volatility and sectoral disparities. The capacity to modify diversification strategies in reaction to fluctuating market conditions is essential for sustaining portfolio resilience and enhancing performance.

Market volatility, a significant characteristic of emerging markets, is demonstrated to be both a challenge and an opportunity. The study emphasises that although high volatility elevates risk, it simultaneously offers possibilities for investors capable of rapidly modifying their portfolios to capitalise on price movements and market swings.

Strategic flexibility enables investors to navigate volatility more adeptly, affording the responsiveness required to address abrupt fluctuations in asset values, economic disturbances, or political occurrences. This versatility enables investors to mitigate losses during downturns and optimise gains during recovery or expansion phases.

The study highlights technological adaptation as a crucial finding, underscoring the increasing significance of technical breakthroughs in influencing investment choices. Emerging markets, typically marked by swift technical advancement, provide both dangers and opportunities for investors. Recognising, anticipating, and responding to technology advances is essential for sustaining a competitive advantage. Investors that strategically link their portfolios with areas undergoing technological advancement are more likely to attain greater returns. Conversely, those who do not adapt to technological upheavals may incur substantial losses, especially in sectors susceptible to obsolescence. The research concludes that incorporating technology foresight into investment decision-making is essential for strategic flexibility.

This study concludes that regulatory changes play a substantial influence. Regulatory environments in emerging markets are frequently unstable, characterised by continual changes in government policies, legal frameworks, and institutional practices. These alterations can either improve or impede investment performance, contingent upon the promptness and efficacy of investors' responses. The research indicates that strategic flexibility is crucial for mitigating regulatory risk, enabling investors to modify their portfolios in reaction to emerging rules, governmental incentives, or sector-specific policies. Furthermore, the study emphasises that regulatory modifications frequently interact with additional variables, like market volatility and technology progress, so complicating the investment environment. Strategic flexibility allows investors to manage this complexity, ensuring their portfolios are consistent with current regulatory changes.

Based on these findings, the study indicates that strategic flexibility serves as a crucial mediating element connecting the independent variables—portfolio diversification, market volatility, technological adaptability, and regulatory changes—with investment performance. By persistently observing market circumstances and modifying portfolios in real-time, investors can improve their capacity to endure market disruptions, capitalise on new opportunities, and maximise long-term returns. Strategic flexibility is a dynamic and continuous process that necessitates investors to be watchful, adaptive, and forward-thinking in their portfolio management strategy.

Theoretical, Managerial and Policy Implications

This study's theoretical implications for strategic flexibility in investment portfolios are complex, enriching discussions across various academic disciplines, such as finance, strategic management, and innovation theory. The study enhances our comprehension of the role of strategic flexibility as a mediator between diverse market dynamics and investment success, especially in emerging economies. This study enhances the theoretical framework by investigating the combined influence of flexibility in managing particular elements, such as market volatility, portfolio diversification, and regulatory changes, which have been the focus of much prior studies. It underscores the dynamic interaction among these variables, indicating that strategic flexibility is both reactive and proactive, enabling investors to foresee and adapt to changes in market conditions. The research contests conventional static investment theories by promoting a more dynamic model that continually adapts to environmental influences.

The study's focus on technical adaptability as a fundamental element of strategic flexibility presents a significant theoretical contribution to the investment strategy literature. It highlights the increasing importance of technology foresight in investment decisions, especially in contexts where technological innovations are swiftly transforming the competitive landscape. This enhances the theoretical comprehension of the intersection of innovation, technology, and financial markets, expanding the framework of strategic management theory by incorporating technological disruption as a vital component of portfolio management.

The study's conclusions hold substantial significance for investment managers and financial institutions, especially those engaged in or aiming to penetrate emerging markets. A crucial managerial insight is the necessity to incorporate flexibility as a fundamental tenet in the portfolio management process. Investment managers must acknowledge that inflexible, long-term strategies—though frequently successful in stable markets—are ill-suited for the volatility and unpredictability of emerging economies. This necessitates a transformation in managerial perspective, highlighting agility, adaptability, and ongoing evaluation of portfolio composition in reaction to real-time market changes.

The research indicates that managers ought to prioritise the incorporation of technology into their investment methodologies. This entails investing in areas propelled by technology innovation and utilising advanced data analytics, machine learning, and artificial intelligence to improve decision-making processes. By employing these tools, managers can more accurately forecast market trends, evaluate risks, and recognise emerging opportunities, thus improving the strategic adaptability of their portfolios. The significance of fostering a culture of adaptation within financial institutions is underscored, wherein decision-making processes are decentralised and attuned to the swiftly evolving external landscape. Investment managers must cultivate a proactive stance towards regulatory and technological changes, ensuring their teams are prepared to make prompt judgements as required.

Furthermore, the study's findings regarding regulatory modifications underscore the imperative for investment managers to implement more advanced risk management procedures. In emerging markets, characterised by fluid and unpredictable regulatory regimes, managers must possess a thorough comprehension of the political and economic context in which they function. This indicates that investment managers must not only observe regulatory developments but also proactively interact with lawmakers and industry stakeholders to foresee prospective regulatory alterations. This engagement enables managers to match their portfolios with advantageous policies and to quickly adapt to unfavourable regulatory changes.

The study presents significant implications for policymakers, especially for governments and regulatory authorities in emerging markets. The results indicate that regulatory stability and openness are essential for attracting and retaining foreign investment. Inconsistent or abrupt regulation alterations can generate uncertainty, prompting investors to adopt a more conservative strategy or, in certain instances, withdraw funds from the market entirely. Policymakers must prioritise the establishment of stable, predictable regulatory frameworks that promote long-term investment. This entails not only formulating explicit norms and regulations but also guaranteeing consistent enforcement and transparent communication with the investment community.

The report emphasises the government's responsibility in promoting technological innovation, especially in sectors vital for economic development. Policymakers must acknowledge that technical progress is a crucial catalyst for economic expansion, particularly in emerging nations where technological leapfrogging can create new investment opportunities. Governments should contemplate providing incentives, such as tax reductions, grants, or subsidies, to enterprises and investors that foster the advancement of essential technology in order to stimulate investment in innovative areas. Furthermore, regulatory frameworks should be constructed to facilitate the integration of new technologies, guaranteeing that obsolete restrictions do not impede innovation or obstruct investors from using rising technology trends.

The study emphasises the interplay between regulatory changes and market volatility, highlighting the necessity for more coordinated policy responses during periods of economic turbulence. Governments in emerging countries frequently have substantial difficulties in navigating political and economic crises, resulting in sudden policy changes that exacerbate market instability. The research indicates that governments ought to use a more strategic and long-term methodology for crisis management, balancing immediate stabilisation initiatives with the necessity of fostering a conducive investment climate. This may entail formulating contingency plans that offer investors a definitive framework for regulatory measures during crises, so mitigating uncertainty and enhancing market trust.

This study has extensive theoretical, managerial, and policy ramifications. It theoretically enhances the comprehension of strategic flexibility as a dynamic, integrative concept that connects market forces with investment performance, especially within emerging markets. From a managerial perspective, it underscores the necessity for agility, technological integration, and advanced risk management measures in portfolio management. The report advocates for enhanced regulatory stability, support for technological innovation, and coordinated crisis management to create a more favourable investment environment. These consequences offer significant insights for both scholars and practitioners aiming to understand the intricacies of investing in swiftly evolving global marketplaces.

Limitations and Recommendations for Future Studies

The study on strategic flexibility in investment portfolios in emerging markets offers useful insights, however it has its limitations. These limitations are crucial to recognise since they delineate the parameters of the study's conclusions and indicate avenues for more investigation. Comprehending the limitations of this research facilitates more accurate interpretations of its findings and paves the way for future investigations to fill the existing gaps.

A key limitation of this study is the intrinsic complexity and variability of emerging markets. Emerging economies are not homogeneous; they vary considerably in their economic frameworks, political stability, regulatory conditions, and technological advancement. For example, China, characterised by its advanced technological infrastructure and stringent regulatory framework, offers a markedly distinct investment climate in contrast to smaller, less developed economies in Sub-Saharan Africa. The variability may hinder the generalisation of this study's findings across all emerging markets. Future study may adopt a more detailed approach by concentrating on certain areas or nations to enhance comprehension of how strategic flexibility functions within the distinct setting of each market. Future research could provide more personalised insights by performing comparative evaluations of various emerging markets, considering the unique characteristics influencing investment performance in each region.

A further restriction is the dependence on past data to assess the influence of factors such as market volatility, technological adaptation, and regulatory changes on investment success. Although historical data offers a significant foundation for comprehending trends and correlations, it may inadequately reflect the swiftly evolving dynamics of emerging markets, especially regarding technology progress. The velocity of technological disruption is accelerating, rendering historical trends potentially unreliable as predictors of future advancements. This poses a dilemma for investors who depend on historical data to guide future decisions. Future research may include additional real-time data or formulate predictive models that consider the non-linear dynamics of technological and regulatory changes. Advanced modelling tools, including machine learning and artificial intelligence, may be utilised to forecast the evolution of these factors and their influence on investment strategies in real-time, providing a more anticipatory view on strategic flexibility.

A pertinent restriction is the challenge in measuring specific qualitative dimensions of strategic flexibility, especially with technical adaptation and regulatory responsiveness. Although quantitative metrics for market volatility and portfolio diversification are well-defined, accurately capturing the subtleties of investor adaptation to technological advancements or regulatory alterations is more complex. These factors frequently entail intricate decision-making processes, the application of cutting-edge financial tools, and subjective assessments of prospective market situations. Consequently, the study may inadequately encompass the intricacies of strategic flexibility in application. Future study may employ more advanced qualitative methodologies, such as comprehensive interviews with portfolio managers or case studies of particular investment firms, to gain deeper insights into the operationalisation of flexibility in actual investment decision-making. Integrating these qualitative observations with quantitative models would yield a more comprehensive understanding of strategic flexibility in emerging markets.

A further weakness is the study's concentration on major institutional investors and portfolio managers, potentially neglecting the experiences and strategies of smaller investors, including retail investors and family offices, in emerging markets. Large institutional investors frequently possess resources, technologies, and experience unavailable to smaller investors, allowing them to employ more advanced strategic flexibility methods. Nonetheless, smaller investors may demonstrate adaptability through alternative means, such as concentrating on specialist areas or utilising local expertise to manoeuvre through turbulent markets. Future research may investigate the manifestation of strategic flexibility among various investor groups, ranging from huge institutional entities to smaller, localised market actors. This will facilitate a comprehensive understanding of how diverse investors utilise flexibility to mitigate risk and capitalise on opportunities in emerging markets.

Furthermore, the study does not thoroughly investigate the potential long-term trade-offs linked to strategic flexibility. Although flexibility is typically regarded as a beneficial quality that improves investment outcomes in volatile conditions, there are instances where excessive flexibility results in overreaction or inadequate decision-making. Frequent adjustments to portfolio allocations in reaction to short-term market changes may elevate transaction costs or lead to missed opportunities for long-term growth. This indicates a potential equilibrium between preserving sufficient flexibility to respond to market dynamics and preventing excessive turnover that could undermine portfolio performance. Future study may explore this equilibrium by assessing the ideal level of flexibility across various market conditions and for distinct categories of investors. Comprehending the location of this equilibrium could assist investors in executing flexibility in a more calculated and efficient manner.

The study primarily examines the financial aspects of strategic flexibility, including portfolio diversification and risk management strategies, yet it does not thoroughly investigate the increasingly pertinent social, environmental, and governance (ESG) factors in emerging markets. As ESG issues increasingly integrate into investment strategies, they may affect investors' approach to flexibility, especially in areas with significant social and environmental risks. In emerging nations characterised by inadequate environmental regulations or pronounced social inequality, investors may need to modify their strategy to address these non-financial risks, which could affect long-term performance. Future research may explore the application of strategic flexibility in the realm of ESG investment, analysing how investors reconcile financial and non-financial factors in response to market dynamics.

Several critical topics merit additional investigation for future research. Future studies should prioritise the development of more complete models that incorporate the intricate relationships among market volatility, technological advancements, and regulatory changes. These models could integrate real-time data and predictive analytics to more effectively reflect the dynamic and rapidly shifting characteristics of emerging economies. Secondly, there is a necessity for additional empirical research that investigates the implementation of strategic flexibility in particular businesses or sectors within emerging economies, especially those significantly affected by technology disruption, such as fintech, renewable energy, or e-commerce. By concentrating on sector-specific dynamics, academics can deliver more nuanced insights into the functioning of flexibility within certain contexts, so delivering practical advise for investors.

REFERENCES

Ahammad, M. F., Basu, S., Munjal, S., Clegg, J., & Shoham, O. B. (2021). Strategic agility, environmental uncertainties and international performance: The perspective of Indian firms. *Journal of World Business*, 56(4), 101218. DOI: 10.1016/j.jwb.2021.101218

Anand, J., McDermott, G., Mudambi, R., & Narula, R. (2021). Innovation in and from emerging economies: New insights and lessons for international business research. *Journal of International Business Studies*, 52(4), 545–559. DOI: 10.1057/s41267-021-00426-1

Bilyay-Erdogan, S. (2020). Does financial flexibility enhance firm value? A comparative study between developed and emerging countries. *Verslas: teorija ir praktika, 21*(2), 723-736.

FaXing. L., & Loang, O. K. (2024). Green Investing and Financial Education: The Case of China's A-Share Market. In *Technology-Driven Business Innovation: Unleashing the Digital Advantage, Volume 1* (pp. 29-41). Cham: Springer Nature Switzerland.

Fu, T., & Loang, O. K. (2024). The Roles of ESG Disclosure, Innovation in Improving Firm Financial Performance: Evidence from China. In *Artificial Intelligence (AI) and Customer Social Responsibility (CSR)* (pp. 197–221). Springer Nature Switzerland. DOI: 10.1007/978-3-031-50939-1_16

Iriani, N., Agustianti, A., Sucianti, R., Rahman, A., & Putera, W. (2024). Understanding Risk and Uncertainty Management: A Qualitative Inquiry into Developing Business Strategies Amidst Global Economic Shifts, Government Policies, and Market Volatility. *Golden Ratio of Finance Management*, 4(2), 62–77. DOI: 10.52970/grfm.v4i2.444

Loang, O. K. (2023). Corporate governance and Islamic behavioural finance: A review from Malaysia and GCC countries. *Indian Journal of Corporate Governance*, 16(1), 28–51. DOI: 10.1177/09746862231178959

Loang, O. K. (2024). Stability Of Shariah-Compliant Stocks In Indonesia, Malaysia, And Gcc: The Roles Of Monetary And Fiscal Policies And Contagion. *Journal of Islamic Monetary Economics and Finance*, 10(1), 155–176. DOI: 10.21098/jimf.v10i1.1899

Loang, O. K. (2024). Sustainability's impact of ESG-infused policies on leading economic indicators in Asian economies. *Journal of Sustainable Research*, 6(3), e240059. DOI: 10.20900/jsr20240059

Prelipcean, G., & Boscoianu, M. (2020). An Innovative Flexible Investment Vehicle Oriented to Sustainability–The Adaptation of Hedge Funds in the Case of Emerging Markets. *ENTRENOVA-ENTerprise REsearch InNOVAtion*, 6(1), 493–503.

Saeed, M. A., Jiao, Y., Zahid, M. M., Tabassum, H., & Nauman, S. (2021). Organizational flexibility and project portfolio performance: The roles of innovation, absorptive capacity and environmental dynamism. *International Journal of Managing Projects in Business*, 14(3), 600–624. DOI: 10.1108/IJMPB-02-2020-0058

Shahzad, S., & Jasińska, E. (2024). Renewable Revolution: A Review of Strategic Flexibility in Future Power Systems. *Sustainability (Basel)*, 16(13), 5454. DOI: 10.3390/su16135454

Sony, M., Antony, J., & Mc Dermott, O. (2023). How do the technological capability and strategic flexibility of an organization impact its successful implementation of Industry 4.0? A qualitative viewpoint. *Benchmarking*, 30(3), 924–949. DOI: 10.1108/BIJ-09-2021-0541

Suresh, G., & Loang, O. K. (2024). The Rationality Conundrum: Exploring Herd Mentality among Individual Investors in the Indian Stock Market. *Indian Journal of Finance*, 18(6), 26–45. DOI: 10.17010/ijf/2024/v18i6/173967

Tang, H., & Loang, O. K. (2024). Does ESG Performance Improve the Financial Performance of Enterprises in China? The Mediating Role of Financial Constraints. In *Artificial Intelligence (AI) and Customer Social Responsibility (CSR)* (pp. 263–289). Springer Nature Switzerland. DOI: 10.1007/978-3-031-50939-1_20

Vrontis, D., Belas, J., Thrassou, A., Santoro, G., & Christofi, M. (2023). Strategic agility, openness and performance: A mixed method comparative analysis of firms operating in developed and emerging markets. *Review of Managerial Science*, 17(4), 1365–1398. DOI: 10.1007/s11846-022-00562-4

Zahoor, N., & Lew, Y. K. (2023). Enhancing international marketing capability and export performance of emerging market SMEs in crises: Strategic flexibility and digital technologies. *International Marketing Review*, 40(5), 1158–1187. DOI: 10.1108/IMR-12-2021-0350

Chapter 11
The Role of Technological Innovation in Shaping Investment Strategies in Emerging Markets:
A Study on Risk and Return Dynamics

Yang Ze
Universiti Malaya, Malaysia

Ooi Kok Loang
https://orcid.org/0000-0003-0412-8899
Universiti Malaya, Malaysia

ABSTRACT

This study examines the role of technological innovation in shaping investment strategies in emerging markets, focusing on the dynamics of risk and return. By exploring key factors such as technological disruption, innovation adoption rates, market competition intensity, and investor technological awareness, the study provides insights into how these variables influence investment returns. Emerging markets present unique challenges and opportunities due to rapid technological advancements, requiring investors to adapt strategies to maximize returns while managing risks associated with market volatility. The findings emphasize the importance of technological literacy among investors and the need for flexible regulatory frameworks to support innovation-driven investments in these dynamic markets.

DOI: 10.4018/979-8-3693-9380-2.ch011

INTRODUCTION

Technological innovation has become a crucial element in influencing investment strategies, especially in emerging markets where swift transformations can offer both opportunities and threats. The convergence of technological disruption and investment dynamics is intricate, yet increasingly pertinent in the contemporary global economy. In these markets, innovation frequently propels growth, compelling industries to embrace new technologies at a rate that can fundamentally transform market conditions. Consequently, investors must traverse this changing environment to make intelligent choices that enhance their returns while minimising the related risks. This study examines the impact of technological innovation on risk and return dynamics in emerging markets, taking into account key aspects such as technological disruption, rates of innovation uptake, market rivalry intensity, and investor understanding of technology (Loang, 2023).

Technological disruption, a principal catalyst of change in these industries, denotes the transformative effect of emerging technologies that make current products, services, or business models obsolete. In emerging markets, change frequently transpires more swiftly and unpredictably than in developed economies, where industries are well-established and regulatory frameworks are more resilient (Karhade & Dong, 2021). Investors in emerging economies encounter a distinct challenge: they must evaluate both the development potential of companies embracing new technology and the inherent dangers associated with disruptive innovations that can destabilise conventional market frameworks. Technological change can rapidly produce both beneficiaries and detractors, complicating the decision-making process for investors aiming to balance risk and return.

The rates of innovation uptake are a crucial determinant influencing investment strategy in these industries. Emerging economies have varied rates of technological adoption, influenced by variations in infrastructure, regulatory environments, and the willingness of industries to accept change. Certain sectors, such as fintech and telecoms, may swiftly embrace innovative solutions, resulting in substantial development prospects. Entities hindered by antiquated infrastructure or less favourable policy frameworks may fall behind, presenting diminished profits or elevated risks for investors. The disparate adoption rates throughout sectors and locations necessitate that investors exercise discernment in their strategies, as the potential for returns is intricately linked to the timing and extent of innovation adoption in certain markets.

The intensity of market competition significantly complicates the investment landscape in emerging nations. Technological innovation frequently stimulates heightened rivalry as new entrants utilise advanced technologies to undermine incumbents and confront established market participants. Increased competition can stimulate growth and enhance efficiency, but it also brings about volatility. For investors, comprehending the competitive dynamics shaped by technology innovation is essential. Markets marked by fierce rivalry stemming from technological improvements may yield substantial gains for early entrants, although they also pose considerable risks if companies do not adapt to breakthroughs or are outmaneuvered by more agile rivals (Rana et al., 2021).

The technological awareness of investors moderates the impact of technological innovation on investment profits. As technical innovation increasingly integrates into corporate operations, investors possessing a profound comprehension of technological trends and breakthroughs are more adept at seeing possibilities and foreseeing threats. In emerging nations, where technological adoption is sometimes inconsistent, investors with robust technological acumen may surpass their less-informed peers by recognising nascent ideas capable of transforming industries. Furthermore, these investors are inclined to formulate strategies that address the particular risks linked to technology disruption, including legislative alterations, infrastructure constraints, and evolving consumer behaviours.

A notable deficiency exists in the comprehension of investor behaviour, especially with technical savvy. Although it is acknowledged that investors with greater technology literacy are more adept at manoeuvring through emerging markets, there exists a paucity of empirical studies regarding the tangible impact of this awareness on investing strategies and decision-making processes. Furthermore, the current literature insufficiently examines the learning curve related to technological developments (Nyagadza et al., 2022). Investors, especially in underdeveloped economies, may lack the requisite resources or experience to comprehend the ramifications of swift technological progress. This information deficit may lead to poor investment choices, causing investors to either overrate the prospective profits of technical advancements or underrate the associated dangers of disruptive technological shifts. Additional research is required to investigate the correlation among technology awareness, investor behaviour, and actual investment results in various emerging markets.

The lack of comprehension regarding the long-term impacts of technical innovation on market competition intensity also hinders the appropriate prediction of investment returns. (FaXing & Loang, 2024) Although many studies emphasise the immediate effects of disruptive technologies—such as the emergence of new competitors and the displacement of established firms—there is insufficient focus on the long-term durability of these competitive dynamics. In many expanding areas, swift technical advancements may first heighten rivalry, subsequently resulting in consolidation as larger companies purchase smaller, technologically proficient businesses (Suresh & Loang, 2024). This process can establish an investing milieu marked by brief intervals of substantial returns, succeeded by phases of stagnation or consolidation. The absence of longitudinal studies analysing these competitive dynamics over prolonged durations creates a significant void in comprehending the complete lifespan of technical innovation in emerging economies, hence affecting investment risk evaluations.

An other gap concerns the influence of regulatory frameworks on the connection between technical innovation and investment returns. Although regulatory environments are recognised as crucial in influencing technological uptake and market competition, there is little analysis of how differing regulatory strategies in emerging markets affect the success or failure of technology-driven investments. Numerous rising economies possess regulatory frameworks that are either inadequately established or inconsistent, resulting in ambiguity over intellectual property rights, data privacy, and the legal structures governing novel technologies such as artificial intelligence, fintech, and blockchain. The interplay between regulatory uncertainties and investment strategies is inadequately examined, resulting in little guidance for investors on managing regulatory risks in technologically advanced sectors. Future research may examine the moderating influence of regulation on technology disruption and its effects on long-term investment returns (Loang, 2024a).

There exists a significant gap in comprehending the impact of social and cultural aspects on the adoption and success of technology breakthroughs in emerging economies. Existing research predominantly emphasises economic or infrastructural catalysts of technological change; nonetheless, social acceptance, cultural attitudes towards technology, and consumer readiness are equally crucial in ascertaining the success of innovations. In areas with limited technology literacy or cultural opposition to new technologies, even significantly disruptive inventions may struggle to attain general acceptance, therefore diminishing their potential for earning investment returns. This gap underscores the necessity for a more interdisciplinary methodology in examining technological innovation in emerging markets, integrating perspectives from sociology, anthropology, and consumer behaviour with conventional economic and financial analysis. Investment strategies that heavily depend on technology innovation may overrate return potential and underrate dangers linked to restricted market acceptance without a comprehensive comprehension of these social dynamics (Loang, 2024b).

LITERATURE REVIEW

Underlying Theory: Disruptive Innovation Theory

The Disruptive Innovation Theory, established by Clayton Christensen in 1997, has proven fundamental for comprehending how technological improvements can fundamentally transform companies and marketplaces. The theory asserts that specific innovations, instead of merely enhancing existing products or services, fundamentally upset dominant market players by launching new items that are initially of inferior quality but ultimately adapt to satisfy the requirements of mainstream consumers. Disruptive innovations generally penetrate the market via niche or underdeveloped niches, which incumbent enterprises sometimes neglect due to initially poor profit margins or a perceived lack of significance. Over time, these ideas enhance and achieve market traction, ultimately displacing or substantially transforming the competitive landscape (Xu & Loang, 2024a). This concept holds considerable ramifications for investors, particularly in emerging economies, where the velocity and effects of disruptive technologies can be notably severe and unpredictable.

A fundamental characteristic of disruptive innovation is its frequent disregard by established companies, who often concentrate on sustaining profitability by incremental enhancements to current products or services. This establishes a market void that smaller, more nimble enterprises might capitalise on (Xu & Loang, 2024b). Initially, disruptive technologies generally focus on low-end consumers or niche markets, providing solutions that may be qualitatively or functionally inferior but are more economical or accessible. As these inventions advance, they acquire a wider clientele, ascend the market hierarchy, and ultimately jeopardise the supremacy of established companies. In this context, disruptive innovations contest the conventional belief that successful companies can preserve their dominance by concentrating on sustaining innovations—those that progressively enhance current products or services. For investors, comprehending the dynamics of disruptive innovation is essential, as it can destabilise conventional market structures and generate new avenues for growth (Anand et al., 2021).

In emerging markets, the potential for disruptive innovation is significantly heightened. Numerous emerging economies lack the established infrastructure and market leaders that define more mature countries. This fosters an environment conducive to disruptive technologies that can transform industries. In markets with restricted access to banking services, fintech innovations like mobile payment platforms have swiftly acquired popularity, circumventing established financial institutions and providing users with more accessible and cost-effective services (Deng et al., 2020). Industries like telecommunications, healthcare, and energy are especially vulnerable to disruptive innovations in emerging nations, as technical progress might provide remedies for enduring infrastructure issues. Investors in these areas must be cognisant of the potential for disruptive innovations to generate new growth possibilities, along with the risks posed by the displacement of established enterprises (Nascimento et al., 2021).

The Disruptive Innovation Theory emphasises the significance of time in investment strategies. Disruptive innovations generally commence with gradual growth and restricted market penetration, subsequently reaching a tipping point where they swiftly acquire market share and disrupt established sectors. For investors, recognising this pivotal moment is essential. Premature investment in a disruptive breakthrough may lead to losses if the innovation fails to achieve momentum or encounters unexpected obstacles. Conversely, delayed investment may lead to missed chances, as innovation has already reshaped the industry and competitors have secured control. This scheduling difficulty is particularly pertinent in emerging nations, where the uptake of new technology may be erratic, shaped by elements such as legislative frameworks, infrastructure advancement, and consumer behaviour. Consequently, investors must meticulously evaluate the market's preparedness for disruptive breakthroughs and formulate strategies that consider the unpredictability associated with their adoption and growth trajectory (Karhade & Dong, 2021).

Moreover, Disruptive Innovation Theory emphasises the significance of resource distribution and strategic decision-making within organisations. Christensen's research indicates that incumbent organisations frequently struggle to adapt to disruptive technologies due to limitations imposed by their current business models and resource allocation mechanisms. Incumbents typically prioritise sustaining innovations—those that enhance current products or services—since these innovations correspond with their established client base and yield more rapid returns. Conversely, disruptive breakthroughs may necessitate alternative business structures, novel capabilities, and an openness to accept reduced margins in the short term. This presents investors with both risks and opportunities. Established companies may exhibit sluggishness in adapting to disruptive developments, hence creating opportunities for new entrants to capture market share. Simultaneously, companies that adeptly manage disruptive innovation by investment in new technology or by altering their business strategies may yield substantial long-term gains. Comprehending how companies distribute resources in reaction to disruptive developments can yield significant insights about their prospective growth potential (Din et al., 2022).

In emerging economies, the dynamics of disruptive innovation are further complicated by external variables including legal frameworks, infrastructure advancement, and socio-cultural influences. In contrast to more developed markets, which typically possess established and predictable regulatory frameworks, developing economies may exhibit regulatory regimes that are either underdeveloped or subject to change (Zhan, 2021). This can generate both possibilities and threats for disruptive ideas. Regulatory loopholes can facilitate the proliferation of disruptive innovations, exemplified by the swift emergence of mobile banking in economies with minimal regulatory supervision of financial services. Nonetheless, abrupt regulatory changes or governmental interventions can provide substantial risks to investors, as disruptive technologies may be hindered by new legislation or policies that favour entrenched enterprises or sectors. Consequently, investors must meticulously assess the regulatory environment when analysing the prospects for disruptive inventions in emerging economies (Rana et al., 2021).

Technological disruption is a recognised term in academic literature, with researchers continuously emphasising its transformative impact on companies and marketplaces. Clayton Christensen's seminal research on disruptive innovation has been extensively utilised to examine how emerging technologies supplant established market leaders and transform industries. Subsequent research has broadened this concept, investigating how disruptive technologies like digital platforms, artificial intelligence, and blockchain might transform the competitive landscape by reducing entry barriers and facilitating new business models. Research in emerging markets indicates that technology disruption frequently transpires more swiftly in these areas, propelled by the absence of established infrastructure and the demand for cost-effective, scalable solutions. Research on mobile telecommunications and digital banking has demonstrated how disruptive technology can surpass existing systems, providing services to marginalised communities and transforming sectors. Nevertheless, a significant portion of the literature continues to concentrate on the impacts of technological disruption in established markets, resulting in a deficiency of comprehension regarding how these dynamics manifest in the more unstable and fragmented economies of developing nations. This vacuum necessitates comprehensive research on the interaction between disruptive innovation and market-specific variables, including regulatory frameworks, infrastructure preparedness, and consumer behaviour in these countries (Bustamante et al., 2021).

The rate of innovation adoption is a significant variable examined in the literature, especially within the context of technology diffusion models. Everett Rogers' "Diffusion of Innovations" hypothesis offers a robust framework for comprehending the dissemination of innovations among various demographic segments. Rogers' model classifies adopters into categories including innovators, early adopters, and laggards, asserting that the adoption rate is influenced by criteria such as relative advantage, compatibility, complexity, trialability, and observability. This hypothesis has been utilised across multiple industries to elucidate the process by which new technologies infiltrate markets and achieve widespread adoption. In emerging markets, the adoption rate of technological advancements is generally inconsistent, frequently hindered by infrastructural, economic, and cultural obstacles. The literature indicates that adoption rates in these regions may vary considerably across sectors. Financial technologies (fintech) have been adopted more swiftly in emerging nations since they offer solutions to neglected groups, while sectors like healthcare and education may experience delays owing to regulatory obstacles or insufficient infrastructure. Although numerous studies examine the determinants of innovation adoption in emerging countries, there is a paucity of data regarding the impact of disparate adoption rates across sectors on investment strategies. The relationship between innovation adoption and investment returns is a poorly explored topic in academic literature, especially with swiftly changing emerging economies.

The intensity of market competition is a thoroughly examined variable in the literature, especially regarding technical innovation. Michael Porter's research on competitive strategy offers a fundamental comprehension of how companies react to competition in their respective industries. Porter's Five Forces framework delineates the principal competitive challenges confronting organisations, encompassing the threat of new entrants, the bargaining power of customers and suppliers, and the intensity of rivalry among current competitors. The research indicates that technological innovation intensifies competition by allowing new entrants to upset established firms and by reducing costs or generating new value propositions. Research indicates that technical innovation can significantly transform competitive dynamics in emerging markets. Research on the African telecom sector indicates that the advent of mobile telecoms technology has heightened competition among companies, resulting in reduced pricing and enhanced services. Likewise, the emergence of e-commerce platforms in markets such as China and India has intensified competition in the retail industry, empowering small and medium-sized firms (SMEs) to contest established market leaders. Nevertheless, the literature frequently emphasises short-term competitive dynamics, while paying insufficient attention to the long-term implications of technical innovation on market structure and competitiveness in emerging markets. Further research is required to comprehend the evolution of these competitive dynamics over time and the influence of technological innovation on the competitive environment across various sectors.

The literature has comparatively overlooked investor technical knowledge relative to other variables. The notion of investor awareness has been examined through the framework of behavioural finance, which investigates the impact of cognitive biases, information asymmetries, and market sentiment on investment choices. Studies indicate that investors possessing enhanced access to information and superior experience are more adept at seeing opportunities and managing risks in intricate markets. In the realm of technological innovation, investor technical awareness denotes the extent to which investors comprehend and assess the ramifications of emerging technology on market dynamics. Research indicates that investors with greater technological expertise are more adept at recognising early-stage innovations and investing in companies poised to capitalise on disruptive technology. This insight is especially crucial in emerging nations, where technical innovations can swiftly transform the investing environment. The literature regarding the impact of investor technology understanding on investment strategies within the realm of emerging market innovation is limited. Numerous studies concentrate on the significance of technological awareness within venture capital and private equity contexts, where investors typically possess specialised expertise in technology areas. Further research is required to understand the influence of technological knowledge on the investment decisions of institutional investors, retail investors, and other stakeholders in emerging markets, where technology adoption is less predictable and innovation-related risks are elevated (Nyagadza et al., 2022).

In conclusion, the research on technological disruption, innovation adoption rates, market rivalry intensity, and investor technological awareness offers significant insights into the impact of these variables on investment returns. Nonetheless, substantial gaps persist, especially in emerging nations, where the distinctive traits of these economies necessitate a more sophisticated comprehension of the relationship between technical innovation and investment patterns. By correcting these deficiencies, subsequent research can provide a more thorough understanding of how technology innovation influences investment strategies and results in the swiftly changing markets of the developing world (Geddes & Schmidt, 2020).

Research Methodology

This study utilises both qualitative and quantitative research methodologies to provide a thorough framework for analysing the intricate interaction between technological innovation and investment strategies in emerging markets. The study seeks to amalgamate these two techniques to encapsulate both the intricate, subjective experiences of investors and firms, alongside the factual, data-driven trends that influence risk and return dynamics in these markets.

The qualitative aspect of the research aims to deliver profound, contextual understanding of the impact of technical innovation on decision-making among principal stakeholders, including investors, policymakers, and business leaders in emerging markets. Semi-structured interviews will be performed with a purposive sample of investors, encompassing venture capitalists, institutional investors, private equity firms, and executives from companies using or advancing technical advances. The semi-structured format of the interviews facilitates flexibility in examining themes that may arise during discussions, while still preserving a level of comparability among interviews. The purpose of these interviews is to elucidate investors' perceptions of technological disruption, identify the elements that impact their investment decisions about specific breakthroughs, and examine their strategies for managing the risks associated with disruptive technology. Additionally, interviews with business leaders will examine how companies in emerging economies adjust to technology advancements, their methods for embracing new ideas, and the obstacles they encounter in very competitive settings.

The qualitative phase will encompass case studies of certain industries or companies that have seen substantial technological disruption. These case studies will offer a comprehensive analysis of how technological innovation has transformed industrial dynamics and the competitive landscape in emerging markets. By concentrating on specific sectors such as fintech, telecommunications, or e-commerce, the research might yield a sector-specific comprehension of the impact of innovation on investor returns. A case study of the mobile payments market in sub-Saharan Africa may demonstrate how little infrastructure expenses and swift adoption rates have generated distinctive chances for disruptive technology, providing insights for investors in various areas or industries. Case studies will be constructed through the triangulation of data obtained from interviews, secondary sources like industry reports, and firm-level data to guarantee a thorough and comprehensive examination.

The study will employ several statistical methodologies to empirically analyse the correlation between technological innovation and investment returns. This portion of the research will entail the gathering and examination of secondary data from several sources, including financial databases, governmental reports, and industry publications. The emphasis will be on critical measures such organisational success, market competitiveness, and rates of technological adoption. The study will utilise econometric studies to measure the effects of variables such as technological disruption, innovation adoption rates, and market rivalry intensity on investment returns in emerging markets. The quantitative method will facilitate the testing of specific hypotheses, such as whether elevated rates of technological adoption correlate with enhanced investment returns, or whether intensified rivalry resulting from technological disruption contributes to increased market volatility and risk.

The quantitative analysis will utilise regression models to evaluate the influence of independent variables (technological disruption, innovation adoption rate, market competitive intensity, and investor technical awareness) on the dependent variable, investment returns. This will include utilising both cross-sectional and time-series data to analyse the interaction of these variables across time and across various marketplaces. Panel data analysis can be employed to evaluate the correlation between the adoption of fintech innovations in different nations and the subsequent changes in market competition and investor returns over a specified timeframe. Employing rigorous econometric methods, such as fixed-effects or random-effects models, will mitigate unobserved variation across countries or sectors, so ensuring that the results remain unbiased by omitted variables.

The study will utilise structural equation modelling (SEM) to examine the correlations among the variables and investigate the mediating or moderating effects of certain factors, including regulatory frameworks and investor technology savvy. Structural Equation Modelling (SEM) is especially advantageous for this research, as it facilitates the concurrent examination of many variable correlations and offers a more intricate comprehension of the complicated interactions involved. The model may indicate whether investor technological knowledge influences the relationship between technological disruption and investment returns, or if the intensity of market rivalry mediates the impact of innovation adoption rates on returns.

To strengthen the rigour of the quantitative analysis, the study will utilise sensitivity analyses, such Monte Carlo simulations or bootstrapping techniques, to evaluate the stability of the results across varying assumptions or situations. This is especially significant in emerging countries, where data availability and quality may be constrained, and market volatility can bring uncertainties into the research. The study's supplementary analyses guarantee that its conclusions are not excessively reliant on particular data points or assumptions, thereby offering a more dependable and generalisable comprehension of the correlation between technological innovation and investment returns.

The mixed-methods approach, integrating qualitative and quantitative research, is essential for addressing the complex character of the research subject. The qualitative insights obtained from interviews and case studies will guide the formulation of the quantitative models, ensuring that the variables used in the study are rooted in the actual experiences of investors and enterprises in emerging economies. In contrast, the quantitative results will offer empirical support for the qualitative insights, allowing the study to formulate more rigorous and practical conclusions. This amalgamation of methodologies facilitates a comprehensive comprehension of the influence of technology innovation on investing strategies, providing both theoretical perspectives and pragmatic advice for investors in swiftly changing markets.

Conceptual Framework

Figure 1. Conceptual framework

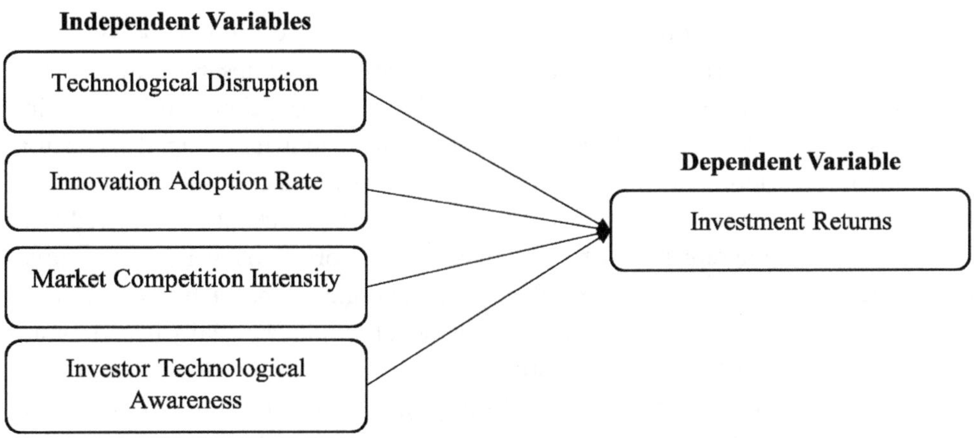

This study's conceptual framework provides a roadmap for comprehending the relationship between technical innovation and investment strategies in emerging markets, emphasising the dynamics of risk and return. The independent variables at the foundation of this paradigm include technological disruption, innovation adoption rate, market competitive intensity, and investor technological knowledge, which jointly influence the dependent variable: investment returns (Nascimento et al., 2021). The framework synthesises theories of disruptive innovation, technology diffusion, market rivalry, and investor behaviour to create a complete model illustrating how technical developments affect financial results in volatile and rapidly changing markets (Anand et al., 2021).

Technological disruption is a fundamental component of the conceptual framework. Based on Clayton Christensen's Disruptive Innovation Theory, this variable reflects how emerging technologies can fundamentally alter sectors by presenting revolutionary products or services that ultimately eclipse established market leaders. In emerging markets, technological disruption exerts a pronounced impact due to the lack of established infrastructure or dominant entities, enabling new entrants to surpass conventional business strategies. The paradigm asserts that technological disruption profoundly impacts investment returns by modifying market dynamics, generating both growth potential and hazards of instability. In sectors like telecommunications and financial services, where technological disruption is significant, investors must manoeuvre through changing market conditions as established firms attempt to retain market share while new, technologically adept entrants seize substantial market portions. The concept posits that the extent and speed of technological disruption within a market will significantly influence the unpredictability of investment returns, as companies either leverage or are supplanted by these advances (Zhan, 2021).

The pace of innovation uptake is a vital element of the framework. Based on Rogers' "Diffusion of Innovations" thesis, this variable elucidates the rate and extent of technical innovation adoption within a market. The adoption rate in emerging economies can differ markedly among sectors and countries, shaped by factors including infrastructural availability, legal frameworks, and cultural perceptions of technology. The theory posits that accelerated adoption rates are associated with increased investment returns, especially for early investors who leverage first-mover advantages. The approach also considers the risks linked to premature investments in technologies that may fail to attain widespread adoption, especially in economies lacking enough infrastructure or governmental support to foster innovation growth. This aspect of the framework underscores the significance of timing in investment choices, indicating that investors who accurately predict the adoption curve of technological advancements can achieve considerable returns, whereas those who miscalculate market readiness may encounter significant risks (Rana et al., 2021).

The intensity of market competition is the third variable in the framework, indicating the level of competitive pressure within an industry as shaped by technical innovation. This variable, based on Michael Porter's competitive strategy theories, analyses how emerging technologies heighten competition by reducing entry barriers, allowing new corporations to contest incumbent entities, and promoting market fragmentation. The concept asserts that in markets characterised by heightened technical innovation, investment returns may exhibit increased volatility due to firms participating in price wars, rapid expansion, and aggressive client acquisition tactics. Nonetheless, it indicates that heightened competition spurred by technical advancements may result in enhanced efficiencies, reduced consumer prices, and ultimately, improved total market growth. The concept emphasises the dual function of market competition intensity, indicating that it can either augment or diminish investment returns based on the sector and the characteristics of the technical innovation involved. In the fintech industry of numerous emerging nations, heightened competition has resulted in increased consumer acceptance and diminished profitability margins for companies, hence creating a challenging landscape for investors to traverse.

The investor's technological awareness is the final independent variable in the framework and acts as a moderating element in the link between technological innovation and investment returns. This variable, informed by behavioural finance and decision-making theories, signifies the knowledge and expertise investors possess in assessing technological advances and their prospective effects on market dynamics. The theory posits that investors possessing elevated technological acumen are more adept at recognising chances for substantial returns, especially in emerging markets where the dangers of technological upheaval are heightened. These investors can more precisely evaluate the potential of emerging technologies to transform sectors, embrace nascent breakthroughs, and alleviate risks linked to market fluctuations. In contrast, investors with limited technological awareness may either overrate the prospective returns of emerging technologies or overlook the risks linked to swift technology advancements. The framework asserts that technology awareness is dynamic and may be cultivated by experience, exposure to innovative fields, and access to specialised knowledge. This element is especially crucial in emerging markets, where the rapidity and unpredictability of technical advancements necessitate that investors consistently adjust their strategy in reaction to new developments (Xu & Loang, 2024a).

The dependent variable in this paradigm, investment returns, results from the interactions among the independent factors. The concept asserts that the interplay of technological disruption, innovation adoption rates, market rivalry intensity, and investor technological awareness influences the potential for returns in emerging markets. Nevertheless, it recognises that these variables do not function independently.

They interact in intricate manners, with technological disruption possibly expediting innovation adoption rates, market competitive intensity affecting investment risk profiles, and investor technical awareness influencing decision-making processes (Deng et al., 2020). A market marked by swift technological disruption and fierce competition may yield significant profits for investors who possess technological acumen and can foresee changes in the competitive environment. Conversely, investors in markets characterised by slower innovation uptake or diminished competitive intensity may experience lower returns alongside mitigated risks.

The conceptual framework acknowledges the importance of external moderating factors, like regulatory settings, economic situations, and infrastructural development, on the link between independent and dependent variables (Bustamante et al., 2021). In markets with weak or inconsistent regulatory frameworks, the effects of technology disruption may be limited, hence diminishing the possibility for substantial gains. In contrast, in markets where governments actively promote technical innovation through advantageous laws, investment returns may be enhanced. The paradigm posits that these external elements must be meticulously assessed when appraising the potential for returns in emerging economies, as they can either augment or detract from the impacts of technological innovation.

CONCLUSION

This study's conclusion highlights the essential significance of technical innovation in influencing investment strategies and results in emerging countries, stressing the complex relationship between risk and return. The evolution of these markets, along with the swift advancement of technology, provides substantial opportunity for investors, while also introducing distinct obstacles. This study aims to elucidate these complexity by analysing critical variables such technology disruption, innovation adoption rates, market competitive intensity, and investor technological awareness, all of which influence the volatility and potential of investment returns.

The study's primary finding is the transformative effect of technological disruption on businesses and markets in emerging economies. Disruptive technological advances do not simply improve existing processes or products; they frequently revolutionise whole sectors. This disruption is particularly evident in emerging markets, where the absence of established infrastructure and legal frameworks facilitates more dynamic and swift transformations. Firms in these areas, being less constrained by legacy systems, can more rapidly adapt to or adopt new technology, hence generating significant growth potential and high returns for investors who accurately predict these transitions. Nonetheless, this trait simultaneously elevates the risk profile of investments, as technological upheavals may induce market volatility, replace established entities, and generate unpredictable market dynamics.

The study emphasises the significance of the adoption rate of innovations across various sectors and geographies in emerging markets. Certain industries, such fintech and telecommunications, have experienced swift adoption of innovation, whilst others fall behind due to infrastructural limitations, legal obstacles, or cultural influences. The disparate adoption results in a multifaceted environment for investors, necessitating navigation through a wide array of risk profiles based on sector and geography. The swift adoption of innovation can yield substantial profits, especially for early adopters; but, it may also exacerbate risks in markets lacking the necessary infrastructure or legal framework to facilitate wider implementation. Consequently, time and market selection are essential elements of any investment strategy in these areas.

The intensity of market rivalry, a notable conclusion of this study, illustrates that technological breakthroughs not only create new growth opportunities but also exacerbate competitive pressures inside markets. This intensification arises as new entrants, frequently armed with advanced technology, contest incumbent competitors, thereby heightening market fragmentation and diminishing profitability for all stakeholders. For investors, this indicates that although the possibility of profits is present, the journey towards achieving those returns is frequently characterised by intensified competition, pricing pressures, and the necessity for companies to rapidly scale in order to secure market share. This dynamic is especially pertinent in emerging markets, where the prevalence of numerous small- and medium-sized enterprises (SMEs) and startups indicates that rivalry is not confined to huge incumbents but may arise from other sources. Investors must recognise these intensified competitive factors, since they might substantially modify the risk-return equilibrium.

This study significantly contributes by highlighting the influence of investor technology understanding on the relationship between innovation and investment returns. The results demonstrate that investors with elevated technology literacy and awareness are more adept at recognising early-stage breakthroughs and evaluating the dangers linked to new technologies. In marketplaces characterised by swift and unpredictable technological development, such knowledge is a crucial instrument for manoeuvring through the intricacies of innovation-driven sectors. Investors possessing heightened technological acumen can more adeptly evaluate the long-term sustainability of breakthroughs, mitigate the tendency to overrate possible rewards, and navigate the hazards linked to disruptive technology. This understanding enables investors to distinguish between short-term trends and long-term technological transformations, facilitating more informed investment decisions that equilibrate risk and return.

The study highlights the broader contextual elements, including regulatory regimes and infrastructure development, that influence the impact of technical innovation on investment returns. Emerging markets sometimes exhibit undeveloped or uneven regulatory frameworks, which can either impede or facilitate the adoption of new technology. In markets where governments facilitate technological innovation by policy initiatives, infrastructural investment, or advantageous regulatory frameworks, the potential for substantial returns is markedly increased. Conversely, in markets characterised by significant regulatory impediments or inadequate infrastructure, even the most promising ideas may have difficulties in achieving momentum. For investors, comprehending these external factors is essential, since they can significantly affect the risk-return dynamics of technology-driven investments in these areas.

This study's conclusion underscores that technology innovation offers significant prospects for investors in emerging nations, necessitating a meticulous and sophisticated strategy. The significant uncertainty and volatility inherent in these markets necessitate that investors have a profound comprehension of the underlying technology, the competitive environment, and the external influences that drive innovation adoption. Furthermore, the swift rate of technical advancement in these areas necessitates that investors remain nimble, consistently adjusting their plans in reaction to emerging advances and fluctuating market conditions.

This study enhances the debate on technical innovation in emerging countries by providing a conceptual framework that synthesises many characteristics of innovation and investment. The results offer significant insights for academic academics and practitioners, emphasising the necessity for a balanced strategy regarding risk and return in technology-driven investments. Subsequent research ought to further investigate the changing dynamics of technology disruption in these sectors, with a specific focus on the enduring effects on market structures, regulatory frameworks, and investor conduct. As emerging economies expand and assimilate into the global economy, the significance of technological innovation will intensify, and comprehending its impact on investment strategies will persist as a vital topic of investigation.

Theoretical, Managerial and Policy Implications

The theoretical ramifications of this study are substantial, enhancing the current understanding of technical innovation and investment strategies, especially within emerging countries. The research elaborates on Disruptive Innovation Theory by illustrating the distinct behaviours of technological disruptions in emerging markets vs industrialised economies. This study highlights the distinct attributes of emerging economies, where infrastructure, legislation, and market structures tend to be more dynamic, contrasting with the predominant focus of disruptive innovation literature on established industries in mature countries. The study emphasises that technological innovations can bypass traditional development trajectories in these markets, challenging established theories of market evolution and highlighting the necessity for new theoretical frameworks that reflect the swift and uneven nature of technological advancement in developing areas. Furthermore, the study incorporates aspects of Diffusion of Innovation Theory, broadening its application from human and organisational behaviour to the macroeconomic setting, where innovation adoption rates are influenced by overarching market and regulatory conditions. This enhances a comprehensive understanding of the dissemination of innovations in emerging markets and the factors that either promote or obstruct this process.

This study's conceptual approach also integrates behavioural finance principles, particularly emphasising investor technology awareness. The theoretical implications are significant, since they underscore a largely neglected facet of investor behaviour: the capacity to evaluate and react to technological changes. Conventional financial theories typically presume rational decision-making predicated on accessible market information; yet, this study indicates that technology knowledge, or its absence, adds a another dimension of complexity to investment choices. Investors possessing substantial technology acumen can more effectively assess the potential of disruptive technologies, whereas those with insufficient expertise may misread technological indicators, resulting in inefficient investment decisions. This indicates that future research may investigate the relationship between technological literacy and investing behaviour, potentially resulting in novel models of investor decision-making that consider knowledge asymmetries in swiftly evolving technological contexts.

The study's managerial implications are significant, providing practical recommendations for corporate leaders engaged in or contemplating investments in emerging markets. The study emphasises the significance of agility and adaptation in navigating the dangers and possibilities presented by technological upheaval. In emerging markets, the rapidity of technology advancement necessitates that enterprises adopt flexible long-term planning to accommodate swift strategic adjustments in response to new developments. This necessitates that managers concentrate not only on technological integration within their organisations but also on the ongoing observation of wider market and technological trends. Companies that swiftly adapt to new technologies, or preferably, spearhead their adoption, are more likely to sustain competitive advantages in marketplaces that are becoming progressively competitive due to technological breakthroughs. The study emphasises the imperative for managers to cultivate a culture of innovation inside their organisations, wherein staff are motivated to experiment with novel technology and procedures, and where failure is perceived as a learning opportunity rather than a hindrance.

From a strategic management viewpoint, the analysis indicates that companies must meticulously evaluate the timing of technology implementation. The premature adoption of disruptive technology might provide competitive benefits, although it also entails hazards, especially if the wider market is unprepared for the breakthrough. Managers must evaluate the prospective advantages of first-mover status against the dangers linked to untested technologies and the likelihood of market opposition. Furthermore, as technology disruption heightens competition, managers must be equipped to manoeuvre through a swiftly evolving competitive environment, where new entrants with creative business models can rapidly contest existing entities. This necessitates that companies be both inventors and proficient in purchasing or collaborating with rising startups that have developed new technologies, thereby establishing a hybrid strategy that integrates internal innovation capabilities with external relationships.

For investors, the managerial implications emphasise the necessity of technology proficiency in portfolio management. The research indicates that investors, especially those concentrating on emerging markets, must have a profound comprehension of the technologies propelling innovation across diverse sectors. This necessitates a transition from conventional financial analysis to a more interdisciplinary methodology that integrates perspectives from technology specialists, industry analysts, and policymakers. Investors capable of precisely evaluating the potential of emerging technologies are more adept at identifying high-yield possibilities while minimising risks linked to market fluctuations and competitive dynamics. This suggests that asset managers and institutional investors ought to cultivate in-house proficiency in emerging technologies or establish collaborations with technology consultants for continuous analysis and advising.

The policy ramifications of this study are significant, especially for governments and regulatory authorities in emerging markets. The results demonstrate that regulatory frameworks significantly influence the adoption of technical breakthroughs, either by helping or obstructing it. In markets characterised by ambiguous, inconsistent, or excessively stringent laws, technology disruptions may have difficulties in gaining traction, hence constraining their capacity to foster economic growth and innovation. In markets where governments actively promote technology innovation through advantageous legislation, infrastructure enhancement, and educational investment, the likelihood of technological disruptions positively affecting industries is markedly increased. This indicates that policymakers should implement a proactive regulatory strategy that balances the promotion of innovation with the prevention of excessive market volatility due to technology disruptions.

Policymakers ought to prioritise the establishment of regulatory frameworks that foster innovation, including the provision of tax incentives for technology companies, investment in research and development, and the safeguarding of intellectual property laws to protect both innovators and consumers. Moreover, legislators must guarantee that the regulatory framework is flexible to accommodate emerging technology, as inflexible regulations may become outdated when technical progress surpasses legal structures. The swift ascent of fintech in numerous emerging nations has underscored the necessity for adaptable regulatory frameworks that can embrace innovative business models while ensuring financial stability. As artificial intelligence, blockchain, and other disruptive technologies proliferate, governments must design regulations that address the ethical and societal ramifications of these advances while promoting their development and implementation.

Limitations and Recommendations for Future Studies

This study's shortcomings stem from its scope, methodology, and the intricate nature of the subject, especially considering the fast-paced evolution of technological innovation and its influence on investment strategies in emerging nations. A significant constraint stems from the difficulty of generalising results across various emerging markets. These economies exhibit significant heterogeneity, marked by diverse levels of infrastructure development, regulatory frameworks, political stability, and cultural influences. Consequently, technological innovation and its impact on market rivalry, adoption rates, and investor behaviour may vary considerably across different regions. This heterogeneity imposes constraints on the generalisability of the study's conclusions. Although the study offers a conceptual framework relevant to various countries, the particular dynamics of technology disruption and innovation adoption may not be consistently applicable across all emerging markets.

A further barrier arises from the accessibility and dependability of data in emerging markets. The quality of data, especially concerning technological adoption rates and market rivalry, can differ significantly among areas, with certain markets missing complete, transparent, and current information. This constraint hinders the capacity to perform longitudinal research or to precisely compare trends across various marketplaces. Emerging markets typically have insufficient or inconsistent data collecting, hence constraining the robustness of empirical conclusions. Despite attempts to alleviate this disadvantage by meticulous data source selection and methodological precision, the intrinsic data constraints in emerging countries provide a challenge to the study's conclusions. Therefore, the results must be interpreted cautiously, especially when applying them to markets with potentially incorrect or missing data.

Another constraint is to the ever-evolving nature of technological innovation. The study examines variables like technological disruption, innovation adoption rate, and market competitive intensity, all of which are prone to swift alterations. Technological landscapes can change suddenly, and emerging markets may feel these changes more intensely due to their unstable economic and regulatory conditions. The swift progression of technical improvements indicates that the results of this study may soon become obsolete as new discoveries arise and transform businesses.

While the conceptual framework outlined in this study is intended to be flexible, it is nevertheless difficult to comprehensively assess the long-term impacts of technology disruption in a rapidly evolving context.

The mixed-methods technique employed in the study, although offering both depth and breadth, has inherent limits. The qualitative component, dependent on interviews and case studies, may be prone to prejudice, especially regarding the subjective experiences and viewpoints of participants. Semi-structured interviews, while providing rich and nuanced insights, may inadequately reflect broader market dynamics, particularly when respondents are swayed by their personal opinions or corporate agendas. Moreover, the quantitative study, notwithstanding its rigour, is limited by the accessibility of dependable data in emerging economies, as previously mentioned. The twin constraints in both qualitative and quantitative approaches indicate that the study's findings, albeit substantial, should be regarded as components of an evolving research corpus rather than as conclusive evidence.

In light of these constraints, the paper presents multiple recommendations for subsequent research. An essential domain for future research is the examination of regional and sectoral disparities within developing markets. As noted, emerging economies are not homogeneous, and future research could gain from concentrating on particular areas or industries to yield more detailed insights into the impact of technical advancements on investment returns. For instance, research on the finance industry in sub-Saharan Africa or the telecoms sector in Southeast Asia may uncover distinct patterns of technological adoption and disruption that markedly diverge from general trends. Future study could yield more thorough and useful insights for investors and policymakers by concentrating on specific industries or areas.

A further direction for future research entails the longitudinal examination of technology progress and its influence on investment strategies across time. Considering the evolving nature of technology and its uncertain path, longitudinal research examining the long-term impacts of particular inventions could yield significant insights into the sustainability of technological disruption and its consequences on market competition and investment returns. Such studies could examine how organisations and investors adjust to persistent technological advancements, providing a more thorough comprehension of the evolution of strategies in reaction to ongoing innovation. This would mitigate a fundamental weakness of this study, namely the difficulty of documenting long-term impacts in a swiftly evolving technology environment.

Subsequent studies may further investigate the impact of investor technical awareness. This study has recognised investor awareness as a pivotal element in influencing the impact of technology innovation on investment returns; nevertheless, additional research is necessary to comprehensively comprehend how investors obtain, analyse, and respond to technological knowledge. This may entail analysing how various investor categories—such as institutional investors, venture capitalists, and individual retail investors—cultivate technical literacy and how this affects their investment choices. Furthermore, studies may investigate the influence of investor networks and the dissemination of technological information inside investing communities. Comprehending these characteristics may yield significant insights for investors aiming to enhance their proficiency in manoeuvring through technology-driven markets.

A crucial domain for future investigation pertains to the influence of regulatory frameworks on the uptake of technical advancements. This study emphasises the significance of regulatory frameworks; nonetheless, further extensive investigations are required to ascertain how various regulatory approaches affect the success or failure of technological disruptions. Comparative analyses among nations or regions with differing regulatory frameworks could illuminate the most efficacious strategies for promoting innovation while ensuring market stability. Furthermore, as emerging markets progressively embrace technologies such as artificial intelligence, blockchain, and digital currencies, future study ought to investigate the impact of rules in these domains on innovation and investment returns. Comprehending the regulatory obstacles and opportunities in these areas will be essential as these technologies gain prevalence.

REFERENCES

Anand, J., McDermott, G., Mudambi, R., & Narula, R. (2021). Innovation in and from emerging economies: New insights and lessons for international business research. *Journal of International Business Studies*, 52(4), 545–559. DOI: 10.1057/s41267-021-00426-1

Bustamante, C. V., Mingo, S., & Matusik, S. F. (2021). Institutions and venture capital market creation: The case of an emerging market. *Journal of Business Research*, 127, 1–12. DOI: 10.1016/j.jbusres.2021.01.008

Deng, P., Liu, Y., Gallagher, V. C., & Wu, X. (2020). International strategies of emerging market multinationals: A dynamic capabilities perspective. *Journal of Management & Organization*, 26(4), 408–425. DOI: 10.1017/jmo.2017.76

Din, S. U., Arshad Khan, M., Khan, M. J., & Khan, M. Y. (2022). Ownership structure and corporate financial performance in an emerging market: A dynamic panel data analysis. *International Journal of Emerging Markets*, 17(8), 1973–1997. DOI: 10.1108/IJOEM-03-2019-0220

FaXing. L., & Loang, O. K. (2024). Green Investing and Financial Education: The Case of China's A-Share Market. In *Technology-Driven Business Innovation: Unleashing the Digital Advantage, Volume 1* (pp. 29-41). Cham: Springer Nature Switzerland.

Geddes, A., & Schmidt, T. S. (2020). Integrating finance into the multi-level perspective: Technology niche-finance regime interactions and financial policy interventions. *Research Policy*, 49(6), 103985. DOI: 10.1016/j.respol.2020.103985

Karhade, P., & Dong, J. Q. (2021). Information technology investment and commercialized innovation performance: Dynamic adjustment costs and curvilinear impacts. *Management Information Systems Quarterly*, 45(3), 1007–1024. DOI: 10.25300/MISQ/2021/14368

Loang, O. K. (2023). Corporate governance and Islamic behavioural finance: A review from Malaysia and GCC countries. *Indian Journal of Corporate Governance*, 16(1), 28–51. DOI: 10.1177/09746862231178959

Loang, O. K. (2024). Stability Of Shariah-Compliant Stocks In Indonesia, Malaysia, And Gcc: The Roles Of Monetary And Fiscal Policies And Contagion. *Journal of Islamic Monetary Economics and Finance*, 10(1), 155–176. DOI: 10.21098/jimf.v10i1.1899

Loang, O. K. (2024). Sustainability's impact of ESG-infused policies on leading economic indicators in Asian economies. *Journal of Sustainable Research*, 6(3), e240059. DOI: 10.20900/jsr20240059

Nascimento, L. D. S., Reichert, F. M., Janissek-Muniz, R., & Zawislak, P. A. (2021). Dynamic interactions among knowledge management, strategic foresight and emerging technologies. *Journal of Knowledge Management*, 25(2), 275–297. DOI: 10.1108/JKM-01-2020-0044

Nyagadza, B., Pashapa, R., Chare, A., Mazuruse, G., & Hove, P. K. (2022). Digital technologies, Fourth Industrial Revolution (4IR) & Global Value Chains (GVCs) nexus with emerging economies' future industrial innovation dynamics. *Cogent Economics & Finance*, 10(1), 2014654. DOI: 10.1080/23322039.2021.2014654

Rana, S., Prashar, S., Barai, M. K., & Hamid, A. B. A. (2021). Determinants of international marketing strategy for emerging market multinationals. *International Journal of Emerging Markets*, 16(2), 154–178. DOI: 10.1108/IJOEM-09-2019-0742

Suresh, G., & Loang, O. K. (2024). The Rationality Conundrum: Exploring Herd Mentality among Individual Investors in the Indian Stock Market. *Indian Journal of Finance*, 18(6), 26–45. DOI: 10.17010/ijf/2024/v18i6/173967

Xu, M., & Loang, O. K. (2024). Industrial Agglomeration, Technological Innovation, and Poverty Alleviation: Evidence from China. In *Artificial Intelligence (AI) and Customer Social Responsibility (CSR)* (pp. 223–236). Springer Nature Switzerland. DOI: 10.1007/978-3-031-50939-1_17

Xu, X., & Loang, O. K. (2024). Fostering Future Entrepreneurs: The Impact of Education, Self-Efficacy, and Financial Support on Entrepreneurial Intentions. *International Journal of Advanced Research in Economics and Finance*, 6(2), 188–203.

Zhan, J. X. (2021). GVC transformation and a new investment landscape in the 2020s: Driving forces, directions, and a forward-looking research and policy agenda. *Journal of International Business Policy*, 4(2), 206–220. DOI: 10.1057/s42214-020-00088-0

Compilation of References

A, C., & R, K. (2016). IMPACT OF SELECTED BEHAVIOURAL BIAS FACTORS ON INVESTMENT DECISIONS OF EQUITY INVESTORS. *ICTACT Journal on Management Studies, 2*(2), 297–311. https://doi.org/DOI: 10.1016/j.jhe.2015.02.003

Abhijith, R., & Bijulal, D. (2024). Heuristic biases influencing individual stock investment decisions: A hybrid fuzzy DELPHI-AHP-DEMATEL approach. *Journal of Advances in Management Research*, 21(4), 627–648. DOI: 10.1108/JAMR-03-2024-0093

Adil, M., Singh, Y., & Ansari, M. S. (2022). How financial literacy moderate the association between behaviour biases and investment decision? *Asian Journal of Accounting Research*, 7(1), 17–30. DOI: 10.1108/AJAR-09-2020-0086

Ahammad, M. F., Basu, S., Munjal, S., Clegg, J., & Shoham, O. B. (2021). Strategic agility, environmental uncertainties and international performance: The perspective of Indian firms. *Journal of World Business*, 56(4), 101218. DOI: 10.1016/j.jwb.2021.101218

Aharoni, Y. (2015). *The foreign investment decision process*. Routledge.

Ahmad, A., & Shah, S. (2020). Cognitive biases affecting investment decision-making. *International Journal of Applied Behavioral Economics*, 7(3), 15–28. DOI: 10.4018/IJABE.2018070102

Ahmad, I., Shah, Z., & Mahmood, K. (2018). The impact of cognitive biases on financial decision-making: Evidence from the Pakistani stock market. *International Journal of Finance & Banking Studies*, 7(3), 14–25.

Ahmad, M. (2020). Does underconfidence matter in short-term and long-term investment decisions? Evidence from an emerging market. *Management Decision*, 59(3), 692–709. DOI: 10.1108/MD-07-2019-0972

Ahmad, M. (2022). The role of cognitive heuristic-driven biases in investment management activities and market efficiency: A research synthesis. *International Journal of Emerging Markets*, 19(2), 273–321. DOI: 10.1108/IJOEM-07-2020-0749

Ahmad, M., & Shah, S. Z. (2020). Overconfidence heuristic-driven bias in investment decision-making and performance: Mediating effects of risk perception and moderating effects of financial literacy. *Journal of Economic and Administrative Sciences*, 38(1), 60–90. DOI: 10.1108/JEAS-07-2020-0116

Ahmad, M., Shah, S. Z., & Abbass, Y. (2020). The role of heuristic-driven biases in entrepreneurial strategic decision-making: Evidence from an emerging economy. *Management Decision*, 59(3), 669–691. DOI: 10.1108/MD-09-2019-1231

Ahmad, M., & Wu, Q. (2023). Heuristic-driven biases as mental shortcuts in investment management activities: A qualitative study. *Qualitative Research in Financial Markets*, 16(2), 291–309. DOI: 10.1108/QRFM-10-2022-0167

Ahmad, M., Wu, Q., & Abbass, Y. (2022). Probing the impact of recognition-based heuristic biases on investment decision-making and performance. *Kybernetes*, 52(10), 4229–4256. DOI: 10.1108/K-01-2022-0112

Akhtar, S., Faff, R., Oliver, B., & Subrahmanyam, A. (2011). The power of bad: The negativity bias in Australian consumer sentiment announcements on stock returns. *Journal of Banking & Finance*, 35(5), 1239–1249. DOI: 10.1016/j.jbankfin.2010.10.014

Alam, N., Khan, M. S., Azad, I., Shahid, F., & Dar, A. A. (2024). Identifying the approach to financial sustainability: Navigating the complexities of earning and spending. *Edelweiss Applied Science and Technology*, 8(4), 995–1006. DOI: 10.55214/25768484.v8i4.1477

Aljanabi, A. R. A. (2023). The impact of economic policy uncertainty, news framing and information overload on panic buying behavior in the time of COVID-19: A conceptual exploration. *International Journal of Emerging Markets*, 18(7), 1614–1631. DOI: 10.1108/IJOEM-10-2020-1181

Alshebami, A. S., & Seraj, A. H. (2022). Investigating the impact of institutions on small business creation among Saudi entrepreneurs. *Frontiers in Psychology*, 13, 897787. Advance online publication. DOI: 10.3389/fpsyg.2022.897787 PMID: 35769726

Anand, J., McDermott, G., Mudambi, R., & Narula, R. (2021). Innovation in and from emerging economies: New insights and lessons for international business research. *Journal of International Business Studies*, 52(4), 545–559. DOI: 10.1057/s41267-021-00426-1

Anderson, A. G., & Larkin, Y. (2012). Does non-informative text affect investor behavior? SSRN *Electronic Journal*. https://doi.org/DOI: 10.2139/ssrn.2181195

Anderson, C. W., Fedenia, M., Hirschey, M., & Skiba, H. (2011). Cultural influences on home bias and international diversification by institutional investors. *Journal of Banking & Finance*, 35(4), 916–934. DOI: 10.1016/j.jbankfin.2010.09.006

Arellano, M., & Bond, S. (1991). Some tests of specification for panel data: Monte Carlo evidence and an application to employment equations. *The Review of Economic Studies*, 58(2), 277–297. DOI: 10.2307/2297968

Arnold, G. (2012). *The Financial Times Guide to Investing: The definitive companion to investment and the financial markets*. Pearson UK.

Asongu, S., Akpan, U. S., & Isihak, S. R. (2018). Determinants of foreign direct investment in fast-growing economies: Evidence from the BRICS and MINT countries. *Financial Innovation*, 4(1), 1–17. DOI: 10.1186/s40854-018-0114-0

Ayaa, M. M., Peprah, W. K., Mensah, M. O., Owusu-Sekyere, A. B., & Daniel, B. (2022). Influence of heuristic techniques and biases in investment decision-making: A conceptual analysis and directions for future research. *International Journal of Academic Research in Business & Social Sciences*, 12(5). Advance online publication. DOI: 10.6007/IJARBSS/v12-i5/13339

Babalos, V., Kostakis, A., & Philippas, N. (2015). Herding behavior in REITs: Novel tests and the role of financial crisis. *International Review of Financial Analysis*, 40, 25–34. DOI: 10.1016/j.irfa.2015.03.002

Bai, R. (2023). Impact of financial literacy, mental budgeting and self control on financial wellbeing: Mediating impact of investment decision making. *PLoS One*, 18(11), e0294466. DOI: 10.1371/journal.pone.0294466 PMID: 37963159

Baker, H. K., Kumar, S., Goyal, N., & Gaur, V. (2019). Behavioral biases among Indian investors: The moderating role of demographic and socioeconomic factors. *Emerging Markets Finance & Trade*, 55(8), 1843–1868. DOI: 10.1080/1540496X.2018.1508561

Baker, H. K., & Nofsinger, J. R. (2002). Psychological biases of investors. *Financial Services Review*, 11(2), 97–116.

Baker, H. K., & Nofsinger, J. R. (2010). *Behavioral finance: Investors, corporations, and markets*. John Wiley & Sons. DOI: 10.1002/9781118258415

Baker, S. R., Bloom, N., & Davis, S. J. (2016). Measuring economic policy uncertainty. *The Quarterly Journal of Economics*, 131(4), 1593–1636. DOI: 10.1093/qje/qjw024

Ball, R., Gerakos, J., & Shivakumar, L. (2010). The role of risk aversion in financial decision-making. *Review of Financial Studies*, 23(3), 885–918.

Banerjee, A. V. (1992). A simple model of herd behavior. *The Quarterly Journal of Economics*, 107(3), 797–817. DOI: 10.2307/2118364

Bao, J., & Saunders, D. (2021). The influence of listing prices on buyer behavior: Evidence from the real estate market. *Journal of Real Estate Research*, 43(1), 35–54.

Barber, B. M., & Odean, T. (2011). The behavior of individual investors. SSRN *Electronic Journal*. https://doi.org/DOI: 10.2139/ssrn.1872211

Barber, B. M., Lee, Y. T., Liu, Y. J., & Odean, T. (2007). Is the aggregate ınvestor reluctant to realise losses? evidence from Taiwan. *European Financial Management*, 13(3), 423–447. DOI: 10.1111/j.1468-036X.2007.00367.x

Barber, B. M., & Odean, T. (2000). Trading is hazardous to your wealth: The common stock investment performance of individual investors. *The Journal of Finance*, 55(2), 773–806. DOI: 10.1111/0022-1082.00226

Barber, B. M., & Odean, T. (2001). Boys will be boys: Gender, overconfidence, and common stock investment. *The Quarterly Journal of Economics*, 116(1), 261–292. DOI: 10.1162/003355301556400

Barberis, N., & Thaler, R. (2003). A survey of behavioral finance. In G. M. Constantinides, M. Harris, & R. Stulz (Eds.), Handbook of the Economics of Finance (Vol. 1B, pp. 1053–1128). Elsevier. https://doi.org/DOI: 10.1016/S1572-3089(03)01028-8

Barberis, N., & Thaler, R. (2003). A survey of behavioral finance. In *Handbook of the Economics of Finance* (pp. 1053–1128). Elsevier.

Barberis, N., & Xiong, W. (2009). What drives the disposition effect? An analysis of the investor's perspective. *Journal of Financial Economics*, 92(3), 348–363.

Barrie, C., & Ho, J. C. T. (2021). academictwitteR: An R package to access the Twitter academic research product track v2 API endpoint. *Journal of Open Source Software*, 6(62), 3272. DOI: 10.21105/joss.03272

Baumeister, R. F., Bratslavsky, E., Finkenauer, C., & Vohs, K. D. (2001). Bad is stronger than good. *Review of General Psychology*, 5(4), 323–370. DOI: 10.1037/1089-2680.5.4.323

Bazerman, M. H., & Samuelson, W. (1983). I won the auction but don't want the prize. *The Journal of Conflict Resolution*, 27(4), 618–634. DOI: 10.1177/0022002783027004003

Becker, J., Hopp, D., & Kriebel, M. (2020). Mental accounting of public funds–The flypaper effect in the lab. *Journal of Economic Behavior & Organization*, 176, 321–336. DOI: 10.1016/j.jebo.2020.04.026

Becker, J., Rai, A., Ringle, C. M., & Völckner, F. (2013). Discovering unobserved heterogeneity in structural equation models to avert validity threats. *Management Information Systems Quarterly*, 37(3), 665–694. DOI: 10.25300/MISQ/2013/37.3.01

Belke, A., & Volz, U. (2018). Capital flows to emerging market and developing economies. Global liquidity and uncertainty versus country–specific pull factors (Working Paper No. 23/2018). German Development Institute.

Bems, R., Catao, L., Koczan, Z., Lian, W., Poplawski-Ribeiro, M., Jiang, H., Liu, Y., & Yang, H. (2016). Understanding the slowdown in capital flows to emerging markets. In World economic.

Beracha, E., Fedenia, M., & Skiba, H. (2014). Culture's impact on institutional investors' trading frequency. *International Review of Financial Analysis*, 31, 34–47. DOI: 10.1016/j.irfa.2013.10.002

Berger, J., & Milkman, K. L. (2012). What makes online content viral? *JMR, Journal of Marketing Research*, 49(2), 192–205. DOI: 10.1509/jmr.10.0353

Biais, B., Hilton, D., Mazurier, K., & Pouget, S. (2005). Judgmental overconfidence, self-monitoring, and trading performance in an experimental financial market. *The Review of Economic Studies*, 72(2), 287–312. DOI: 10.1111/j.1467-937X.2005.00333.x

Bikhchandani, S., Hirshleifer, D., & Welch, I. (1992). A theory of fads, fashion, custom, and cultural change as informational cascades. *Journal of Political Economy*, 100(5), 992–1026. DOI: 10.1086/261849

Bikhchandani, S., & Sharma, S. (2001). Herd behavior in financial markets. *IMF Staff Papers*, 47(3), 279–310. DOI: 10.2307/3867650

Bilyay-Erdogan, S. (2020). Does financial flexibility enhance firm value? A comparative study between developed and emerging countries. *Verslas: teorija ir praktika, 21*(2), 723-736.

Bogunjoko, A. (2021). *Impact of Behavioral Finance on Investment decisions Investigation in to how psychological factors affect Investment decisions among millennial Investors in Nigeria* (Doctoral dissertation, Dublin, National College of Ireland).

Bokhari, S., & Geltner, D. (2011). Loss aversion in commercial real estate transactions: Implications for pricing strategies. *Real Estate Economics*, 39(4), 587–620. DOI: 10.1111/j.1540-6229.2011.00308.x

Brunnermeier, M. K. (2009). Deciphering the liquidity and credit crunch 2007-2008. *The Journal of Economic Perspectives*, 23(1), 77–100. DOI: 10.1257/jep.23.1.77

Bryman, A., & Bell, E. (2011). *Business research methods 3e*. Oxford University Press.

Busenitz, L. W., & Barney, J. B. (1997). Differences between entrepreneurs and managers in large organizations: Biases and heuristics in strategic decision-making. *Journal of Business Venturing*, 12(1), 9–30. DOI: 10.1016/S0883-9026(96)00003-1

Bussy, A., & Zheng, H. (2023). Responses of FDI to geopolitical risks: The role of governance, information, and technology. *International Business Review*, 32(4), 102136. DOI: 10.1016/j.ibusrev.2023.102136

Bustamante, C. V., Mingo, S., & Matusik, S. F. (2021). Institutions and venture capital market creation: The case of an emerging market. *Journal of Business Research*, 127, 1–12. DOI: 10.1016/j.jbusres.2021.01.008

Calvo, G. A., Leiderman, L., & Reinhart, C. M. (2011). Capital inflows and real exchange rate appreciation in Latin America: The role of external factors. *Staff Papers - International Monetary Fund. International Monetary Fund*, 40(1), 108–151. DOI: 10.2307/3867379

Carril-Caccia, F., & Pavlova, E. (2018). Foreign direct investment and its drivers: A global and EU perspective. *Economic Bulletin Articles*, 4, 60–78.

Cascão, A. I., Ferreira, M. P., & da Silva, D. C. (2023). The influence of behavioral biases on real estate investment decisions: A review. *Real Estate Management and Valuation*, 31(1), 58–68. DOI: 10.2478/remav-2023-0006

Case, K. E., & Shiller, R. J. (1989). The efficiency of the market for single-family homes. *The American Economic Review*, 79(1), 125–137.

Case, K. E., & Shiller, R. J. (2003). Is there a bubble in the housing market? *Brookings Papers on Economic Activity*, 2003(2), 299–342. DOI: 10.1353/eca.2004.0004

Cepoi, C.-O. (2020). Asymmetric dependence between stock market returns and news during COVID-19 financial turmoil. *Finance Research Letters*, 36, 101658. DOI: 10.1016/j.frl.2020.101658 PMID: 32837370

Cerutti, E., Claessens, S., & Rose, A. K. (2019). How important is the global financial cycle? Evidence from capital flows. *IMF Economic Review*, 67(1), 24–60. DOI: 10.1057/s41308-019-00073-5

Cevik, E., Kirci Altinkeski, B., Cevik, E. I., & Dibooglu, S. (2022). Investor sentiments and stock markets during the COVID-19 pandemic. *Financial Innovation*, 8(1), 69. DOI: 10.1186/s40854-022-00375-0 PMID: 35814528

Chalissery, N., Tabash, M. I., Nishad, T. M., Aburezeq, I. M., & Daniel, L. N. (2023). Does the investor's trading experience reduce susceptibility to heuristic-driven biases? The moderating role of personality traits. *Journal of Risk and Financial Management*, 16(7), 325. DOI: 10.3390/jrfm16070325

Chang, C., Chang, Y., & Ho, W. (2016). The anchoring effect on housing markets: The role of brokers' price expectations. *Journal of Housing Economics*, 34, 54–67. DOI: 10.1016/j.jhe.2016.08.001

Chang, E. C., Cheng, J. W., & Khorana, A. (2000). An examination of herd behavior in equity markets: An international perspective. *Journal of Banking & Finance*, 24(10), 1651–1679. DOI: 10.1016/S0378-4266(99)00096-5

Chaudary, S. (2019). Does salience matter in investment decision? *Kybernetes*, 48(8), 1894–1912. DOI: 10.1108/K-09-2018-0490

Chauhan, Y., Ahmad, N., Aggarwal, V., & Chandra, A. (2019). Herd behaviour and asset pricing in the Indian stock market. *IIMB Management Review*, 32(2), 143–152. DOI: 10.1016/j.iimb.2019.10.008

Cheung, C., Wong, K., & Li, L. (2022). Availability bias and its implications in real estate investment: Evidence from Hong Kong. *International Journal of Housing Markets and Analysis*, 15(2), 249–265. DOI: 10.1108/IJHMA-03-2021-0051

Chinloy, P., & Pappas, M. (2016). The role of big data in real estate investment decision making. *Journal of Property Investment & Finance*, 34(3), 218–234. DOI: 10.1108/JPIF-05-2015-0055

Choe, H., & Eom, Y. (2009). The disposition effect and investment performance in the futures market. *Journal of Futures Markets*, 29(6), 496–522. DOI: 10.1002/fut.20398

Chou, R., Engle, R. F., & Kane, A. (1992). Measuring risk aversion from excess returns on a stock index. *Journal of Econometrics*, 52(1-2), 201–224. DOI: 10.1016/0304-4076(92)90070-8

Cici, G. (2012). The prevalence of the disposition effect in mutual funds' trades. *Journal of Financial and Quantitative Analysis*, 47(4), 795–820. DOI: 10.1017/S0022109012000348

Clarke, R. G., Mendoza, J. A., & Carter, D. A. (2014). Herding behavior among credit rating agencies: Effects on bond spreads and trading volume. *Journal of Fixed Income*, 23(4), 72–84. DOI: 10.3905/jfi.2014.23.4.072

Clauretie, T. M., & Thistle, P. D. (2007). Distance and the housing market: The impact of location on property values. *Journal of Real Estate Research*, 29(2), 155–178.

Cooper, A. C., Folta, T. B., & Woo, C. (1995). Entrepreneurial information search. *Journal of Business Venturing*, 10(2), 107–120. DOI: 10.1016/0883-9026(94)00022-M

Cordell, D. M., Smith, R., & Terry, A. (2011). Overconfidence in financial planners. *Financial Services Review*, 20(4).

Corr, P., & Plagnol, A. (2023). *Behavioral economics: The basics*. Routledge. DOI: 10.4324/9781003166900

Daniel, K., & Hirshleifer, D. (2015). Overconfident investors, predictable returns, and excessive trading. *The Journal of Economic Perspectives*, 29(4), 61–88. DOI: 10.1257/jep.29.4.61

Dar, A., & Anuradha, N. (2018). Use of orthogonal arrays and design of experiment via Taguchi L9 method in probability of default. *Accounting*, 4(3), 113–122.

De Bondt, W. F., & Thaler, R. H. (1985). Does the stock market overreact? *The Journal of Finance*, 40(3), 793–805. DOI: 10.1111/j.1540-6261.1985.tb05004.x

de Mello Ferreira, V. R. (2021). Financial literacy and behavioral economics: Knowledge, nudging, and the psychology of decision-making. In *The Routledge Handbook of Financial Literacy* (pp. 489–504). Routledge. DOI: 10.4324/9781003025221-37

De Vita, G., & Kyaw, K. S. (2008). Determinants of capital flows to developing countries: A structural VAR analysis. *Journal of Economic Studies (Glasgow, Scotland)*, 35(4), 304–322. DOI: 10.1108/01443580810895608

Deng, C., Liang, C., Hong, Y., & Jiang, Y. (2023). CCTV news' asymmetric impact on the Chinese stock market during COVID-19: A combination analysis based on the SVAR and NARDL models. *Emerging Markets Finance & Trade*, 59(4), 1232–1246. DOI: 10.1080/1540496X.2022.2123219

Deng, P., Liu, Y., Gallagher, V. C., & Wu, X. (2020). International strategies of emerging market multinationals: A dynamic capabilities perspective. *Journal of Management & Organization*, 26(4), 408–425. DOI: 10.1017/jmo.2017.76

Dhar, S., & Bose, I. (2020). Emotions in Twitter communication and stock prices of firms: The impact of Covid-19 pandemic. *Decision (Washington, D.C.)*, 47(4), 385–399. DOI: 10.1007/s40622-020-00264-4

Dhawan, D., Bekalu, M., Pinnamaneni, R., McCloud, R., & Viswanath, K. (2021). COVID-19 news and misinformation: Do they matter for public health prevention? *Journal of Health Communication*, 26(11), 799–808. DOI: 10.1080/10810730.2021.2010841 PMID: 34865604

Din, S. U., Arshad Khan, M., Khan, M. J., & Khan, M. Y. (2022). Ownership structure and corporate financial performance in an emerging market: A dynamic panel data analysis. *International Journal of Emerging Markets*, 17(8), 1973–1997. DOI: 10.1108/IJOEM-03-2019-0220

Dua, P., & Garg, R. (2015). Macroeconomic determinants of foreign direct investment: Evidence from India. *Journal of Developing Areas*, 49(1), 133–155. DOI: 10.1353/jda.2015.0025

Dumitrescu, E.-I., & Hurlin, C. (2012). Testing for granger non-causality in heterogeneous panels. *Economic Modelling*, 29(4), 1450–1460. DOI: 10.1016/j.econmod.2012.02.014

Eberhardt, M., & Bond, S. (2009). *Cross-section dependence in nonstationary panel models: A novel estimator (MPRA Paper 17692)*. University Library of Munich.

Edwards, S. (2001). Capital mobility and economic performance: Are emerging economies different? (Working Paper No. 8076). National Bureau of Economic Research.

Eissa, M. A., & Elgammal, M. M. (2020). Foreign direct investment determinants in oil exporting countries: Revisiting the role of natural resources. *Journal of Emerging Market Finance*, 19(1), 33–65. DOI: 10.1177/0972652719880153

Elangovan, R., Irudayasamy, F. G., & Parayitam, S. (2022). Testing the market efficiency in Indian stock market: Evidence from Bombay Stock Exchange broad market indices. *Journal of Economics, Finance and Administrative Science*, 27(54), 313–327. DOI: 10.1108/JEFAS-04-2021-0040

Ellis, A., & Freeman, D. J. (2024). Revealing choice bracketing. *The American Economic Review*, 114(9), 2668–2700. DOI: 10.1257/aer.20210877

Evanega, S., Lynas, M., Adams, J., Smolenyak, K., & Insights, C. G. (2020). Coronavirus misinformation: Quantifying sources and themes in the COVID-19 'infodemic'. *JMIR Preprints*, 19(10), 2020. DOI: 10.2196/preprints.25143

F¨orster, M., Jorra, M., & Tillmann, P. (2014). The dynamics of international capital flows: Results from a dynamic hierarchical factor model. *Journal of International Money and Finance*, 48, 101–124. DOI: 10.1016/j.jimonfin.2014.07.004

Fajri, A., & Setiawati, E. (2023). The Influence of Over Confidence, Illusion of Control, Availability, Anchoring Bias and Financial Literacy on Investment Decision Making in the Community of Demak District As Beginning Investors. *The International Journal of Business Management and Technology*, 7(4), 187–198.

Fama, E. F. (1970). Efficient capital markets: A review of theory and empirical work. *The Journal of Finance*, 25(2), 383. DOI: 10.2307/2325486

FaXing. L., & Loang, O. K. (2024). Green Investing and Financial Education: The Case of China's A-Share Market. In *Technology-Driven Business Innovation: Unleashing the Digital Advantage, Volume 1* (pp. 29-41). Cham: Springer Nature Switzerland.

Fedenia, M., Shafer, S., & Skiba, H. (2013). Information immobility, industry concentration and institutional investors' performance. *Journal of Banking & Finance*, 37(6), 2140–2159. DOI: 10.1016/j.jbankfin.2013.01.034

Filip, A. M., & Pochea, M. M. (2023). Intentional and spurious herding behavior: A sentiment driven analysis. *Journal of Behavioral and Experimental Finance*, 38, 100810. DOI: 10.1016/j.jbef.2023.100810

Fogel, K., & Berry, T. (2010). Disposition bias and its impact on investment decisions: Evidence from real estate. *The Journal of Real Estate Finance and Economics*, 41(1), 27–50.

Forbes, K. J., & Warnock, F. E. (2012). Capital flow waves: Surges, stops, flight, and retrenchment. *Journal of International Economics*, 88(2), 235–251. DOI: 10.1016/j.jinteco.2012.03.006

Fratzscher, M. (2012). Capital flows, push versus pull factors and the global financial crisis. *Journal of International Economics*, 88(2), 341–356. DOI: 10.1016/j.jinteco.2012.05.003

Frazzini, A. (2006). The disposition effect and underreaction to news. *The Journal of Finance*, 61(4), 2017–2046. DOI: 10.1111/j.1540-6261.2006.00896.x

Friedman, J., & Wenzel, T. (2006). The effects of past performance on investment decisions. *Financial Analysts Journal*, 62(3), 70–84. DOI: 10.2469/faj.v62.n3.4021

Fromlet, H. (2001). Behavioral finance – theory and practical application. *Business Economics (Cleveland, Ohio)*, 7(1), 63–69.

Fukasawa, M., Kawakami, N., Nakayama, C., & Yasumura, S. (2021). Relationship between use of media and radiation anxiety among the residents of Fukushima 5.5 years after the nuclear power plant accident. *Disaster Medicine and Public Health Preparedness*, 15(1), 42–49. DOI: 10.1017/dmp.2019.132 PMID: 31779727

Fuster, A., Kaplan, G., & Zafar, B. (2021). What would you do with $500? Spending responses to gains, losses, news, and loans. *The Review of Economic Studies*, 88(4), 1760–1795. DOI: 10.1093/restud/rdaa076

Fu, T., & Loang, O. K. (2024). The Roles of ESG Disclosure, Innovation in Improving Firm Financial Performance: Evidence from China. In *Artificial Intelligence (AI) and Customer Social Responsibility (CSR)* (pp. 197–221). Springer Nature Switzerland. DOI: 10.1007/978-3-031-50939-1_16

Gajewski, J. F., Heimann, M., Meunier, L., & Ohadi, S. (2024). Nudges for responsible finance? A survey of interventions targeted at financial decision making. *Corporate Social Responsibility and Environmental Management*, 31(2), 1203–1219. DOI: 10.1002/csr.2625

Gallimore, P. (1996). The role of appraisals in real estate markets: A critical analysis of their impact on decision-making. *Journal of Property Research*, 13(1), 23–44.

Garduno, J. C. (2022). *Financial Advisor Decisions and Behavioral Biases*. California Baptist University.

Garfin, D. R., Silver, R. C., & Holman, E. A. (2020). The novel coronavirus (COVID-2019)outbreak: Amplification of public health consequences by media exposure. *Health Psychology*, 39(5), 355–357. DOI: 10.1037/hea0000875 PMID: 32202824

Gatzlaff, D. H., & Tirtiroglu, D. (1995). Real estate market efficiency: Issues and evidence. *Journal of Real Estate Literature*, 3(2), 157–189. DOI: 10.1080/10835547.1995.12090046

Gavrilakis, N., & Floros, C. (2021). The impact of heuristic and herding biases on portfolio construction and performance: The case of Greece. *Review of Behavioral Finance*, 14(3), 436–462. DOI: 10.1108/RBF-11-2020-0295

Geddes, A., & Schmidt, T. S. (2020). Integrating finance into the multi-level perspective: Technology niche-finance regime interactions and financial policy interventions. *Research Policy*, 49(6), 103985. DOI: 10.1016/j.respol.2020.103985

Geltner, D., Miller, N., Clayton, J., & Eichholtz, P. (2007). *Commercial real estate analysis and investments*. South-Western Cengage Learning.

Genesove, D., & Mayer, C. (2001). Loss aversion and seller behavior: Evidence from the Boston housing market. *The Quarterly Journal of Economics*, 116(4), 1233–1259. DOI: 10.1162/00335530175326556l

Gigerenzer, G., & Gaissmaier, W. (2011). Heuristic decision making. *Annual Review of Psychology*, 62(1), 451–482. DOI: 10.1146/annurev-psych-120709-145346 PMID: 21126183

Gilardi, F., Gessler, T., Kubli, M., & Müller, S. (2022). Social media and political agenda setting. *Political Communication*, 39(1), 39–60. DOI: 10.1080/10584609.2021.1910390

Glaser, M., & Weber, M. (2007). Overconfidence and trading volume. *The Geneva Risk and Insurance Review*, 32(1), 1–36. DOI: 10.1007/s10713-007-0003-3

Green, T. C., & Jame, R. (2013). Company name fluency, investor recognition, and firm value. *Journal of Financial Economics*, 109(3), 813–834. DOI: 10.1016/j.jfineco.2013.04.007

Groner, R., Groner, M., & Bischof, W. F. (1983). The role of heuristics in models of decision. *Advances in Psychology*, 16, 87–108. DOI: 10.1016/S0166-4115(08)62195-0

Gyourko, J., & Keim, D. B. (1992). What does the stock market tell us about the real estate market? *Real Estate Economics*, 20(2), 193–218. DOI: 10.1111/1540-6229.00591

Hadri, K. (2000). Testing for stationarity in heterogeneous panel data. *The Econometrics Journal*, 3(2), 148–161. DOI: 10.1111/1368-423X.00043

Hair, J. F., Risher, J. J., Sarstedt, M., & Ringle, C. M. (2019). When to use and how to report the results of PLS-SEM. *European Business Review*, 31(1), 2–24. DOI: 10.1108/EBR-11-2018-0203

Hannan, S. A. (2018). Revisiting the determinants of capital flows to emerging markets: A survey of the evolving literature (Working Paper No. 18/214). International Monetary Fund.

Hannan, S. A. (2017). The drivers of capital flows in emerging markets post global financial crisis. Journal of International Commerce. *Economic Policy*, 8(02), 1750009.

Hans, A., Choudhary, F. S., & Sudan, T. (2024). Behavioral determinants of investment decisions: evidence from Indian retail equity investors in the wake of COVID-19 induced financial risks. *International Journal of Accounting & Information Management.*

Haroon, O., & Rizvi, S. A. R. (2020). COVID-19: Media coverage and financial markets behavior–A sectoral inquiry. *Journal of Behavioral and Experimental Finance*, 27, 100343. DOI: 10.1016/j.jbef.2020.100343 PMID: 32427152

Harrison, J. R., & Johnson, R. (2006). How to improve decision-making in real estate investments. *Real Estate Issues*, 31(1), 19–30.

Hasan, M., Ahmed, S. S., Mustafa, S., & Aziz, A. (2023). Risk perception as a mediator between heuristic biases and investment decision making: Case study of Pakistan stock exchange. *NICE Research Journal*, 16(4), 35–55. DOI: 10.51239/nrjss.v16i4.434

Hasso, T., Pelster, M., & Breitmayer, B. (2020). Who trades cryptocurrencies, how do they trade it, and how do their trades affect the cryptocurrency market? *Journal of International Financial Markets, Institutions and Money*, 65, 101–141.

Hayes, A. F. (2013). *Introduction to mediation, moderation, and conditional process analysis: A regression-based approach*. Guilford Press.

Helmina, M. R. A., Rosari, N., Yusniar, M. W., & Utaminingsih, N. S. (2023). Mind Matters in Investments: Unveiling the Psychological Forces Shaping Decision Making Behavior. [Jurnal Dinamika Manajemen]. *Journal of Database Management*, 14(2), 273–285.

Hertwig, R., & Pachur, T. (2015). Heuristics, history of. *International Encyclopedia of the Social & Behavioral Sciences*, 829-835. https://doi.org/DOI: 10.1016/B978-0-08-097086-8.03221-9

Hilary, G., & Menzly, L. (2006). Does past success lead analysts to become overconfident? *Management Science*, 52(4), 489–500. DOI: 10.1287/mnsc.1050.0485

Hirshleifer, D. (2001). Investor psychology and asset pricing. *The Journal of Finance*, 56(4), 1533–1597. DOI: 10.1111/0022-1082.00379

Hirshleifer, D., & Teoh, S. H. (2003). Herd behavior and cascading in capital markets: A review and synthesis. *European Financial Management*, 9(1), 25–66. DOI: 10.1111/1468-036X.00207

Hon, T. Y., Moslehpour, M., & Woo, K. Y. (2021). Review on behavioral finance with empirical evidence. *Advances in Decision Sciences*, 25(4), 1–30.

Hopkin, P. (2018). *Fundamentals of risk management: understanding, evaluating and implementing effective risk management*. Kogan Page Publishers.

Hoxha, M., & Hasani, A. (2022). Regret aversion and its impact on investor behavior in real estate markets. *International Journal of Financial Studies*, 10(3), 78. DOI: 10.3390/ijfs10030078

Huang, J., Antonides, G., & Nie, F. (2020). Is mental accounting of farm produce associated with more consumption of own-produced food? *Journal of Behavioral and Experimental Economics*, 88, 101594. DOI: 10.1016/j.socec.2020.101594

Hussain, S. M., Korkeamäki, T., Xu, D., & Khan, A. H. (2015). What drives stock market growth? a case of a volatile emerging economy. *Emerging Markets Finance & Trade*, 51(1), 209–223. DOI: 10.1080/1540496X.2015.1011533

Ilmanen, A. (2003). Expected returns on stocks and bonds. *Journal of Portfolio Management*, 29(2), 7–27. DOI: 10.3905/jpm.2003.319869

Im, K. S., Pesaran, M. H., & Shin, Y. (2003). Testing for unit roots in heterogeneous panels. *Journal of Econometrics*, 115(1), 53–74. DOI: 10.1016/S0304-4076(03)00092-7

Iram, T., Bilal, A. R., & Latif, S. (2024). Is awareness that powerful? Women's financial literacy support to prospects behaviour in prudent decision-making. *Global Business Review*, 25(5), 1356–1381. DOI: 10.1177/0972150921996185

Iriani, N., Agustianti, A., Sucianti, R., Rahman, A., & Putera, W. (2024). Understanding Risk and Uncertainty Management: A Qualitative Inquiry into Developing Business Strategies Amidst Global Economic Shifts, Government Policies, and Market Volatility. *Golden Ratio of Finance Management*, 4(2), 62–77. DOI: 10.52970/grfm.v4i2.444

Islam, M. A., Khan, M. A., Popp, J., Sroka, W., & Ol'ah, J. (2020). Financial development and foreign direct investment the moderating role of quality institutions. *Sustainability (Basel)*, 12(9), 3556. DOI: 10.3390/su12093556

Itzkowitz, J., Itzkowitz, J., & Rothbort, S. (2015). ABCs of trading: Behavioral biases affect stock turnover and value *. *Review of Finance*, 20(2), 663–692. DOI: 10.1093/rof/rfv012

Jain, A., Hisam, M. W., Azad, I., Dar, A. A., Malhotra, M., & Khan, M. S. (2024). Digitalization's Revolutionary Effect on Education and Career Development. *Information Sciences Letters*, 13(1), 149–157. DOI: 10.18576/isl/130112

Jain, J., Walia, N., Singla, H., Singh, S., Sood, K., & Grima, S. (2023). Heuristic biases as mental shortcuts to investment decision-making: A mediation analysis of risk perception. *Risks*, 11(4), 72. DOI: 10.3390/risks11040072

Jain, R., Sharma, D., Behl, A., & Tiwari, A. K. (2022). Investor personality as a predictor of investment intention – mediating role of overconfidence bias and financial literacy. *International Journal of Emerging Markets*, 18(12), 5680–5706. DOI: 10.1108/IJOEM-12-2021-1885

Jaiyeoba, H. B., Adewale, A. A., Haron, R., & Che Ismail, C. M. (2018). Investment decision behaviour of the Malaysian retail investors and fund managers. *Qualitative Research in Financial Markets*, 10(2), 134–151. DOI: 10.1108/QRFM-07-2017-0062

Kahneman, D., & Tversky, A. (2013). Prospect theory: An analysis of decision under risk. In *Handbook of the fundamentals of financial decision making: Part I* (pp. 99-127).

Kahneman, D., & Tversky, A. (2013). Prospect theory: An analysis of decision under risk. *World Scientific Handbook in Financial Economics Series*, 99-127. https://doi.org/DOI: 10.1142/9789814417358_0006

Kahneman, D., & Tversky, A. (1979). Prospect theory: An analysis of decision under risk. *Econometrica*, 47(2), 263–291. DOI: 10.2307/1914185

Kahn, R. N. (2018). *The future of investment management*. CFA Institute Research Foundation. DOI: 10.2139/ssrn.3474545

Kang, J. K., & Stulz, R´. M. (1997). Why is there a home bias? An analysis of foreign portfolio equity ownership in Japan. *Journal of Financial Economics*, 46(1), 3–28. DOI: 10.1016/S0304-405X(97)00023-8

Kao, C., & Chiang, M.-H. (2001). On the estimation and inference of a cointegrated regression in panel data. In Baltagi, B. H. (Ed.), *Nonstationary panels, panel cointegration, and dynamic panels*. Emerald Group Publishing Limited.

Karhade, P., & Dong, J. Q. (2021). Information technology investment and commercialized innovation performance: Dynamic adjustment costs and curvilinear impacts. *Management Information Systems Quarterly*, 45(3), 1007–1024. DOI: 10.25300/MISQ/2021/14368

Kasoga, P. S. (2021). Heuristic biases and investment decisions: Multiple mediation mechanisms of risk tolerance and financial literacy—a survey at the Tanzania stock market. *Journal of Money and Business*, 1(2), 102–116. DOI: 10.1108/JMB-10-2021-0037

Kathpal, S., Akhtar, A., Zaheer, A., & Khan, M. N. (2021). COVID-19 and heuristic biases: Evidence from India. *Journal of Financial Services Marketing*, 26(4), 305–316. DOI: 10.1057/s41264-021-00116-x

Kengatharan, L., & Kengatharan, N. (2014). The influence of behavioral factors in making investment decisions and performance: Study on investors of Colombo stock exchange, Sri Lanka. *Asian Journal of Finance & Accounting*, 6(1), 1. DOI: 10.5296/ajfa.v6i1.4893

Kenton, W. (2019). *What are short-term investments?*https://www.investopedia.com/terms/s/shorterminvestments.asp

Khan, R., Rustam, F., Kanwal, K., Mehmood, A., & Choi, G. S. (2021). US based COVID-19 tweets sentiment analysis using TextBlob and supervised machine learning algorithms [Conference session]. International Conference on Artificial Intelligence (ICAI), Islamabad, Pakistan, IEEE, pp. 1–8. DOI: 10.1109/ICAI52203.2021.9445207

Khan, A., Bashir, M., & Islam, T. (2021). Cognitive biases in investment decision-making: A study on real estate investors in Pakistan. *Journal of Behavioral Finance*, 22(2), 113–127. DOI: 10.1080/15427560.2020.1794083

Khan, I., Afeef, M., Jan, S., & Ihsan, A. (2021). The impact of heuristic biases on investors' investment decision in Pakistan stock market: Moderating role of long term orientation. *Qualitative Research in Financial Markets*, 13(2), 252–274. DOI: 10.1108/QRFM-03-2020-0028

Khan, R., Awais, M., & Malik, Q. A. (2023). Innovation, Sentiment, Great Market Crash and Stock Market Value Reflection: A case of Over-confidence and Attribution Bias of Stock's Investors. [JTHS]. *Journal of Tourism, Hospitality, and Services Industries Research*, 3(2), 1–15.

Khan, R., Bafakih, A., & Ali, M. (2024). Financial literacy and investment decision-making: Insights from the real estate sector. *Journal of Property Investment & Finance*, 42(1), 12–26. DOI: 10.1108/JPIF-06-2022-0080

Kinatta, K., Uwais, A., & Yusuf, R. (2022). The psychology of herding in financial markets: Evidence from Indonesia. *Journal of Behavioral Finance*, 23(4), 451–470. DOI: 10.1080/15427560.2022.2050604

Kirera, F. K., & Mburugu, B. M. (2019). IMPACT OF HEURISTIC BIASES ON INDIVIDUAL INVESTOR DECISION MAKING PROCESS AT NAIROBI SECURITIES EXCHANGE: A SURVEY OF INDIVIDUAL INVESTORS IN MERU COUNTY. *Journal of Environmental Sustainability Advancement Research, 5.*

Klamer, A., de Groot, H., & van der Laan, J. (2017). The influence of historical prices on property valuations: Evidence from the Dutch real estate market. *Real Estate Economics*, 45(3), 645–672.

Koepke, R. (2019). What drives capital flows to emerging markets? A survey of the empirical literature. *Journal of Economic Surveys*, 33(2), 516–540. DOI: 10.1111/joes.12273

Kok, R., & Acikgoz Ersoy, B. (2009). Analyses of FDI determinants in developing countries. *International Journal of Social Economics*, 36(1/2), 105–123. DOI: 10.1108/03068290910921226

Kubilay, B., & Bayrakdaroglu, A. (2016). An empirical research on investor biases in financial decision-making, financial risk tolerance and financial personality. *International Journal of Financial Research*, 7(2). Advance online publication. DOI: 10.5430/ijfr.v7n2p171

Kumar, A., & Ghosh, S. (2014). Availability bias in real estate investment: A behavioral perspective. *International Journal of Housing Markets and Analysis*, 7(4), 494–508. DOI: 10.1108/IJHMA-01-2014-0002

Kumar, P., Islam, M. A., Pillai, R., & Sharif, T. (2023). Analysing the behavioural, psychological, and demographic determinants of financial decision making of household investors. *Heliyon*, 9(2), e13085. DOI: 10.1016/j.heliyon.2023.e13085 PMID: 36793953

Kurniawati, D., & Sutrisno, S. (2019). The Benchmark of Investor Decisions to Invest In the Initial Public Offering (IPO). Riset Akuntansi dan Keuangan Indonesia, 4(2), 166-176.

Langer, E. J. (2016). *The power of mindful learning*.

Lantushenko, V., & Nelling, E. (2017). Herding behavior in financial markets: Evidence from institutional investors. *Journal of Behavioral Finance*, 18(4), 360–376. DOI: 10.1080/15427560.2017.1335269

Lavazza, A., & Farina, M. (2020). The role of experts in the Covid-19 pandemic and the limits of their epistemic authority in democracy. *Frontiers in Public Health*, 8, 356. https://www.frontiersin.org/articles/10.3389/fpubh.2020.00356. DOI: 10.3389/fpubh.2020.00356 PMID: 32760690

Leamer, E. E. (2007). Housing is the business cycle. NBER Working Paper No. 13428.

Lekkas, D., Gyorda, J. A., Price, G. D., Wortzman, Z., & Jacobson, N. C. (2022). Using the COVID-19 pandemic to assess the influence of news affect on online mental health-related search behavior across the United States: Integrated sentiment analysis and the circumplex model of affect. *Journal of Medical Internet Research*, 24(1), e32731. DOI: 10.2196/32731 PMID: 34932494

Leković, M. (2020). Cognitive biases as an integral part of behavioral finance. *Economic Themes*, 58(1), 75–96. DOI: 10.2478/ethemes-2020-0005

Ling, D. C., & Archer, W. R. (2013). *Real estate principles: A value approach*. McGraw-Hill Education.

Lin, H., Zhang, J., & Hu, J. (2018). The role of herding behavior in price formation during IPOs: Evidence from the Chinese market. *Journal of Empirical Finance*, 47, 227–244. DOI: 10.1016/j.jempfin.2018.04.008

Loang, O. K. (2023). Corporate governance and Islamic behavioural finance: A review from Malaysia and GCC countries. *Indian Journal of Corporate Governance*, 16(1), 28–51. DOI: 10.1177/09746862231178959

Loang, O. K. (2024). Stability Of Shariah-Compliant Stocks In Indonesia, Malaysia, And Gcc: The Roles Of Monetary And Fiscal Policies And Contagion. *Journal of Islamic Monetary Economics and Finance*, 10(1), 155–176. DOI: 10.21098/jimf.v10i1.1899

Loang, O. K. (2024). Sustainability's impact of ESG-infused policies on leading economic indicators in Asian economies. *Journal of Sustainable Research*, 6(3), e240059. DOI: 10.20900/jsr20240059

Lusardi, A., & Mitchell, O. S. (2014). The economic importance of financial literacy: Theory and evidence. *Journal of Economic Literature*, 52(1), 5–44. DOI: 10.1257/jel.52.1.5 PMID: 28579637

Lütje, T., & Menkhoff, L. (2007). What drives home bias? evidence from fund managers' views. *International Journal of Finance & Economics*, 12(1), 21–35. DOI: 10.1002/ijfe.309

Mahapatra, M. S., & Mishra, R. (2020). Behavioral influence and financial decision of individuals: A study on mental accounting process among Indian households. *Cogent Economics & Finance*, 8(1), 1827762. DOI: 10.1080/23322039.2020.1827762

Maia, V. M., Tommasetti, R., & da Silva Macedo, M. A. (2021). Australian market response to COVID-19 as moderated by social media. *Pacific Accounting Review*, 33(5), 625–635. DOI: 10.1108/PAR-09-2020-0138

Malmendier, U., & Tate, G. (2005). CEO overconfidence and corporate investment. *The Journal of Finance*, 60(6), 2661–2700. DOI: 10.1111/j.1540-6261.2005.00813.x

Marney, A., & Fakhry, M. (2024). Behavioral biases and economic stability: A framework for housing markets. *The Journal of Economic Perspectives*, 38(1), 63–82.

Mathiyarasan, M., & Krishnamoorthi, M. (2024). The role on heuristic biases over investor decision making—A risk perception as mediator. *Studies in Systems, Decision and Control*, 637-646. https://doi.org/DOI: 10.1007/978-3-031-50939-1_49

Mayfield, C., Perdue, G., & Wooten, K. (2008). Investment management and personality type. *Financial Services Review*, 17(3), 219–237.

Mazur, M., Dang, M., & Vega, M. (2021). COVID-19 and the March 2020 stock market crash. Evidence from S&P1500. *Finance Research Letters*, 38, 101690. DOI: 10.1016/j.frl.2020.101690 PMID: 32837377

Menkhoff, L., Schmeling, M., & Schmidt, U. (2010). Are All Professional Investors Sophisticated? *German Economic Review*, 11(4), 418–440. DOI: 10.1111/j.1468-0475.2009.00497.x

Mercado, R. V.Jr, & Park, C.-Y. (2011). What drives different types of capital flows and their volatilities in developing Asia? *International Economic Journal*, 25(4), 655–680. DOI: 10.1080/10168737.2011.636628

Merton, R. C.MERTON. (1987). A simple model of capital market equilibrium with incomplete information. *The Journal of Finance*, 42(3), 483–510. DOI: 10.1111/j.1540-6261.1987.tb04565.x

Metawa, N., Hassan, M. K., Metawa, S., & Safa, M. F. (2019). Impact of behavioral factors on investors' financial decisions: Case of the Egyptian stock market. *International Journal of Islamic and Middle Eastern Finance and Management*, 12(1), 30–55. DOI: 10.1108/IMEFM-12-2017-0333

Mishra, K., & Metilda, M. J. (2015). A study on the impact of investment experience, gender, and level of education on overconfidence and self-attribution bias. *IIMB Management Review*, 27(4), 228–239. DOI: 10.1016/j.iimb.2015.09.001

Mitchell, O., & Lusardi, A. (Eds.). (2020). *Remaking Retirement: Debt in an Aging Economy*. Oxford University Press. DOI: 10.1093/oso/9780198867524.001.0001

Mohammed, S., Dar, A. A., Khan, M. S., Azad, I., Jayaraman, G., & Albalawi, O. (2024). Goodwill Valuation Enhancement through Capitalization Method and Statistical Impact Analysis. *Journal of Risk and Financial Management*, 17(6), 226. DOI: 10.3390/jrfm17060226

Mokoaleli-Mokoteli, T., Taffler, R. J., & Agarwal, V. (2009). Behavioural bias and conflicts of interest in analyst stock recommendations. *Journal of Business Finance & Accounting*, 36(3–4), 384–418. DOI: 10.1111/j.1468-5957.2009.02125.x

Montier, J. (2002). *Behavioural Finance: Insights into Irrational Minds and Markets*. John Wiley & Sons., DOI: 10.1057/9781137366290.0014

Montier, J. (2009). *Behavioural investing: A practitioner's guide to applying behavioural finance*. John Wiley & Sons.

Moore, D. A., & Healy, P. J. (2008). The trouble with overconfidence. *Psychological Review*, 115(2), 502–517. DOI: 10.1037/0033-295X.115.2.502 PMID: 18426301

Moscone, F., & Tosetti, E. (2009). A review and comparison of tests of cross-section independence in panels. *Journal of Economic Surveys*, 23(3), 528–561. DOI: 10.1111/j.1467-6419.2008.00571.x

Mouna, A., & Anis, J. (2015). A study on small investors' sentiment, financial literacy and stock returns: Evidence for emerging market. *International Journal of Accounting and Economics Studies*, 3(1), 10. DOI: 10.14419/ijaes.v3i1.4098

Naeem, S. B., & Bhatti, R. (2020). The Covid-19 'infodemic': A new front for information professionals. *Health Information and Libraries Journal*, 37(3), 233–239. DOI: 10.1111/hir.12311 PMID: 32533803

Nair, P. S., & Shiva, A. (2023). Specifying and validating overconfidence bias among retail investors: A formative index. *Managerial Finance*, 50(5), 1017–1036. DOI: 10.1108/MF-04-2023-0237

Nanda, A. P., & Banerjee, R. (2021). Consumer's subjective financial well-being: A systematic review and research agenda. *International Journal of Consumer Studies*, 45(4), 750–776. DOI: 10.1111/ijcs.12668

Naqvi, B., Rizvi, S. K. A., Mirza, N., & Umar, M. (2023). Financial market development: A potentiating policy choice for the green transition in G7 economies. *International Review of Financial Analysis*, 87, 102577. DOI: 10.1016/j.irfa.2023.102577

Nascimento, L. D. S., Reichert, F. M., Janissek-Muniz, R., & Zawislak, P. A. (2021). Dynamic interactions among knowledge management, strategic foresight and emerging technologies. *Journal of Knowledge Management*, 25(2), 275–297. DOI: 10.1108/JKM-01-2020-0044

Naseem, U., Razzak, I., Khushi, M., Eklund, P. W., & Kim, J. (2021). COVIDSenti: A large-scale benchmark Twitter data set for COVID-19 sentiment analysis. *IEEE Transactions on Computational Social Systems*, 8(4), 1003–1015. DOI: 10.1109/TCSS.2021.3051189 PMID: 35783149

Nguyen, C. P., & Lee, G. S. (2021). Uncertainty, financial development, and FDI inflows: Global evidence. *Economic Modelling*, 99, 105473. DOI: 10.1016/j.econmod.2021.02.014

Northcraft, G. B., & Neale, M. A. (1987). Experts and amateurs: The role of experience in pricing decisions. *Organizational Behavior and Human Decision Processes*, 39(3), 298–315. DOI: 10.1006/obhd.1995.1081

Northcraft, G. B., & Neale, M. A. (1987). Experts, amateurs, and real estate: An anchoring-and-adjustment perspective on property pricing decisions. *Organizational Behavior and Human Decision Processes*, 39(1), 84–97. DOI: 10.1016/0749-5978(87)90046-X

Nteso, D. C. (2021). *Mental accounting of saving and debt in South Africa*. University of Johannesburg.

Nyagadza, B., Pashapa, R., Chare, A., Mazuruse, G., & Hove, P. K. (2022). Digital technologies, Fourth Industrial Revolution (4IR) & Global Value Chains (GVCs) nexus with emerging economies' future industrial innovation dynamics. *Cogent Economics & Finance*, 10(1), 2014654. DOI: 10.1080/23322039.2021.2014654

Odean, T. (1999). Do investors trade too much? *The American Economic Review*, 89(5), 1279–1298. DOI: 10.1257/aer.89.5.1279

Oehler, A., Rummer, M., & Wendt, S. (2008). Portfolio selection of german investors: On the causes of home-biased investment decisions. *Journal of Behavioral Finance*, 9(3), 149–162. DOI: 10.1080/15427560802341434

Ojala, M., & Hallikas, J. (2006). Investment decision-making in supplier networks: Management of risk. *International Journal of Production Economics*, 104(1), 201–213. DOI: 10.1016/j.ijpe.2005.03.006

Otuteye, E., & Siddiquee, M. (2015). Overcoming cognitive biases: A heuristic for making value investing decisions. *Journal of Behavioral Finance*, 16(2), 140–149. DOI: 10.1080/15427560.2015.1034859

Ozili, P. K., & Arun, T. (2023). Spillover of COVID-19: Impact on the global economy. In *Managing inflation and supply chain disruptions in the global economy* (pp. 41–61). IGI Global., DOI: 10.4018/978-1-6684-5876-1.ch004

Ozkan, M., & Ozkan, O. (2020). Financial evaluation of mental accounting.

Palm, R., & Andersson, H. (2020). The effect of cognitive biases on the valuation of real estate: Evidence from Swedish appraisers. *Journal of Property Research*, 37(3), 214–232.

Pandey, A., & Jessica, D. (2018). Behavioral biases in investment decisions: A case study of real estate investors. *International Journal of Economic Perspectives*, 12(2), 589–601.

Pang, A. (2013). Social media hype in times of crises: Nature, characteristics and impact on organizations. *Asia Pacific Media Educator*, 23(2), 309–336. DOI: 10.1177/1326365X13517189

Pathak, D. D., & Thapa, B. S. (2024). Beyond market anomalies: How heuristics and perceived efficiency shape investor behavior in developing markets. *Investment Management and Financial Innovations*, 21(3), 1–14. DOI: 10.21511/imfi.21(3).2024.01

Pedroni, P. (2019). Panel cointegration techniques and open challenges. In Tsionas, M. (Ed.), *Panel data econometrics* (pp. 251–287). Elsevier. DOI: 10.1016/B978-0-12-814367-4.00010-1

Pikulina, E., Renneboog, L., & Tobler, P. N. (2017). Overconfidence and investment: An experimental approach. *Journal of Corporate Finance*, 43, 175–192. DOI: 10.1016/j.jcorpfin.2017.01.002

Pillay, P. (2021). *Households' Review of their Budgets to Deal with the Paradox of Covid-19 Financial Disruptions and Increased Health-Related Expenses: A Mental Accounting Approach* (Master's thesis, University of Pretoria (South Africa)).

Pompian, M. M. (2021). *Behavioral Finance and Your Portfolio: A Navigation Guide for Building Wealth*. John Wiley & Sons.

Poterba, J. M. (1991). House price dynamics: The role of tax policy and demographics. *Real Estate Economics*, 19(3), 226–246. DOI: 10.1111/1540-6229.00619

Prelipcean, G., & Boscoianu, M. (2020). An Innovative Flexible Investment Vehicle Oriented to Sustainability–The Adaptation of Hedge Funds in the Case of Emerging Markets. *ENTRENOVA-ENTerprise REsearch InNOVAtion*, 6(1), 493–503.

Prosad, R. S., Kapoor, A., & Sengupta, S. (2015). The impact of disposition bias on real estate investment decisions: An empirical analysis. *Real Estate Review*, 45(1), 1–16.

Puaschunder, J. (2020). *Behavioral economics and finance leadership*. Springer Books. DOI: 10.1007/978-3-030-54330-3

Ramakrishnan, T., Mohan Gift, M. D., Chitradevi, S., Jegan, R., & Subha Hency Jose, P. Nagaraja, Rajneesh Sharma H.N., Selvakumar P., Sintayehu Mekuria Hailegiorgis, (2022). "Study of Numerous Resins Used in Polymer Matrix Composite Materials", Advances in Materials Science and Engineering, vol. 2022, Article ID 1088926, 8 pages, 2022. https://doi.org/DOI: 10.1155/2022/1088926

Rana, S., Prashar, S., Barai, M. K., & Hamid, A. B. A. (2021). Determinants of international marketing strategy for emerging market multinationals. *International Journal of Emerging Markets*, 16(2), 154–178. DOI: 10.1108/IJOEM-09-2019-0742

Rasool, S., & Ullah, S. (2020). The impact of herding behavior on stock market returns: Evidence from Pakistan. *Journal of Behavioral and Experimental Finance*, 27, 100344. DOI: 10.1016/j.jbef.2020.100344

Raut, R. K., Das, N., & Mishra, R. (2018). Behaviour of individual investors in stock market trading: Evidence from India. *Global Business Review*, 21(3), 818–833. DOI: 10.1177/0972150918778915

RavenPack. (2023). Coronavirus media monitor [dataset]. https://coronavirus .ravenpack.com/

Razmdoost, K., Dimitriu, R., & Macdonald, E. K. (2015). The effect of overconfidence and Underconfidence on consumer value. *Psychology and Marketing*, 32(4), 392–407. DOI: 10.1002/mar.20787

Read, D., Loewenstein, G., Rabin, M., Keren, G., & Laibson, D. (2000). Choice bracketing. *Elicitation of preferences*, 171-202.

Research methods for business: A skill building approach. (1993). *Long Range Planning, 26*(2), 136. https://doi.org/DOI: 10.1016/0024-6301(93)90168-F

Results - OpenURL Connection - EBSCO. (n.d.). https://search.ebscohost.com/login .aspx?direct=true&profile=ehost&scope=site&authtype=crawler&jrnl=22494561 &AN=119728965&h=V%2BVpbk08dKwQWZsrOFly0%2Br1EiAFTltLQCCq vJjhaceQ0krgFQPbQ3q7vD5TZWfNYp80StbJ1Q4cNse46hQL8g%3D%3D&crl=c

Rikberg, O. (2023). The Impact of Behavioural Biases on Individual Investors' Decision-Making: An Analysis of Cognitive and Emotional Biases in Investment Choices.

Ringle, C. M., Da Silva, D., & Bido, D. D. (2014). Modelagem de Equações Estruturais com Utilização do Smartpls. *Revista Brasileira de Marketing*, 13(2), 56–73. DOI: 10.5585/remark.v13i2.2717

Rohana Kumara, R. M., & Kawshala, B. A. (2021). The impact of heuristic biases on investors' investment decision making; Evidence from Colombo stock exchange. *Journal of Business and Technology*, 86-103. https://doi.org/DOI: 10.4038/jbt.v5i0.55

Romanycia, M. H., & Pelletier, F. J. (1985). What is a heuristic? *Computational Intelligence*, 1(1), 47–58. DOI: 10.1111/j.1467-8640.1985.tb00058.x

Ro, S., Chiang, Y.-C., & Lin, B. X. (2019). Herding in real estate markets. *Journal of Property Research*, 36(2), 124–141. DOI: 10.1080/09599916.2019.1602466

Russell, C. (2024). *The aging experience*. Taylor & Francis. DOI: 10.4324/9781032683720

Sadhu, S., Poddar, V., Paul, P., Hansda, S., Saha, R., Chakraborty, A., Paul, T., & Mondal, . (2022). Sentiment analysis on COVID-19 Twitter data. *American Journal of Electronics & Communication*, 3(2), 21–29. DOI: 10.15864/ajec.3205

Saeed, K. (2019). Impact of heuristic biases on investment decision locus of control playing a moderating role. SSRN *Electronic Journal*. https://doi.org/DOI: 10.2139/ssrn.3499658

Saeed, M. A., Jiao, Y., Zahid, M. M., Tabassum, H., & Nauman, S. (2021). Organizational flexibility and project portfolio performance: The roles of innovation, absorptive capacity and environmental dynamism. *International Journal of Managing Projects in Business*, 14(3), 600–624. DOI: 10.1108/IJMPB-02-2020-0058

Sattar, M. A., Toseef, M., & Sattar, M. F. (2020). Behavioral finance biases in investment decision making. *International Journal of Accounting. Finance and Risk Management*, 5(2), 69.

Sayrani, M., Razmjoy, & Samari, R. (2023). The Impact of Heuristic Biases in Investment Decision-Making and Perceived Market Efficiency a Survey at the Tehran Stock Exchange. *Financial and Behavioral Researches in Accounting*, 3(1), 1–16.

Schoemaker, P. (2012). *Profiting from uncertainty: Strategies for succeeding no matter what the future brings*. Simon and Schuster.

Seiler, M. J., Haurin, D. R., & O'Neill, R. (2008). The impact of regret on the decision to sell a home. *Real Estate Economics*, 36(1), 49–74. DOI: 10.1111/j.1540-6229.2008.00213.x

Seiler, M. J., Seiler, V. L., Harrison, J. L., & Lane, W. R. (2012). The impact of initial listing price on sales price: An analysis of the residential real estate market. *Journal of Real Estate Research*, 34(1), 1–20.

Selvakumar, P. (2023). Biomedical applications of polymers in biosensors, cancer vaccines and drug delivery systems. *Biopolimery i Kletka*, 39(4), 245–256. DOI: 10.7124/bc.000AA0

Selvakumar, P., Mariappan, P., Shunmugam, S., Paul, R., & Jabez, S. (2024). Removal of chemicals from effluent using photobioreactor technology to improve environmental and health impacts. *Zeitschrift für Physikalische Chemie*, 2024(7), 1295–1302. Advance online publication. DOI: 10.1515/zpch-2023-0450

Serfas, S. (2011). The impact of cognitive biases on capital investments. *Zeitschrift für Planung & Unternehmenssteuerung*, 21(4), 427–446. DOI: 10.1007/s00187-011-0120-0

Shah, S. Z., Ahmad, M., & Mahmood, F. (2018). Heuristic biases in investment decision-making and perceived market efficiency. *Qualitative Research in Financial Markets*, 10(1), 85–110. DOI: 10.1108/QRFM-04-2017-0033

Shahzad, S., & Jasińska, E. (2024). Renewable Revolution: A Review of Strategic Flexibility in Future Power Systems. *Sustainability (Basel)*, 16(13), 5454. DOI: 10.3390/su16135454

Sharpe, W. F. (1964). Capital asset prices: A theory of market equilibrium under conditions of risk. *The Journal of Finance*, 19(3), 425. DOI: 10.2307/2977928

Shefrin, H. M., & Thaler, R. H. (1992). Mental accounting, saving, and self-control. *Choice over time*, 287-330.

Sheldrake, R. (2016). Students' intentions towards studying science at upper-secondary school: The differential effects of underconfidence and over-confidence. *International Journal of Science Education*, 38(8), 1256–1277. DOI: 10.1080/09500693.2016.1186854

Sherani, A. W., Naeem, A., & Shah, M. (2023). Following the crowd or making informed choices? the impact of heuristic and prospect biases on portfolio management and performance: Evidence from Pakistan's stock market downturn IN 2022. *International Journal of Business and Management Sciences*, 4(1), 203–221.

Shiller, R. J. (2000). *Irrational exuberance*. Princeton University Press.

Shiller, R. J. (2000). Irrational exuberance: Explanations and policy implications. *Financial Analysts Journal*, 56(2), 18–24. DOI: 10.2469/faj.v56.n2.2334

Shiller, R. J. (2008). *The subprime solution: How today's global financial crisis happened, and what to do about it*. Princeton University Press.

Shiller, R. J. (2017). *Narrative economics: How stories go viral and drive major economic events*. Princeton University Press. DOI: 10.3386/w23075

Shimizu, C., & Nishimura, J. (2006). Disposition bias in real estate investment: Evidence from Japan. *The Journal of Real Estate Finance and Economics*, 32(3), 271–286.

Shukla, A., Rushdi, D. N. J., & Katiyar, D. R. C. (2020). Impact of behavioral biases on investment decisions 'a systematic review'. *International Journal of Management*, 11(4).

Silva, E. M., de Lacerda Moreira, R., & Bortolon, P. M. (2023). Mental Accounting and Decision Making: A systematic review of the literature. *Journal of Behavioral and Experimental Economics*, 107, 102092. DOI: 10.1016/j.socec.2023.102092

Silver, E. A., Victor, R., Vidal, V., & De Werra, D. (1980). A tutorial on heuristic methods. *European Journal of Operational Research*, 5(3), 153–162. DOI: 10.1016/0377-2217(80)90084-3

Simon, H. A. (1955). A behavioral model of rational choice. *The Quarterly Journal of Economics*, 69(1), 99. DOI: 10.2307/1884852

Simon, H. A. (1956). Rational choice and the structure of the environment. *Psychological Review*, 63(2), 129–138. DOI: 10.1037/h0042769 PMID: 13310708

Singh, H., Singh, A., & Nagpal, E. (2022). Demystifying behavioral biases of traders using machine learning. *EAI/Springer Innovations in Communication and Computing*, 179-188. https://doi.org/DOI: 10.1007/978-3-030-82763-2_16

Singh, R., Pandey, N., & Mohan, V. (2023). Behavioral biases in financial decision-making: A systematic review. *Behavioral Sciences (Basel, Switzerland)*, 13(3), 1–25. DOI: 10.3390/bs13030104

Sinha, A., & Ghosh, T. (2021). Impact of economic policy uncertainty on FDI inflows: Evidence from India. In *Recent developments in Asian economics international symposia in economic theory and econometrics*. Emerald Publishing Limited. DOI: 10.1108/S1571-038620210000028009

Sinnewe, E., & Nicholson, G. (2023). Healthy financial habits in young adults: An exploratory study of the relationship between subjective financial literacy, engagement with finances, and financial decision-making. *The Journal of Consumer Affairs*, 57(1), 564–592. DOI: 10.1111/joca.12512

Skwara, F. (2023). Effects of mental accounting on purchase decision processes: A systematic review and research agenda. *Journal of Consumer Behaviour*, 22(5), 1265–1281. DOI: 10.1002/cb.2193

Sobkow, A., Garrido, D., & Garcia-Retamero, R. (2020). Cognitive abilities and financial decision making. *Psychological perspectives on financial decision making*, 71-87.

Sony, M., Antony, J., & Mc Dermott, O. (2023). How do the technological capability and strategic flexibility of an organization impact its successful implementation of Industry 4.0? A qualitative viewpoint. *Benchmarking*, 30(3), 924–949. DOI: 10.1108/BIJ-09-2021-0541

Spindler, G. (2011). Behavioural finance and investor protection regulations. *Journal of Consumer Policy*, 34(3), 315–336. DOI: 10.1007/s10603-011-9165-6

Spuchľakova, E., Michalikova, K. F., & Misankova, M. (2015). Risk of the collective investment and investment portfolio. *Procedia Economics and Finance*, 26, 167–173. DOI: 10.1016/S2212-5671(15)00910-7

Stout, L. A. (1995). Are stock markets costly casinos-disagreement, market failure, and securities regulation. *Virginia Law Review*, 81(3), 611. DOI: 10.2307/1073496

Stulz, R. M. (2008). Rethinking risk management. In *Corporate risk management* (pp. 87–120). Columbia University Press. DOI: 10.7312/chew14362-005

Sugumaran, K. M. D., Pandiyarajan V., Y. B S, Selvakumar P. and M. S, (2024). "Analysis of Electromyography Signals for Control of Mechanical Prosthesis using Machine Learning Techniques," 2024 2nd International Conference on Intelligent Data Communication Technologies and Internet of Things (IDCIoT), Bengaluru, India, 2024, pp. 1059-1067, DOI: 10.1109/IDCIoT59759.2024.10467707

Suh, J. (2005). Home bias among institutional investors: A study of the economist quarterly portfolio poll. *Journal of the Japanese and International Economies*, 19(1), 72–95. DOI: 10.1016/j.jjie.2003.12.003

Sui, L., Sun, L., & Geyfman, V. (2021). An assessment of the effects of mental accounting on overspending behaviour: An empirical study. *International Journal of Consumer Studies*, 45(2), 221–234. DOI: 10.1111/ijcs.12613

Suresh, G., & Loang, O. K. (2024). The Rationality Conundrum: Exploring Herd Mentality among Individual Investors in the Indian Stock Market. *Indian Journal of Finance*, 18(6), 26–45. DOI: 10.17010/ijf/2024/v18i6/173967

Swamy, V., & Narayanamurthy, V. (2018). What drives the capital flows into BRICS economies? *World Economy*, 41(2), 519–549. DOI: 10.1111/twec.12606

Talpsepp, T. (2011). Reverse disposition effect of foreign investors. *Journal of Behavioral Finance*, 12(4), 183–200. DOI: 10.1080/15427560.2011.606387

Teal, F., & Eberhardt, M. (2010). *Productivity analysis in global manufacturing production (Technical report)*. University of Oxford.

Thaler, R. H. (1980). Toward a positive theory of consumer choice. *Journal of Economic Behavior & Organization*, 1(1), 39–60. DOI: 10.1016/0167-2681(80)90051-7

Thaler, R. H. (1990). Anomalies: Saving, fungibility, and mental accounts. *The Journal of Economic Perspectives*, 4(1), 193–205. DOI: 10.1257/jep.4.1.193

Thaler, R. H. (1999). Mental accounting matters. *Journal of Behavioral Decision Making*, 12(3), 183–206. DOI: 10.1002/(SICI)1099-0771(199909)12:3<183::AID-BDM318>3.0.CO;2-F

Thaler, R. H. (2016). Behavioral economics: Past, present, and future. *The American Economic Review*, 106(7), 1577–1600. DOI: 10.1257/aer.106.7.1577

Thaler, R. H., & Sunstein, C. R. (2008). *Nudge: Improving decisions about health, wealth, and happiness*. Yale University Press.

The effect of optimism bias and over confidence on investment decisions in Aceh mediated by herding. (2023). *Quality-Access to Success, 25*(198). https://doi.org/ DOI: 10.47750/QAS/25.198.19

Tiwari, A. K., Abakah, E. J. A., Bonsu, C. O., Karikari, N. K., & Hammoudeh, S. (2022). The effects of public sentiments and feelings on stock market behavior: Evidence from Australia. *Journal of Economic Behavior & Organization*, 193, 443–472. DOI: 10.1016/j.jebo.2021.11.026

Tversky, A., & Kahneman, D. (1973). Availability: A heuristic for judging frequency and probability. *Cognitive Psychology*, 5(2), 207–232. DOI: 10.1016/0010-0285(73)90033-9

Tversky, A., & Kahneman, D. (1973). Judgment under uncertainty: Heuristics and biases. https://doi.org/DOI: 10.21236/AD0767426

Tversky, A., & Kahneman, D. (1974). Judgment under uncertainty: Heuristics and biases. *Science*, 185(4157), 1124–1131. DOI: 10.1126/science.185.4157.1124 PMID: 17835457

Twin, A. (2019). *What are long-term investments?*https://www.investopedia.com/terms/l/longterminvestments.asp

Tyson, E. (2020). *Investing for dummies*. John Wiley & Sons.

Ülkü, S., Hydock, C., & Cui, S. (2020). Making the wait worthwhile: Experiments on the effect of queueing on consumption. *Management Science*, 66(3), 1149–1171. DOI: 10.1287/mnsc.2018.3277

Valle-Cruz, D., Fernandez-Cortez, V., López-Chau, A., & Sandoval-Almazán, R. (2022). Does Twitter affect stock market decisions? Financial sentiment analysis during pandemics: A comparative study of the H1N1 and the COVID-19 periods. *Cognitive Computation*, 14(1), 372–387. DOI: 10.1007/s12559-021-09819-8 PMID: 33520006

van Dijck, J., & Alinejad, D. (2020). Social media and trust in scientific expertise: Debating the Covid-19 pandemic in The Netherlands. *Social Media + Society*, 6(4), 2056305120981057. DOI: 10.1177/2056305120981057

Van Raaij, W. F. (2016). *Understanding consumer financial behavior: Money management in an age of financial illiteracy*. Springer. DOI: 10.1057/9781137544254

Vijayakumar, G., Rajkumar, M., Rajiv Chandar, N., Selvakumar, P., & Duraisamy, R. (2024). Muniyandi Rajkumar, Rajiv Chandar N, Selvakumar P and Ramesh Duraisamy, (2024). Environmentally friendly TDS removal from waste water by electrochemical ion exchange batch-type recirculation (EIR) technique. *Environmental Science. Water Research & Technology*, 10(4), 826–835. DOI: 10.1039/D3EW00793F

Vrontis, D., Belas, J., Thrassou, A., Santoro, G., & Christofi, M. (2023). Strategic agility, openness and performance: A mixed method comparative analysis of firms operating in developed and emerging markets. *Review of Managerial Science*, 17(4), 1365–1398. DOI: 10.1007/s11846-022-00562-4

Wang, L., & Li, S. (2018). Determinants of foreign direct and indirect investments from the institutional perspective: A comparative analysis between emerging and mature markets. *International Journal of Emerging Markets*, 13(5), 1330–1347. DOI: 10.1108/IJoEM-01-2018-0038

Wangzhou, X., Chen, Z., & Liu, H. (2021). Disposition bias in commercial real estate: Evidence from transaction data. *Real Estate Economics*, 49(3), 613–635.

Wangzhou, Z., Li, J., & Liu, Y. (2021). Regret aversion and risk perception in investment decision-making: The moderating role of financial literacy. *International Review of Economics & Finance*, 76, 145–159. DOI: 10.1016/j.iref.2021.06.014

Waweru, N. M., Munyoki, E., & Uliana, E. (2008). The effects of behavioural factors in investment decision-making: A survey of institutional investors operating at the Nairobi stock exchange. *International Journal of Business and Emerging Markets*, 1(1), 24. DOI: 10.1504/IJBEM.2008.019243

Weimann, G., & Brosius, H.-B. (2017). Redirecting the agenda: Agenda-setting in the online Era. *The Agenda Setting Journal*, 1(1), 63–102. DOI: 10.1075/asj.1.1.06wei

Weixiang, S., Qamruzzaman, M., Rui, W., & Kler, R. (2022). An empirical assessment of financial literacy and behavioral biases on investment decision: Fresh evidence from small investor perception. *Frontiers in Psychology*, 13, 977444. DOI: 10.3389/fpsyg.2022.977444 PMID: 36225674

West, C. R. (2021). *Windfalls of Time and Money: Effects on Wellbeing and Decision-Making*. University of California.

Westerlund, J. (2005). New simple tests for panel cointegration. *Econometric Reviews*, 24(3), 297–316. DOI: 10.1080/07474930500243019

Westerlund, J. (2007). Testing for error correction in panel data. *Oxford Bulletin of Economics and Statistics*, 69(6), 709–748. DOI: 10.1111/j.1468-0084.2007.00477.x

Xie, Z., & Li, J. (2017). Export intensity, domestic competition, and product innovation in an emerging economy. *International Journal of Technology Management*, 74(1–4), 96–121. DOI: 10.1504/IJTM.2017.083612

Xu, X., & Loang, O. K. (2024). Fostering Future Entrepreneurs: The Impact of Education, Self-Efficacy, and Financial Support on Entrepreneurial Intentions. *International Journal of Advanced Research in Economics and Finance*, 6(2), 188–203.

Yang, A., & Saffer, A. J. (2019). Embracing a network perspective in the network society: The dawn of a new paradigm in strategic public relations. *Public Relations Review*, 45(4), 101843. DOI: 10.1016/j.pubrev.2019.101843

Yao, Y., & Zhou, Y. (2019). Research on Outward Direct Investment in Emerging Economies. In 3rd International Seminar on Education Innovation and Economic Management (SEIEM 2018) (pp. 300–303). Atlantis Press. DOI: 10.2991/seiem-18.2019.78

Yarba, I., & Güner, Z. N. (2020). Uncertainty, macroprudential policies and corporate leverage: Firm-level evidence. *Central Bank Review*, 20(2), 33–42. DOI: 10.1016/j.cbrev.2020.03.005

Zahoor, N., & Lew, Y. K. (2023). Enhancing international marketing capability and export performance of emerging market SMEs in crises: Strategic flexibility and digital technologies. *International Marketing Review*, 40(5), 1158–1187. DOI: 10.1108/IMR-12-2021-0350

Zainuri, Z., Viphindrartin, S., & Wilantari, R. N. (2021). The impacts of the COVID-19 pandemic on the movement of composite stock price index in Indonesia. The Journal of Asian Finance. *Economics and Business*, 8(3), 1113–1119. DOI: 10.13106/jafeb.2021.vol8.no3.1113

Zargar, F. N., & Kumar, D. (2023). Market fear, investor mood, sentiment, economic uncertainty and tourism sector in the United States amid COVID-19 pandemic: A spillover analysis. *Tourism Economics*, 29(2), 551–558. DOI: 10.1177/13548166211052803

Zhang, L., & Miao, Y. (2018). The role of automated valuation models in mitigating behavioral biases in real estate. *International Journal of Housing Markets and Analysis*, 11(4), 623–645.

Zhang, Y. A., Li, Y., & Li, H. (2014). FDI spillovers over time in an emerging market: The roles of entry tenure and barriers to imitation. *Academy of Management Journal*, 57(3), 698–722. DOI: 10.5465/amj.2011.0351

Zhan, J. X. (2021). GVC transformation and a new investment landscape in the 2020s: Driving forces, directions, and a forward-looking research and policy agenda. *Journal of International Business Policy*, 4(2), 206–220. DOI: 10.1057/s42214-020-00088-0

Zhou, J., Xue, J., & Huang, S. (2015). Behavioral biases and real estate prices: Evidence from Beijing. *The Journal of Real Estate Finance and Economics*, 51(3), 343–366. DOI: 10.1007/s11146-015-9537-3

About the Contributors

Xiong Xu is an accomplished academic with a strong background in management and global collaboration. He holds a Bachelor's and Master's degree from Chengdu University and a PhD in Management from City University Malaysia. Since 2010, Dr. Xu has served as an Associate Professor at Chengdu International Studies University, where he oversees global collaboration and partnership initiatives.

Ooi Kok Loang, LLM, CMIIA, CIA, is with the Department of Finance at the University of Malaya, renowned for his expertise in behavioural finance and capital markets. His professional journey includes significant roles as an auditor and business consultant at KPMG (Big 4 Audit Firms) and Deputy Dean at two prestigious private universities. Dr. Ooi holds a Master in Finance and a PhD in Behavioral Finance from Universiti Sains Malaysia (QS137), a Master of Laws (Business Law) from the International Islamic University Malaysia (QS Top 300 by subject), and is a US Certified Internal Auditor. With a strong portfolio of publications and active contributions as a reviewer for top international SCI and Scopus-indexed journals, Dr. Ooi is keen to mentor passionate PhD students, offering a vibrant environment for research and academic excellence.

***

Pankaj Singh Chandel is an Assistant Professor in the Department of Tourism Management at Dev Sanskriti Vishwavidyalaya, Haridwar, where he has been teaching since 2014. He holds a PhD in Tourism and a PGDM in Tourism and Travel Services Management from the Indian Institute of Tourism and Travel Management. His expertise lies in homestay tourism, and he is recognized as a skilled orator on travel knowledge. Dr. Chandel has published research articles in Scopus-indexed journals and has contributed to publications with IGI Global, demonstrating his commitment to academic scholarship in the field of tourism. His research focuses on sustainable tourism practices and the development of homestay tourism in India. As an active member of several professional organizations, including the Travel Agents Association of Uttarakhand and ATOAI, Dr. Chandel actively participates in initiatives promoting sustainability in the tourism industry. His involvement in these organizations allows him to bridge the gap between academic research and industry practices. Dr. Chandel's ORCID (https://orcid.org/0000-0002-4135-8194) showcases his research outputs and professional activities.

Ann Mary Cherian is an academic in the Department of Economics at Christ College (Autonomous), Irinjalakuda, located in Thrissur, Kerala.With a passion for economics and a commitment to academic excellence, she has made significant contributions to the field through her research and teaching. Her areas of interest include rural development, tourism economics, and the socio-economic impact of public policies. She is a dedicated educator, guiding students in understanding complex economic concepts while conducting insightful studies in her field.

Parihar Suresh Dahake is working as an Assistant Professor at Shri Ramdeobaba College of Engineering and Management in the Department of Management Technology. He received his BTech, MBA, and Ph.D. from the Rashtrasant Tukdoji Maharaj Nagpur University and PGDIBO, M.Com from Indira Gandhi National Open University (IGNOU). Dr.Parihar dahake has Qualified SET(Commerce) and SET (Management). He has 14 Years of Teaching Experience and 13 years of Research Experience. His areas of expertise are Consumer behavior, Organizational Behaviour, Marketing management, and IMC.

Amir Ahmad Dar is the Faculty in the Department of Mathematics at Lovely Professional University Punjab. The area of interest: Financial mathematics, financial economics, statistics and business mathematics.

Chadalavada Lakshmi Nath, Qualifications: MBA, PGDFM, PGDHRM, M.Phil., Ph. D, ORCID ID: 0000 0002 2972 1560, Experience:- 28 Years, International Journal Publications: 12, National Journal Publications: 18, UGC Care: 05, Papers Presented in Workshops, Conferences, Seminars & Symposium: 36, Seminars, Conferences, Workshops Organized: 07, Research Projects Completed with AICTE Funding 02, Consultancy Services: Regularly to various Small, Medium and Large Scale Business Entities., Ph.D. Guidance: 02 Scholars pursuing., FDPs/ QIPs Attended:- 18

Raj Kumar Mishra is an Assistant Professor at the Institute of Management Sciences, University of Lucknow, with 13 years of teaching experience. He has also gained valuable experience working at prestigious institutions like PSIT Kanpur and

BBD University. He has authored one book, holds one patent, and has published 12 research papers in esteemed national and international journals. With a Ph.D. in Management specializing in Marketing, his current research focuses on the influence of emerging technologies such as AI and Big Data on consumer behaviour and brand engagement. He also explores the effectiveness of personalized and healthcare marketing, as well as the role of ethical advertising in fostering consumer trust.

Mohit Nain is currently working as an Assistant Professor (Statistics) in the Department of Mathematics and Statistics, Lovely Professional University, Phagwara, since September 2021. He published more than 15 research papers and book chapters in different reputed journals. He also attended more than 6 national and international conferences and participated many workshops related to statistical data analysis. His area of interest is design of experiments, regression modeling and trend analysis.

Junior Ntabanganyimana is a motivated person who is devoted to both social and personal development. I enthusiastically pursued my education, doing well academically and participating in extracurricular activities that encouraged community service and leadership. My early passion for math and statistics inspired me to pursue higher education, and I eventually graduated with a degree in statistics from Lovely Professional University.

P. Selvakumar is currently an Associate Professor in the Department of Science and Humanities at Nehru Institute of Technology, Coimbatore, Tamil Nadu, India. Since 2023, he has served as the Department IQAC Coordinator at the institute. Prior to joining Nehru Institute of Technology, he held positions as an Assistant Professor in the Department of Science and Humanities various engineering colleges in Coimbatore, Tamil Nadu, India, spanning from 2011 to 2023. Dr.P. Selvakumar's academic and research interests lie primarily in the field of phytochemistry. He has made significant contributions to his field, with an impressive record that includes 30 journal publications, 12 patents, and 20 conference papers. Additionally, he has organized 5 seminars and conferences, further demonstrating his commitment to academic and scientific exchange. Throughout his career, Dr. P.Selvakumar has been recognized for his dedication and excellence in teaching, having been honored with several awards, including the Best Teacher Awards. He holds a prominent position in the academic community, contributing actively to research.

R. Sethumadhavan is a seasoned academician and management expert with 23 years of experience in the field. He currently serves as a faculty member at the School of Management, Presidency University in Bangalore, Karnataka. Holding a PhD in Management, Dr. Sethumadhavan brings a wealth of knowledge and expertise to his teaching and research endeavors. His extensive experience spans various aspects of management, making him a valuable resource for students and professionals alike.

Partap Chahal Singh is committed to teaching and research in Finance and Investment domain since last 16 years+. His qualification is PhD (Commerce), M.Com, MBA. He has rich work experience in the field of Teaching, administration and research as well. He held various responsibilities like Editor, Co-editor, and Editorial Board member, Associate Editor in number of national and international journals. He has been regularly been receiving offers for writing books from the top publishing houses of India and received many letter of thanks& compliments for giving valuable suggestions and commendable views concerning improvement of many leading Publications/Books. He has written and published 5 books namely Financial Management, Risk Management, working capital Mana

Chirayu Vats is a dedicated lecturer in the Department of Psychology at Dev Sanskriti Vishwavidyalaya (DSVV), Haridwar. With a strong academic background and a passion for teaching, Chirayu has contributed significantly to the field of psychology through both education and research. At DSVV, She is involved in various interdisciplinary research projects that aim to integrate traditional Indian psychological concepts with modern psychological practices. Her work often explores the cultural and spiritual dimensions of psychology, reflecting the university's emphasis on holistic education. Chirayu is also actively engaged in promoting the understanding of Indian cultural practices, such as Yagya, and their relevance to contemporary psychological well-being. Her commitment to education and research has made her a valuable member of the DSVV faculty, where she continues to inspire students and contribute to the advancement of psychological studies in India

Index

M

O

P

R

S

T

U

www.ingramcontent.com/pod-product-compliance
Lightning Source LLC
LaVergne TN
LVHW081340300926
849161LV00008B/2034